HEBREW AND HELLENE IN VICTORIAN ENGLAND

NEWMAN, ARNOLD, AND PATER

Hebrew and Hellene
in Victorian England

NEWMAN, ARNOLD, AND PATER

By David J. DeLaura

UNIVERSITY OF TEXAS PRESS
AUSTIN & LONDON

Standard Book Number 292–78404–X
Library of Congress Catalog Card No. 75–79539
Copyright © 1969 by David J. DeLaura
All Rights Reserved
Printed by The University of Texas Printing Division, Austin
Bound by Universal Bookbindery, Inc., San Antonio

FOR ANN

ACKNOWLEDGMENTS

"Arnold and Newman: Humanism and the Oxford Tradition," which appeared in an earlier form in *Texas Studies in Literature and Language* (VI, Supplement, 1965), is reprinted by permission of the editors and of the University of Texas Press. "Pater and Newman: The Road to the Nineties," also in an earlier version, appeared in *Victorian Studies* (X, 1966), and is reprinted by their permission. I also wish to thank the following for permission to reprint excerpts from previously published materials: A. & C. Black Ltd., London: Stanford University Press, California, for passages from *The Mind of the Oxford Movement*, ed. Owen Chadwick; the University of Michigan Press, for passages from *The Complete Prose Works of Matthew Arnold*, ed. R. H. Super; Mrs. Mary Moorman, for passages from Mrs. Humphry Ward, *A Writer's Recollections*; Oxford University Press, for quotations from *The Letters of Matthew Arnold to Arthur Hugh Clough*, ed. H. F. Lowry, *The Note-Books of Matthew Arnold*, ed. H. F. Lowry, K. Young, and W. H. Dunn, and *The Poetical Works of Matthew Arnold*, ed. C. B. Tinker and H. F. Lowry; and Yale University Press, for passages from *Unpublished Letters of Matthew Arnold*, ed. Arnold Whitridge, and A. Dwight Culler, *The Imperial Intellect*.

The book has benefited from detailed criticism and comment from a number of readers. I am especially grateful to Warren D. Anderson, of the University of Iowa; Barbara Charlesworth Gelpi, of Brandeis University; U. C. Knoepflmacher, of the University of California, Berkeley; William Robbins, of the University of British Columbia; R. H. Super, of the University of Michigan; Martin J. Svaglic, of Loyola University, Chicago; and Geoffrey Tillotson, of Birkbeck College, the University of London. Collectively, these readings represent a quite uncommon degree of generosity, and have greatly enhanced my sense of the profession as both community and fraternity. I wish the book were a more perfect demonstration of my gratitude.

Thanks are due to Professor Arnold Whitridge, Matthew Arnold's grandson, for unfailing kindness and support over several years, and for giving me a free hand to use unpublished correspondence. Professor Arthur Kyle Davis, Jr., of the University of Virginia, generously allowed me to examine the collection of Arnold letters he has formed over many years. To the Reverend C. Stephen Dessain, of the Birmingham Oratory, I am indebted in several ways, above all for his generosity in sharing with me his unparalleled knowledge of Newman. For advice and help of various kinds I wish to thank William Beautyman, Jay Claiborne, Lawrence G. Evans, and Gerald C. Monsman.

I am indebted to the University of Texas Research Institute for two summer research grants that materially advanced my work. My deepest obligation is expressed in my dedication.

INTRODUCTION

This book comprises three studies investigating in detail the intellectual and personal relations existing among three dominating figures in nineteenth-century English thought and culture. These studies are fundamentally concerned with the humanistic vision of Matthew Arnold and Walter Pater and emphasize their adaptation of the traditional religious culture to the needs of the later nineteenth century. John Henry Newman enters as a figure of central importance, a far greater importance than he has hitherto been accorded, because of his commanding position in the thought of both younger men and because the contrasts and continuities in Arnold and Pater often become clearest in relation to him. I am concerned with nothing less than the total "vision" of Arnold and Pater though I have not by any means entered into every aspect of their thought. I have attempted to give a sense of motive and progression to both careers by concentrating on the ways in which the religious problems of the Victorian period centrally affected their evolving humanistic syntheses.

Graham Hough[1] has traced the heritage of English aestheticism and "Decadence" through its best-known figures—Ruskin, Rossetti, Pater, Morris, the Rhymers, and Yeats. He stresses the increasing dominance of the "aesthetic" norm in English art, religion, and life and underlines some of the ways in which English religious attitudes were transformed in the process. But Pater seems distinctly out of place in this scheme; Hough does not establish the long-supposed link between Ruskin and Pater, and he does not adequately account for the place of religious concerns in Pater's distinctive synthesis. I have attempted to work out the "other" line leading from traditional norms to the nineties. This line has not gone entirely unnoticed, especially by the late

[1] Graham Hough, *The Last Romantics*.

T. S. Eliot, but its full implications are by no means clear. Eliot's conception of continuity and diminution among the three—that Arnold's "degradation" of religion was "competently" continued by Pater—has been constantly before me in these studies although his viewpoint is not precisely my own and his interests not my exclusive concerns. By establishing Arnold's and Pater's extensive indebtedness to Newman and by analyzing the nature of their "use" of his ideas, it is easier to account for the peculiar and complex role of traditional religion (especially as mediated through Newman) in their successors, notably Oscar Wilde and Lionel Johnson, though this is an extension of the topic I have not taken up here.[2]

These studies have been conducted in great, though I hope not stupefying, detail: a benefit of the method may be an understanding of the density and elaborate interconnectedness of the intellectual currents of High and Late Victorian culture. Only by examining the immense interweaving of interests, arguments, and goals, in a much more unified culture than our own, can we detect the full flavor of these men's work as well as measure the full weight of the polemics and preoccupa-

---

[2] John Pick ("Divergent Disciples of Walter Pater," *Thought: Fordham University Quarterly*, XXIII [March 1948], 114–128) pointed out that nearly all of Pater's disciples "fastened upon the Pater of the 'Conclusion' to the *Renaissance*" and read into his later works the earlier ideals. Barbara Charlesworth (*Dark Passages: The Decadent Consciousness in Victorian Literature*, pp. 81–95) notes, however, that three chief influences on Lionel Johnson, the admitted anomaly, were Newman, Arnold, and Pater. Moreover, studies of Wilde seem consistently to miss the religious quality in his work and (as revealed in his letters) his significant attraction, perhaps through Arnold and Pater, to Newman and Catholicism. For the conflict of "Christian Idealism" and Hellenism in Wilde's poetry, see Aatos Ojala, *Aestheticism and Oscar Wilde*, Part I: *Life and Letters*, pp. 158–171. There is reason to question the statement of Wendell V. Harris ("Pater as Prophet," *Criticism*, VI [Fall 1964], 350) concerning Pater's role in the nineties: "The more one knows about the lives of the members of the 'decadent' coterie, the less importance has Pater in determining either their art or their personal tragedies." Even apart from the notorious case of Wilde, a book like George Moore's *Confessions of a Young Man* (1886), important in establishing the climate of the nineties in England, is suffused, quite explicitly, by vulgarized Paterian rhetoric. Ruth Z. Temple, in "The Ivory Tower as Lighthouse" (*Edwardians and Late Victorians*, ed. Richard Ellmann, pp. 28–49) suggests the wide extent of Pater's influence, not only on the nineties but also on the fiction and criticism of the twentieth century. See Enid Starkie (*From Gautier to Eliot: The Influence of France on English Literature, 1851–1939*, p. 57) on Pater: "The nineties would not have been possible without him."

tions themselves. The uniquely satisfying quality of Victorian prose arises in part from the sense of rich and diverse talent in a small, geographically close-knit, and "centripetal" intellectual community. The public statements of Victorian critics and essayists (and sometimes of poets and novelists) are often best regarded as refutation, qualification, or approval of some other writer's views. In particular, I have sought to define the mechanics of the process by which the substance of dogmatic Christianity was transformed, within one or two generations, into the fabric of aestheticism. I have endeavored to describe the pressures generating a response, the precise elements of transvaluation, and the shared and unshared factors in a shifting cultural equation, by which the conservative humanism of Newman, at once religious and literary, could be exploited, with a strong sense of meaningful continuity, in the fluid, relativistic, and "aesthetic" humanism of Pater. That the development of aestheticism, especially in Arnold and Pater, is fundamentally bound to changes in religious doctrine and expression has long been acknowledged; but the dearth of detailed studies has obscured this major line of inheritance in Victorian culture. Although deliberately emphasizing the transformation of values and categories in Newman, Arnold, and Pater—one of the most closely interwoven successions in intellectual history—I have tried everywhere, in righting a false balance, to escape the danger of making myself liable to the charge of the fallacy of the unique source.

The most revealing transformation can be seen in the history of certain phrases and ideas. For example, the "inwardness" that Newman insists on as man's essential spiritual quality is secularized as part of Arnold's criticism and culture and emerges finally as Pater's "impassioned contemplation"—that detached observation of "the individual in his isolation," the "solitary prisoner" whose dream of a world consists of certain traditional states of mind apart, ultimately, from real objects. Equally important is the emphasis all three place on an *elite* culture; that is, their shared sense that the highest organization of the human powers was "aristocratic," a privileged mode of perception endangered in a rapidly democratizing society. In all three, too, culture is defined almost as much in religious as in secular terms: if there is a shift, it is, paradoxically, toward the progressive *religionizing* of the idea of culture and its attendant intellectual qualities. As one moves from Newman to Arnold to Pater, the ideal of culture acquires more and more "religious" graces derived from the traditional culture. Arnold and Pater both were free of Newman's suspicion of the corrective and self-transcending power of secular culture, viewed in broad historical perspective, and were consequently free, again paradoxically, to identify it increasingly with the function of historic religion. Moreover, all three men were continuously involved with the problematic role of religion and of religious experience in the modern world, a concern that, as much as any other theme, reveals the true proportions and progression of their three disparate careers.

Newman's role was that of the supremely adequate nineteenth-century apologist of orthodoxy in terms comprehensible to his contemporaries. The chief effort of the final two decades of Arnold's life, in both the religious writings and the later literary criticism, was precisely to defend the validity of Christian ethics and Christian feeling, even while acknowledging the disappearance of God announced by contemporary agnosticism and science. Moreover, he continually violated his own self-imposed intellectual limitations by suggesting a transcendent source or power or tendency whose name was the "Eternal." In Pater's most Christian phase, religion remained only the supreme "hope" or "possibility" but still a "necessity." Even in his early, most antipathetic mood, when traditional religion was presented largely as the forerunner of certain ideal modes of apprehension, the "religious graces" remained as the crown of life, the reward of the highest human striving.

Newman's important role in the history of nineteenth-century aestheticism seems virtually to have escaped detection. At the base of the large number of suggestive phrases and ideas from Newman which resonate through Arnold's and Pater's work is the extraordinary openness of Newman's Christian humanism to the diversity and unpredictability of human experience, even of secular experience. This openness is best conveyed in the *Idea of a University,* above all in the too little known essays of the second half, and in the *Grammar of Assent.* Perhaps the "miracle" both Arnold and Pater found in Newman is the astonishing fact that this, the most powerful defender of the claims of religion upon the modern mind, was also the most adequate definer, in prose of incomparable lucidity and suavity, of an ideal of totality, comprehensiveness, inclusiveness, at a time when the image of the distinctively human was being either fragmented or radically reduced. Arnold's religionizing of culture in the sixties had ample precedent in Newman's transference, almost verbatim, of the description of the supernatural virtues in the Oxford sermons to his description of secular education in Discourse V of the *Idea of a University*. Moreover, Newman's early view that "Poetry . . . is our mysticism" anticipates Arnold's view in the literary essays of his final decade. No doubt Pater found it easy to turn to his own uses Newman's discussion of the "beauty of our moral being" and "the beauty of grace" (*Idea*, p. 108).[3] Perhaps most important, Arnold, Pater, and their successors live out the full consequences of Newman's prediction, expressed in an 1841 review of Henry Hart Milman, that, on the liberal Anglican premises, Christian revelation will "have done no more than introduce a *quality* into our moral life, not anything that can be contemplated by itself, obeyed and perpetuated" (*ECH*, II, 242).

Newman could be important to these two men in part because orthodox Christianity, although imperiled, remained a decisive cultural force in England, close to the mainstream of national life and of consequence to intellectuals, long after its importance had receded on the Continent. The picturesque medievalism of the Romantic and Victorian poets unquestionably lay behind, and gave impetus to, both the Oxford Movement and aestheticism.[4] The lines traced here present, I think,

---

[3] Robert L. Peters (*Victorians on Literature and Art*, p. 56) suggests interestingly that in such a passage Newman "was supplying, though unwittingly, a rationale for the Cyrenaicism of Pater and the aesthetes." But surely he is misleading when he states that Newman "equated the scholar's 'beauty of intellect' with the artist's 'beauty of feature and form,' the poet's 'beauty of mind,' and the preacher's 'beauty of grace' ": the main point of Newman's passage is that "Every thing has its own perfection . . . and the perfection of one is not the perfection of another."

[4] John Beer's essay, "Newman and the Romantic Sensibility" (*The English Mind: Studies in the English Moralists presented to Basil Willey*, ed. Hugh Sykes Davies and George Watson, pp. 193–218), is valuable in suggesting the wide extent of Newman's romanticism. Beer demonstrates that Newman escaped the dangers of his own romantic sensibility: "To have remained in Oxford as it was . . . would have been to enclose himself in a walled garden of sensibility: his religious quest for per-

a more serious side of the nineteenth century's encounter with its "medieval" past. To combine Hough's approach with my own is suddenly to throw the Late Victorian cultural situation into a new perspective: it can be meaningfully seen as Protestant England's partial rediscovery and recapturing of its disavowed European, and thus "Catholic," past. Hence, part of the fascination Catholicism exercised over both Arnold and Pater: hence, also, the impression that this Catholic emphasis, which marks in one respect the end of Protestant England, comes too late in the day to be of the most vital use in a rapidly deteriorating religious and cultural situation.[5] It is probably Newman who, above all, accounts for Arnold's and Pater's calling for a "Catholic" religious humanism, even though no longer on the basis of belief in Newman's sense of the term. To that extent, the Tractarians, and especially Newman after the publication of the *Apologia* in 1864, were important agents in putting an end to "Protestant" England, though its successor was not an England any of the principals in this book would have approved—for reasons similar to those later voiced by T. S. Eliot in his sociological essays. It is tempting to say that if there had not been the "miracle" of Newman—the subtle defender of religious orthodoxy who was also the adequate definer of a humanist consciousness—Late Victorian literary life might well have been less "religious" than it was, and that without him it is impossible otherwise to account for the precise religious tone suffusing much of the work of the period.

The special reasons for Arnold's and Pater's attraction to Newman must begin and end with the force of the Oxford tradition itself, a distinctive tradition of personal and intellectual formation that I have called "theological humanism." Unquestionably, the writings of the

---

manence must have died into an aestheticism that circled in its own harmonies, leaving no road open to action."

[5] The rise of a "literary" Catholicism, often very different from the actual Catholic culture around it, in such Victorian and Late Victorian figures as Coventry Patmore, the Wards, the Meynells, Aubrey De Vere, Francis Thompson, Lionel Johnson, and Gerard Manley Hopkins is heavily indebted to Newman's example and influence but has never been coherently examined from this point of view. Newman's role in the still unfinished "Modernist" episode in the Roman Catholic Church, as well as its reverberations in the Church of England, has also escaped close examination.

three men reflect the progressive detachment of the older Oxford from the realities of contemporary society; it is increasingly a theme for picturesque, nostalgic treatment, like one of Morris' or Rossetti's medieval subjects.[6] But it is equally true that the Oxford consciousness and "sentiment," which Arnold found embodied in Newman and passed on to Pater, was very close to the center of the practical work of his critical career. Newman was attractive to Arnold because he provided the fullest definition and exemplification of the highest, most complex use of the human faculties, a complex of values both men saw as increasingly under attack from an insurgent scientific naturalism and a newly refurbished rationalism. Newman was thus the supreme practitioner of that refined intellectual and spiritual perception that is the link between Arnold's intellectual and religious writings. Moreover, Newman had best described and accounted for changes in religious dogma as the result of changes in general culture: his doctrine of development, itself an acknowledgment of the new nineteenth-century demand for an "historical" view of things, was admirably adapted to the needs of an Arnold increasingly attuned to the whispers of the *Zeitgeist*. Pater found in Newman the fullest formulation of the psychological grounds of faith and the act of belief—one-half of his final, awkwardly maintained dualism. He was responding, again, to

[6] Paul Elmer More (*The Drift of Romanticism: Shelburne Essays, Eighth Series,* pp. 105–107) sees the weakness in Pater as deriving precisely from the "withdrawal from life" represented in the Oxford tradition, its monastic ideal of "faith fleeing the world" leading to "a worship of beauty isolated from, and in the end despised by, the real interests of life." "Paterism might without great injustice be defined as the quintessential spirit of Oxford emptied of the wholesome intrusions of the world—its pride of isolation reduced to sterile self-absorption, its enchantment of beauty alembicated into a faint Epicureanism, its discipline of learning changed into a voluptuous economy of sensations, its golden calm stagnated into languid elegance" (p. 108).

Though marred by sentimentality and lack of interpretative power, William S. Knickerbocker's *Creative Oxford: Its Influence in Victorian Literature* usefully explores the idea of "rationalism and Catholicism" in contention for the soul of Victorian Oxford, especially in "Oxford's four great humanists"—Newman, Arnold, Ruskin, and Pater. His brief treatment of Arnold and Newman (pp. 148–149) is in line with my own thesis: "To have heard Newman, to have read him, to have caught the cadence of his style and his high, poetic realisation of Oxford's uniqueness and significance, tended to unify and to give point to all his [Arnold's] own varied efforts."

Newman's prophetic sense of the special character of any apologetic adequate to the needs of the nineteenth century, a sense first clearly enunciated in the Introduction to the *Development of Christian Doctrine* (1845). Further, Newman had worked out a "personalist" theory of literature which best embodied Pater's idea of the special function of literature in modern times. And finally, to both Arnold and Pater, Newman had presented the image of European—and Christian—civilization as an enduring source of value satisfying the permanent ethical and aesthetic needs of man: in effect, the basis of a culture superior to the anarchic individualism of the nineteenth century.[7]

This book converges, in ways I had not originally anticipated, on Pater. For example, by an instructive paradox not previously worked out, Pater's final religious position is seen to be as much indebted to Newman's orthodoxy as it is to Arnold's "natural" Christianity. It is important to insist that in emphasizing the complex uses to which Pater puts his Arnoldian borrowings, I am not claiming too much or the wrong things for Arnold as a source; indeed, none of these studies is conceived as a "source" study in the narrow sense. I have deliberately neglected many of the known sources of Pater's interest in art for art's sake and other doctrines (for example, Goethe, Swinburne, Hegel, Heine), but there is no other author whose phrases, ideas, arguments, and attitudes so completely saturate Pater's writings at all stages as do Arnold's, and the apparent echoes illuminate as much by contrast as by likeness. A close examination of the full significance of the Arnoldian matrix clarifies and readjusts our apprehension of the unifying motives and directions of Pater's career. Moreover, the chronological reading of Pater's works from the points of view I have adopted (his response to Arnold, his dialectical struggle with the Christian-pagan dichotomy, his reliance on Newman in working out his later religious position) reveals with, I hope, new clarity and precision the central motifs, the

---

[7] I have been greatly helped in this matter by the sustained reflection of A. Dwight Culler: in *The Imperial Intellect: A Study of Cardinal Newman's Educational Ideal*; "Method in the Study of Victorian Prose," *The Victorian Newsletter*, No. 9 (Spring 1956), pp. 1–4; and his introductions to Newman's *Apologia pro Vita Sua* and *Poetry and Criticism of Matthew Arnold*.

polemical intentions, and the shifts in thought which seem still to be ignored in most readings of Pater.

The central topic of the present book is a Victorian embodiment of one of the great recurrent and unifying "myths" of European history: the conflict of Apollo and Christ, Rome and Jerusalem, intelligence and belief, the secular and the sacred impulses in society. This culture conflict as it is worked out in Arnold and Pater is *not* a thrice-told tale. Indeed, its full implications can only be grasped in a very long look ahead to our present situation, a look we seem even today scarcely prepared to take. For the full dimensions of *secularity* in the modern world, especially as it has exhibited itself in phenomena of the mid-twentieth century like religious and atheistic existentialism and "secular" Christianity, are the long-delayed fruits of "Modernist" speculation in the late nineteenth century. The importance of the Christian-pagan theme in Arnold and Pater is its inconclusiveness. Despite his avowed agnosticism, his pose of empiricism, and his resistance to the transcendental and metaphysical, Arnold persistently appeals to a covert supernaturalism in the religious writings and in the literary writings of the final decade, whether in his periphrases for God or in his generally unrecognized openness to the "mystery" of existence and to a universal morality of history. In the final reckoning he confessed his inability to fuse reason and faith, ideas and morality, in a higher, post-Christian synthesis. For Pater there is a similar exhaustion of thought after the careful irresolution of *Marius*, and his subsequent failure to define the "mixed" culture he aspired to, or what the "third condition" of man, transcending historic dualisms, might be.

The "failure" of Arnold and Pater is significant because they insist, in effect, that a "religious" reading of human nature involving a complex vision of man's permanent moral and aesthetic needs is requisite in any adequate modern humanism. They remain figures of living importance even today because, with unparalleled force and fullness in their own generation, they insisted on a humanistic vision alive on the one hand to the implications of nineteenth-century evolutionary science and on the other to a comprehensive retention of those qualities of mind, emotion, and imagination which have defined what it has meant to be fully "human" in the European past.[8] More specifically, the issue is that of the place of religion in an increasingly embattled literary humanism. The older tradition of "literae humaniores," in which letters (including history) shared room, perhaps the smaller room, with philosophy and theology, was the shifting synthesis within which European civilization, "theological humanism," defined itself. Only in the rapid breakdown of that tradition in the nineteenth century did letters move to the center of the humanist scheme, filling the void created by the discrediting or even disappearance of the more ratiocinative components of the traditional educational program; "reason" itself was increasingly confined to the methods of science and technology and denied a significant role in metaphysical or theological speculation. In any event, modern apologists for letters, whether theologically orthodox or not, tend to adopt a religious tone and to assign to poetry a central function in the preservation of humane values—a function previously shared with the more normative disciplines.[9]

[8] My "The Place of the Classics in T. S. Eliot's Christian Humanism" (Frederic Will, ed., *Hereditas: Seven Essays on the Modern Experience of the Classical*, pp. 153–197) takes up a more advanced stage of the same process in a more decisively secular and metaphysically neutral climate. Partly because of his greater perspective, Eliot has a clearer apprehension than either Arnold or Pater, of what the issues are and of what is at stake for both religion and culture. Norman Friedman ("Newman, Aristotle, and the New Criticism: On the Modern Element in Newman's Poetics," *PMLA*, LXXXI [June 1966], 271) strikingly concludes: "nineteenth- and twentieth-century poetry and poetics represent what may be a last-ditch attempt to rescue the subjective life of the free individual from the encroachments of Western technological civilization."

[9] Richard Foster, *The New Romantics: A Reappraisal of the New Criticism*, describes in detail the movement of representative American New Critics from a formalist position to something like a religious or even mystical view of the role of letters in society. He centers his discussion on Arnold's statement of 1880 that "The future of poetry is immense."

William A. Madden's "The Divided Tradition of English Criticism" (*PMLA*, LXXIII [March 1958], 69–80) is the best discussion of the theological presuppositions of modern criticism. He sees an "unbridgeable gap" between those who view art as "handmaiden" (Hulme, Eliot) and those who take art as "savior" (Arnold, Pater, Yeats, I. A. Richards, Herbert Read). Madden brings up important continuities between Arnold and Pater, but I would question his failure to distinguish both in mood and substance Arnold's poetry from his prose, and (though he correctly sees the importance of religion in Pater) his virtual denial of any genuine Christian elements in his thought. Madden's *Matthew Arnold: A Study of the Aesthetic Tempera-*

Arnold and Pater provide necessary points of departure for any survey of the evolution of this modern rationale of letters or the "humanities" in a hostile environment because they are the first conservative literary thinkers to defend letters while fully acknowledging the challenge of radical, reductive modern thought. I think it no exaggeration to say that the contemporary defense of letters (illogical, unstable, and necessary) cannot be understood without a strong sense of the complex of values, deriving from the experience of Oxford itself, which the three principals of this book centrally defended throughout their entire careers. And so if the Oxford humanists, Newman, Arnold, and Pater, are foster parents, however problematical, of aestheticism, the issues they raise reach well beyond the abortive productions of a special moment in late nineteenth-century culture. The fate of their shared concern for the maintenance of certain inherited modes of human consciousness was involved in the collapse of the older Oxford tradition itself and thus with the collapse of the unity and dynamism of European education as a whole. To perpetuate the values that Arnold and Pater subsumed under the term "culture"—despite the absence of older sustaining religious and social beliefs and an increasing divorce from the actualities of modern society—remains, I believe, the tragically unfulfilled aspiration of twentieth-century literary humanists. The sustaining and growing conviction, then, out of which this book has grown is that the definition of the humanist consciousness linking Newman, Arnold, and Pater, an effort made, significantly, with a strong and increasingly defensive sense of an entire scale of values in grave, perhaps terminal, crisis, is even today the indispensable basis of our dis-

---

ment in Victorian England, which appeared too late to be used in this study, is the fullest case yet argued for the "aesthetic" as the dominating motif of Arnold's career. But the book errs, in my judgment, by simplifying Arnold and by discounting or ignoring Arnold's later interests, especially religious, which I have tried to account for in this book.

Vincent Buckley, in *Poetry and Morality*, reflects in detail and helpfully on the ways in which Arnold's moralism distorts and limits his criticism, especially as the result of his defective views of religion and of poetic "form." Though he dwells centrally on "The Study of Poetry" (1880), he might have found Arnold's dilemmas in even sharper form, and self-confessed, in the comparatively neglected "Literature and Science" (1882).

cussion of literature and the role of literature in the humanizing process. Indeed, the confusions and failure of historical perspective of the Leavis-Snow debate and our mandatory and perennial anguish over the "crisis in the humanities" repeat without much advancing that earlier line of thought. The issues in the on-going debate—literary, religious, and broadly cultural—have by no means been worked out to their ultimate conclusion or even to some sort of stability. Far from comprising an "episode" of a past culture, the issues first raised with some clarity and penetration by Newman, Arnold, and Pater are the issues defining the quality of our future.

CONTENTS

Acknowledgments vii
Introduction ix
Abbreviations xxiii

ARNOLD AND NEWMAN: HUMANISM AND THE OXFORD TRADITION

PART I   THE OXFORD SENTIMENT 5

CHAPTER   1. The Oriel Inheritance 5
CHAPTER   2. The Quarrel of Reason and Faith 26
CHAPTER   3. The Onslaught on the Philistines 39
CHAPTER   4. Newman and the Religion of Culture 61

PART II   THE RELIGION OF THE FUTURE 81

CHAPTER   5. Development and the *Zeitgeist* 81
CHAPTER   6. Literature and Dogma 101
CHAPTER   7. Catholicism and the Future of Religion . . . 121
CHAPTER   8. Newman and the Future of Poetry 139
CHAPTER   9. Newman and the Center of the Arnoldian Vision . 152

ARNOLD, PATER, AND THE DIALECTIC OF HEBRAISM AND HELLENISM

PART I   THE SCARCE REMEDIABLE CLEAVAGE 165

CHAPTER 10. The Dialectical Impulse 165
CHAPTER 11. The Hellenism of Arnold and Pater 171
CHAPTER 12. The Sources 181

PART II   ARNOLD, PATER, AND THE REINSTATEMENT
          OF MAN   192

CHAPTER 13. "Coleridge" and the Higher Morality   192
CHAPTER 14. "Winckelmann" and Pagan Religious
             Sentiment   202
CHAPTER 15. Arnold, Pater, and the Supreme, Artistic
             View of Life   222
CHAPTER 16. The Renaissance   230
CHAPTER 17. Arnold, Pater, and the Complete Religion
             of the Greeks   245

PART III   PATER AND THE THIRD CONDITION OF HUMANITY .   .   256

CHAPTER 18. Toward *Marius*: Aesthetic Worship   256
CHAPTER 19. *Marius* and the Necessity of Religion   263
CHAPTER 20. Gaston and the Lower Pantheism   285
CHAPTER 21. Plato and Pater's Double Vision   296

PATER AND NEWMAN: THE ROAD TO THE NINETIES

CHAPTER 22. Newman and the Rhetoric of Aestheticism   .   .   .   305
CHAPTER 23. Newman and the Theology of *Marius*   314
CHAPTER 24. The "Style" of Humanism   329
CHAPTER 25. Newman, Arnold, Pater, and the Future   .   .   .   339

Appendix I   345
Appendix II   347
Bibliography   349
Index   361

ABBREVIATIONS

The following abbreviations are used in citing Newman's works: the publisher in all cases except *EDD* is Longmans, Green, and Co.:

Apologia   *Apologia Pro Vita Sua,* ed. Charles Frederick Harrold. New York, 1947.

D&A   *Discussions and Arguments on Various Subjects.* London, 1897.

DofA   *Certain Difficulties Felt by Anglicans in Catholic Teaching.* 2 vols. London, 1897.

ECH   *Essays Critical and Historical.* 2 vols. London, 1897.

EDD   *An Essay on the Development of Christian Doctrine.* London: J. Toovey, 1845.

GA   *An Essay in Aid of a Grammar of Assent,* ed. Charles Frederick Harrold. New York, 1947.

Idea   *The Idea of a University,* ed. Charles Frederick Harrold. New York, 1947.

LCJHN   *Letters and Correspondence of John Henry Newman,* ed. Anne Mozley. 2 vols. London, 1898.

LG   *Loss and Gain: The Story of a Convert.* 9th ed. London, 1891.

OUS   *Fifteen Sermons Preached before the University of Oxford.* London, 1898.

PPS   *Parochial and Plain Sermons.* 8 vols. London, 1899.

Verses   *Verses on Various Occasions.* London, 1896.

The following abbreviations are used in citing Arnold's works:

CPW   *The Complete Prose Works of Matthew Arnold,* ed. R. H. Super. Vol. I: *On the Classical Tradition* (1960); Vol.

III: *Lectures and Essays in Criticism* (1962); Vol. V: *Culture and Anarchy* (1965). Ann Arbor: University of Michigan Press, 1960————.

DA   *Discourses in America.* New York: The Macmillan Company, 1896.

EC-2   *Essays in Criticism, Second Series.* London: Macmillan and Company, 1895.

ELR   *Essays, Letters, and Reviews by Matthew Arnold,* ed. Fraser Neiman. Cambridge, Massachusetts: Harvard University Press, 1960.

GB   *God and the Bible.* New York: Macmillan and Company, 1883.

L   *Letters of Matthew Arnold, 1848–1888,* ed. G. W. E. Russell. 2 vols. in one. New York: The Macmillan Company, 1900.

LC   *The Letters of Matthew Arnold to Arthur Hugh Clough,* ed. Howard Foster Lowry. London and New York: Oxford University Press, 1932.

LD   *Literature and Dogma.* New York: The Macmillan Company, 1883.

MxE and   *Mixed Essays* and *Irish Essays and Others.* 2 vols. in one.
IEO   New York: The Macmillan Company, 1883.

NB   *The Note-books of Matthew Arnold,* eds. Howard Foster Lowry, Karl Young, and Waldo Hilary Dunn. London: Oxford University Press, 1952.

PW   *The Poetical Works of Matthew Arnold,* eds. C. B. Tinker and H. F. Lowry. London: Oxford University Press, 1950.

SPP and   *St. Paul and Protestantism* and *Last Essays on Church and*
LECR   *Religion.* 2 vols. in one. New York: Macmillan and Co., 1883.

UL   *Unpublished Letters of Matthew Arnold,* ed. Arnold Whitridge. New Haven: Yale University Press, 1923.

The following abbreviations are used in citing Pater's works; with the exception of *Ren-1*, all are in the Library Edition (London: Macmillan & Co., 1910):

Appr.   *Appreciations.*
EG   *Essays from 'The Guardian'.*
GL   *Gaston de Latour: An Unfinished Romance.*
GS   *Greek Studies.*
ME   *Marius the Epicurean: His Sensations and Ideas.* 2 vols.
MS   *Miscellaneous Studies.*
PP   *Plato and Platonism.*
Ren-1   *Studies in the History of the Renaissance.* London: Macmillan and Co., 1873.
Ren-3   *The Renaissance: Studies in Art and Poetry.* 3rd ed.

HEBREW AND HELLENE IN VICTORIAN ENGLAND

NEWMAN, ARNOLD, AND PATER

Arnold and Newman:
Humanism and the Oxford Tradition

PART I

THE OXFORD SENTIMENT

CHAPTER ONE The Oriel Inheritance

Matthew Arnold and John Henry Newman met only twice. The first meeting took place on May 13, 1880, when Arnold was invited to a reception given by the Duke of Norfolk at his house in St. James's Square in honor of Newman, who had been made a Cardinal in Rome in May of the preceding year. Arnold was fifty-seven years old, with the bulk of his poetry and criticism behind him; Newman, then seventy-nine, had felt that "the cloud is lifted" in the bestowal of the hat, but the major writings had ended ten years before, and the remaining decade of his life was spent out of the public eye.

Arnold received the invitation on Thursday, the day of the reception, but had to attend a dinner first. His friend Arthur Stanley, himself a former Rugbeian and Oxonian and now a leader of the Broad-Church party, was present. Arnold later gave his sister Fan a delightful vignette of Stanley, always something of a social climber, "who was deeply interested and excited at my having the invitation to meet the Cardinal; he hurried me off the moment dinner was over, saying, 'This is not a thing to lose!' " (*L*, II, 196) That very night, when he arrived home, Arnold wrote Stanley the following account:

Newman stood in costume, in a reserved part of the drawing room, supported by a chaplain and by the D. of Norfolk. Devotees, chiefly women, kept pressing up to him; they were named to him, knelt, kissed his hand, got a word or two and passed on. I don't know that I should have had the courage to cleave the press, but Lady Portsmouth took charge of me and conveyed me safe to the chaplain who whispered my name to Newman. I made the most deferential of bows, he took my hand in both of his and held it there during our interview, which of course was very short. He said: "I ventured to tell the Duchess I should like to see you," and I said I was glad of the opportunity to tell him how much I owed him. He asked me a question or two about myself, and then about Tom and his troubles; nothing of any interest passed, but I am glad to have spoken to him and shaken hands with him. The sentiment of him, of his sermons, of his position in the Church and in English religion, filled Oxford when I was there; it suited the place, and I am glad, and always shall be glad, to have been there at that moment, and grateful to Newman for the atmosphere of feeling he then created for me.[1]

The "sentiment" of Newman, "the atmosphere of feeling" he created in Arnold's young manhood, suffused much of Arnold's later career. How much Arnold "owed" Newman, however, in two of his most persistent concerns—the role and stance of the critic, and the religious future of England—has never been fully recorded.

Forty years ago the late Henry Tristram in a helpful study suggested a number of connections between the two men, especially in their common attack on "Liberalism."[2] What remains unexplored in its range and complexity is Arnold's life-long involvement with Newman, as a man and as an intellectual stimulus—and the two are not easily separated. For example, Newman is a constantly invoked presence in Arnold's religious writings of the eighteen-seventies, and not always as the "adversary," even though Newman's religious position is, for Arnold, frankly "impossible" (*DA*, p. 139). The sheer mass and importance of direct and indirect reference to Newman in Arnold's writings, when combined with an extended correspondence between the two men, force the conclusion that Newman was more central and more essential to Arnold's development than is generally

[1] Unpublished letter in the possession of Mr. Seymour Adelman of Philadelphia, by whose generosity it is presented here.

[2] Henry Tristram, "Newman and Matthew Arnold," *The Cornhill*, N.S. LX (March 1926), 309–319.

believed. The precise weight and tone of Arnold's attitudes toward
a number of crucial matters—criticism and the qualities of the critic;
culture, Liberalism, Philistinism; religious "development," the Oxford Movement, the Roman Catholic Church; the relation of religion
to poetry—cannot be caught without reference to Arnold's relation
to Newman. Beyond these matters of belief and opinion, however,
there remains the enigma of the two men—both subtle, both masters
of style and the public manner, and, despite the barrier of twenty
years and incompatible commitments, bound together in an almost
unique (though long-distance) master-disciple relationship com-
pounded of affection, respect, flattering mutual interest, and a kind
of awed and wary incomprehension.

When Matthew Arnold entered Balliol College in the autumn of
1841, John Henry Newman, until recently the acknowledged leader
of the Tractarians, was unquestionably the most spiritually attractive
figure at Oxford. But Arnold's enrollment almost exactly coincided
with the ebbing of the Tractarian tide. Tract 90 appeared in February,
1841, its burden being that the Thirty-Nine Articles "do not oppose
Catholic teaching; they but partially oppose Roman dogma; they for
the most part oppose the dominant errors of Rome" (*Apologia*, p. 72).
In the deafening din of repudiation, Newman retired to Littlemore,
and, as he says in the *Apologia*, "From the end of 1841, I was on my
death-bed, as regards my membership with the Anglican Church"
(*Apologia*, p. 133). For the observation of this scene of acute spiritual
and intellectual turmoil, Matthew Arnold brought special qualifications: his father, Thomas Arnold, had been for some years perhaps
Newman's most bitter and outspoken public enemy.

In the decade before he went up to Oxford, Matthew Arnold must
have heard a great deal, much of it decidedly unfavorable, about the
Tractarian Movement and its leading spirit. Almost unbelievably,
Newman and Thomas Arnold met only twice. In 1828, Newman had
disputed with Arnold for his B.D. degree, "merely to keep Arnold
company" (*LCJHN*, I, 158, 159). And in February 1842, four
months before Arnold's death, they met again; reflecting, two years
later, on their relations, Newman regretfully describes the elder Ar-

nold as "a man whom I have always separated from the people he was
with, always respected, always defended, though from an accident
he got a notion that I was a firebrand, and particularly hostile to *him*"
(*LCJHN*, II, 395). Between the two meetings stretches the phenom-
enon of Tractarianism, the meaning of which Thomas Arnold remained to the last stubbornly unable to comprehend.[3] His blindness
to its theological richness and to the value of its practical side, the
quest for a religion of holiness, may have sprung from his closeness
to its chief figures. Oriel College is the key. Both Dr. Arnold and Newman had held fellowships at Oriel, and consequently had a great many
mutual friends and acquaintances.[4] There, in John Keble and in Hurrell Froude, Newman had found the companions suited to create a
climate favorable to the aims of the Oxford Movement. There, too,
Dr. Arnold found, in liberals like Richard Whately, Renn Dickson
Hampden, and Edward Copleston, support for his own Latitudinarian
theology and for a reading of Scripture which minimized the traditional force of prophecy and miracle.

Matthew Arnold's standing with regard to these two incompatible
Oriel traditions is of the utmost importance in understanding his own
complex theological disposition—at once liberal and conservative,
poetic and rationalistic. To the Oxford Movement, and above all to
Newman, Arnold was to look for that temper of mind which he was to
recommend as perhaps the chief substance of his critical and social
essays. From the "Oriel Noetics," men like Whately and Hampden,
Arnold learned the chief method of his religious criticism of the
eighteen-seventies—the sharp distinction between the explicative language of theology and the symbolic and "approximative" language of
the Bible.[5] The two original lines of antagonistic thought grew, significantly, by mutual repulsion. One of the chief purposes of Hampden's
Scholastic Theology Considered in its Relation to Christian Theology

[3] See Thomas Mozley, *Reminiscences, Chiefly of Oriel College and the Oxford
Movement*, II, 54; and Arnold Whitridge, *Dr. Arnold of Rugby*, p. 170.

[4] T. W. Bamford, *Thomas Arnold*, p. 95. Long ago Leslie Stephen (*Studies of a
Biographer*, II, 99–102) broached the subject of Matthew Arnold's dual Oxford inheritance.

[5] See William Blackburn, "Matthew Arnold and the Oriel Noetics," *Philological
Quarterly*, XXV (January 1946), 70–78.

(the Bampton lectures for 1832) was precisely to discredit the views on tradition held by the men of the Oxford Movement. That movement, born officially in July 1833, defined itself from the first as a "counter-movement" bent upon resisting "the assault of Liberalism upon the old orthodoxy of Oxford and England" (*Apologia*, p. 53), a Liberalism centered very strongly in the person of Thomas Arnold. This was the "Liberalism" that Matthew Arnold in the sixties was to insist that he and Newman were joined together in repulsing. In fact Matthew Arnold, who won an Oriel fellowship in March 1844, claimed *both* Oriel traditions as his own, though undoubtedly he was never willing or able to resolve the deep ambiguities of their union in his thinking. At times, to be sure, Matthew Arnold expressed impatience with that whole generation of Oriel thinkers, their common defect being, it would seem, their taint of provinciality—so abhorrent to Arnold. In 1869, after reading John Taylor Coleridge's *Memoir* of John Keble (who was Matthew Arnold's godfather), Arnold complained to his mother: "my one feeling when I close the book is of papa's immense superiority to all the set, mainly because, owing to his historic sense, he was so wonderfully, for his nation, time, and profession, European, and thus so got himself out of the narrow medium in which, after all, his English friends lived" (*L*, II, 5; February 20, 1869). However, in the last essay Arnold wrote—published three months after his death in 1888—he looks back to that Oriel generation, and sees them all as one in "tone, bearing, dignity." Speaking of such figures as Shelley, Godwin, Hunt, and Byron in his review of Edward Dowden's life of Shelley, Arnold suddenly, and for unclear reasons, exclaims:

what a set! The history carries us to Oxford, and I think of the clerical and respectable Oxford of those old times, the Oxford of Copleston and the Kebles and Hawkins, and a hundred more. . . . I appeal to Cardinal Newman, if perchance he does me the honour to read these words, is it possible to imagine Copleston or Hawkins declaring himself safe "while the exalted mind of the Duke of Norfolk protects me with the world?" (*EC-2*, p. 238)

The conflation of all these disparate men, Edmund Copleston, John and Thomas Keble, Edward Hawkins, and Newman, as well as the grounds for his admiration, suggest the complexity, and perhaps the confusion, of Matthew Arnold's religious position. It also suggests that when Arnold speaks, again and again, of the Oxford of the "old times" he is thinking of the eighteen-twenties, thirties, and forties, of the Oriel of Thomas Arnold's and John Henry Newman's generation.

Thomas Arnold was involved in one of the great spiritual crises of Newman's life. In May 1833, while traveling alone in Sicily, Newman fell seriously ill; in his feverish state, he subjected himself to an intense examination of his own spiritual "hollowness." In the account he later wrote, Newman explained: "Arnold in his letter to Grant about me, accuses me among others of identifying high excellence with certain peculiarities of my own—i.e. preaching myself."[6] The letter to Grant does not survive; the closest we may come to its contents is a letter to A. P. Stanley, of May 1836:

Now with regard to the Newmanites. I do not call them bad men, nor would I deny their many good qualities. . . . but fanaticism is idolatry . . . a fanatic worships something which is the creature of his own devices, and thus even his self-devotion in support of it is only an apparent self-sacrifice, for it is in fact making the parts of his nature or his mind, which he least values, offer sacrifice to that which he most values. The moral fault . . . is in the idolatry,—the setting up some idea which is most kindred to our own minds, and then putting it in the place of Christ. . . . it is clear to me that Newman and his party are idolators.[7]

The manner is, for all its characteristically "explosive" tone,[8] surprisingly balanced for the man whose article on the "Oxford Malignants" had appeared in the preceding month.

Sometime earlier than Newman's illness of May 1833 occurred an episode that was to plague the personal relations of these two men of Oriel. At Rome, when asked whether a particular interpretation of

---

[6] John Henry Newman, *Autobiographical Writings,* ed. Henry Tristram, p. 125. Father Tristram's comments: "it is not clear whether he admitted the truth of the impeachment or not" (p. 143).

[7] Arthur Penrhyn Stanley, *The Life and Correspondence of Thomas Arnold,* II, 46–47, May 24, 1836.

[8] Mozley, *Reminiscences,* II, 54.

Scripture held by Thomas Arnold was Christian, Newman replied,
"But is *he* a Christian?" (*Apologia*, p. 30). By June of 1834 an "innocent" Newman complains that Hurrell Froude is abandoning him over
this "strange mishap":

> only think how mildly I have always spoken of Arnold, and how bitterly
> you; never did I use a harsh word against him, I think, except that once,
> and then at Rome, and with but one or two friends. Yet even from Rome
> these words are dragged forth, and I have to answer for them, in spite of
> my very great moderation and charity as touching him. (*LCJHN*, II, 42)

The unpleasantness was increased by the open bitterness of Thomas
Arnold's treatment of Newman in an Appendix (on the Apostolical
Succession) to Volume III of his *Sermons* (*LCJHN*, II, 82). By
January of 1836, Newman and Thomas Arnold had come to be looked
upon as the symbolic leaders of the opposing extremes at the University (*LCJHN,* II 146). Newman himself referred to the Liberals now
as "the school of Dr. Arnold" (*Apologia*, p. 191); and Newman saw
that Arnold's party was growing, throughout the thirties, in numbers
as well as in "breadth and definiteness of doctrine": above all, "by
the accession of Dr. Arnold's pupils, it was invested with an elevation of character which claimed the respect even of its opponents"
(*Apologia*, p. 264). Thomas Arnold's own lack of "mildness" and
"moderation" reached a kind of crescendo in the famous *Edinburgh*
article of April 1836, titled (though this was not Arnold's phrase)
"The Oxford Malignants." Newman and E. B. Pusey had both written works attacking Hampden as heretical, and the Tractarians made
his being offered the Regius Professorship of Divinity the occasion
for a violent *furor theologicus.* Arnold, convinced of the ill will of
the Tractarian party, plunged into the fray with his attack on "the
Oxford conspirators, . . . the formalist Judaizing fanatics," and "the
pretended holiness" of their lives: "But the attack on Dr. Hampden
bears upon it the character . . . of *moral wickedness.* . . . in such a proceeding we see nothing of Christian zeal, but much of the mingled
fraud, and baseness, and cruelty of fanatical persecution." Arnold
is convinced he is dealing with men "blinded by wilful neglect of the

highest truth" or "corrupted by the habitual indulgence of evil passions."[9]

This is the Arnold who, as a contemporary remarked, "wielded his pen as if it were a ferule";[10] he went to his grave without any clearer grasp of the real bearing of the Oxford Movement. The irony, perhaps even the tragedy and waste, of much of Thomas Arnold's controversial career, was that he and Newman were at one in their efforts to deepen the spiritual lives of the young men who came under their influence, and each was to leave a mark on the Church of England—on its piety and its theology—which would remain indelible for many years. Newman seems to have had a kind of tolerant contempt for Arnold as an ecclesiastical thinker, judging that "there is so little intellectual *consistency* in his bases" regarding the chimerical doctrine of the identification of the perfect State and the perfect Church. On the other hand, Newman could generously grant, on the appearance of A. P. Stanley's edition of the *Life and Correspondence* in 1844, that "it is very pleasant to think that his *work* has been so good a one—the reformation of public schools—this seems to have been blessed and will survive him."[11] Newman claimed, in a letter written to John Keble three months after Thomas Arnold's death: "I think I never spoke harshly of him except on the occasion which gave me the opportunity of doing so, and which I really cannot reproach myself with" (*LCJHN*, II, 359–360). That single remark, however, remained to trouble Newman for some years; only the conversion to Catholicism of Matthew Arnold's brother, Thomas Arnold, Jr., put that specter to rest. In 1856, two years after Tom Arnold's conversion, Newman wrote him: "I knew your father a little, and I really think I never had any unkind feeling towards him. . . . If I said ever a harsh thing against him I am very sorry for it. In seeing you, I should have a sort of pledge that he at the moment of his death made it all up with me."[12]

---

[9] Cited in Whitridge, *Dr. Arnold of Rugby,* p. 235.

[10] See *ibid.,* pp. 170–171.

[11] John Henry Newman, *Correspondence of John Henry Newman with John Keble and Others,* pp. 321–322.

[12] Mrs. Humphry Ward, *A Writer's Recollections,* p. 21.

In the absence of direct testimony, it is dangerous to speculate too closely on the motives for Matthew Arnold's abandonment of the Christianity of his boyhood home. Nevertheless, it has recently been shown that the loss of religious faith in such representative early Victorian agnostics as F. W. Newman (John Henry Newman's brother), J. A. Froude (brother of Newman's close friend, Hurrell Froude), and George Eliot was not due, in the first place, to the usually suggested reasons—the rise of evolutionary theory in geology and biology and the Higher Criticism of the Bible. Instead, in each life the dominant factor was a growing repugnance toward the *ethical* implications of what each had been taught to believe as essential Christianity—especially the set of interrelated doctrines: Original Sin, Reprobation, Baptismal Regeneration, Vicarious Atonement, Eternal Punishment.[13] Only after this alienation was fixed did the skeptical trio show serious interest in the Higher Criticism (as support for attacking offensive orthodox teachings) and evolution (as indicating a way of life more in harmony with the meliorist ethic of the age). Despite Matthew Arnold's rather tepid defense of the Christian "system of morality" in 1863 against John Stuart Mill's indictment of its negative character (*CPW*, III, 133), it is precisely the familiar arguments of the nineteenth-century agnostics based on ethical revulsion which Arnold urges in his own full-dress assault on Evangelical theology in *Saint Paul and Protestantism* (1870). He contemptuously rejects the "monstrous" vision of a capricious God who deals in election and predestination and cruelly emphasizes the crass commercial quality of the Puritan catchwords, "covenant," "ransom," "redeem," "purchase," "bargain" (*SPP*, pp. 7–11).

Arnold's loss of faith, whatever its cause, came early and was remarkably undramatic; it was not the turbulent spiritual struggle J. A. Froude endured (reflected in his semiautobiographical novels, *Shadows of the Clouds*, 1847, and *The Nemesis of Faith*, 1849), nor was it the

---

[13] See Howard R. Murphy, "The Ethical Revolt Against Christian Orthodoxy in Early Victorian England," *American Historical Review*, LX (July 1955), 800–817. Professor Charles Coulston Gillispie (*Victorian Studies*, II [December 1958], 166–169) would include Darwin and Leslie Stephen for the same reasons.

years-long diminution of belief which flickers painfully through the
letters of Arthur Hugh Clough.[14] By the time of his Oxford residency
whatever crisis Arnold had undergone seems to have passed. Even in
1840 and 1841 he was reluctant to avow the Thirty-Nine Articles or
accept the Athanasian Creed;[15] and Clough testifies that Arnold's
chapel attendance was irregular (*LC*, p. 25). Froude resented Arnold's
tone of being *au-dessus de la mêlée*, of being aloof from the spectacle
of religious struggle going on all about him. So fixed was Arnold by
1849 in the attitude of lofty impassivity, which is one of the moods
of the poems of this period, that Froude could complain to Clough,
obviously alluding to his own torment: "I admire Matt—to a very
great extent. Only I don't see what business he has to parade his calmness and lecture us on resignation when he has never known what a
storm is and doesn't know what he has to resign himself to—I think
he only knows the shady side of nature out of books."[16]

It is not surprising, then, that Arnold, like his brother Tom, never
"showed . . . the smallest tendency to 'Newmanism' " in any formal
sense while at Oxford.[17] Mrs. Humphry Ward, Tom's daughter,
writes:

Matthew Arnold occasionally went, out of admiration, my father used to
say, for that strange Newmanic power of words, which in itself fascinated
the young Balliol poet, who was to produce his own first volume of poems
two [*sic*] years after Newman's secession to the Church of Rome. But he
was never touched in the smallest degree by Newman's opinions. He and
my father and Arthur Clough, and a few other kindred spirits, lived indeed
in quite another world of thought. They discovered George Sand, Emerson
and Carlyle, and orthodox Christianity no longer seemed to them the sure
refuge that it had always been to the strong teacher who trained them as
boys.[18]

[14] Alan Harris wrote ("Matthew Arnold: The 'Unknown Years'," *Nineteenth
Century*, CXIII [April 1933], 499–500) that Arnold "seems, indeed, to have shed
his orthodox beliefs with few of the usual struggles."

[15] *LC*, pp. 23–24, citing a letter of Edward Walford, *The Times* (London), Friday,
April 20, 1880, p. 13.

[16] Arthur Hugh Clough, *The Correspondence of Arthur Hugh Clough*, ed. Frederick L. Mulhauser, I, 251.

[17] Mrs. Humphry Ward, *Recollections*, p. 11.

[18] *Ibid.*, pp. 11–12.

But her father, while supporting her view of the reason for the attraction, suggests a more intense and prolonged personal involvement with Newman. Tom writes: "The perfect handling of words, joined to the delicate presentation of ideas, attracted him powerfully to John Henry Newman, whose afternoon Sunday sermons at St. Mary's he for a long time regularly attended. But, so far as I know, Newman['s] teaching never made an impression upon him."[19] Tom himself was scarcely under the influence of Newman the man or the preacher:

Of Newman, in my undergraduate time, I had seen scarcely anything. I went certainly once—perhaps twice— to hear one of his afternoon sermons at St. Mary's, but the delicacy and refinement of his style were less cognisable by me than by my brother, and the multiplied quotations from Scripture, introduced by "And again"— "And again," the intention of which I only half divined, confused and bewildered me.[20]

What Matthew Arnold sought and found in the sermons he attended "for a long time" is not easily expressed. "The strange Newmanic power of words," "The perfect handling of words, joined to a delicate presentation of ideas"—these are the unquestioned attractions, and the burden of Arnold's praise of Newman in the sixties is precisely Newman's urbanity and intellectual delicacy. Further, in the 1883 lecture on "Emerson" Newman is presented as a figure of refined aesthetic interest in himself—a man of "imagination," "genius," "charm," and "style," a "spiritual apparition" (*DA*, pp. 139–141).

Exactly what did Arnold hear in Newman's sermons preached between the autumn of 1841 and September 25, 1843, the date of his last sermon in the Anglican Church? First, it is important to note that he did *not* hear either of the famous quotations rather misleadingly given in the "Emerson" lecture forty years later: these belong to 1838 and 1839. Only three of the *Parochial and Plain Sermons* belong to this era (Sermons X and XI of Volume VII, and Sermon XVI of Volume VIII), and only one of the *Oxford University Sermons*, "The Theory of Developments in Religious Doctrine" (despite its title, a rather distant forecast of the *Essay on the Development of Christian Doctrine*).

---

[19] Thomas Arnold, [Jr.], *Passages in a Wandering Life*, p. 57.
[20] *Ibid.*, p. 150.

The bulk of the sermons Arnold could have heard were sixteen of those appearing in *Sermons Bearing on Subjects of the Day*, which, notwithstanding its title, is almost exclusively concerned with devotional matters. Only very occasionally is a note struck which will be heard again in Arnold's religious writings: for example, Newman's dwelling on the small "elect remnant" who provide the nexus between the Jewish and the Christian Churches will be recalled in Arnold's lecture on "Numbers; or, The Majority and the Remnant"; and Newman's sermon on the Kingdom of God as "a kingdom *founded, based* in righteousness" finds an echo later in Arnold's increasing emphasis on "the kingdom of God or the reign of righteousness."[21] Above all, the Arnold who preached the "method of Jesus" as the overcoming of "faults of temper and faults of sensuality" by strictness of conscience ("inwardness"), and "the secret of Jesus" as "self-renouncement" leading to *peace, joy, life,* and the "element" of "mildness" and "sweet reasonableness" would have responded with great sympathy to Newman's exhortation: "Whatever is right, whatever is wrong, in this perplexing world, we must be right in 'doing justly, in loving mercy, in walking humbly with our God;' in denying our wills, in ruling our tongues, in softening and sweetening our tempers, in mortifying our lusts; in learning patience, meekness, purity, forgiveness of injuries, and continuance in well-doing."[22] These are, of course, all matters of direct concern to Arnold many years afterward and if Newman's sermons did indeed influence these passages in Arnold's writings, it is more likely that Arnold reread the *Sermons* after they were reissued in 1869.

The little direct evidence of Newman's influence on Arnold during Arnold's Oxford days is inconclusive. In 1843, in a letter to his friend, John Duke Coleridge, concerning his father's sermons, Arnold praised his own "utter want of prejudice" in finding it "perfectly possible to admire" both his father's *and* Newman's sermons.[23] On the other hand,

---

[21] See John Henry Newman, *Sermons Bearing on Subjects of the Day*, pp. 193 ff., and *DA*, pp. 15 ff. (Newman is cited directly, in a related context, *DA*, p. 6); and *Sermons*, pp. 237 ff., and *LD*, pp. 337 ff.

[22] See *Sermons*, p. 13, and *LD*, Chapter VII (Newman is brought into the argument on *LD*, p. 211).

[23] See Appendix I.

when A. P. Stanley's *Life and Correspondence of Thomas Arnold* appeared in May 1844, it was precisely Thomas Arnold's letter of May 1836, already cited above, attacking the Newmanites as "idolators," that Arnold singled out for approval. He wrote his mother in late May or early June: "What I have always thought clean conclusive, as he [Dr. Arnold] would have said, against the completeness of Newman's system, making it impossible that it should ever satisfy the whole of any man's nature, and which I have no doubt now I may have heard him say, is most characteristically put in the CXXX^th Letter."[24] The point of Arnold's objection to Newman's "system" is not clear, although the idea of satisfying the whole of a man's nature is suggested in Thomas Arnold's definition of Tractarian idolatry as "setting up some idea which is most kindred to our own minds, and then putting it in the place of Christ, who alone cannot be made an idol, and cannot inspire fanaticism, because He combines all ideas of perfection, and exhibits them in their just harmony and combination." But of course by 1844, although he might well refrain from telling his mother so, Arnold's own notion of the "ideas of perfection" in their "just harmony and combination" had advanced well beyond his father's. At least as regards Arnold's Oxford days, his brother Tom's judgment seems roughly correct: "Newman's teaching never made an impression upon him." How true this is, is seen by contrast in Arthur Hugh Clough, who had been bitten deeply by the Tractarian bug. In January 1838 Clough was reading Newman's sermons, and in April he reports that he likes "the great Newman" increasingly. In May, though no "thoroughgoing convert ad Neomanism," he was obviously filled with the heady theological disputes of the movement.[25] And as late as October 1843, the familiar Clough was struggling over the Thirty-Nine Articles and not "particularly inclined to become a Puseyite" but was prevented by his "Puseyitic position" from becoming anything else.[26] For Arnold there could be no such immersion in theological politics, and a letter

[24] Unpublished letter, dated only "Balliol, Sunday," in the possession of Arnold Whitridge; dating fixed by sentence, "you shall have my exhibition before June ends." For Thomas Arnold's letter, see note 7, above.

[25] Clough, *Correspondence*, I, 66, 69, 71–72.

[26] *Ibid.*, I, 124.

of his of March 1845, just a few months before Newman's conversion to the Catholic Church, is a "satire on Tractarianism," although its exact point is rather hard to specify (*LC*, pp. 55–57, and Lowry's note).

What remains, then, of the effect on Arnold of Newman and the Oxford Movement during this period? Owen Chadwick has recently reminded us:

> There is a certain continuity of piety between the Evangelical movement and the Oxford Movement. There were other reasons why the high churchmen should learn not to be afraid of the feelings—romantic literature and art, the sense of affection and the sensibility of beauty pervading European thought, the flowering of poetry, the medievalism of the novel or of architecture. But in religion the Evangelicals taught the Oxford men not to be afraid of their feelings. . . .
>
> Probably it is this element of feeling, the desire to use poetry as a vehicle of religious language, the sense of awe and mystery in religion, the profundity of reverence, the concern with the conscience not only by way of beauty, but by growth towards holiness, which marks the vague distinction between the old-fashioned high churchmen and the Oxford men.[27]

Surely it is these latter qualities to which Arnold could and did respond most strongly in the Oxford Movement, and above all in Newman. If one-half of Newman's influence on Arnold was to center on such matters as Liberalism and culture in the sixties, the rest was to affect the tone—and to some extent even the ideas—of the religious writings of the seventies. Only if Newman's "teaching" is restricted to his theological propositions and to Anglican ecclesiastical politics, can Tom Arnold's statement be said to be strictly true. For all of Matthew Arnold's plunge, during and after the Oxford years, into Goethe, Emerson, Carlyle, Spinoza, and George Sand, the experience of Newman's sermons over a "long time" was almost certain to provide Arnold with key attitudes that he developed later in *Literature and Dogma* and elsewhere. Feeling as an essential element of religion, the close tie between religion and poetry, the profound concern with conscience and morality—all of these Tractarian emphases survived the period of Arnold's greatest alienation from Christianity. Perhaps most important,

[27] Owen Chadwick, ed., *The Mind of the Oxford Movement*, p. 27.

these residual attitudes were to make Arnold unhappy, in the sixties, with the rather joyless stoicism that he had developed as an alternative to Christianity during the preceding two decades.

Not surprisingly, Newman's is a somewhat wraithlike presence in Arnold's early poetry. The bulk of the poetry falls during the forties and fifties, and his early critics soon saw that a "perfectly natural feeling of regret towards a departing faith" was "the principal source of the mournful and pathetic inspiration" of the early collections.[28] The poetry is, in fact, unintelligible except as the expression of Arnold's struggle to clear some standing room in a world where he can accept neither past, nor present, nor future. With regard to that past, which is in large part Christianity, Arnold may feel intense regret at the departure of faith, but never in this period does he hesitate in his rejection of Christianity, nor does he make the slightest movement toward reconciliation. What the poetry insists upon is the obligation of renouncing false props from the past and of accepting unblinkingly the implications of a naturalistic universe. He could have little sympathy for or patience with what he regarded (in "Thyrsis," 1866) as Clough's wavering and perhaps his spiritual cowardice. Throughout this period Arnold's attitude toward Christianity has a double aspect related to his later views; now his interest is in forging a philosophy outside the context of historical Christianity, whereas later his philosophy of man and of history will be explicitly "Christian." In both periods, however, he displays undisguised contempt for official religion and a kind of intense gaiety in exposing the pretensions of self-consciously religious people. He writes Clough in 1849, admitting that he is "more snuffing after a moral atmosphere to respire in than ever before in my life"; but he makes clear that he and Clough are above merely religious people like Arnold's brother Tom, who was soon to follow Newman into the Catholic Church. Only he and Clough are "The children of the second birth /Whom the world could not tame";[29] the others, those preoccupied with religion, are "mystics and such cattle": Tom is not "in any sense cattle or even a mystic but he has not a 'still, considerate mind' "

---

[28] J. B. Selkirk, *Ethics and Aesthetics of Modern Poetry*, p. 43.

[29] A quotation from Arnold's poem, "Stanzas in Memory of the Author of 'Obermann' " (*PW*, p. 310).

(*LC,* pp. 109–110; September 23, 1849). The "cattle" whom Arnold seems most to have contemned were precisely agnostics like J. A. Froude and F. W. Newman, whose torments of conscience had become matters of public controversy.

In Arnold's *Cromwell,* the 1843 Newdigate prize poem at Oxford, Mrs. Tillotson claims to hear, "faintly, the voice of Newman."[30] She may be alluding to Arnold's almost Tractarian interest in the seventeenth-century Anglican Church, evident in the portraits of Laud, "In priestly garb, . . . like a saint at rest," and of Charles I: "the monarch wept alone, / Between a ruin'd church and shatter'd throne!" (*PW,* pp. 476, 477). Ironically, as C. B. Tinker and H. F. Lowry remark, "The selection of the subject may well have been intended to turn the attention of young enthusiasts back to the principles of Puritanism, and away from the pernicious doctrines of Catholicism with which Pusey and Newman had infected the University."[31] If in "Stanzas from the Grande Chartreuse," first published in 1855, Newman's voice can, as Mrs. Tillotson says,[32] be heard more clearly, it is in a deeply ambiguous context. Conceived as far back as Arnold's Oxford days, and written perhaps from 1851 on,[33] the "Grande Chartreuse" not only suggests the reasons for Arnold's growing dissatisfaction with his painful interim state, conveyed in the early poems, of a lofty, impassive stoicism; it also suggests in detail Arnold's attitudes toward the place of historic Christianity in the modern world—and with obvious references to Newman and the Oxford Movement.

The poem is not so much a lament for a lost Christianity as an expression of Arnold's hopelessness over the impotence to which his melancholy, withdrawn stoicism has reduced him. At least four different attitudes are considered in the poem: (1) Christian faith, which has simply "gone" (l. 84;) (2) Arnold's own "outworn" and "outdated code (ll. 100,106) gained from the "rigorous teachers" and

[30] Kathleen Tillotson, "Matthew Arnold and Carlyle" (Warton Lecture on English Poetry), *Proceedings of the British Academy,* XLII (1956), 139.

[31] C. B. Tinker and H. F. Lowry, *The Poetry of Matthew Arnold: A Commentary,* p. 323. Hereafter cited as *Commentary.*

[32] Tillotson, "Matthew Arnold and Carlyle," p. 149.

[33] Tinker and Lowry, *Commentary,* pp. 248–249.

"masters of the mind" of his youth, who are the "shy recluses" of
l. 192; (3) the attitude of the present, the "world" (l. 97), which is
entirely insensitive to the melancholy demeanor of "the race of them
who grieve" (l. 110); and (4) the vision of a far-distant renewed
world, now "powerless to be born" (l. 86), but in waiting for which
Arnold and his fellow recluses ask allowance for their "tears" (l. 162).
And so the "children" beneath the "abbey-wall" are not, as some commentators have assumed, *Christians,* but people like Arnold, post-
Christians, who have nevertheless been schooled in a philosophy of
meditative withdrawal and therefore are as unfitted for the life of
"action and pleasure" offered by the modern world (ll. 194 ff.) as are
the traditional Christians like the monks. Rather wistfully, Arnold
sees himself as too far committed to the "reverie" and seclusion of his
shy masters (l. 206), and resigns himself to his "desert" (l. 210).
Arnold's sense of being totally unfitted for activity in the world, as the
result of his early ethical discipline, is clear, and the poem thus becomes
entirely consistent with Arnold's relative indifference to Christianity
in this period. The tone of regret with regard to his present state is
unmistakable.

By the mid-fifties, then, the two "faiths" that Matthew Arnold had
successively held—that of Christian orthodoxy, and that which bade
him aspire to "the high, white star of Truth"—were both of the "dead"
world of the past. He seems, even if reluctantly, to accept the view of
the despised "world" that orthodox religious faith "is now / But a
dead time's exploded dream" (ll. 97–98). Tinker and Lowry are
correct, certainly, in seeing Dr. Arnold and Rugby Chapel, and Newman and St. Mary's, as one of the real subjects of the poem. The implication is strong that, for Arnold, then as later, Christian theology
was an "exploded dream," intellectually indefensible.[34] As he was to

[34] *Ibid.,* p. 252. The identification by Kenneth Allott (ed., *The Poems of Matthew
Arnold,* p. 288 n) of Arnold's two lost faiths as "The Protestant and Catholic forms
of Christian orthodoxy" is unintelligible in terms of the reading presented here. A.
Dwight Culler (*Imaginative Reason: The Poetry of Matthew Arnold,* p. 271) as part
of his otherwise admirable exegesis, follows Mrs. Tillotson in seeing Dr. Arnold as
"certainly" one of Arnold's "rigorous teachers"—a contention that upsets the delicate
balance of forces in the poem, in which Dr. Arnold figures with Newman as the representative of a dead *religious* tradition.

say of Newman in 1883, "he has adopted, for the doubts and difficulties which beset men's minds to-day, a solution which, to speak frankly, is impossible" (*DA*, p. 139). Also, it seems likely that Arnold is referring to both groups, the "last of the race of them who grieve" and the "last of the people who believe," in his remark, "the best are silent now" (ll. 110–114). Was Newman in the eighteen-fifties, like Dr. Arnold and like Arnold's favorite sages, one of the now "silent"?[35] At any rate, the image for the intellectual confusion of the age, as expressed by Arnold in the conclusion of "Dover Beach,"[36]

> And we are here as on a darkling plain
> Swept with confused alarms of struggle and flight,
> Where ignorant armies clash by night,

may well have been derived in part from the conclusion of one of Newman's most impressive Oxford sermons: "Controversy, at least in this age, does not lie between the hosts of heaven, Michael and his Angels on the one side, and the powers of evil on the other; but it is a sort of night battle, where each fights for himself, and friend and foe stand together. When men understand each other's meaning, they see, for the most part, that controversy is either superfluous or hopeless."[37]

During the eighteen-fifties the shape of Newman's long-term in-

---

[35] The Achilles who "ponders in his tent" (l. 115) may, according to Sir Edmund Chambers, have referred to Newman (see Tinker and Lowry, *Commentary*, p. 249 n). Harvey Kerpneck claims (" 'Kings of Modern Thought'," *Modern Language Quarterly*, XXIV [December 1963], 392–395), though not very convincingly, that the stanza refers to the Achilli trial of 1851–1853.

[36] Published in 1867 but "probably composed much earlier" (Tinker and Lowry, *Commentary*, p. 173).

[37] *OUS*, p. 201; Tinker and Lowry (*Commentary*, p. 175) point to Thucydides as the ultimate source. Clough used the image in *The Bothie* (1848); see Allott, *Poems of Matthew Arnold*, p. 243 n. Carlyle had also used the image in the conclusion of "Characteristics," (Kathleen Tillotson, "Matthew Arnold and Carlyle," p. 148). The possible influence of Newman's sermon was noted by Charles Frederick Harrold (*John Henry Newman: An Expository and Critical Study of His Mind, Thought and Art*, p. 336). Allott (pp. 46–47) offers strong evidence for the conjecture that "The Voice" in the poem of that title (written perhaps as early as the mid-forties) is that of Newman. If so, Newman's "thrilling" and "melancholy" summons is presented as a profound and disturbing temptation that the speaker has nevertheless successfully overcome. Culler (*Imaginative Reason*, pp. 88–90) argues even more fully for Newman as the subject of the poem.

fluence on Arnold—both in Arnold's view of Newman's significance as a man, as well as in certain substantive intellectual debts—becomes clear. In March 1853, Arnold writes his wife from Cambridge: "Yet I feel that the Middle Ages and all their poetry and impressiveness are in Oxford and not here" (*L*, I, 30). This feeling anticipates the Preface to *Essays in Criticism*, written twelve years later, where Arnold describes Oxford and "her ineffable charm," "whispering from her towers the last enchantments of the Middle Age"—words that Arnold later explicitly referred to Newman.[38] In October 1854 Arnold writes again, this time from Oxford:

[I] felt the peculiar *sentiment* of this country and neighbourhood as deeply as ever. But I am much struck with the apathy and *poorness* of the people here, as they now strike me, and their petty pottering habits compared with the students of Paris, or Germany, or even of London. Animation and interest and the power of work seem so sadly wanting in them. And I think this is so; and the place, in losing Newman and his followers, has lost its religious movement, which after all kept it from stagnating, and has not yet, so far as I see, got anything better. (*L*, I, 44–45)

Arnold's intense interest in Newman's activities continued, as a letter of 1855, written to his brother Tom in New Zealand, reveals:

As to Church matters, I think people in general concern themselves less with them than they did when you left England. Certainly religion is not, to all appearance at least, losing ground here: but since the great people of Newman's party went over, the disputes among the comparatively unimportant remains of them do not excite much interest. I am going to hear Manning at the Spanish Chapel next Sunday. Newman gives himself up almost entirely to organising and educating the Roman Catholics, and is gone off greatly, they say, as a preacher.[39]

---

[38] See *CPW*, III, 290; and *DA*, p. 142. Arnold's usual attitude toward the Middle Ages was more complex; he wrote in December 1860: "I have a strong sense of the irrationality of that period, and of the utter folly of those who take it seriously and play at restoring it; still, it has poetically the greatest charm and refreshment possible for me. The fault I find with Tennyson in his *Idylls of the King* is that the peculiar charm and aroma of the Middle Age he does not give in them. There is something magical about it, and I will do something with it before I have done" (*L*, I, 147). He may have kept this promise in "Pagan and Mediaeval Religious Sentiment" (1864).

[39] Mrs. Humphry Ward, *Recollections*, p. 53.

Tom was received into the Roman Catholic Church in January 1856, in Tasmania, and returned to England in October, his post of school inspector having been made untenable by reason of his conversion. At this time he saw Matthew once again but left almost at once to take up, at Newman's invitation, his duties as Professor of English Literature at the Catholic University in Dublin.[40] In May 1857, having just won election to the Poetry Professorship at Oxford, Matthew Arnold wrote to Dublin, in answer to Tom's congratulations, a letter filled with references to the Oxford of "The Scholar-Gipsy," and remarked that "the sentiment of the place is overpowering to me when I have leisure to feel it."[41] Arnold's letters also reveal, interestingly, that the High Church party at Oxford had put up an opposition candidate; Arnold was plainly elated when it turned out that "Keble voted for me after all."[42]

Arnold's enduring interest, then, in Newman and in a peculiar version of the Oxford "sentiment" with which he was henceforth habitually to link Newman is evident as early as the eighteen-fifties. The intellectual debt is more difficult to trace, but is seems entirely likely that Arnold would read with great interest Newman's *Discourses on the Scope and Nature of University Education, Addressed to the Catholics of Dublin,* published late in 1852. These lectures almost certainly played an important role in the formation of Arnold's teaching on "criticism" and "culture" in the following decade. But the direct influence may perhaps have begun much earlier with the Preface to the *Poems* of 1853, dated October 1. Certainly in one essential matter Arnold's views of poetry did not accord with Newman's. If in 1852 Arnold knew Newman's much earlier essay on "Poetry, with Reference to Aristotle's Poetics" (1829), he would have known that Newman in that discussion treated Aristotle's conception of tragedy in a highly Romantic manner, deprecating plot and emphasizing the power of "the characters, sentiments, and diction" (*ECH*, I, 1–2). As Charles Harrold puts it, Newman was at one with Wordsworth and Coleridge "in preferring suggestiveness, irregularity, vagueness above Greek

[40] *Ibid.*; Thomas Arnold, *Passages*, p. 159.
[41] Mrs. Humphry Ward, *Recollections*, p. 54.
[42] *Ibid.*, pp. 54–56.

clarity and form."[43] Though Arnold had other critics in mind, he could almost be thinking of Newman's essay when he complains: "We have critics who seem to direct their attention merely to detached expressions, to the language about the actions, not to the action itself" (*PW*, p. xxiii). And of course Arnold goes on to praise Goethe's ideal of "*Architectonicè* in the highest sense; that power of execution, which creates, forms, and constitutes: not the profoundness of single thoughts, not the richness of imagery, not the abundance of illustration" (*PW*, p. xxv).

On two key points treated by Newman in 1852, however, Arnold and Newman coincide. First, in Arnold's emphasis on "disinterested objectivity," in his refusal to acknowledge that the poet owes his age "service," and in his insistence that poets, wishing "neither to applaud nor to revile their age," want instead "to educe and cultivate what is best and noblest in themselves"—in all of these matters Arnold is giving a first statement of the "disinterested" half of his later doctrine of "criticism" and "culture." This doctrine may have been partially derived from Newman's extended emphasis, in the Dublin discourses, on knowledge as "an end in itself" and of only limited service to society at large. In the second place, and more important for the moment, is the precise quality of mind which Arnold recommends to the poet amid "the bewildering confusion of our times" (*PW*, p. xxx). Anxious to escape the modern tendency toward "the dialogue of the mind with itself," with its accompaniment of "doubts" and "discouragement," Arnold seeks an antidote for "an age of spiritual discomfort" (*PW*, pp. xvii, xxix). He omits *Empedocles* from the 1853 collection precisely on the grounds that it exhibits "suffering" that "finds no vent in action" and "a continuous state of mental distress" (*PW*, p. xviii). Above all, the poet must strive to banish "from his mind all feelings of contradiction, and irritation, and impatience" (*PW*, p. xxx). Arnold's suggested means for achieving "the calm, the cheerfulness, the disinterested objectivity" of the early Greeks is that "commerce with the ancients" which produces "a steadying and composing effect" upon the judgment (*PW*, pp. xvii, xxviii). This quality of the mind

[43] Harrold, *John Henry Newman*, p. 248.

is of course similar to the one Arnold ten years later ascribed to Goethe, whom Spinoza "calmed" and "composed" (*CPW*, III, 182, 177); it is also akin to that "true grace and serenity . . . of which Greece and Greek art suggest the admirable ideals of perfection," as Arnold was to describe it in *Culture and Anarchy* (*CPW*, V, 125). Newman had described, even if with less emphasis on the spiritual climate of the age, the effects of "this illuminative reason and true philosophy," which was the goal of a university education, in terms strikingly similar to those Arnold used a year later. Such a quality, Newman explains, "puts the mind above the influences of chance and necessity, above anxiety, suspense, unsettlement, and superstition, which is the lot of the many." Such a mind cannot be "partial," "exclusive," "impetuous": instead, it is ever "patient, collected, and majestically calm" (*Idea*, p. 122). The man of such disciplined powers has "the repose of a mind which lives in itself, while it lives in the world" (*Idea*, p. 158). Newman might almost be speaking for Arnold when he says that a liberal education creates a "habit of mind . . . of which the attributes are, freedom, equitableness, calmness, moderation, and wisdom" (*Idea*, p. 90). Finally it should be recalled that Newman openly defends his Oxonian and "classical" cast of mind against the "modern disciples" of Lockean utilitarianism, the point of whose famous *Edinburgh* article of 1810 was the charge that "The study of the Classics had been made the basis of the Oxford education" (*Idea*, pp. 142 ff.).

CHAPTER TWO   The Quarrel of Reason and Faith

With the inauguration in the early eighteen-sixties of Arnold's public role as critic—and it must be remembered that a very heavy proportion of Arnold's first essays were as much religious as literary—begins a complex of interrelated allusions to Newman, Oxford, and the Tractarian Movement. Moreover, it becomes clear that Arnold, always tortuously conscious of his public stance and tone, looked to Newman above all others for the qualities of mind and the tone of public discourse which he not only sought to emulate but which were, to a large extent, the very substance of his message in the sixties. Also during this period begins a regular exchange of volumes leading to a surprising frequency of correspondence between the two men. Above all, the implicit reliance in certain crucial matters on key ideas and attitudes of Newman's is so voluminous and so central to the Arnoldian view of life that a reassessment of the relations of the two men is in order.

Arnold himself was to acknowledge in 1868, while in the midst of writing *Culture and Anarchy*, that Newman's influence was "mixed up with all that is most essential in what I do and say."[1] In November 1871 Arnold, now deep into *Literature and Dogma,* specified that Newman's effect "consists in a general disposition of mind rather than in a particular set of ideas" (*UL*, p. 56). This is made even clearer in the following May when Newman is said to be one of the figures from whom Arnold had "learnt habits, methods, ruling ideas, which are constantly with me" (*UL*, pp. 65–66). Moreover, Arnold added, "I am sure in details you must recognize your own influence often" (*UL*, p. 66). Neither the habits and ruling ideas on the one hand, nor the details on the other, have been sufficiently identified and defined. Without a knowledge of them, several central informing strands in the texture of Arnold's thought cannot be recognized in their precise strength and color.

Arnold's notebooks for 1863 reveal him, apparently late in the year, reading widely in Roman Catholic sources like Lacordaire, Wiseman, Manning, and the *Dublin Review* (*NB*, pp. 22–23).[2] Among the citations are two from Jules Gondon, *Notice biographique sur le R. P. Newman*, a work published ten years earlier. One sentence, which Arnold took down, suggests some of the reasons for his continuing

---

[1] Henry Tristram, "Newman and Matthew Arnold," *The Cornhill*, N.S. LX (March 1926), 311.

[2] References to Francis of Assisi seem to point ahead to "Pagan and Mediaeval Religious Sentiment," published in April 1864.

interest in Newman and the Catholic Church: "Newman in his letter
to Jelf. Le siècle tend vers je ne sais quel inconnu—and the Church of
Rome appears alone in possession of this inconnu—giving, *elle seule*,
un essor libre et régulier aux sentiments intimes d'adoration, de mysti-
cisme, de tendresse, et à tant d'autres sentiments qui peuvent s'appeler
plus spécialement catholiques" (*NB*, p. 23). As E. K. Brown remarks, Arnold's interest in Roman Catholic history, doctrine, and practice was part of his campaign to broaden the range of operative ideas
and sympathies of his High Victorian audience.[3]

Even earlier, in January 1863, Arnold was publicly using Newman's testimony in a highly suggestive context. In condemning Bishop
Colenso's egregious treatise on the accuracy of the Pentateuch, Arnold
argues that the book does not advance "the culture of England and
Europe, . . . 'either by edifying the little-instructed, or by further informing the much-instructed' " (*CPW*, III, 43). The reason he gives
is that "The highly-instructed few, and not the scantily-instructed many,
will ever be the organ to the human race of knowledge and truth,"
and among the several "great teachers, divine and human," he brings
forward is Newman: " 'The few (those who can have a saving knowledge) can never mean the many,' says, in one of his noblest sermons,
Dr. Newman" (*CPW*, III, 43–44).[4] Moreover this phrase, to be recalled twenty years later in "Numbers" (*DA*, p. 6), seems to have
suggested the flourish at the end of "Heinrich Heine" (August 1863)
concerning the latter's "want of moral balance": "there is so much
power, so many seem able to run well, so many give promise of running well;—so few reach the goal, so few are chosen. *Many are called,
few chosen*" (*CPW*, III, 132).

Two of Newman's most characteristic teachings—on the existence
of a privileged spiritual elite and on the sharp discrimination of moral
from intellectual truth—are suggested by this citation and are two
ideas that absorb a great deal of Arnold's attention during these crucial
first years of the formation of his critical doctrine. Newman, perhaps
reflecting the Calvinism of his own background, used the text of the

---

[3] E. K. Brown, *Matthew Arnold: A Study in Conflict*, pp. 92–93.

[4] The sermon, entitled "Many Called, Few Chosen" and preached in 1837, appears
in *PPS*, V, 254–269; the phrase quoted appears on p. 268.

Many called, Few chosen, again and again.[5] Newman's early poems, which Arnold in 1868 claimed to know already,[6] are likewise strewn with references to God's hidden saints: "These are the chosen few,/ The remnant fruit of largely-scatter'd grace"; "The chosen are few, few the deeds well done, / For scantness is still Heaven's might" (*Verses*, pp. 43, 81). After his visit to Greece in 1833 Newman asked of the sages and poets of the ancient world:

> But is their being's history spent and run,
> Whose spirits live in awful singleness,
> Each in its self-form'd sphere of light or gloom?
> (*Verses*, p. 109)

The last stanza of Newman's "The Course of Truth" would have been very congenial to Arnold:

> Still is the might of Truth, as it has been:
> Lodged in the few, obey'd, and yet unseen.
>   Rear'd on lone heights, and rare,
>   His saints their watch-flame bear,
> And the mad world sees the wide-circling blaze,
> Vain searching whence it streams, and how to quench its rays.
> (*Verses*, p. 97)

And in 1840, in his sermon on "Implicit and Explicit Reason," Newman said: "It is not too much to say that the stepping by which great geniuses scale the mountains of truth is as unsafe and precarious to men in general, as the ascent of a skilful mountaineer up a literal crag. It is a way which they alone can take; and its justification lies in their success. And such mainly is the way in which all men, gifted or not gifted, commonly reason,—not by rule, but by an inward faculty" (*OUS*, p. 257). About this passage William Robbins comments: "We find Newman here speaking of the 'great geniuses' in the same way that Arnold speaks of the 'sublime solitaries'."[7] The Arnold who was painfully beginning to define the role of criticism would undoubtedly

---

[5] See two sermons of 1836: "The Individuality of the Soul" and "The Visible Church for the Sake of the Elect" (*PPS*, IV, 80–93, 150–167).

[6] Tristram, "Newman and Matthew Arnold," p. 311.

[7] William Robbins, *The Ethical Idealism of Matthew Arnold*, p. 235, n. 10.

be interested in that "inward faculty," which Newman in the same sermon described as "a living spontaneous energy within us, not an art," as opposed to the merely reflective or analytical intellect. Further, a look backward to Arnold's earliest poems shows that intellectual vision and insight are frequently associated with mountain imagery whereas a look ahead to a passage in *Culture and Anarchy* reveals that one of Arnold's chief objects is "inculcating the belief that excellence dwells among high and steep rocks, and can only be reached by those who sweat blood to reach her" (*CPW*, V, 152).

More specifically, these passages from Newman's work recall the running theme in Arnold's writings little noticed by most critics, his concern for the special role in history of a small elite fraternity who possess a privileged insight into truth. In the poetry the elite was composed of Arnold's admired solitary sages, such as Senancour, who claims place with "The Children of the Second Birth," the "small transfigured band" (*PW*, pp. 310–311). In a poem of 1860, "The Lord's Messengers," Arnold speaks pessimistically of the "men of genius" sent by the Lord to "carry my peace upon earth":

> Hardly, hardly shall one
> Come, with countenance bright,
> At the close of day, from the plain.
> (*PW*, pp. 216–217)

"Rugby Chapel," first published in 1867, takes up the theme again; Dr. Arnold is one with "the noble and great who are gone," "souls temper'd with fire, / Fervent, heroic, and good" (*PW*, pp. 290, 291). But it was with "The Bishop and the Philosopher" (January 1863) that Arnold began a notable attempt to define the historical role of the "individual genius," the "superior man," an important variant of the nineteenth-century cult of genius. Arguing against the hyperdemocratic idea that destructive religious books like Bishop Colenso's are suitable even for "the little-instructed," Arnold insists: "Knowledge and truth, in the full sense of the words, are not attainable by the great mass of the human race at all. . . . Old moral ideas leaven and humanise the multitude: new intellectual ideas filter slowly down to them from the thinking few; and only when they reach them in this manner do they adjust themselves to their practice without convulsing it" (*CWP*, III, 44). As a witness to this truth Newman's testimony was invoked.

The theme was continued the following month in "Dr. Stanley's Lectures on the Jewish Church," where Arnold, calling upon the lofty but ill-defined privileges of "criticism," proceeds to describe four attitudes toward the "religious life." Stanley's book, unlike Colenso's, satisfies two classes, "those who prosecute the religious life, or those who need to prosecute it"; but there is a third class: "There remain a few of mankind who do not come to him [Stanley] with these demands, or acknowledge these needs." Arnold does not deny that these last men *have* such needs ("this is a matter which literary criticism does not try"), but

a very few of mankind aspire after a life which is not the life after which the vast majority aspire, and to help them to which the vast majority seek the aid of religion. . . . the ideal life—the *summum bonum* for a born thinker, for a philosopher like Parmenides, or Spinoza, or Hegel—is an eternal series of intellectual acts. . . . this life treats all things, religion included, with entire freedom as subject-matter for thought, as elements in a vast movement of speculation. The few who live this life stand apart, and have an existence separate from that of the mass of mankind; . . . the region which they inhabit is a laboratory wherein are fashioned the new intellectual ideas which, from time to time, take their place in the world. (*CPW*, III 65–66)

These are also the few individuals who live the "purely intellectual life, . . . whose life, whose ideal, whose demand, is thought, and thought only" (*CPW*, III, 66). Literary criticism regards these few as "exempt from all concern with edification"; they have "the right of treating religion with absolute freedom" (*CPW*, III, 79–80).

This line of thought represents a major effort on Arnold's part to mark out a realm of lofty pure intellectualism inhabited by a few great sages like Parmenides, Spinoza, and Hegel; implicit here also is the second important matter, that of the sharp discrimination between intellectual and moral truth. That Arnold was not perfectly happy with the result is suggested both by his failure to reprint his review of Stanley's *Lectures* or to include the relevant passages from "The Bishop and the Philosopher" in the later essay, "Spinoza and the Bible" (December 1863), and by a significant distinction made in that second Spinoza essay. There he insists that, to be great, the remarkable philosopher "must have something in him which can influence character, which is edifying; he must, in short, have a noble and lofty character himself, a character . . . *in the grand style*" (*CPW*, III, 181). This elite of privileged sages appears rather steadily in Arnold's writings for several years—for example, in the essays on "Joubert" (January 1864) and "The Function of Criticism" (November 1864).[8] Theirs are the very qualities that Arnold, in his farewell lecture at Oxford, was to attribute to that history-making elite of "the men of Oxford" of Newman's and Dr. Arnold's generation, who "prepared currents of feeling" and "kept up . . . communications with the future" (*CPW*, V, 106). The truly "great men of culture," says Arnold, are able to "humanise" the best thought, "to make it efficient outside the clique of the cultivated and learned, yet still remaining the *best* knowledge and thought of the time, and a true source, therefore, of sweetness and light" (*CPW*, V, 113).

Newman was, then, deeply involved, both in the substance of Arnold's teaching and as a sage himself, in these two essential and interrelated ideas of Arnold's early criticism—the historical role of an elite and the mutual exclusiveness of the moral and intellectual spheres. Even the phrasing is very close at times. For example, when Arnold says, in "The Bishop and the Philosopher," "The great mass of the human race have to be softened and humanised through their heart and imagination, before any soil can be found in them where knowledge may strike living roots" (*CPW*, III, 44), he echoes the characteristic assertions in Newman's "Tamworth Reading Room" (1841). "The heart," says Newman, "is commonly reached, not through the reason,

---

[8] "Joubert" discusses "the famous men of genius" in literature—the Homers, the Dantes, the Shakespeares—whose "criticism of life . . . is permanently acceptable to mankind." These are "the great abounding fountains of truth," "the sacred personages" (*CPW*, III, 209). In "The Function of Criticism" the man who gives himself to the "very subtle and indirect action," which Arnold assigns to criticism—an idea associated with Newman— will be one of "a very small circle" practicing the virtues of a holy sage: "the Indian virtue of detachment," "the greatest sincerity" (*CPW*, III, 274–275).

but through the imagination, by means of direct impressions, by the testimony of facts and events, by history, by description" (*D&A*, p. 293). He adds: "After all, man is *not* a reasoning animal; he is a seeing, feeling, contemplating, acting animal" (*D&A*, p. 294). And finally, "Instances and patterns, not logical reasonings, are the living conclusions which alone have a hold over the affections, or can form the character" (*D&A*, p. 297). (Remarkably, this last sentence of Newman's appears four times in Arnold's own notebooks, beginning in 1879: *NB*, pp. 326, 335, 350, 515.) These statements reveal a distinctive view of man's nature and the modes of human apprehension in which the temperament and the teaching of the two men coincide. Both men were, in a certain mood, acutely aware of the distinction between intellect and morality. Newman, relying ultimately on a theology of nature and grace and attacking the Liberal assumption that knowledge is a means of moral improvement, had flatly stated in "The Tamworth Reading Room": "To know is one thing, to do is another; the two things are altogether distinct" (*D&A*, p. 262).[9] Arnold, within a naturalistic frame and attempting dialectically to work out an alternative fusion of these two aspects of man's life, almost impatiently admits that, although Hebraism and Hellenism "are profound and admirable manifestations," nevertheless

we can hardly insist too strongly on the divergence of line and of operation with which they proceed. . . . The difference whether it is by doing or by knowing that we set most store, and the practical consequences which follow from this difference, leave their mark on all the history of our race and its development. . . . They are, truly, borne towards the same goal; but the currents which bear them are infinitely different. . . . underneath the superficial agreement the fundamental divergence still subsists. (*CPW*, V, 166–67)

Part of the similarity between Newman and Arnold is derived from a shared skepticism concerning the efficacy and validity of metaphysical propositions, especially as regards the religious life. For example, in Tract 85 of *Tracts for the Times* (1838), Newman attacks "free in-

---

[9] And see *Idea*, p. 106: "Knowledge is one thing, virtue is another; good sense is not conscience, refinement is not humility, nor is largeness and justness faith."

quiry" in religious matters, pursued for its own sake, as leading to skepticism. He denies that reason is dangerous to faith, or that argument will not "advance the cause of truth"; yet

obedience | after all, if a man does nothing more than argue, if he has nothing deeper
at bottom, if he does not seek God by some truer means, by obedience, by
faith prior to demonstration, he will either not attain truth, or attain a
shallow, unreal view of it, and have a weak grasp of it. Reason will prepare
for the reception, will spread the news and secure the outward recognition
of the truth; but in all we do we ought to seek edification, not mere knowledge. (*D&A*, p. 201)

There are a number of places in Arnold's 1863 essays— "The Bishop and the Philosopher," "Dr. Stanley's Lectures," "Marcus Aurelius," "Spinoza and the Bible"—in which Arnold, in very similar terms, seeks to protect religious life from the corrosive effects of the merely rational intellect operating without a due regard for edification. Stanley's book is praised for fulfilling "the indispensable duty of edifying at the same time that it informs" (*CPW*, III, 65). In defining the elevated sphere of intellect where the solitary sages dwell, Arnold had been "re-proached with wishing to make free-thinking an aristocratic privilege, while a false religion is thrown to the multitude to keep it quiet" (*CPW*, III, 79). To this, Arnold replies: "those on whose behalf I de-mand from a religious speaker edification are more than this multitude; and their cause and that of the multitude are one. They are all those who acknowledge the need of the religious life. The few whom literary criti-cism regards as exempt from all concern with edification, are far fewer than is commonly supposed" (*CPW*, III, 79). Even "the educated mi-nority" for the most part still "retain their demand upon the religious life"; they must realize that their advanced intellectual culture "is not without its dangers to the religious life. . . . the moment they enter the sphere of religion, they too ask and need to be edified, not informed only" (*CPW*, III, 80).

Arnold's point here, against men like Bishop Colenso, is that a clergyman, "speaking to the religious life, . . . may honestly be silent about matters which he cannot yet use to edification" (*CPW*, III, 80). Arnold's characteristically hopeful prediction is that "Some day the religious life will have harmonised all the new thought with itself, will be able to use it freely"; but he immediately adds, "it cannot use it yet" (*CPW*, III, 81). Religious life and the "free inquiry" of the modern skeptical intellect were not then reconciled, as indeed they were not to be twenty years later at the time of Arnold's Rede lecture ("Literature and Science"). Arnold's practical prescription in the circumstances is both traditional and typically Newmanesque:

Certainly, Christianity has not two doctrines, one for the few, another for the many; but as certainly, Christ adapted His teaching to the different stages of growth in His hearers, and for all of them adapted it to the needs of the religious life. He came to preach moral and spiritual truths; and for His purpose moral genius was of more avail than intellectual genius, St. Peter than Solomon. (*CPW*, III, 80–81)

This "adaptation" of a religious message to the state of its hearers is the "economy" of faith, or "accommodation," which engaged Newman's close attention during his Anglican years and was to figure centrally in 1864 in the *Apologia*.

In an important sermon of 1843 ,which Arnold may very well have heard, Newman explained that there are many cases

in which we are obliged to receive information needful to us, through the medium of our existing ideas, and consequently with but a vague apprehension of its subject-matter. Children, who are made our pattern in Scripture, are taught, by an accommodation, on the part of their teachers, to their immature faculties and their scanty vocabulary. To answer their questions in the language which we should use towards grown men, would be simply to mislead them, if they could construe it at all. We must dispense and "divide" the word of truth, if we would not have it changed, as far as they are concerned, into a word of falsehood; for what is short of truth in the letter may be to them the most perfect truth, that is, the nearest approach to truth, compatible with their condition. (*OUS*, pp. 340–341)[10]

Newman maintained that "economies"—such as "mythical representa-

---

[10] Significantly, perhaps, at this very point in the sermon occurs the note ("Hence it is not more than an hyperbole to say that, in certain cases, a lie is the nearest approach to truth") which Kingsley used as the motto of his pamphlet, "What, Then, Does Dr. Newman Mean?" (*Apologia*, p. 373 n) For Newman's discussion of the Economy, see *Apologia*, pp. 245 ff., and Note F, pp. 310 ff.

tions," "certain narratives of martyrdoms," and "alleged miracles"—
are necessary because of the great gap between "supernatural and eternal laws" and our difficulty in understanding and representing them.
He frankly expresses his fear "of employing Reason, not in carrying
out what is told us, but in impugning it; not in support, but in prejudice of Faith. . . . Reason can but ascertain the profound difficulties of
our condition, it cannot   remove them" (*OUS*, pp. 342–343, 344,
351). So dubious was Newman at times concerning the role of reason
in religious life, that he could say, as he did in "The Tamworth Reading
Room," that "physics, taken by themselves, tend to infidelity," and that
"the study of Nature, when religious feeling is away, leads the mind,
rightly or wrongly, to acquiesce in the atheistic theory as the simplest
and the easiest" (*D&A*, pp. 299, 300). In his analysis, the following
year in the *Apologia,* of the role of "the wild living intellect of man"—
"the power of that universal solvent, which is so successfully acting
upon religious establishments," "the all-corroding, all-dissolving scepticism of the intellect in religious inquiries"—Newman was to declare:
"considering the faculty of reason actually and historically . . . its
tendency is towards a simple unbelief in matters of religion" (*Apologia*, pp. 221–222).[11]

Arnold thus followed Newman in this crucial matter of the division
between Reason and what may be called, broadly, Faith. Of course
there were strong counterpulls in both men which sought to assert a
unified ideal *above* duality and division. Even in "The Tamworth
Reading Room" Newman insists, "I have no fanatical wish to deny
to any whatever subject of thought or method of reason a place altogether, if it chooses to claim it, in the cultivation of the mind. . . . the
great and true maxim is to sacrifice none—to combine, and therefore
to adjust, all" (*D&A*, p. 274). The precise structure of Newman's
Christian humanist ideal was suggested in 1852 in his *Idea of a Uni-*

---

[11] See *Ibid.*, p. 237, where Liberalism "at present" is described as "nothing else
than that deep, plausible scepticism, . . . as being the development of human reason,
as practically exercised by the natural man." Sidney M. B. Coulling ("The Background of 'The Function of Criticism at the Present Time'," *Philological Quarterly,*
XLII [January 1963], 40) remarks that Arnold's objection to the timing of Colenso's
destructive criticism was "the same point" Newman was to make in the *Apologia* the
following year.

versity: "We attain to heaven by using this world well, though it is to pass away; we perfect our nature, not by undoing it, but by adding to it what is more than nature, and directing it towards aims higher than its own" (*Idea*, p. 109).[12] Similarly, in Arnold a search for a holistic ideal harmonizing all of man's instincts marks his entire critical career. In fact, as Lionel Trilling asserts, Arnold's criticism, at least in intention, "is the reconciliation of the two traditions whose warfare had so disturbed his youth—rationalism and faith."[13] It is in this light that the ideal of the "imaginative reason" as it is introduced suddenly at the end of "Pagan and Mediaeval Religious Sentiment" (April 1864) should be placed. The imaginative reason, the characteristic demand of "the modern spirit," which is best conveyed in the greatest Greek poets, somehow reconciles the senses and the understanding, the heart and the imagination; it strikes a balance between "the thinking-power" and "the religious sense" (*CPW*, III, 230–231). Similarly, the central intention of *Culture and Anarchy* is surely the definition of an ideal which will cancel the historical oscillation of Hebraism and Hellenism, the extremes of moralism and intellectualism, by somehow combining them in a higher synthesis.

Yet, for all their shared drive toward "harmonizing" man's impulses, the numerous citations indicate that both Newman and Arnold remain, for complex reasons, remarkably alike in their sense of the strong division between Faith and Reason. Much of the cause, for both men, lies in their Oxford experience. Newman throughout his life was subject, without question unfairly, to the accusation of being (in Owen Chadwick's words) "a sceptic, not an honest doubter, not even a man with a *fides quaerens intellectum*, but a sceptic who held his scepticism about the rational intellect in a dual harness with religious credulity." As Chadwick says, "His teaching encouraged Ward to make the absolute division between the conscience and the metaphysical in-

---

[12] See *Apologia*, pp. 224–225: "She [the Church] does not teach that human nature is irreclaimable, else wherefore should she be sent? not, that it is to be shattered and reversed, but to be extricated, purified, and restored; not, that it is a mere mass of hopeless evil, but that it has the promise upon it of great things, and even now, in its present state of disorder and excess, has a virtue and a praise proper to itself."

[13] Lionel Trilling, *Matthew Arnold*, pp. 176–177.

tellect, even though he rejected Ward's conclusions."[14] In all the Tractarians, Chadwick notes "a streak of scepticism about the metaphysical
realm": "The whole Movement was fighting the aridity (as it believed) of Paley and Whately and the school of religious philosophers,
was engaged in showing the lack of value, *for religious purposes*, of the
logical intellect." Newman's marked division sprang from his habitual
use of Reason as the analytical reason, and of Faith as "more a principle of action than of intellectual assent."[15] Newman hesitates to affirm
that evidence is a source of faith: "for faith, though confirmed by evidence, has another source—in the moral judgment and the religious
feelings, acted upon by the grace of God."[16]

The peculiar relevance to Arnold of this emphasis is clear in Newman's 1843 sermon on the "economy," in which one of the main difficulties he takes up is the objection that "The words 'Person,' 'Substance,' 'Consubstantial,' 'Generation,' 'Procession,' 'Incarnation,'
'Taking of the manhood into God,' and the like, have either a very
abject and human meaning, or none at all" (*OUS*, p. 338). It is precisely to meet that objection that the doctrine of the economy, as Newman explains it, was developed. With great frankness Newman admits
that in this world we see in a glass darkly; here "we are allowed such an
approximation to the truth as earthly images and figures may supply to
us" (*OUS*, p. 340). He simply admits "a profound sense of our ignorance of Divine Verities" (*OUS*, p. 349). Whole chapters of Arnold's
religious books like *Literature and Dogma* and *God and the Bible* are
devoted to ridiculing "metaphysical theology," embodied in the Christian creeds, as utter "blunder." Arnold's streak of skepticism about the
metaphysical realm was very broad indeed, and it would not do to ex-
aggerate Newman's skepticism or to underplay the profound religious
differences separating him from Arnold. But it remains that Arnold
very likely acquired his suspicion of the metaphysical intellect, especially in religious matters, at Oxford. If the liberal school of Dr. Arnold

[14] Owen Chadwick, ed., *The Mind of the Oxford Movement*, p. 42. The classical
statement of the charge is in Thomas Mozley's *Reminiscences, Chiefly of Oriel College
and the Oxford Movement*, II, 434 ff. Mozley, like Chadwick, rejects the imputation.
[15] Chadwick, *Mind of the Oxford Movement*, p. 43.
[16] *Ibid.*, p. 44.

would have contributed greatly to the tendency, so would the deeply antimetaphysical bias of the Tractarian movement, above all represented in the works of John Henry Newman.

CHAPTER THREE   The Onslaught on the Philistines

The preceding chapter drew out certain aspects of Newman's view of human nature and of the human powers that were the basis for Arnold's attraction to Newman in the eighteen-sixties. Dover Wilson some years ago suggested the outlines of Newman's more specific influence on Arnold in this decade:

the spirit of the Oxford Movement, which he associated with the traditions and beauty of the city itself, . . . may be seen in everything he wrote. And but for Newman's *Idea of a University* it is likely that *Culture and Anarchy* would never have seen the light; different as the two works are in tone and in the circumstances which produced them, their hearts beat as one. . . . when he [Arnold] speaks of "culture" he is thinking of the "liberal education" of which Newman writes made available for the whole of England by an indefinite multiplication of non-residential Rugby schools under state supervision.[1]

Oxford, the Oxford Movement, and Newman's *Idea of a University* are the acknowledged channels of Newman's influence upon Arnold during these years. Yet, except to study certain long-recognized similarities of style, that influence has never been examined in detail. This lack of analysis is all the more surprising because Arnold himself, while writing *Culture and Anarchy,* was aware that (as his letter of January 1868 indicates) Newman's "influence and writings" were "mixed up with all that is most essential in what I do and say." Newman's in-

[1] Matthew Arnold, *Culture and Anarchy*, ed. J. Dover Wilson, p. xiii.

fluence extends far beyond a rather generalized coincidence of attitude.

The key to Arnold's renewed and intensified interest in Newman was the publication of Newman's *Apologia Pro Vita Sua*, which appeared in weekly pamphlets between April 21 and June 2, 1864, with an Appendix on June 16, and in book form later in June. The work would have held Matthew Arnold's fascinated attention for several reasons. First, it threw light on the man Newman, whose career Arnold had followed with great interest, and on his personal quest for religious truth. Next, there was the evocation of Oxford and its history, as well as the complex of intellectual, aesthetic, and spiritual values which Arnold habitually associated with Oxford. Further, Newman reconstructed the mood of theological debate at Oxford during the thirties and forties, in which Arnold's father had figured prominently. Again, the *Apologia*, appearing as it did at the precise moment of Arnold's most intensive concern over his own critical stance and tone, represented in itself a highly distinguished example of a public controversial manner. Finally, the *Apologia* apparently sent Arnold back to earlier writings of Newman, and increasingly through these years what can be called Newman's theory and practice of criticism becomes the model of Arnold's own critical theory and practice.

Several of these claims on Arnold's attention converge in the use to which Arnold put the *Apologia* in his crucial essay, "The Literary Influence of Academies," which appeared in August 1864. Arnold seems at first to introduce Newman's name obliquely, parenthetically, in order to make a minor logical point:

In a production which we have all been reading lately, a production stamped throughout with a literary quality very rare in this country, and of which I shall have a word to say presently—*urbanity*; in this production, the work of a man never to be named by any son of Oxford without sympathy, a man who alone in Oxford of his generation, alone of many generations, conveyed to us in his genius that same charm, that same ineffable sentiment which this exquisite place itself conveys,—I mean Dr. Newman,—an expression is frequently used which is more common in theological than in literary language, but which seems to me fitted to be of general service; the *note* of so and so, the note of catholicity, the note of antiquity, the note of sanctity, and so on. (*CPW*, III, 244)

Only later does Arnold more directly discuss Newman's qualities: "In England there needs a miracle of genius like Shakespeare's to produce balance of mind, and a miracle of intellectual delicacy like Dr. Newman's to produce urbanity of style" (*CPW*, III, 250). Two major themes are sounded here—first, that Newman represents, supremely, the "charm" and the "ineffable sentiment" of Oxford; and second, that his writings display the "intellectual delicacy" and the "urbanity of style" which come close to the center of Arnold's developing definition of criticism and culture.

What should also be stressed is that the first quoted passage concerns a matter, central in Arnold, in which he closely, if implicitly, followed Newman: "I say that in the bulk of the intellectual work of a nation which has no centre, no intellectual metropolis like an academy, . . . there is observable *a note of provinciality*" (*CPW*, III, 244–245). Sainte-Beuve and Renan are invoked as sponsors of the ideal of "a centre of correct taste," as against pervasive English provinciality, but just as clearly it is to Newman, with his "urbanity of style," that Arnold also looks for his ideal in practice. Almost certainly Arnold would apply to the *Apologia* the qualities he sums up in the term "urbanity": "the tone of the city, of the centre, the tone which always aims at a spiritual and intellectual effect, and not excluding the use of banter, never disjoins banter itself from politeness, from felicity" (*CPW*, III, 249). Clearly, Arnold would have been very much taken by the matter and the lively manner of Newman's first two pamphlets, "Mr. Kingsley's Method of Disputation" and "True Mode of Meeting Mr. Kingsley," published on April 21 and April 28—so lively that Newman entirely changed his tone in subsequent pamphlets, and suppressed the two sarcastic pieces in the second edition (1865) of the *Apologia*.[2] Much of Newman's attention in these two pieces was devoted to a scathing analysis of Kingsley's "method of disputation"—for example, how, "By insinuation, or by

[2] Wilfrid Ward, *The Life of John Henry Cardinal Newman*, II, 18–19.

implication, or by question, or by irony, or by sneer, or by parable, he enforces again and again a conclusion which he does not categorically enunciate" (*Apologia*, p. 378). In one especially brilliant section Newman puts words into Kingsley's mouth ("he seems to make answer"), and has him call himself " 'the immaculate lover of Truth, so observant (as I have told you) of "*hault courage* and strict honour,"—and (aside)—"and not as this publican" ' " (*Apologia*, p. 377). This of course is neither banter nor politeness and cannot quite be called urbanity, although it has much of felicity. What it recalls is the Matthew Arnold of *Essays in Criticism* and *Culture and Anarchy*, providing long and devastating fictitious speeches for his opponents— whether the egregious Alderman-Colonel Wilson, or the fictitious "eloquent advocate" of the middle class who "cries": " 'We are all . . . Philistines together . . . Let us have no nonsense about independent criticism, and intellectual delicacy, and the few and the many'," the very qualities Newman himself represented (*CPW*, V, 131–132; *CPW*, III, 276).

More substantially, the matter of a "centre of correct taste" as an antidote to "provinciality" is one that Arnold undoubtedly had seen in Newman's writings. The chief burden of "The Literary Influence of Academies" is that an academy, by providing "an authority" and "a standard higher than one's own habitual standard in intellectual matters," promotes Arnold's favored qualities—"a quick and flexible intelligence," an urbanity not excluding banter, balance of mind, moderation, proportion, "the fitness, the measure, the centrality, which is the soul of all good criticism"—and resists those enemies of the critical spirit, "hap-hazard, crudeness, provincialism, eccentricity, violence, blundering" (*CPW*, III, 238, 236, 237, 249, 252, 253, 241). Similarly, in *Culture and Anarchy* Arnold seeks a "strict standard of excellence," harks back to his earlier remarks on an "authoritative centre" of "correct information, taste, and intelligence," calls for "a high standard of right reason," and speaks (in a passage otherwise bearing Newmanesque overtones) of excellence dwelling "among high and steep rocks" (*CPW*, V, 147, 150, 152). For the most part, ity," the representative of our "best self," to be the State (*CPW*, V, in his later writings Arnold conceives this "sound centre of author-

155, 134–135). In his *Idea of a University* Newman, whose concern is everywhere with the totality and unity of knowledge and with the existence of a central historical tradition of learning and intellectual formation, had asserted that at Oxford and Cambridge there is to be found "a characteristic tone of thought, a recognized standard of judgment" (*Idea*, p. 130). He insisted that for the student the scope and result of "the cultivation of the intellect" for its own sake, which he calls "Liberal Education," should be made the "standard of excellence." "To set forth the right standard, and to train according to it"—this, says Newman, is "the business of a University" (*Idea*, p. 135). Dwight Culler has reminded us that "the whole effort" of Arnold's mature thought in such matters as an English Academy or the idea of the State "was to establish some standard or source of values, larger than the self and perfectly distinct from it." His effort, however imperfect, "is of the same character in the field of humanism as Newman's was in the more decisive sphere of religion."[3] As the preceding citations indicate, Newman's search for a center of authority extended into areas of secular, intellectual culture as well; the parallels thus become all the more striking.

The process whereby Newman was absorbed into the total texture of Arnold's thought was next significantly furthered in November of 1864, in the most important statement of the *Essays in Criticism*, "The Function of Criticism at the Present Time." Newman is not mentioned by name, but his presence is very marked. Midway through the essay, Arnold prosecutes the case for disinterestedness by complaining that the various political and religious journals of England—unlike the *Revue des Deux Mondes*—stifle the free play of mind by subserving partisan and sectarian interests:

And so on through all the various fractions, political and religious, of our society; every fraction has, as such, its organ of criticism, but the notion of combining all fractions in the common pleasure of a free disinterested play of mind meets with no favour. Directly this play of mind wants to have more scope, and to forget the pressure of practical considerations a little, it is checked, it is made to feel the chain. We saw this the other day in the

---

[3] John Henry Newman, *Apologia Pro Vita Sua*, ed. A. Dwight Culler, pp. xvii–xviii.

extinction, so much to be regretted, of the *Home and Foreign Review*. Perhaps in no organ of criticism in this country was there so much knowledge, so much play of mind; but these could not save it. The *Dublin Review* subordinates play of mind to the practical business of English and Irish Catholicism, and lives. (*CPW*, III, 271)

Arnold must have been fully aware that Newman was deeply involved in the controversy over the *Home and Foreign Review*, a controversy that had far-reaching effects on the freedom of intellectual life within the Roman Catholic Church in England. Although Arnold misstates the exact issues, he knew that Newman had, for several months in 1859, edited the *Home and Foreign's* predecessor, the *Rambler*. And he knew that Newman was deeply committed to the intellectual freedom for which Sir John Acton, as editor, had made the *Home and Foreign* a byword. The first issue had appeared in July 1862, and Newman's letters indicate that he sympathized with many of the periodical's aims, even though he was still pained by the flippancy and bishop-baiting of such contributors as Richard Simpson, whose tone resembled that which had earlier led to the extinction of the *Rambler*.[4] Significantly, Newman would not allow his name to be associated with the *Dublin*, Wiseman's official organ and the preserve of Wiseman, Manning, and William George Ward, the extreme ultramontanes, from whom Newman wished to be dissociated, especially on the question of the Temporal Power of the Papacy.[5] Newman's aims, basically Acton's own, were (in Newman's words) "to create a body of thought as against the false intellectualism of the age, to surround Catholicism with defences necessary for and demanded by the age, to take a Catholic view of the theories, and give a Catholic interpretation to the discoveries of the age."[6] This ideal was not, to be sure, the exact equivalent of Arnold's disinterestedness, but it did lead, in both the *Rambler* and the *Home and Foreign*, to the dissemination of a great deal of "knowledge" (concerning, for example, the work of the

[4] Wilfrid Ward, *Newman*, I, 538, 539: Newman's role in the controversy and that of Arnold's brother Tom (a contributor to both the *Rambler* and the *Home and Foreign*) is best discussed in Joseph Altholz, *The Liberal Catholic Movement in England: The "Rambler" and its Contributors, 1848–1864.*

[5] Wilfrid Ward, *Newman*, I, 548.

[6] *Ibid.*, p. 549.

Munich Catholic historian, Döllinger) and to "a free play of the mind" unprecedented in an English religious journal. Through the whole controversy over ecclesiastical condemnation of the *Home and Foreign* Newman sought, as Wilfred Ward says, "to prevent collisions between the *Dublin* and the *Home and Foreign*, earnestly desirous that variety of opinion should be tolerated."[7] The important point for the present study is that Arnold is closely linking Newman's ideals and associates with his own ideals of *criticism*—as the disinterested pursuit of the best that is known and thought in the world, in order "to create a current of true and fresh ideas" (*CPW*, III, 270)— in its most central and explicit statement.

Moreover, the words given by Arnold to his archetypal British Philistine—"Let us have no nonsense about independent criticism, and intellectual delicacy, and the few and the many" (*CPW*, III, 276)— are all associated with Newman. Further, this essay of Arnold's contains a famous passage that echoes Newman:

the British Constitution itself, which, seen from the practical side, looks such a magnificent organ of progress and virtue, seen from the speculative side,—with its compromises, its love of facts, its horror of theory, its studied avoidance of clear thoughts . . . seen from this side, our august Constitution sometimes looks . . . a colossal machine for the manufacture of Philistines. (*CPW*, III, 275)

In a series of letters published in 1855 on the Crimean War and titled "Who's to Blame?" Newman had analyzed the British constitution and the character of John Bull in terms that clearly anticipated Arnold's view of the constitution and of the British Philistine. Newman's point was that John Bull was illogical in blaming military and political leaders for the disasters of the War, since it was the British constitution itself, the very mirror of John Bull's intense and eccentric individualism and his abhorrence of centralization, which hampered the leaders in conducting the war that John Bull had called for. His main contention is that "a constitutional government cannot efficiently control a war, and should therefore be slow to enter into one."[8] Again

[7] *Ibid.*, p. 556.
[8] Ward's summary, *ibid.*, p. 353.

and again these letters suggest Arnold's view and his characteristic methods, nowhere more than in the following satiric passage:

England, surely, is the paradise of little men, and the purgatory of great ones. May I never be a Minister of State or a Field-Marshall! I'd be an individual, self-respecting Briton, in my own private castle, with the *Times* to see the world by, and pen and paper to scribble off withal to some public print, and set the world right. Public men are only my *employés*; I use them as I think fit, and turn them off without warning. Aberdeen, Gladstone, Sidney Herbert, Newcastle, what are they muttering about services and ingratitude? were they not paid? hadn't they their regular quarterday? Raglan, Burgoyne, Dundas,—I cannot recollect all the fellows' names,—can they merit aught? can they be profitable to me their lord and master? (*D&A*, 343)[9]

The reader at once thinks ahead to the chapter "Doing as One Likes" in *Culture and Anarchy*, where "the old ways of the Constitution," "our system of liberty," are subjected to very close scrutiny, and the middle class is made responsible for the collapse of civil order because of its insistence that the "Government must neither have any discretionary power nor act resolutely on its own interpretation of the law if any one disputes it" (*CPW*, V, 117, 119, 123).

Several final and important parallels link "The Function of Criticism" to Newman. Near the close of his essay Arnold, in a long and complicated sentence, sums up his views of the unity of European culture:

But, after all, the criticism I am really concerned with,—the criticism which alone can much help us for the future, the criticism which, throughout Europe, is at the present day meant, when so much stress is laid on the importance of criticism and the critical spirit,—is a criticism which regards Europe as being, for intellectual and spiritual purposes, one great confederation, bound to a joint action and working to a common result; and whose members have, for their proper outfit, a knowledge of Greek, Roman, and Eastern antiquity, and of one another. (*CPW*, III, 284)

---

[9] Henry Tristram ("Newman and Matthew Arnold," *The Cornhill*, N.S. LX [March 1926], 315) notes: "Philistinism, as a political force, is the object of attack in the Pamphlet 'Who's to Blame?'"

In "Christianity and Letters," a lecture in the second half of the *Idea of a University*, Newman had, as Father Tristram saw, "anticipated Arnold in his specifically Arnoldian message that the 'Apostolic Succession' in culture is to be traced through Rome to Greece, and in particular to Athens."[10] In Newman this was, as Dwight Culler remarks, "the image of Civilization as a great, distinct, and objective fact, an *orbis terrarum* which was co-extensive with Christianity and more than coeval in point of time."[11] This vision of losing the self in the object of knowledge, also found in "The Literary Influence of Academies," Culler sees as "the truth upon which the humanism of Matthew Arnold is based": "the whole effort of Arnold's critical essays was to give to the body of world literature the character of an objective standard of excellence. The diseases of his countrymen were all diseases of self—on the one hand, the eccentricities of Romantic individualism, and on the other, the partisan zeal of political and religious conflict—and the cure for these diseases was a system of value which was larger than the self and perfectly distinct from it. Such a system Arnold found in culture, 'the best that is known and thought in the world'."[12]

Arnold's doctrine of criticism and culture, especially in its characteristic dualism, levied extensively upon Newman's thought. "The Function of Criticism," Arnold's most important statement of his critical principles, is suffused with Newmanesque thinking and phrasing. Everywhere the parallels are striking. When Arnold says that the object of criticism is, in all branches of knowledge, "to see the object as in itself it really is" (*CPW*, III, 258), he echoes Newman's assertion that a university training teaches a man "to see things as they are, to go right to the point" (*Idea*, p. 157). Arnold further argues, "A polemical practical criticism makes men blind even to the ideal imperfection of their practice, makes them willingly assert its ideal perfection, in order the better to secure it against attack; and clearly this is narrowing and baneful to them" (*CPW*, III, 271). Newman had similarly said that those who lacked a harmonious unity in their thought will display "nar-

[10] *Ibid.*, p. 317.
[11] A. Dwight Culler, *The Imperial Intellect: A Study of Newman's Educational Ideal*, p. 235.
[12] *Ibid.*, p. 234.

rowness of mind," since "Men, whose minds are possessed with some one object, take exaggerated views of its importance, are feverish in the pursuit of it," whereas "the intellect, which has been disciplined to the perfection of its powers, . . . cannot be partial, cannot be exclusive, cannot be impetuous, cannot be at a loss" (*Idea*, pp. 120, 122). Finally, the limited exterior goal of Arnold's criticism, as "a distinterested endeavour to learn and propagate the best that is known and thought in the world," was "to establish a current of fresh and true ideas" (*CPW*, III, 282). Newman's statement of the goal of a university training is strikingly similar: "it aims at raising the intellectual tone of society, at cultivating the public mind, at purifying the national taste, at supplying true principles to popular enthusiasm and fixed aims to popular aspiration, at giving enlargement and sobriety to the ideas of the age" (*Idea*, p. 157).

The full extent of Newman's influence on Arnold's *Essays in Criticism* can be measured only by the great rhapsodic invocation to the spirit of Oxford in the Preface, published in February 1865:

Beautiful city! so venerable, so lovely, so unravaged by the fierce intellectual life of our century, so serene!

       "there are our young barbarians, all at play!"

And yet, steeped in sentiment as she lies, spreading her gardens to the moonlight, and whispering from her towers the last enchantments of the Middle Age, who will deny that Oxford, by her ineffable charm, keeps ever calling us nearer to the true goal of all of us, to the ideal, to perfection,—to beauty, in a word, which is only truth seen from another side?—nearer, perhaps, than all the science of Tübingen. Adorable dreamer, whose heart has been so romantic! who hast given thyself so prodigally, given thyself to sides and to heroes not mine, only never to the Philistines! home of lost causes, and forsaken beliefs, and unpopular names, and impossible loyalties! . . . Apparitions of a day, what is our puny warfare against the Philistines, compared with the warfare which this queen of romance has been waging against them for centuries, and will wage after we are gone? (*CPW*, III, 290)

Surely Arnold, in referring to the "ineffable charm" of Oxford, is speaking here as that "son of Oxford" who had seen in Newman the representative par excellence of the "charm" and the "ineffable sentiment which this exquisite place itself conveys" (*CPW*, III, 244).

Moreover, the attack on Philistinism and the implicit reference to the Oxford Movement in "lost causes" and "forsaken beliefs" point ahead to the famous passage on Newman in *Culture and Anarchy*, shortly to be considered. How essentially *Essays in Criticism* was associated in Arnold's mind with Newman is proved by a comment in Arnold's 1883 essay on Emerson; referring to Newman's Oxford sermons, Arnold remarks: "Somewhere or other I have spoken of those 'last enchantments of the Middle Age' which Oxford sheds around us, and here they were!" (*DA*, p. 142). It is not surprising that he sent Newman a copy in March 1865, inscribing it, "From one of his old hearers" (*L*, I, 292).

Newman must have entered Matthew Arnold's thoughts more than once in 1865, since, after a break with Newman and a relapse into religious skepticism, Tom Arnold left Newman's Oratory school in Birmingham and re-established himself at Oxford.[13] However, Arnold's next public reference to Newman occurred in the first of the lectures on Celtic literature, delivered on December 6, 1865. Referring to Eugene O'Curry's lectures delivered at the Catholic University in Dublin, Arnold remarks in passing,

it is touching to find that these lectures, a splendid tribute of devotion to the Celtic cause, had no hearer more attentive, more sympathising, than a man, himself, too, the champion of a cause more interesting than prosperous, —one of those causes which please noble spirits, but do not please destiny, which have Cato's adherence, but not Heaven's,—Dr. Newman. (*CPW*, III, 305; and see *Apologia*, p. 194)

Arnold here reflects a judgment made not infrequently during the last decades of Newman's career, that he was a noble but wasted talent somewhat after the pattern in which Arnold liked to present Christ. It seems Newman's disastrous "cause" is not, in Arnold's mind, merely the Catholic University, but the Roman Catholic Church and the whole of Newman's spiritual career.[14]

On June 7, 1867, Arnold delivered his farewell lecture as Professor

[13] Thomas Arnold, [Jr.], *Passages in a Wandering Life*, pp. 179–180, 185–186, 191.

[14] See Tristram, "Newman and Matthew Arnold," p. 319.

of Poetry at Oxford, "Culture and its Enemies," later to become, as "Sweetness and Light," the first chapter of *Culture and Anarchy*. The famous passage on Oxford, the Oxford Movement, Liberalism, and John Henry Newman is at the heart of the lecture's thesis. Arnold is arguing that "beauty and sweetness are essential characters of a complete human perfection":

When I insist on this, I am all in the faith and tradition of Oxford. I say boldly that this our sentiment for beauty and sweetness, our sentiment against hideousness and rawness, has been at the bottom of our attachment to so many beaten causes, of our opposition to so many triumphant movements. . . . We have not won our political battles, we have not carried our main points, we have not stopped our adversaries' advance, we have not marched victoriously with the modern world; but we have told silently upon the mind of the country, we have prepared currents of feeling which sap our adversaries' position when it seems gained, we have kept up our communications with the future. Look at the course of the great movement which shook Oxford to its centre some thirty years ago! It was directed, as any one who reads Dr. Newman's *Apology* may see, against what in one word may be called "Liberalism." Liberalism prevailed; it was the appointed force to do the work of the hour; it was necessary, it was inevitable that it should prevail. . . . But what was it, this Liberalism, as Dr. Newman saw it, and as it really broke the Oxford movement? It was the great middle-class Liberalism, which had for the cardinal points of its belief the Reform Bill of 1832, and local self-government, in politics; in the social sphere, free-trade, unrestricted competition, and the making of large industrial fortunes; in the religious sphere, the Dissidence of Dissent and the Protestantism of the Protestant religion. I do not say that other and more intelligent forces than this were not opposed to the Oxford movement; but this was the force which really beat it; this was the force which Dr. Newman felt himself fighting with. (*CPW*, V, 106–107)

Arnold sees "this great force of Philistinism" as "thrust into the second rank" by a new power; in other words, "the world of middle-class Liberalism" seemed, in this year of the Second Reform Bill, to be superseded by "the world of democracy," the way for which had been prepared by "the currents of feeling created by Dr. Newman's movement, the keen desire for beauty and sweetness which it nourished, the deep aversion it manifested to the hardness and vulgarity of middle-class Liberalism, the strong light it turned on the hideous and grotesque illusions of middle-class Protestantism" (*CPW*, V, 107). Thus Arnold sees "the sentiment of Oxford for beauty and sweetness," embodied above all in "Dr. Newman's movement," as ultimately the long-term civilizing and even "political" force for which *Culture and Anarchy, Friendship's Garland*, and all his social essays of the late seventies and eighties were to argue. Again and again he was to speak of "the pedantry, bigotry, and narrowness of our middle-class, which disfigure the civilisation we have to offer [the Irish]," the class "with a defective type of religion, a narrow range of intellect and knowledge, a stunted sense of beauty, a low standard of manners; and averse, moreover, to whatever may disturb it in its vulgarity" (*IEO*, pp. 329, 400). In his well-known letter to Newman of November 29, 1871, Arnold avowed that Newman's influence consisted in "a general disposition of mind rather than in a particular set of ideas" and immediately added: "In all the conflicts I have with modern Liberalism and Dissent, and with their pretensions and shortcomings, I recognise your work" (*UL*, pp. 56–57).

The question remains, was Arnold fully justified in considering Newman an ally in his lifelong campaign to civilize the English middle class? Arnold's lecture was printed in July 1867, and in August Henry Sidgwick, the future Cambridge philosopher, tellingly pursued the theme of Arnold's "dilettante humour," carefully searching out the ethical flaw in Arnold's argument. One of his main contentions was that by making religion merely the subduer of "the obvious faults of our animality, . . . a sort of spiritual police," Arnold had neglected both the emotional and the intellectual dimensions of religious experience.[15] So sensitive was Arnold to the truth of this charge that in his writings from 1869 onward he worked precisely to eliminate from his view of religion the taint of aestheticism and self-centeredness. Sidgwick went on to argue that a proof of the inadequacy of Arnold's "languid patronage to religion" was his quite mistaking Newman's conception of "Liberalism" and his views of "the functions of re-

[15] Henry Sidgwick, "The Prophet of Culture," *Macmillan's Magazine,* XVI (August 1867), 275.

ligion and its place in the social organism": "Dr. Newman fought for a
point of view which it required culture to appreciate, and therefore he
fought in some sense with culture; but he did not fight for culture,
and to conceive him combating side by side with Mr. Matthew Arnold is almost comical."[16] Certainly there seems, at first glance, a good
deal of justification for Sidgwick's charge. For example, the antitheses
that Arnold invokes are almost entirely aesthetic—beauty, sweetness,
feeling, as opposed to hideousness, rawness, hardness, vulgarity, the
grotesque. Moreover, a reading of the *Apologia* seems to support Sidgwick, too, and to suggest that Arnold was illegitimately extending
Newman's definition of "Liberalism."

Certainly Arnold was following the *Apologia*, verbally, when he
said that Liberalism "really broke the Oxford movement" and that
"this was the force which Dr. Newman felt himself fighting with";
for Newman explains concerning his departure from the Anglican
Church:

> The most oppressive thought, in the whole process of my change of opinion,
> was the clear anticipation, verified by the event, that it would issue in the
> triumph of Liberalism. Against the Anti-dogmatic principle I had thrown
> my whole mind; yet now I was doing more than anyone else could do, to
> promote it. I was one of those who had kept it at bay in Oxford for so many
> years; and thus my very retirement was its triumph. The men who had
> driven me from Oxford were distinctly the Liberals; it was they who had
> opened the attack upon Tract 90, and it was they who would gain a second
> benefit, if I went on to abandon the Anglican Church. But this was all . . .
> there are but two alternatives, the way to Rome, and the way to Atheism:
> Anglicanism is the halfway house on the one side, and Liberalism is the
> halfway house on the other. How many men were there, as I knew full well,
> who would not follow me now in my advance from Anglicanism to Rome,
> but would at once leave Anglicanism and me for the Liberal camp. (*Apolo-
> gia*, pp. 184–185)

But even there, it is evident, Newman was defining Liberalism as "the
anti-dogmatic principle"; and earlier he had called it "the principle of

16 *Ibid.*, pp. 276–277.

the Movement of 1833" (*Apologia*, pp. 44–45). Further, in the long note on "Liberalism" added to the *Apologia* in the 1865 edition, Newman had defined Liberalism in precise and limited *theological* terms:

Now by Liberalism I mean false liberty of thought, or the exercise of thought upon matters, in which, from the constitution of the human mind, thought cannot be brought to any successful issue, and therefore is out of place. Among such matters are first principles of whatever kind; and of those the most sacred and momentous are especially to be reckoned the truths of Revelation. Liberalism then is the mistake of subjecting to human judgment those revealed doctrines which are in their nature beyond and independent of it, and of claiming to determine on intrinsic grounds the truth and value of propositions which rest for their reception simply on the external authority of the Divine Word. (*Apologia*, p. 261)

Newman sees "the rudiments of the Liberal party" in the "select circle or class of men" who had reformed and awakened Oxford in the first decades of the century (*Apologia*, pp. 260-261)—among them, of course, the Oriel Noetics. The first generation "introduced into Oxford a license of opinion" which was not, however, consciously heterodox theologically; but "The party grew, all the time that I was in Oxford, even in numbers, certainly in breadth and definiteness of doctrine, and in power. And, what was a far higher consideration, by the accession of Dr. Arnold's pupils, it was invested with an elevation of character which claimed the respect even of its opponents" (*Apologia*, pp. 261–262, 264). These, then, were the men, the theological Liberals associated with Matthew Arnold's father, and hence in a sense members of Arnold's own theological party, whom Newman referred to as the Liberals "who had driven me from Oxford"; this was the Liberalism "which Dr. Newman felt himself fighting with." There is nothing here directly about self-government, free trade, or the hideousness of middle-class Protestantism.

A further caution against accepting Arnold's apparently too easy identification of his sense of Philistinism and Liberalism with Newman's is suggested by Newman himself. Newman saw that Liberalism had changed greatly in the preceding three or four decades and that even the circle around Hampden, Whately, and Thomas Arnold was not liberal in its theology "in the sense in which the bulk of the educated classes through the country are liberal now" (*Apologia*, p. 261). Liberalism had changed and broadened its character and influence through the century. He explains:

> I am not going to criticize here that vast body of men, in the mass, who at this time would profess to be liberals in religion; and who look towards the discoveries of the age, certain or in progress, as their informants, direct or indirect, as to what they shall think about the unseen and the future. The Liberalism which gives a colour to society now, is very different from that character of thought which bore the name thirty or forty years ago. Now it is scarcely a party; it is the educated lay world. When I was young, I knew the word first as giving name to a periodical, set up by Lord Byron and others. Now, as then, I have no sympathy with the philosophy of Byron. Afterwards, Liberalism was the badge of a theological school, of a dry and repulsive character, not very dangerous in itself, though dangerous as opening the door to evils which it did not itself either anticipate or comprehend. At present it is nothing else than that deep, plausible scepticism, of which I spoke above, as being the development of human reason, as practically exercised by the natural man. (*Apologia,* p. 237)

This is, again, the Newman who frankly admitted that the tendency of "the faculty of reason actually and historically . . . is toward a simple unbelief in matters of religion" (*Apologia*, p. 221).

What residue of truth, then, if any, remains in Arnold's claim that Newman's writings inform "all the conflicts I have with modern Liberalism and Dissent"? Certainly there is evidence that Newman did in fact extend his understanding of the term Liberalism to include nontheological matters, although religion remains—as it did not with Arnold—the central and controlling element, and other considerations are judged largely as they affect the status in society of supernatural Christianity. Here, as in so many other places, Arnold echoes Newman. To be sure, there is little enough in Newman of what Arnold calls the exact objects of "the great Liberal party in the last thirty years": "the advocacy of free-trade, of Parliamentary reform, of abolition of church-rates, of voluntaryism in religion and education, of noninterference of the State between employers and employed, and of marriage with one's deceased wife's sister" (*CPW*, V, 128). But Newman himself could on occasion deal a smart smack at Liberal politicians, as when he remarks of Lord Brougham, in "The Tamworth Reading Room," "after parsons no men quote Scripture more familiarly than Liberals and Whigs" (*D&A*, p. 287).[17] Even the *Apologia* at least glancingly suggests that opposition to such complex political causes as those for Catholic Emancipation and for the Reform Bill of 1832, both of which seemed to threaten the prerogatives and exclusiveness of the Established Church, was in fact a very strong motive in the formation of the Oxford Movement (*Apologia*, pp. 263-264, 27–28). More specifically, when Arnold speaks of Bright's values, derived largely from "the world of middle-class liberalism," as leading to self-deluding praise of "cities," "railroads," and "manufactures" (*CPW*, V, 108), he recalls Newman's damning quotations from Sir Robert Peel on the glories of "steamboats and railroads," "producer and consumer" (*D&A*, p. 257); the comments of the two men on this frame of mind reveal the essential kinship of their own minds. Arnold remarks, just after the passage on Newman, "It is the same fashion of teaching a man to value himself not on what he *is*, not on his progress in sweetness and light, but on the number of railroads he has constructed, or the bigness of the tabernacle he has built" (*CPW*, V, 108). Newman's reply, too, stresses inwardness against what he calls "a chief error of the day"—"that our true excellence comes not from within, but from without; not wrought out through personal struggles and sufferings, but following upon a passive ex-

---

[17] A passage on a Conservative, Sir Robert Peel, has the very ring of Arnold disdainfully taking on a politician of the sixties: "He tells us that his great aim is the peace and good order of the community, and the easy working of the national machine. With this in view, any price is cheap, everything is marketable; all impediments are a nuisance" (*D&A*, p. 284). Howard W. Fulweiler ("Tractarians and Philistines: *The Tracts for the Times* versus Victorian Middle-Class Values," *Historical Magazine of the Protestant Episcopal Church*, XXXI [March 1962], 52, 53) shows that although they express primarily a spiritual ideal, the tracts challenged "the complacency and faith in material progress of the Victorian Middle class" and "the secular ideals of the middle class in their opposition to liberal reforms, their indifference to material progress, and their implicit denial of the economic views of the political economists."

posure to influences over which we have no control" (*D&A*, p. 266).
Newman, like Arnold, is asking in essence what the sources of "satisfaction and inward peace" really are (*D&A*, p. 260).

Newman had also spoken in terms closer to Arnold's conception of
Liberalism in his 1850 lectures on the Oxford Movement, called
Certain Difficulties Felt by Anglicans in Catholic Teaching. Almost
certainly these lectures lay behind the long passage on Newman and
the Oxford Movement in Arnold's farewell lecture. For example, in
asserting that the movement "has created a mere party in the National
Church" and that there is an "extreme want of congeniality . . . between the movement of 1833 and the nation at large," Newman had
anticipated some of Arnold's argument by quoting from Hurrell
Froude's *Remains*: "How is it we are so much in advance of our generation?" (*DofA*, I, 34, 35, 37). Even closer to Arnold, Newman
had briefly connected the movement with a reaction against Liberal
legislation; as part of his case on the Erastian character of the Church
of England, Newman remarks: "As the nation changes its political,
so may it change its religious views; the causes which carried the Reform
Bill and Free Trade may make short work with orthodoxy" (*DofA*,
I, 9). And in contending that the Catholic Church is "the one great
principle of unity and concord which the world has seen," he adds
somewhat sardonically: "In this day, I grant, scientific unions, free
trade, railroads, and industrial exhibitions are put forward as a substitute for her influence, with what success posterity will be able to
judge" (*DofA*, I, 304).

Not surprisingly, Arnold and Newman also coincided in their contempt for radical, religiously and politically subversive solutions to
the problems of the century—for example, Benthamism and Comteanism, which might be regarded as extreme extensions of Liberal
principles. In "The Tamworth Reading Room" Newman had spoken
of Bentham, who "had not a spark of poetry in him," at some length
and with entire scorn; and in the *Idea of a University* Bentham is seen,
along with Hobbes and Hume, as "simply a disgrace" (*D&A*, 262–
263, 269–270, 272, 277; *Idea*, p. 276, and see p. 351). Arnold, too,
spoke of Utilitarianism as being "doomed to sterility," and of Bentham as the "great, dissected master" of his disciples (*CPW*, III, 136,

289). Only a few paragraphs below the discussion of Newman in the farewell lecture, Arnold speaks contemptuously of Bentham's claim to be "the renovator of modern society" (*CPW*, V. 111). Of "the ways of Jacobinism" Arnold found most objectionable "its addiction to an abstract system" (*CPW*, V, 109). This line of reasoning was, as suggested above, what attracted Arnold to Newman's views in "The Tamworth Reading Room," in which Letter 6 is devoted to the idea that men are not touched by reason, conclusions, opinions, logic, syllogisms, argument, inferences, proofs, evidences, analysis, demonstrations, or speculations. Instead, "man is a seeing, feeling, contemplating, acting animal"; "to act you must assume, and that assumption is faith"; and, as Arnold was to quote several times in his notebooks, "instances and patterns, not logical reasonings, are the living conclusions which alone have a hold over the affections, or can form the character" (*D&A*, pp. 292 ff.). Arnold thus prepares the reader to accept, though with reservations, Father Tristram's perhaps surprisingly unqualified view that

Arnold was always girding at what he called the Philistinism of the country, and Newman, although he avoids the terms, plainly anticipated Arnold by a decade in his assault upon the common enemy. Philistinism, as a religious force, is the object of attack in "The Present Position of Catholics"; Philistinism, as an educational force, is the object of attack in the "Idea of a University"; and Philistinism, as a political force, is the object of attack in the pamphlet "Who's to Blame?"[18]

One might add that Philistinism, as a religious and educational and political force, is the object of attack in "The Tamworth Reading Room."

Certainly, then, Newman's writings did provide Arnold with many of the ideas, phrases, and strategies of his battle with Liberalism and Dissent. But one should be cautious in interpreting the role of the Oxford Movement in this central line of Arnold's thought. Despite the rhetoric of the farewell lecture, in which Arnold seems to associate himself with the Tractarians as with other Oxford causes ("we in Oxford," "our attachment to . . . beaten causes," "we have prepared cur-

18 Tristram, "Newman and Matthew Arnold," p. 315.

rents of feeling"), and despite the fact that Arnold clearly wishes to suggest that the Liberalism the Oxford Movement opposed is his opponent too, the evidence is strong that in no essential way did he ever see the Oxford Movement itself as his cause. In other words, when Arnold insists that "I am all in the faith and tradition of Oxford" (*CPW*, V, 106), that sense of a shared faith and tradition is felt to extend far more broadly than to the precise theological and ecclesiastical issues that exercised the Tractarians. On the occasion of his receiving the D.C.L. at Oxford in June 1870, Arnold wrote his mother, "I felt sure I should be well received, because there is so much of an Oxford character about what I have written" (*L*, II, 40). The reference is in very significant measure to crucial passages in, above all, *Essays in Criticism* and *Culture and Anarchy* in which the "Oxford sentiment"—conceived as the "sentiment for beauty and sweetness" and as a unique ideal of perfected human intelligence and character—is repeatedly associated with the person and writings of John Henry Newman. But with regard to the Tractarian Movement itself, of which Newman had been the leader, and to its fortunes after 1845, Arnold's habitual attitude is, with the one important exception of the passage in the farewell lecture, a combination of impatience, condescension, occasional grudging admiration, and almost unbroken intellectual contempt.

John Taylor Coleridge's *Memoir* of John Keble, published in 1869, impressed Arnold with the "narrow medium" in which the Oxford "set" of his father's generation lived.[19] Arnold's impatience is obviously with the Oxford theological politics of *both* parties, and the charge against them all is that of *provinciality*, supposedly the very

---

[19] See page 9 above. Coleridge, in his *Memoir of John Keble*, nevertheless did bring Newman and "the old Oxford ἦθος" (II, 384) vividly before Arnold's mind just as he was to turn his full attention to the contemporary religious crisis. Keble's speaking, on June 14, 1855, of his wish "to counteract the terrible secular spirit which has come over the place [Oxford], naturally enough by the re-action consequent on Newman's secession, and other such things" (II, 388), is close to the tone and tenor of Arnold's already cited letter of October 1854 (*L*, I, 44–45). Keble's disturbed sense in the fifties of "a deep and gradually swelling tide of Rationalism, in unison with the revolutionary spirit" (II, 423), is not far distant from Arnold's concern, in *Literature and Dogma*, with the influence of T. H. Huxley and Bradlaugh over the masses.

quality from which Newman, the great exemplar of *urbanity*, had been declared exempt. It is certainly possible that Newman, at least in his role as intellectual and religious leader, would not have been excluded from that condemnation. For Ritualism, the High Church inheritor of the traditions of the Oxford Movement after the defection of Newman, Arnold had ill-concealed disdain. Speaking in 1877 of the English lack of "lucidity of mind and largeness of temper," Arnold gives as an example "that question of not the most strong-minded portion of the clergy and laity," the Ritualists. They are the camp of the "Simpletons," as against the Dissenters, the camp of the "Savages" (*ME*, p. 175).[20] More fundamentally at issue, however, was a question that went far beyond Romanizing enthusiasts within the Church of England; at stake was Matthew Arnold's gradually evolving picture of the future of human life. In an important letter of March 1881, written to Ernest Fontanès, the French Protestant theologian, Arnold ruthlessly rejected both orthodox Christianity and those alternative rationalized "religions of the future" which the nineteenth century spawned so optimistically. With a daring and imaginative scope he rarely permitted himself in public print, Arnold quite simply and radically rejected "the old religious theory of human life" and demanded a richer conception of human nature and man's "instincts," presumably in accord with the holistic theory affirmed in *Culture and Anarchy* in the sixties and enriched after the period of the religious writings in the seventies. He wrote:

I do not think Miss Cobbe has any real influence,[21] neither do I think that the Ritualists, about whom you enquire, have any real influence. But the two

[20] This essay is further interesting in that Falkland, who is called "our martyr of sweetness and light, of lucidity of mind and largeness of temper" (*ME*, p. 177), is one of the very select company whose qualities recall Arnold's portrait of Newman. This sense is confirmed when Arnold uses, about Falkland, a memorable and evocative phrase he used in *Culture and Anarchy* about Newman and the Oxford Movement: "He and his friends . . . kept open their communications with the future, lived with the future" (*ME*, p. 174). On Ritualism, see the scathing reference in *Literature and Dogma* (*LD*, pp. 279–280) to "the energumens during the celebration of the Communion in some Ritualistic church, their gestures and behaviour, the floor of the church strewn with what seem to be the dying and the dead, progress to the altar almost barred by forms suddenly dropping as if they were shot in battle."

[21] Arnold's quarrel with Frances Cobbe, an enthusiastic religious rationalist who

cases are different; the Ritualists have a large body of clamorous supporters, Miss Cobbe has a small body of earnest sympathisers. The force which is shaping the future is with neither; nor is this force, it seems to me, either with any of the orthodox religions, or with any of the neo-religious developments which propose to themselves to supersede them. Both the one and the other give to what they call religion, and to religious ideas and discussions, too large and absorbing a place in human life; man feels himself to be a more various and richly-endowed animal than the old religious theory of human life allowed, and he is endeavouring to give satisfaction to the long suppressed and still imperfectly-understood instincts of this varied nature. . . . The moral is that whoever treats religion, religious discussions, questions of churches and sects, as absorbing, is not in vital sympathy with the movement of men's minds at present. (*L*, II, 220–221)

This judgment is repeated and amplified in September 1882 in "A Liverpool Address":

Or take a very different movement from that of the Salvation Army, a movement of far higher dignity, reach, and import. . . . The [Ritualist] movement is full of interest. It has produced men to be respected, men to be admired, men to be loved—produced men of learning, men of genius, men of goodness and charm. But can one resist the truth that lucidity would have been fatal to it? The movers of all these questions about apostolical succession, church, patristic authority, primitive usage, symbolism, postures, investments —questions so passionately debated, and on which I will by no means seek to cast ridicule—do they not all begin by taking for granted something no longer possible or receivable, build on this basis as if it were indubitably solid, and fail to see, that, their basis not being solid, all they build upon it is fantastic?[22]

The opposition between the humanisms of Matthew Arnold and John Henry Newman could not be stated more starkly; and this is the abiding opposition to be borne in mind through the massive physical bulk of Newman's evident influence on Arnold's ideas and practice. It prepares the critic, in the face of the almost reverential public references

---

had defended Colenso, began as far back as 1864, in "The Function of Criticism" (*CPW*, III, 278–280).

[22] Matthew Arnold, *Five Uncollected Essays of Matthew Arnold,* ed. Kenneth Allott, p. 92.

of the sixties and in private correspondence until a far later date, for the complex and more negative use of Newman's works in Arnold's religious writings. When, in 1883, Arnold remarked that Newman "has adopted, for the doubts and difficulties which beset men's minds today, a solution which, to speak frankly, is impossible (*DA*, p. 139), Arnold is using language he habitually used in referring, not merely to Roman Catholics, but to all public religionists—both the orthodox and the compromising rationalists—those "mystics and such cattle" he had so despised in his Oxford days. Arnold could never quite reverse his contemptuous and almost angry opinion that they, unlike Matthew Arnold, had not frankly acknowledged what he saw as insuperable intellectual obstacles to traditional supernaturalism in the nineteenth century, and had not spoken directly to "the doubts and difficulties which beset men's minds to-day."

CHAPTER FOUR Newman and the Religion of Culture

Up to this point, I have discussed how Newman enters directly, or by strong implication, into many of Arnold's major concerns in the eighteen-sixties. The effect may seem somewhat scattered because of the sheer variety of contexts in which Newman figures. I have deliberately withheld for full consideration until now a matter of sustained concern to Arnold in this period. This is the development of his central doctrine of criticism and culture, in which the example of Newman almost certainly provided Arnold with many of his basic notions and terms and which very likely inspired the deep-running dualism that a number of readers have detected in Arnold's ideal. Of course Newman was, as many of the preceding pages have demonstrated, a chief source of Arnold's ideal of intellectual excellence and a model for the tone and manner of his critical activity. But it is when one follows the series of progressive reshapings and restatements of Arnold's ideals of criticism and culture through the decade of the sixties that the most permanent stamp of Newman's characteristic thought upon Arnold's writings becomes evident. Both in stating his positive ideal, the qualities of mind which criticism and culture were to sponsor, and in defining the social aims of his ideal, Arnold found support in the *Idea* and elsewhere in Newman.

The connection between Newman and Arnold in this regard has been asserted before, at least briefly, by Dover Wilson and Father Tristram.[1] More recently Raymond Williams has put the problem in historical perspective by seeing Arnold's discussion of culture as the inheritor of a long line of culture criticism—the setting up of an ideal, usually derived from the institutions of the past, against which society can be judged, an ideal which draws especially on Edmund Burke, Samuel Taylor Coleridge, Thomas Carlyle, and John Henry Newman.[2] Williams plausibly argues that when Newman deplores the lack of "some definite word" in English to cover the "cultivation" and "perfection" of the intellect he is describing, he is searching for Arnold's term, "culture."[3]

Arnold's first extended statement of his intellectual ideal occurred in his inaugural lecture at Oxford, "The Modern Element in Literature," delivered in November 1857. There he states the ideal of human nature which he labels Sophoclean and which will be normative for him through the sixties: "human nature developed in a number of directions, politically, socially, religiously, morally developed—in its completest and most harmonious development in all these directions" (*CPW*, I, 28). As a foundation for this holistic theory, Arnold strongly emphasizes the complexity and interconnection of all knowledge. He speaks of "the collective life of humanity": "everywhere there is connexion, everywhere there is illustration: no single event, no single

[1] Henry Tristram, "Newman and Matthew Arnold," *The Cornhill*, N.S. LX (March 1926), 316, 317; Dover Wilson, ed., Preface to Matthew Arnold's *Culture and Anarchy*.

[2] Raymond Williams, *Culture and Society, 1780–1950*, p. 125.

[3] *Ibid.*, p. 120; *Idea*, pp. 110–111. As early as 1841, in "The Tamworth Reading Room," Newman had spoken of "the culture of the mind" and "the cultivation of the mind" (*D&A*, pp. 259, 274).

literature, is adequately comprehended except in its relation to other events, to other literatures." For the most adequate comprehension, representation, and interpretation of an age we must look to its poetry, which demands "the most energetic and harmonious activity of all the powers of the human mind." As a first tentative definition of "the critical power," Arnold finds "the supreme characteristic" of a "modern" age to be "the manifestation of a critical spirit, the endeavour after a rational arrangement and appreciation of facts" (*CPW*, I, 20–21, 22, 25). Newman had made this theme central in the fourteenth of his *Oxford University Sermons*. His subject is "Wisdom"— that "orderly and mature development of thought," "science and philosophy," which was to be the real subject of the *Idea*; in fact, whole paragraphs of this sermon appear almost verbatim in Discourse VI of the *Idea*. In the sermon (delivered in 1841) Newman had described this condition of the intellect as "enlargement or expansion of mind, . . . a wise and comprehensive view of things" and had argued that knowledge, though an essential *condition,* is not the cause of the enlargement:

this enlargement consists in the comparison of the subjects of knowledge one with another. We feel ourselves to be ranging freely, when we not only learn something, but when we also refer it to what we knew before. It is not the mere addition to our knowledge which is the enlargement, but the change of place, the movement onwards, of that moral centre, to which what we know and what we have been acquiring, the whole mass of our knowledge, as it were, gravitates. And therefore a philosophical cast of thought, or a comprehensive mind, or wisdom in conduct or policy, implies a connected view of the old with the new; an insight into the bearing and influence of each part upon every other; without which there is no whole, and could be no centre. It is the knowledge, not only of things, but of their mutual relations. It is organized, and therefore living knowledge. (*OUS,* p. 287; see *Idea*, pp. 118–119)

In the *Idea* itself, anticipating Arnold's remarks on the "energetic and harmonious activity" of all the powers of the mind, Newman prefaced this passage with the following: "The enlargement consists, not merely in the passive reception into the mind of a number of ideas hitherto unknown to it, but in the mind's energetic and simultaneous action upon and towards and among those new ideas, which are rushing in upon it" (*Idea*, p. 118). This was the encyclopedic and synthetic ideal of Discourse V where liberal knowledge is described as "a comprehensive view of truth in all its branches, of the relations of science to science, of their mutual bearings, and their respective values" (*Idea*, p. 91).

Six years later, in 1863, Arnold once more undertook the detailed establishment of a lofty and pure "intellectual sphere" apart from practical and even moral considerations. In the two essays on Spinoza and in that on Stanley's lectures, discussed above, Arnold's decisive separation of reason and morality follows the example of Newman's exaggerated Tractarian view of the distinction between faith and reason. At the end of "Pagan and Mediaeval Religious Sentiment," published in April 1864, occurred the abrupt and undeveloped statement of an ideal that stood *above* division—the "imaginative reason" that somehow combined "the senses and understanding" and "the heart and imagination" and that was (alternatively) a balance between "the thinking-power" and "the religious sense" (*CPW*, III, 230–231). This rich synthetic ideal, which foreshadowed the goal of "culture" and "total perfection" to be set forth in *Culture and Anarchy* and which had a complex historical origin in sources as various as Aristotle, Hugh of St. Victor, Bacon, and Coleridge, colored and complicated all of Arnold's subsequent views on the role of reason in modern life. Culture itself—and the word occurs repeatedly in suggestive contexts long before *Culture and Anarchy*—was not, as Trilling explains, simply a method of the abstract "critical" reason, "but an attitude of spirit contrived to receive truth. It is a moral orientation, involving will, imagination, faith. . . . Culture may best be described as religion with the critical intellect super-added."[4] The chief terms in Arnold's prolonged public discussion of the place of intelligence in man's life and in the life of society were, of course, the overlapping and evolving ones, "criticism" and "culture." But there is a certain continuity in the attendant terms that he uses again and again, almost as incantations, to

[4] Lionel Trilling, *Matthew Arnold*, p. 241. The sources of Newman's ideal of universality and his view of the unity of knowledge are admirably developed in A. Dwight Culler, *The Imperial Intellect: A Study of Newman's Educational Ideal*.

suggest the qualities of mind he desires—such terms as imaginative reason, disinterestedness, urbanity, intellectual delicacy, sweetness and light, and the "element" of Jesus ("mildness and sweetness").

It is important to note that both halves of Arnold's (hopefully superable) division, symbolized by an expression like "imaginative reason," have a basis in Newman's thought. In a sermon of 1840 on "Implicit and Explicit Reason" (Number XIII of the *Oxford University Sermons*), Newman had distinguished the spontaneous "simple faculties and operations of the mind" from "the process of analyzing and describing them, which takes place upon reflection." The first operation, Implicit Reason, Newman calls "unconscious reasoning," which is analogous to Faith; it involves "impulse, instinct, conscience, imagination, habit," and later Newman speaks of it as "an instinctive Reason, which is prior to argument and proof" (*OUS*, pp. 256, 259; and Sermon XIV, p. 280). Citing the immediately following passage on the "great geniuses" who "scale the mountains of truth," a passage used earlier in this book, William Robbins notes that "The reason, as Arnold uses it, is often intuition, imaginative insight, or experimental memory," and that this process is akin to Newman's "implicit" reason, "a unique combination of powers blended of instinct, unconscious memory, and practised skill."[5] The passage itself, it will be recalled, speaks of this as reasoning "not by rule, but by an inward faculty," "a living spontaneous energy within us, not an art" (*OUS*, p. 257). To Explicit Reason, the second, reflective process of the mind, belong, says Newman, such terms as "science, method, development, analysis, criticism, proof, system, principles, rules, laws" (*OUS*, p. 259). Sermon XIV develops this second process under the heading of the supernatural gift of "Wisdom," which is the counterpart "in earthly language" of "science and philosophy"; and in this sermon occur those numerous passages on "enlargement or expansion of mind," "a comprehensive view of things," which were to be imbedded at the heart of Newman's *Idea of a University*. In other words, this view of the second process of the mind, "the uses of our critical and analytical powers," was the kernel of the "idea" of reason, science, and philosophy which

---

[5] William Robbins, *The Ethical Idealism of Matthew Arnold*, p. 170.

Newman was to promulgate in the Dublin discourses. It was this second process that, as I shall maintain, Arnold more or less consciously incorporated into his ideal of reason in "The Function of Criticism" and his later writings. At the outset it is important to note that Newman's conception of even "our critical and analytical powers" was never, either in the sermons or the *Idea,* that of some desiccated thinking-machine. For—and this was surely one of the reasons why Arnold, who set as his goal "spontaneity of consciousness" (*CA,* p. 156), was attracted to Newman's view of our mental processes—Newman's idea of reason involved a dynamic process. As a passage in Sermon XIV, quoted above, puts it, it must be a "living knowledge," a "ranging freely," a "movement onwards of that moral centre, to which . . . the whole mass of our knowledge gravitates," and what the *Idea* was to call "the mind's energetic and simultaneous action upon new ideas" (*OUS,* p. 287; *Idea,* p. 118).

It remains to be shown that in almost every aspect of Arnold's continuing experiment at definition the shadow of Newman can be detected. The climactic essay of the early sixties is "The Function of Criticism at the Present time" (November 1864). The key informing word of the essay is "disinterestedness," a concept combining two major themes of Newman's *Idea,* that of knowledge "for its own sake" and that of the carefully delimited social "utility" of liberal knowledge. First, there is Arnold's severely intellectualist view, controlling a large proportion of the essay, that criticism must never quit "the intellectual sphere" (*CPW,* III, 266), that serene playground of genius which he had tried to define in the essays of 1863. This seems to be a partial retreat from the balance of the "imaginative reason" because it moves in the direction of the overly severe dichotomies that had, it seems, so marred an essay like "Dr. Stanley's Lectures" that Arnold never reprinted it. To be sure, "The Function of Criticism" at the beginning and twice elsewhere offers a balanced statement of the social benefits of Arnold's conception of criticism. Arnold starts by repeating a rigorously intellectual definition of the modern critical effort he had made in 1860: "to see the object as in itself it really is" (*CPW,* III, 258; I, 140); but he soon after sees wide if generalized social effects of such criticism: "It tends to establish an order of ideas, if not absolutely true, yet true by comparison with that which it displaces; to make the best ideas prevail. Presently these new ideas reach society, the touch of truth is the touch of life, and there is a stir and growth everywhere; out of this stir and growth come the creative epochs of literature" (*CPW*, III, 261). Nevertheless, the intellectualist and autotelic note remains dominant. For these creative epochs require primarily "many-sided learning," a "long and widely-combined critical effort," and "a thorough interpretation of the world" (*CPW*, III, 263). Great eras like that of Periclean Greece and the Renaissance "were, in the main, disinterestedly intellectual and spiritual movements; movements in which the human spirit looked for its satisfaction in itself and in the increased play of its own activity" (*CPW*, III, 263–264). This emphasis can grow very insistent. Criticism is the exercise of "curiosity," which Arnold defines as "just this disinterested love of a free play of mind on all subjects, for its own sake." Criticism, moreover, "obeys an instinct prompting it to try to know the best that is known and thought in the world, irrespectively of practice, politics, and everything of the kind; and to value knowledge and thought as they approach this best, without the intrusion of any other considerations whatever" (*CPW*, III, 268).

Arnold is, then, the sponsor of the notions "that the mind may be made the source of great pleasure," and that criticism must keep "in the pure intellectual sphere" (*CPW*, III, 269, 271). Only cautiously does he admit the possible social benefits of criticism— and even these appear to be largely in the intellectual and literary realm. As he declares in a famous passage, "I say, the critic must keep out of the region of immediate practice in the political, social, humanitarian sphere, if he wants to make a beginning for that more free speculative treatment of things, which may perhaps one day make its benefits felt even in this sphere, but in a natural and thence irresistible manner" (*CPW*, III, 275). The remoteness of Arnold's social goals here is evident when he indicates that the very thing criticism offers society at large *is* the concept of "the life of the intelligence" for its own sake—"the notion of the free play of the mind upon all subjects being a pleasure in itself, being an object of desire, being an essential provider of elements without which a nation's spirit, whatever compensations it may have for them, must, in the long run, die of inanition" (*CPW*, III, 268).

The parallels with well-known passages in Newman's *Idea* are very extensive and need only be indicated. At the outset of the crucial Discourse (V) on "Knowledge Its Own End," Newman states that a university creates "a pure and clear atmosphere of thought," apparently akin to Arnold's "pure intellectual sphere" (*Idea*, p. 90). Cultivation of mind is "worth seeking for its own sake": it "is desirable, though nothing come of it, as being of itself a treasure, and a sufficient remuneration of years of labour" (*Idea*, p. 101). Where Arnold spoke of the human spirit finding "its satisfaction in itself" and the mind being "made the source of great pleasure," Newman had asserted that by the very "constitution of the human mind" knowledge "is its own reward," and that "we are satisfying a direct need of our nature" in acquiring it (*Idea*, pp. 91–92).[6] Newman is in general as uncompromising as Arnold in protecting the autotelic character of this knowledge: "that alone is liberal knowledge, which stands on its own pretensions, which is independent of sequel, expects no complement, refuses to be *informed* (as it is called) by any end, or absorbed into any art" (*Idea*, pp. 95–96.)[7] Even more cautiously than Arnold, Newman admits that knowledge may have "a result beyond itself" and issue in "tangible fruit," but his primary contention is "that, prior to its being a power, it is a good; that it is, not only an instrument, but an end" (*Idea*, p. 99).

Only later, in Discourse VII, does Newman face directly the demand of the Useful Knowledge School (which he had attacked in "The Tamworth Reading Room" and which he associates with Locke, the *Edinburgh Review*, and "the disciples of a low Utilitarianism") that "Education should be confined to some particular and narrow end, and

---

[6] See *CPW*, V, 91: "a desire after the things of the mind simply for their own sakes and for the pleasure of seeing them as they are" is "natural and proper in an intelligent being."

[7] Where criticism, for Arnold, must refuse to remain in the sphere of "narrow and relative conceptions" and dwell on "what is excellent in itself," Newman had seen his "philosophical" use of reason as that which continually "rises towards general ideas" (*CPW*, III, 274, 271; *Idea*, p. 99).

should issue in some definite work, which can be weighed and measured" (*Idea*, p. 135). He answers by stages. He first repeats "that
intellectual culture is its own end; for what has its *end* in itself, has
its *use* in itself also" (*Idea*, p. 143). He then goes a step further by
admitting that a liberal education, though not a professional education,
can be truly "useful," in the carefully limited sense that it "*tends* to
good, or is the *instrument* of good." The social benefits are, as in
Arnold's view, very generalized: "not useful in any low, mechanical,
mercantile sense, but as diffusing good, or as a blessing, or a gift, or
power, or a treasure, first to the owner, then through him to the world"
(*Idea*, p. 145). A further step in Newman's concession that "utility in
this large sense as the end of Education" means that "general culture
of mind," though it does not lead directly to any trade or profession,
is "the best aid to professional and scientific study" (*Idea*, p. 146).
Newman ends the discourse by postulating a final social good for education, "that of training good members of society" (*Idea*, p. 156). As
shown earlier, this conclusion closely anticipates Arnold. The task of
the critical intelligence, for Arnold, is "to see the object as in itself it
really is"; for Newman, university training teaches the individual "to
see things as they are." As for society, Arnold assigned to criticism the
task of "a disinterested endeavour to learn and propagate the best that
is known and thought in the world, and thus to establish a current of
fresh and true ideas" (*CPW*, III, 282). The social end of education,
for Newman, if somewhat less dynamic, was similar: "it aims at raising the intellectual tone of society, at cultivating the public mind, at
purifying the national taste, at supplying true principles to popular
enthusiasm and fixed aims to popular aspiration, at giving enlargement
and sobriety to the ideas of the age" (*Idea*, p. 157).

Obviously, the intellectual atmosphere that Arnold's "disinterestedness" was designed to counteract was that of the "low Utilitarianism"
and the "Useful Knowledge School" which Newman opposed all his
life. As Trilling put it, in an age of interests and partisanship "it was
the duty of criticism to take the part of science and advance its un-
clouded disinterestedness."[8] Speaking of the tradition that runs from

---

[8] Trilling, *Matthew Arnold*, p. 185.

Burke to Arnold, in which Newman's role is crucial, Raymond Williams remarks: "The work of perfection, which Arnold was to name as Culture, received increasing emphasis in opposition to the powerful Utilitarian tendency which conceived education as the training of men to carry out particular tasks in a particular kind of civilization."[9] In no matter do Arnold and Newman stand more closely allied; they shared a similar conception of reason in its highest reaches and in its most powerful and sensitive organization; they display a similarly motivated reluctance to commit the highly organized intelligence to the clamorous demands of practical life; and the enemies of their conception of reason and its social role belong to a single line of modern thought (roughly speaking, that of British Empiricism) "condemnatory of any teaching which tends to the general cultivation of the mind" (*Idea*, p. 141).

"Criticism" and "culture" are overlapping and chronologically continuous terms; the latter absorbs the former, above all in *Culture and Anarchy*, and adds to it an ideal of man's total—moral and intellectual —perfection. To be sure, "The Function of Criticism" had anticipated *Culture and Anarchy* by asserting the work of criticism to be that of leading man toward "perfection" and "spiritual progression" (*CPW*, III, 271, 273); and, conversely, "Culture and Its Enemies," Arnold's farewell lecture and the first chapter of *Culture and Anarchy*, looked back to the earlier essay in defining one side of man's double nature as "the genuine scientific passion," the "desire to see things as they are." However, culture as the "study of perfection" sees "the moral and social passion for doing good" as its own "main and pre-eminent part" (*CPW*, V, 91). Arnold is setting up a frankly rival ideal to that of historic Christianity. Here Newman could not, of course, follow Arnold, who refers to himself as, "above all, a believer in culture," and looks for grounds on which to rest "a faith in culture" (*CPW*, V, 88–89). The added social, moral, and quasi-religious tone of Arnold's discussion of culture was in large part an effort to retrieve his evolving ideal of human consciousness from the numerous charges leveled against it, often not very justly or coherently, of self-seeking, utilitarianism, aestheticism, and hedonism. Arnold's holistic and naturalistic

---

[9] Williams, *Culture and Society*, pp. 120–121.

ideal, in these years just before he turned his full attention to the religious crisis of the age, is at first declared to be identical with that of religion: "Religion says: *The Kingdom of God is within you*; and culture, in like manner, places human perfection in an *internal* condition, in the growth and predominance of our humanity proper, as distinguished from our animality. It places it in the ever-increasing efficacy and in the general harmonious expansion of those gifts of thought and feeling which make the peculiar dignity, wealth, and happiness of human nature" (*CPW*, V, 94). The social dimension of this aesthetic and intellectual ideal resides almost exclusively in the insistence that this is to be "a *general* expansion," an ideal progressively diffused in the community at large. As such, it is important to note, the ideal of culture never abandons the essential notes that had marked criticism, a complex version of perfected taste and intelligence and a "disinterested" removal from practical concerns. But the radical nature of Arnold's ideal and the measure of his distance from supernatural Christianity in these years are at once clear when he announces that this harmonious expansion of *all* human powers "is not consistent with the over-development of any one power at the expense of the rest. Here culture goes beyond religion, as religion is generally conceived by us" (*CPW*, V, 94).

Newman, for considerations discussed below, but above all because of his rigorous distinction between faith and reason, never worked out a similarly "total" humanistic ideal, an ideal that would overcome the dualism of faith and reason which so concerned both men. Of course, one might argue that implicit in the ideal of liberal education presented in the *Idea* were the materials for an approach to such a concept, even within Christian theological norms, because the *Idea* emphasizes comprehensiveness and versatility, richness and harmony and asserts that education "implies an action upon our mental nature, and the formation of a character; it is something individual and permanent, and is commonly spoken of in connexion with religion and virtue" (*Idea*, pp. xxxiii, xxxv, 101). Even more explicitly, in "The Tamworth Reading Room," within two pages of the passage in which Newman announced, "To know is one thing, to do is another; the two things are altogether distinct," he speaks of the need for working toward "the unity of our complex nature," "an harmonizing of the chaos" (*D&A*, pp. 262, 264). He later asserts that in "the cultivation of the mind," in all the claims on human intelligence from logic to poetry, "the great and true maxim is to sacrifice none—to combine, and therefore to adjust, all" (*D&A*, p. 274). In the same series of letters occurs Newman's insistence, undoubtedly attractive to the Arnold who postulated the "imaginative reason," that the heart is reached not so much by reason and logic as by the imagination: "after all, man is *not* a reasoning animal; he is a seeing, feeling, contemplating, acting animal" (*D&A*, pp. 293, 294).[10] Nevertheless, Newman did not precede Arnold, except incidentally, in formulating a theory attempting to overcome, on the natural plane, the historical dichotomy of man's religious and intellectual experience—with one important exception.

Later in *Culture and Anarchy*, Arnold restates and deepens his distinction between "the scientific passion" and "the passion for doing good" as that between "Hebraism" and "Hellenism": "the governing idea of Hellenism is *spontaneity of consciousness*; that of Hebraism, *strictness of conscience*" (*CPW*, V, 165). The "fundamental divergence" that divides these two essential human impulses is, of course, the same separation that preoccupied Arnold in his essays of 1863. Arnold is now arguing, in terms of his concept of culture, for a rapprochement of the two forces and has enriched his analysis by a new historical scheme. He begins by seeming to attribute equal value to the two, each of which is inadequate: "Hebraism and Hellenism are, neither of them, the *law* of human development, as their admirers are prone to make them; they are, each of them, *contributions* to human development,—august contributions, invaluable contributions; and each showing itself more august, more invaluable, more preponderant over the other, according to the moment in which we take them, and the relation in which we stand to them" (*CPW*, V, 170–171). Further, "by alternations of Hebraism and Hellenism, of a man's intellectual

---

[10] It should be remembered also that Arnold's statement, "culture . . . places human perfection in an *internal* condition," "an inward condition of the mind and spirit" (*CPW*, V, 94–95), echoes Newman's insistence that "true excellence comes . . . from within," and that liberal knowledge is "an inward endowment" (*D&A*, p. 266; *Idea*, p. 100).

and moral impulses, of the effort to see things as they really are and the effort to win peace by self-conquest, the human spirit proceeds; and each of these two forces has its appointed hours of culmination and seasons of rule"—Christianity being the triumph of Hebraism, and the Renaissance, "an uprising and re-instatement of man's intellectual impulses and of Hellenism" (*CPW*, V, 171–172). In fact, however, much of this assumed equivalence of value turns out to be a rhetorical device, since Arnold's projected "larger conception of human nature" *is* Hellenism, the Greek ideal that absorbs the impulse of Hebraism into its own ideal of the harmonious development of all human powers: "a comprehensive adjustment of the claims of both the sides in man, the moral as well as the intellectual, of a full estimate of both, and of a reconciliation of both" (*CPW*, V, 179). Of course, Arnold knew very well that the practical establishment of such a theory of man was not easy or imminent. Writing in a more discouraged mood in 1870, he deplores the actual, unworthy forces which lead English life and which ensure that "the real union between Hebraism and Hellenism can never be accomplished, and our totality is still as far off as ever. Unhappy and unquiet alternations of ascendency [sic] between Hebraism and Hellenism are all that we shall see;—at one time, the indestructible religious experience of mankind asserting itself blindly; at another, a revulsion of the intellect of mankind from this experience, because of the audacious assumptions and gross inaccuracies with which men's account of it is intermingled" (*SPP,* p. xxxv).

Although nineteenth-century thinkers as diverse as Thomas Carlyle and John Stuart Mill had anticipated Arnold's interest in periods of "concentration" and periods of "expansion," it seems likely that these more religious exercises in historical analysis were influenced by a remarkable passage in Newman's *Apologia,* in which he frankly faces the historical "conflict between Infallibility and Reason" within Christendom. He sees this "warfare," with an optimism more characteristic of his Catholic than of his Anglican period, as "necessary for the very life of religion," and their respective claims reconciled *within* "Catholic Christendom." The image he uses, predictive of Arnold's "unhappy and unquiet alternations of ascendency," is the perhaps more orderly one of "Authority and Private Judgment alternately advancing and retreating as the ebb and flow of the tide." His view is that a "high Providence" has provided a remedy for the alleged danger that, under Infallibility, "the restless intellect of our common humanity is utterly weighed down, to the repression of all independent effort and action whatever" (*Apologia*, p. 228). He answers:

The energy of the human intellect "does from opposition grow;" it thrives and is joyous, with a tough elastic strength, under the terrible blows of the divinely-fashioned weapon, and is never so much itself as when it has lately been overthrown. It is the custom with Protestant writers to consider that, whereas there are two great principles in action in the history of religion, Authority and Private Judgment, they have all the Private Judgment to themselves, and we have the full inheritance and the super-incumbent oppression of Authority. But this is not so; it is the vast Catholic body itself, and it only, which affords an arena for both combatants in the awful, never-dying duel. It is necessary for the very life of religion, viewed in its large operations and its history, that the warfare should be incessantly carried on. Every exercise of Infallibility is brought out into act by an intense and varied operation of the Reason, both as its ally and as its opponent, and provokes again, when it has done its work, a re-action of Reason against it; and, as in a civil polity the State exists and endures by means of the rivalry and collision, the encroachments and defeats of its constituent parts, so in like manner Catholic Christendom is no simple exhibition of religious absolutism, but presents a continuous picture of Authority and Private Judgment alternately advancing and retreating as the ebb and flow of the tide;—it is a vast assemblage of human beings with wilful intellects and wild passions, brought together into one by the beauty and the Majesty of a Superhuman Power,—into what may be called a large reformatory or training-school, not as if into a hospital or into a prison, not in order to be sent to bed, not to be buried alive, but (if I may change my metaphor) brought together as if into some moral factory, for the melting, refining, and moulding, by an incessant, noisy process, of the raw material of human nature, so excellent, so dangerous, so capable of divine purposes. (*Apologia*, pp. 228–229)

Within a Christian and Providential framework, Newman, too, saw the possibility of a reconciliation of man's religious and intellectual experience. But his was actual, past and present, *within* history. Perhaps Matthew Arnold's view of history, despite the superintendence of a surrogate-Providence in the *Zeitgeist,* was ultimately less optimistic than John Henry Newman's.

Thus, a series of dualisms unite, and yet subtly distinguish, the views of Newman and of Arnold on the range of reason in its highest and most organized form and on the role of reason in society and in the formation of human character. First, there is the bedrock and persistent recognition of the polarity of "faith" (including such matters as religion, morality, and imagination) and the critical reason. Next, once a high ideal of intellectual excellence has been established, there is the shared reluctance to commit intelligence in its fullest definition to the practical tasks of this world. Perhaps Arnold's conception of disinterestedness is the more extreme, since, even if a bit reluctantly, Newman could say, as one cannot picture Arnold saying, that the practical end of a university course "is that of training good members of society" (*Idea,* p. 156). As Raymond Williams notes, despite Arnold's definition of culture as right knowing and right doing, "his emphasis in detail is so much on the importance of knowing, and so little on the importance of doing, that Culture at times seems very like the Dissenters' Salvation: a thing to secure first, to which all else will then be added."[11] The (perhaps overstated) point of E. K. Brown's study of Arnold is "the oscillation between the poles of detachment and action, of artistic contemplation and practical criticism" throughout his works.[12] Of course Arnold tried, far more consciously and at greater length than Newman did, to synthesize the fundamental impulses of man. But both men had made attempts in this direction by establishing a high and complex ideal of human consciousness, and, as Culler says, by establishing the historical "image of a large human culture" distinguished by apartness, detachment, and catholicity, which would transcend the self.[13] Both failed in this attempt, for different, if complementary, reasons.

There are two central themes in the *Idea* which are never satisfactorily resolved: the need to include religious teaching in a program of

[11] Williams, *Culture and Society,* p. 136.
[12] E. K. Brown, *Matthew Arnold: A Study in Conflict,* p. 179.
[13] John Henry Newman, *Apologia Pro Vita Sua,* ed. A. Dwight Culler, pp. xvii–xviii.

studies, and the fact that cultivation of the mind, rather than professional training, is the object of a university.[14] Fergal McGrath, in his
study of the *Idea*, is at pains to insist that Newman's "mental distinction" between "the intellectual and moral issues" should not be read
as "a real distinction which his other writings and his life-work put
completely out of count."[15] Almost certainly this is glossing over a serious difficulty too easily. For if Newman, in the *Idea*, had viewed Civilization as "a great objective fact" in time and space (and, in Culler's
words, "had set it forth in more satisfactory terms than Arnold would
ever do"), surely Culler is correct in asking: "Why did he not acknowledge the power of that fact, so obviously bigger than any individual or
any nation or any single epoch, to take men out of themselves, to provide a standard by which they could correct and discipline their own
nature?"[16] He suggests three reasons. The first is connected with the
highly competitive English educational system, which Newman saw as
a source of vanity and pride. Second, "the Oriel apologetic for liberal
knowledge" had paradoxically, Newman felt, dissolved "the real defenses of humanism, for it turned the attention of the student away
from the object of knowledge, with the veneration it ought to excite,
toward the contemplation of the self which was being cultivated by
the knowledge." Finally, and most important, Culler sees Newman's
conception of culture as "stubbornly naturalistic," and hence he could
not assign to literary culture the value Arnold gave it.[17] In a word, the
insuperable defect of humanistic culture, for Newman, lay in the fact
that "it still provides no means for transcending the limits of the natural man."[18]

The most telling proof of this defect is Newman's definition of the
"Gentleman," the characteristic product of Oxford and of Newman's
ideal of liberal knowledge, a definition often quoted apart from its
context, as if it were Newman's positive ideal of man. Newman, perhaps the supreme modern defender of the ideal of liberal education,

---

[14] Fergal McGrath, *Newman's University: Idea and Reality*, p. 133.
[15] *Ibid.*, p. 291.
[16] Culler, *Imperial Intellect*, p. 235.
[17] *Ibid.*, pp. 236–238.
[18] *Ibid.*, pp. 238.

introduces the product of this education in Discourse V in this highly qualified way: "It is well to be a gentleman, it is well to have a cultivated intellect, a delicate taste, a candid, equitable, dispassionate mind, a noble and courteous bearing in the conduct of life . . . but still, I repeat, they are no guarantee for sanctity or even for conscientiousness, they may attach to the man of the world, to the profligate, to the heartless,—pleasant, alas, and attractive as he shows when decked out in them" (*Idea*, p. 107). His valuation of this product of his supposed ideal of life is even clearer in Discourse VIII, a large portion of which expands on these qualities, only to suggest that these are "copies" or counterfeits of the qualities of "St. Paul's exemplar of the Christian in his external relations" (*Idea*, pp. 180, 185 ff.). One of the chief (if today generally unacknowledged) objectives of Newman's *Idea* is to warn that the character endowed with the fruits of a liberal education is particularly liable to mistake its real natural virtues for the essential Christian virtues that are of paramount importance. The qualities sponsored by this natural ideal, embraced by what Newman calls "the Religion of Philosophy," remain strictly indifferent to the central issue of life: they can develop "apart from religious principle," and they "partly assist and partly distort the development of the Catholic." They may be found in the saints, as well as in the enemies of religion (*Idea*, p. 187). One is tempted to say that the characteristic product of Arnold's "culture" nicely exemplifies the qualities of Newman's Oxford "gentleman"; but this is to say that, by Newman's standards, Arnold's paragon is a kind of fraudulent copy of St. Paul's "saint."[19]

In Arnold, the failure lies in a different direction. Culler maintains that Arnold's attempt to establish, in "culture," a norm larger than the self failed because when he looks for an interpreter of the norm, "whether in an English Academy or in the idea of the State or in his celebrated 'touchstones' for poetry, he ended by reintroducing the self in another guise."[20] Transcendence of self is a key motif of Arnold's critical, social, and religious writings. May not Arnold's failure to achieve this transcendence explain the "unresolved inner tension," the

[19] The premises of John Griffin's "Defense" of Newman's Gentleman, (*Dublin Review*, No. 505 [Autumn 1965], pp. 245–254) are confused.
[20] Newman *Apologia* (ed. Culler), pp. xvii–xviii.

"divided mind and spirit," which E. K. Brown saw in Arnold's oscillation between "detachment and action"?—an oscillation that can be reshaped meaningfully as that between reason and morality.[21] For, despite his asserted ideal of a human nature brought to perfection on all sides, Arnold was fundamentally too conservative ever to give up, especially after the religious writings of the following decade, the historic Christian dualism between nature and grace, morality and reason —the dualism that proved to be the rock on which Newman's view of "intellectual culture" also foundered. Arnold did suggest, in *Culture and Anarchy,* that a naturalistic culture and "perfection" are "known absolutes," and that they could serve as a substitute for religion, a position that readers of almost all biases have since deplored as confused.[22] A source of Arnold's own confusion and "division" is his intellectual conviction that no theistic absolutes can be validated, whereas imaginative and emotional participation in the great inherited structure of European and world civilization seemed, at least historically, to have demanded something very close to religious faith.[23] Almost at once, in the writings of the following several years, Arnold set about qualifying his Hellenic ideal, and in such forces as "the Eternal" and "the power that makes for righteousness" he sought, however illogically, sanctions for his humanism which were in fact imaginative and emotional equivalents for God. Especially in *Literature and Dogma,* these forces inhabit a realm that can justly be described as the supernatural. Arnold's holistic ideal, though reasserted in the social writings of the final decade of his life, never quite regained its confident tone. His deepened sense of the religious crisis of the age permanently complicated his naturalism. Culler seems to chide Arnold for his failure to pursue to the utmost the idea that values, "which have their origin within us," transcend the self and exercise a corrective power only in the "guise" of "the great, distinct, and objective image of human nature which has been erected in the culture of the past.[24] But this is to view Arnold through twen-

[21] Brown, *Matthew Arnold,* pp. 121, 183.

[22] For recent examples, see Williams, *Culture and Society,* p. 136; and Wayne Shumaker, "Matthew Arnold's Humanism: Literature as a Criticism of Life," *Studies in English Literature,* II (Autumn 1962), 397, 401.

[23] See the discussion of "Literature and Science," Chapter 8, below.

[24] Culler, *Imperial Intellect,* p. 235.

tieth-century spectacles and to ask of him a detachment from metaphysically supported values which, despite his protests against metaphysics,
he was unable—emotionally and imaginatively—to adopt. For Arnold,
as for Newman, the ideal of a perfected intelligence—even an intelligence drawing to itself qualities of imagination, taste, and sympathy—
could never supplant the deep-rooted sense of an ineradicable division
in man between *doing* and *knowing*.

At this point in the analysis it is possible to appreciate the full import
of Arnold's acknowledgment in the letter of January 1868—midway
through the writing of *Culture and Anarchy*—of what Newman had
so far meant to him. Newman had sent him a copy of his newly collected poetry, *Verses on Various Occasions*; Arnold responded: "But
the more inward qualities and excellences of the Poems remind me
how much I, like so many others, owe to your influence and writings;
the impression of which is so profound, and so mixed up with all that
is most essential in what I do and say, that I can never cease to be
conscious of it and to have an inexpressible sense of gratitude and attachment to its author."[25] The reverential, almost filial, tone will per-
dure now till the end, but the extent of the influence, even up to this
moment in 1868, is by no means so exaggerated or merely conventional
as a casual reader might assume.

Perhaps the best way to catch the precise weight and tone of Arnold's
indebtedness is to summarize the immense verbal network that links
the supreme efforts of these two men to define the nature and role of
reason. The sheer mass of identical (or cognate) terms and figures employed to define—and, in the very process, to exemplify—the capacities
of the perfected intelligence caps the argument for intellectual filiation.
For example, in describing the activities of the educated mind, both
Arnold and Newman use these words: relating, combining, adjusting,
connecting, harmonizing, uniting, comprehending. Even more suggestive are the qualities that both men attribute to the liberal and critical
intelligence: energy, spontaneity, freedom, harmoniousness, cultivation, unity, taste, flexibility, interiority and inwardness, beauty, perfection, excellence, power, ease, clarity, comprehensiveness. Equally im-

25 Tristram, "Newman and Matthew Arnold," p. 311.

portant is a series of noncognate terms that tend to suggest *balance* and *elevation* as the highest qualities and effects of the most finely organized intelligence. Arnold recommends fitness, measure, certainty, urbanity, moderation, proportion, delicacy, pliancy, patience, sincerity, simplicity, order, balance, regulation, fineness of temper, security, peacefulness, impersonality. Newman, before him, had spoken of equitableness, calmness, moderation, wisdom, candor, refinement, versatility, dispassionateness, courteousness, self-possession, and repose. To describe mental operations is necessarily to use metaphor; here, too, Arnold and Newman coincide in a series of figures suggesting mental *growth* and *movement*. Arnold speaks of complete harmonious development, blithe movement, a criticism "quietly enlarging" and "ever widening" its knowledge, harmonious expansion, growth, progression, *becoming* (as opposed to *having*), the stream of consciousness. Newman had used the figures of intrinsic fecundity, a living spontaneous energy, enlargement, expansion, movement onwards, a formative power, digestion, growth, locomotion. Finally, the two men commonly use metaphors of *light* and *sight* to convey the unfettered scope and penetration characteristic of the finest intelligence. Arnold speaks of "aerial ease, clearness, and radiancy"; the "warm glow" of the highest style; "to see the object as in itself it really is." These suggest Newman's emphasis on a clear atmosphere of thought, enlightenment, insight, illumination, seeing with the mental eye, clearsightedness, mental vision, seeing things as they are.

PART II

THE RELIGION

OF THE FUTURE

CHAPTER FIVE Development and the *Zeitgeist*

If Newman's role in the unfolding of Arnold's view of intelligence and its place in human development was very far-reaching, his presence in Arnold's religious writings of the eighteen-seventies, especially in *St. Paul and Protestantism* and *Literature and Dogma,* is even more explicit and continuous. William Robbins expresses the received opinion when he says, "Newman was a spiritual ally in Arnold's prolonged campaign against hard, unlovely Puritanism and crassly utilitarian Philistinism, one of the spiritual fathers of *Culture and Anarchy* rather than of the later and distinctively religious works."[1] This is no doubt substantially correct, but it fails to suggest either the sheer bulk of direct references to Newman in the religious works, or the complexity of tone in Arnold's response to and use of Newman's religious writings. In fact, the later relationship has almost entirely escaped discussion; and this is all the more serious an omission in any account of Arnold's intellectual development since Newman would seem to be, next perhaps to Bishop Butler, the most extensively quoted specifically theological writer in Arnold's religious works.

Arnold's most elaborate discussion of Newman's thought anywhere in his writings occurs in "Puritanism and the Church of England"

[1] William Robbins, *The Ethical Idealism of Matthew Arnold*, p. 56.

(*Cornhill*, February 1870), later a chapter in *St. Paul and Protestantism,* which was published in May of that year. It is important to note that from the first Arnold conceived his religious writings to be a continuation of the work of his father's generation. On November 13, 1869, Arnold wrote his mother, noting that the major work of Dr. Arnold's and S. T. Coleridge's time had been "the exploding of the old notions of literal inspiration in Scripture, and the introducing of a truer method of interpretation." He explains that his two recent articles entitled "St. Paul and Protestantism" (*Cornhill*, October and November 1869) had contended that the "old notions about justification will undergo a like change." The articles had in fact attacked the whole Christian "economy" of salvation, especially in the commercial metaphors with which Dissenting theology had imaged forth that process. Now, he says, his purpose in the forthcoming essay will be "to show how the Church [of England], though holding certain doctrines like justification in common with Puritanism, has gained by not pinning itself to those doctrines and nothing else, but by resting on Catholic antiquity, historic Christianity, development, and so on, which open it to an escape from all single doctrines as they are outgrown" (*L*, II, 23–24). The key word is "development."

Late in 1869 Arnold was obviously reading closely in Newman's *An Essay on the Development of Christian Doctrine* (1845), for the center of "Puritanism and the Church of England" is occupied by the appropriation and judgment of Newman's ideas. The Church of England, Arnold argues, does not exist for "special opinions" as Nonconformism does; instead, it serves "religious progress" in "proceeding by development" and allowing "much greater freedom of mind" on the essentials of Christian theology. This is the idea of the "development and gradual exhibiting of the full sense of the Bible and Christianity," which goes forward by "growth and gradual illumination" (*SPP*, pp. 120, 121). This is also the idea, continues Arnold, set forth "persuasively and truly" by "an admirable writer," Dr. Newman, "in a book which is one of his least known works, but which contains, perhaps, even a greater number of profound and valuable ideas than any other one of them" (*SPP*, p. 121). With the reader favorably disposed, Arnold then gives three substantial quotations, conflated and revised, from the *Essay on Development,* in which Newman speaks of apparent variations of Church doctrine under the figures of *growth, increase, expansion,* and *development* (*SPP,* pp. 121–123; *EDD,* pp. 26, 27, 61–62, 95). Arnold accurately enough sums up this "admirably expounded" notion as that of "a gradual understanding of the Bible, a progressive development of Christianity"; moreover, Arnold's three supporting quotations from Butler are also to be found in the *Essay* (*SPP,* pp. 123–124; *EDD,* pp. 111, 114). Arnold concludes this exposition on a note of high praise: "All this is incomparably well said; and with Dr. Newman we may, on the strength of it all, beyond any doubt, 'fairly conclude that Christian doctrine admits of formal, legitimate, and true developments'; that 'the whole Bible is written on the principle of development' " (*SPP,* p. 124; *EDD,* pp. 113, 103).

But at this very moment, Arnold decisively parts company with Newman. The reasons for Arnold's extended demurrer, and the way in which the rejoinder is managed, are indicative of the relations of the two men as well as of the grounds of Arnold's religious humanism. Newman's use of the idea of development "in support of the pretensions of the Church of Rome to an infallible authority on points of doctrine" is, Arnold begins, "arbitrary and condemned by the idea itself" (*SPP,* p. 124). He admits that Newman "with much ingenuity" can challenge Protestants with the fact that their characteristic doctrines are as much developments of the post-Nicene Church as are the characteristically Catholic doctrines of Purgatory and the Canon of Scripture: "And thus Dr. Newman would compel Protestants to admit that which is, he declares, in itself reasonable,—namely, 'the probability of the appointment in Christianity of an external authority to decide upon the true developments and practice in it' " (*SPP,* p. 125; *EDD,* p. 117).[2] But here Arnold suddenly retorts: "Now, asserted in this absolute way, and extended to doctrine as well as discipline, to speculative thought as well as to Christian practice, Dr. Newman's conclusion seems at variance with his own theory of development" (*SPP,* p. 125). What follows is a fascinating example of Arnold's argumentative methods, especially in the religious writings. For

---

[2] The other relevant passages alluded to here by Arnold occur in *EDD,* pp. 6, 16 ff., 98–99.

it seems evident that Arnold never fully understood, or allowed himself
to understand, the real and internal drift of Newman's argument. For
example, Arnold's use of "absolute way" merely exploits popular
prejudice. Moreover, the *Essay on Development* dealt with "doctrine"
and "speculative thought" primarily and from the first and was not
"extended to those areas." Finally, what is more suspicious, Arnold
simply refuses to follow Newman's argumentation through. He seems
to accept Newman's initial arguments, against Protestants, that characteristically Protestant and Catholic doctrines are equally "developments" of the Church. But Newman had gone on to argue, on the basis
of probability, that the appointment of an infallible external authority,
to safeguard developments of Christian doctrine from error, is simply
a "reasonable" extension of the doctrine of development itself. True or
false, the argument is cogent and demands examination and, if false,
refutation. Clearly, Newman's conclusion is antecedently unacceptable
to Arnold; and instead of examination or rejoinder Arnold gives an
alleged refutation, in Newman's own words, that development "comes
of its own innate power of expansion within the mind in its season,
though with the use of reflection and argument and original thought,
more or less as it may happen, with a dependence on the ethical growth
of the mind itself, and with a reflex influence upon it" (*SPP*, pp. 125–
126; *EDD*, p. 113). This, Arnold approvingly comments, is "the
natural, spontaneous, free character of true development" (*SPP*, p.
126). For Newman, these were exactly the perennial qualities of the
devout theologizing mind; but of course, for Arnold, they were precisely the qualities most unlikely to reside in an orthodox Christian
theologian, especially in a Roman Catholic. Hence the effective rhetoric
of "natural, spontaneous, free," the qualities that, as Newman had
clearly seen twenty years before in the *Present Position of Catholics*,
popular English prejudice would refuse to acknowledge in the Roman
Church.

For Arnold himself, though able on occasion to exploit such prejudice, the issue was much wider than contemporary Protestant-Catholic
polemics. He now turns to the ultimate grounds for his refusal to analyze Newman's arguments. At stake was Arnold's view of history and
the nature of Christianity. Implicitly, he recognizes the inherent and

inevitable limitations of the argument of the *Essay on Development*; in that work Newman develops an *argumentum ad hominem* against Protestants who of course already accepted the fundamental dogmas of Christianity and, presumably, the notion of a Providence safeguarding and guaranteeing the truth of those doctrines.[3] Arnold's strategy is to develop a counterargument that attempts to resolve any dispute by transcending parties and bringing into question the validity and truth of all Christian theology. Theological development, says Arnold, "may often require vast periods of time," and he insists "that for its true and ultimate development in this line more time is required, and other conditions have to be fulfilled, than we have had already. So far as Christian doctrine contains speculative philosophical ideas, never since its origin have the conditions been present for determining these adequately; certainly not in the mediaeval Church, which so dauntlessly strove to determine them" (*SPP*, p. 126). In fact, never yet have the "great questions of philosophy and of scientific criticism" which Christianity admittedly raises been answerable within the Christian Churches. The Middle Ages were utterly inadequate to "historic criticism, criticism of style, criticism of nature," and the entire corpus of medieval philosophy and theology is written off at a stroke because its opinions, "being philosophical developments, . . . are made in an age when the forces for true philosophical development are waning or wanting" (*SPP*, pp. 127, 128).[4] In Arnold's drastically simplified and sche-

---

[3] See Anthony Stephenson, "The Development and Immutability of Christian Doctrine," *Theological Studies*, XIX (December 1958), 531.

[4] In Arnold's reading lists for 1870 appear six of the *Quarterly* reviews of Henry Hart Milman collected in May 1870, in *Savonarola, Erasmus, and Other Essays*. Milman, a Liberal Anglican historian close to Dr. Arnold, had died in 1868. One of the essays listed by Arnold (*NB*, p. 587) is Milman's hostile 1846 review of Newman's *Essay on Development*, and Milman's treatment of "the gloom and oppression" of the Middle Ages as an argument against Newman's theory of development suggests that Arnold may have known the review before the publication of "Puritanism and the Church of England" in February. In refuting Newman's case for an alleged "development," Milman ironically brings in the Middle Ages: "Christianity is advancing towards its perfect development, while mankind is degenerating into the darkest barbarism and ignorance." Milman continues: "Yet there is not a poet, from Claudian to Dante, not a philosopher . . . from Boetius (a low point of departure) to Anselm" (p. 325). "It is strange that the clergy, that bishops, that popes, cannot escape the growing ferocity, the all-enveloping ignorance of the times; and yet they

matized view of intellectual history, there had been in Greece before
the appearance of Christianity a "favouring period" for such matters
as "a philosophy of theology" or "a philosophical criticism," and only
with the Renaissance did "the movement of philosophy and criticism"
resume its progress:

this movement was almost entirely outside the Churches, whether Catholic
or Protestant, and not inside them. . . . Philosophy and criticism have become
a great power in the world, and inevitably tend to alter and develop Church-
doctrine, so far as this doctrine is, as to a great extent it is, philosophical
and critical. Yet the seat of the developing force is not in the Church itself,
but elsewhere; its influences filter strugglingly into the Church, and the
Church slowly absorbs and incorporates them. And whatever hinders their
filtering in and becoming incorporated, hinders truth and the natural progress of things. (*SPP*, pp. 128–130)

The agency of this true development is harder to define. Arnold at
one point says, "Thought and science follow their own law of development, they are slowly elaborated in the growth and forward pressure
of humanity, . . . and their ripeness and unripeness, as Dr. Newman
most truly says, are not an effect of our wishing and resolving. Rather
do they seem brought about by a power such as Goethe figures by the
Zeit-Geist or Time-Spirit, and St. Paul describes as a divine power
revealing additions to what we possess already" (*SPP*, pp. 130–131).
Arnold's rhetorical shift toward the postulation of a "divine power"
superintending the development of the human intelligence, is, as it
often is with Arnold in these matters, breathtaking. He wants a "natural, spontaneous, free" development of religious doctrine based on
"philosophy and criticism," a process the conditions of which have
never been achieved *within* the Churches, although since the Renaissance the means are available *outside* the Churches and are now "filtering" or "struggling" in, so as to bring a reluctant Christianity into line
with the large movement of the Western mind which is "the natural

---

are not only faithfully watching the terrible lamp of Christian faith, but they are adding to its lustre. Their wisdom is (as we are to suppose) steadily on the increase,
while every other growth of the human mind is dwindling down almost to utter extinction" (pp. 325–326).

progress of things." This argument is of course a corollary of Arnold's view that Christianity "has practice for its great end and aim"; the Churches, quite literally, have no mind of their own. Seemingly, Arnold's moralized and deintellectualized Christianity will have for its permanently and intellectually viable substance a small body of ethical truths;[5] deprived of any inherent intellectual substance, method, or dynamic, Christianity must submit and adapt itself to the "developing" and (presumably) changing standards of the "philosophy and criticism" of each age for any metaphysical description of the reality that Christianity admittedly speaks to. This is virtually a protodefinition of theological Modernism.

It is not surprising, then, that Newman, elaborately saluted with one hand for statements on the development of doctrine, is with the other rather roughly handled in the deeper implications of his argument and is in fact swept aside either as tiresomely reactionary or as the representative of an a priori "impossible" position. Moreover, Arnold's first careful paraphrases of Newman's view as that of "a gradual understanding of the Bible, a progressive development of Christianity," soon enough give way to the view that philosophy and criticism "tend to *alter* and *develop* Church-doctrine" (my emphasis), a scheme of progress effected by the Time-Spirit, "a divine power" that reveals "additions" to what already exists. Substantial *alteration* and *addition* are precisely what Newman is eager to deprecate in his concept of development.[6] A final and significant paradox is the fact that Newman, though of course holding that the history of doctrinal development is ultimately under the rule of Providence, guaranteed and sanctioned by the authority of the teaching Church, nevertheless clearly holds that the internal *mechanism* of doctrinal development proceeds from man's "use of reflection and argument and original thought"; on the other hand Arnold, the professed advocate of "philosophy and criticism," is far more "mystical" in delivering the whole process to a quasi-Providential "divine power" that "reveals" additions and superintends "the natural

[5] For a typical summation, see the catechism Arnold provides in "A Comment on Christmas" (1885), added in 1887 to the popular edition of *St. Paul and Protestantism,* p. 166. See also *SPP*, pp. 132–134, and *LECR*, pp. 229–231.

[6] See Stephenson, "Christian Doctrine," pp. 531–532.

progress of things." This is what Arnold seems to have meant when he wrote his mother in November 1869: "It is not man who determines what truths shall present themselves to this or that age, or under what aspect; and until the time is come for the new truth or the new aspect, they are presented unsatisfactorily or in vain" (*L*, II, 23).

In the light of *St. Paul and Protestantism* as a whole, as well as of Arnold's other religious writings, it is fairly clear what Christianity's "true and ultimate development in this line" will be: the jettisoning of the entire metaphysical apparatus and methodology of traditional theology as literally meaningless. Arnold's "additions" tend to be *deletions*, his ultimate theology being a collection of religiously tinged moral maxims from the Bible. Arnold's instinct of course is never to argue directly, but to insinuate, to slip behind an opponent by undermining the opponents *type* of argument. For example, the characteristic method of *Literature and Dogma* and *God and the Bible* is to meet all theological objections by denying that metaphysical questions have any meaning. At any rate, this first use of Newman's religious thought is typical of Arnold's treatment of Newman in the religious writings: the man is treated with considerable deference, and his words are quoted, usually somewhat out of context, when Newman's literary and intellectual authority seems helpful to Arnold's argument; but Newman is impatiently thrust aside as soon as his more "arbitrary" and "impossible"— and central—views are glimpsed. Newman on "development" is invoked as a kind of elaborate red herring to endorse a view of theological history which he would abhor, a rationalization and "de-supernaturalization" of Christianity, the emptying out of the content of most of the characteristic doctrines of orthodox theology, and the retention of a Pelagian scheme of self-induced moral transformation using Jesus as a model.

Arnold seems momentarily to throw Newman a crumb by stating: "What may justly be conceded to the Catholic Church is, that in her idea of a continuous developing power in united Christendom to work upon the data furnished by the Bible, and produce new combinations from them as the growth of time required it, she followed a true instinct." But he at once withdraws his tribute: "But the right *philosophical* developments she vainly imagined herself to have had the power to produce, and her attempts in this direction were at most but a prophecy of this power, as alchemy is said to have been a prophecy of chemistry" (*SPP*, p. 131). Strictly speaking, then, "development" operates exclusively in secular "thought and science," which "follow their own line of development" (*SPP*, p. 130). In fact, for Arnold the question of doctrinal development was a kind of intellectual will-o'-the-wisp. Presumably modern thought, on the one hand, and religion on the other, will go on undisturbed, each in its own sphere, a position obviously related to Arnold's view of the extreme dichotomy between the moral and intellectual spheres in the sixties. This desirable severance will be hastened as the churches drop all pretensions to the metaphysical validity of traditional theological categories. Where by "development" Newman meant (among other metaphors) something like the unfolding of the implications of an original germinative thought, Arnold (despite his use of the word "addition") tends to mean something closer to the *alteration, deletion,* and eventual *extirpation* of Christian theology.

Arnold's peculiar imperturbability in the face of such seriously incompatible definitions is evident when, later in the essay, he once more invokes Newman on development. Arnold is arguing that the Nonconformist churches are wrong to separate from the Church of England over matters of *discipline,* since individual "fancies" must be sacrificed to the life of the religious community, or over matters of *dogma,* since, the Church lacking the means of settling philosophical points, people should "concede" them and unite in the *moral* principle, "Let every one that nameth the name of Christ depart from iniquity" (*SPP*, p. 139). In the midst of this argument, Newman is brought in again:

All that Dr. Newman has so excellently said about development applies here legitimately and fully. Existence justifies additions and stages of existence. The living edifice planted on the foundation, *Let every one that nameth the name of Christ depart from iniquity,* could not but grow, if it lived at all. If it grew, it could not but make developments, and all developments not inconsistent with the aim of its original foundation, and not extending beyond the moral and practical sphere of its original foundation, are legitimated by the very fact of the Church having in the natural evolution of its life and growth made them. (*SPP*, p. 136)

The interesting fact is that, with the exception of "additions," all of Arnold's key words here—"stages of existence," "living edifice," "grow," "developments," "evolution"—are compatible with Newman's metaphors of organic growth. And yet, Arnold's words "excellently" and "legitimately" conceal—how consciously is hard to tell— not merely the difference in the two men's concepts but their near opposition. Newman was discussing precisely the development of doctrine, while Arnold holds that Christian "dogma," "theological philosophy," "speculation," and "opinion" have nothing to do with the essence of Christianity and must in fact be jettisoned since "the moral and practical sphere . . . was the sphere of its original foundation."

This inverted parallelism of Newman's and Arnold's ideas is strikingly followed up in the remainder of "Puritanism and the Church of England." Newman is brought in, seconding Hooker in support of the proposition that "the Bible does not exhibit, drawn out in black and white, the precise tenets and usages of any Christian society; some inference and criticism must be employed to get at them" (*SPP*, pp. 145–146; *EDD*, pp. 94 ff.). With Newman, Arnold argues that church discipline and church doctrine were both arrived at by "a process of reasoning and collection" (*SPP*, p. 146). Newman, in the *Essay on Development*, had worked out an *ad hominem* argument against Protestants, that since Protestant and Catholic doctrines were both developments, the existence of some external authority to judge the merits of conflicting Christian claims is probable and reasonable. Arnold, also developing an *ad hominem* argument against Protestants, accepts Newman's claim that both sets of doctrines are "developments," only to argue then that *both* are "unsound developments," and that therefore Protestants should be comprehended into the Church of England, which "does not identify Christianity with these unsound developments." It does not require that members believe in either the Protestant "received doctrine of justification" or the Catholic "doctrine of priestly absolution and of the real presence": "She thus provides room for growth and further change in these very doctrines themselves" (*LD*, p. 147). For "growth" and "change," read "removal" and "repudiation." In effect, Arnold, using a kind of elaborate parody of Newman's argumentation, has undercut all historic Christian positions, Protestant and Catholic, and made of the Church of England a nondoctrinal mediatorial Church of the Future beyond the dreams of all but the most aggressive Latitudinarians. His vision, reminiscent of his father's, is that of a totally comprehensive National Church in which Anglicans and Dissenters could close ranks: "Then there might arise a mighty and undistracted power of joint life, which would transform, indeed, the doctrines of priestly absolution and the real presence, but which would transform, equally, the so-called *Scriptural Protestantism* of imputed righteousness, and which would do more for real righteousness and for Christianity than has ever been done yet" (*SPP*, pp. 150–151). For "transform," again, read "discard."

Finally, in the midst of pursuing, by the perverse aid of Newman's arguments, this line of unity against the *"separatists . . . for the sake of opinions"* (*SPP*, p. 138), Arnold had also elaborately invoked, and very nearly burlesqued, a central contention of Newman's, this time from the *Apologia*:

Dr. Newman has told us what an impression was once made upon his mind by the sentence: *Securus judicat orbis terrarum*. We have shown how, for matters of philosophical judgment, not yet settled but requiring development to clear them, the consent of the world, at a time when this clearing development cannot have happened, seems to carry little or no weight at all; indeed, as to judgment on these points, we should rather be inclined to lay down the very contrary of Dr. Newman's affirmation, and to say: *Securus delirat orbis terrarum*. But points of speculative theology being out of the question, and the practical ground and purpose of man's religion being broadly and plainly fixed, we should be quite disposed to concede to Dr. Newman, that *securus* colit *orbis terrarum*;—those pursue this purpose best who pursue it together. For unless prevented by extraneous causes, they manifestly tend, as the history of the Church's growth shows, to pursue it together. (*SPP*, p. 135; see *Apologia*, pp. 106 ff.)

Once again, then, a crucial idea of Newman's is treated with a kind of levity that seems at odds with the expressions of genuine respect for Newman the man which Arnold, here as elsewhere, employs. This complexity of response informs many of the references to Newman in Arnold's religious writing.

There is no evidence that Arnold sent Newman a copy of *St. Paul and Protestantism* on its appearance in May 1870; and for the reasons given above, it seems unlikely that he would have done so. But in 1871 and 1872 an extraordinary burst of correspondence occurs between the two men which links their thought and cements their hitherto fragmentary personal relations.

Early in November of 1871 Newman issued the two volumes of *Essays Critical and Historical*, a reprinting of sixteen pieces from his Anglican days, with one exception. Arnold must have bought the volumes at once and have begun that close reading in the essays which the works of the next few years reveal. On November 29 he writes Newman, expressing his regret that he had not had time to call on Newman when in Birmingham. On October 16 Arnold had delivered at the Birmingham and Midland Institute the lecture, "A Persian Passion Play," which had now just appeared in the December issue of *Cornhill*. He tells Newman he is having a copy sent him, "because what is said about Mahometanism at the end seems to me to coincide very much with a strain of remark in a reprinted article of yours on Milman which I have just been reading, and to be an unconscious homage to the truth of what you have there said" (*UL,* pp. 55–56).[7]

Arnold's remark seems to have been this one:

All religions but a man's own are utterly false and vain; the authors of them are mere imposters; and the miracles which are said to attest them, fictitious. We forget that this is a game which two can play at; although the believer of each religion always imagines the prodigies which attest his own religion to be fenced by a guard granted to them alone. Yet how much more safe it is, as well as more fruitful, to look for the main confirmation of a religion in its intrinsic correspondence with urgent wants of human nature, in its profound necessity! Differing religions will then be found to have much in common, but this will be an additional proof of the value of that religion which does most for that which is thus commonly recognised as salutary and necessary. (*EC-I,* p. 258)[8]

---

[7] In several places, I have (for the most part silently) corrected Whitridge's text in the light of the original Arnold and Newman letters, photographic copies of which were kindly made available to me by Father Stephen Dessain of the Birmingham Oratory.

[8] "A Persian Passion Play" was added to the third edition of *Essays in Criticism* (1875).

Arnold's implication is that Christianity will stand this test of "nature." Newman's essay alluded to in Arnold's letter is an 1841 review of Milman's *History of Christianity* (1840). Newman was distressed by Milman's Latitudinarian facility for finding "the *resemblance* between the Magianism of the East and Judaism after its return from captivity there" (*ECH*, II, 197). Newman does not "deny the similarity between the two theologies" (*ECH*, II, 197), but to him Milman seems to be saying "that the Jewish theology is worth no more than the Magian" (*ECH*, II, 198); and Milman so presents Christian theology as to emphasize "how like Christianity is to heathenism" (*ECH*, II, 204) and to imply "that great portion of what is generally received as Christian truth, is in its rudiments or in its separate parts to be found in heathen philosophies and religions" (*ECH*, II, 231). From the admitted resemblance, Milman seems to argue, " 'these things are in heathenism, therefore they are not Christian:' we, on the contrary, prefer to say, 'these things are in Christianity, therefore they are not heathen' " (*ECH*, II, 231). Newman expresses his frank fear, "Will Revelation have done more than introduce a *quality* into our moral life, not anything that can be contemplated by itself, obeyed, and perpetuated?" (*ECH*, II, 242). He ends rather plaintively, asking, "where then, after all, and what is Christianity?" (*ECH*, II, 245). At first glance, Arnold's comparison is rather surprising, since his own religious views were far closer to Milman's Broad Church theology, especially in Arnold's rationalizing insistence on Christianity's "natural truth." But apparently Arnold considered that his own views on the uniqueness of Christianity, *even on this naturalistic basis*, align him more closely with an orthodox dogmatic Christian than with a "comprehensive" liberal Christian like Milman. Perhaps it is on such perplexing grounds as this that Arnold would have justified some of his frequent and rather enigmatic assertions about Newman's influence on his own thought.

At any rate, Arnold's second reason for writing Newman was "to give myself an opportunity of explaining, that the *Spectator's* assertion, in a review of your Essays, that some lines of mine were 'a portrait of Mr. Newman,' has its sole ground in the writer's own imagination. What is said in those lines is not what I should have said if I

had been speaking of you, and I should not like you to think it was;
at any rate, said of you it was not; I had quite another personage in
mind" (*UL*, p. 56). In the *Spectator* for November 11, R. H. Hutton
had anonymously reviewed the *Essays* and had observed that these
Anglican controversial writings show "an anxious and difficult movement," and have "less ease, less freedom, less richness of illustration,
and less breadth of thought" than any other of Newman's works,
Anglican or Catholic. These essays, says Hutton, explain "a celebrated
portrait of Dr. Newman, drawn while he was still an Anglican"; he
then quotes lines 182–190 of Arnold's "Scholar-Gipsy":

> . . . amongst us one,
> Who most has suffer'd, takes dejectedly
> His seat upon the intellectual throne;
> And all his store of sad experience he
> Lays bare of wretched days;
> Tells us his misery's birth and growth and signs,
> And how the dying spark of hope was fed,
> And how the breast was soothed, and how the head,
> And all his hourly varied anodynes. (*PW*, p. 260)

Hutton speaks of this as a picture of "spiritual valetudinarianism."[9]
Whatever the intended reference—and there is reason to think Arnold
had in mind Tennyson, about whom he had complained to Newman
in 1868[10]—Arnold hastened to disavow even the suspicion of so un-
flattering a portrait.

At this point occurs Arnold's most extended and most moving acknowledgment of Newman's influence:

I cannot forbear adding, what I have often wished to tell you, that no words
can be too strong to express the interest with which I used to hear you at
Oxford, and the pleasure with which I continue to read your writings now.
We are all of us carried in ways not of our own making and choosing, but

[9] *Spectator,* November 11, 1871, p. 1369.

[10] See Henry Tristram, "Newman and Matthew Arnold," *The Cornhill,* N.S. LX
(March 1926), 311. Tinker and Lowry (*Commentary*, pp. 209–211) note that, although Arnold later referred the words to Goethe, all other evidence points to Tennyson. Moreover, Hutton's assertion that the poem was written while Newman "was
still an Anglican" is simply incorrect since "The Scholar-Gipsy" was first published
in Arnold's 1853 *Poems*.

nothing can ever do away the effect you have produced upon me, for it consists in a general disposition of mind rather than in a particular set of ideas. In all the conflicts I have with modern Liberalism and Dissent, and with their pretensions and shortcomings, I recognize your work; and I can truly say that no praise gives me so much pleasure as to be told (which sometimes happens) that a thing I have said reminds people, either in manner or matter, of you. (*UL*, pp. 56–57)

The words "Liberalism and Dissent" alert us to the likelihood that Arnold now not only thought of Newman as an ally in the general battle against Philistinism, described in "Culture and its Enemies," but also considered, with at least some justice, that Newman had been his guide in using arguments on "development" against the Dissenters in "Puritanism and the Church of England." Arnold then asks Newman two questions. The first, concerning Newman's use of Butler in the *Essay on Development*, indicates that Arnold was at work on Chapter X of *Literature and Dogma* late in November of 1871; its significance must await the discussion of the latter volume, below. The second involves the role of the Churches in modern society, and looks less to Arnold's immediate theological concerns than to his social writings of the late seventies. Apropos of Newman's 1837 essay on the "Fall of la Mennais," Arnold inquires:

Do not you think that what is Tory and anti-democratic in the Church of England (and undoubtedly her Tory, anti-democratic, and even *squirearchical* character is very marked) is one of her great dangers at the present time; and a danger from which the Catholic Church, with its Gregories and Innocents of whom you speak, is much more exempt? I mean, though the R. Catholic Church may in fact have been anti-democratic in modern times on the Continent, there seems nothing in her nature to make her so; but in the nature of the English Church there does; and is not this an additional peril, at the present day, for the English Church? (*UL*, pp. 57–58)[11]

Newman's reply of December 3 suggests that the previous correspondence between the two men had been more extensive than our present evidence reveals: "Your letter, as those which you have writ-

[11] See a letter of May 30, 1872, addressed to another correspondent: "I entirely agree with you that its Tory and squirearchical connexion has been and is of the greatest disservice to the Church of England" (*L*, II, 97).

ten to me before now, is an extremely kind one." In the words "with quite as intimate an interest have I read what you have lately written and also what you now send me" Newman also indicates that he has kept abreast of Arnold's developing religious position, obviously alluding to the only two sections of *Literature and Dogma* to be published in periodical form (*Cornhill*, July and October 1871, comprising the Introduction and Chapters I–IV of the book). He adds, poignantly: "The more so, as regards your letter as well as your writings, for the very reason that I am so sensitively alive to the great differences of opinion which separate us" (*UL*, p. 59). In answer to Arnold's questions concerning Bishop Butler, Newman pleads a lapse of memory, but agrees with Arnold on "what you say about the Anglican and Catholic Churches relatively to democratic ideas." He recalls that Hurrell Froude had felt "that the Church must alter her position in the political world," and had followed Lamennais's progress with sympathy. He notes that there are at least "minute tokens which are showing themselves of the drawings of the Papal policy just now in the direction of the democracy," and that "it may be in the counsels of Providence that the Catholic Church may at length come out unexpectedly as a popular power" (*UL*, pp. 59–61). In his original review of Lamennais's *Affaires de Rome*, Newman had summarized Lamennais's anti-Gallican, ultramontane view that the Pope should "take a high line, exert his spiritual powers, throw off the absolute courts who are his present supporters, and place himself at the head of the democratic movement throughout Europe" (*ECH*, I, 154). He says of Lamennais: "Believing that the Church Catholic was equal to any emergence or variety of human society, he desired her to throw herself upon the onward course of democracy, and to lead a revolutionary movement, which in her first ages she had created. She had risen originally as the champion of suffering humanity; let her now return to her first position" (*ECH*, I, 156). Newman is willing to grant "that popular influence is the life of the papacy," and that "while its carriage is aristocratic, the true basis of its power is the multitude" (*ECH*, I, 162). Nevertheless, Newman's Anglican view, for all his hatred of the quasi-Gallican State domination of the English Church, is conservative, even reactionary, concerning any possible rapprochement between the Churches and democracy. The "democratical party of the day" resembles antichrist in its cry of "liberty," and yet Lamennais "does not seem to recognize . . . that rebellion is a sin": in fact, "what we, in our English theology, should call the lawless and proud lusts of corrupt nature, he almost sanctifies as the instinctive aspirations of the heart after its unknown good" (*ECH*, I, 157–158). Clearly, the Newman of 1871, now a moderate ultramontane himself, is less willing to condemn what in 1837 he called a "drugged and unwholesome" doctrine. At any rate, both Arnold and Newman, in this exchange of letters, seem acute prophets about the way the world was running.

In February and March 1872, three notes passed between the two men. On February 14 Newman wrote from the Oratory:

My dear Mr Arnold

I am going to ask your acceptance of a volume which is now close upon publication.

It is not one of any great interest to you—being made up of odds and ends already published—but I have no other way of showing you the gratitude, which I sincerely feel, for the various instances of your kindness towards me

Yours very sincerely
John H Newman.[12]

The volume, dated January 5, 1872, is *Discussions and Arguments*, a collection of six further essays by Newman, four of them from the period before 1845. The reference to "various instances" of Arnold's kindness may, again, indicate a greater incidence of earlier correspondence and exchange of writings than we can now prove. Arnold hastens to reply the following day, February 15, on Athenaeum Club stationery:

My dear Sir

I need hardly say what pleasure it will give me to receive from you the book you speak of, or how much I shall value it: I write this line, however,

[12] This and the following two letters are published through the assistance of Father Dessain.

to beg you, if the book is not yet sent off, to add to its value by yourself writing my name in it.

With the most sincere thanks and regard, I am always,

> my dear Sir,
> Most truly yours,
> *Matthew Arnold.—*

The Revᵈ Dʳ Newman.

On March 7 Arnold wrote from Harrow, acknowledging the gift:

My dear Sir

I find your book with its kind inscription awaiting me here on my return home, after a period of much family trouble.[13] To read you, always gives me high pleasure; and it always carries me back, besides, to some of the happiest places and times of my life; so the book is particularly welcome to me just now. Accept once more my cordial thanks, and believe me to be, my dear Sir,

> Yours gratefully and sincerely
> *Matthew Arnold.—*

The Revᵈ Dʳ Newman.

P.S. I hope, if I send you from time to time any little thing of mine which I think may have interest for you, you will not put yourself to the trouble of writing to acknowledge it. To send would be a satisfaction to me; but it is a satisfaction I should deny myself if I thought I could not have it without compelling you to write a letter as the price of it.

The postscript of this last letter is explained by a letter of Newman's dated May 24, 1872, in which he thanks Arnold for a copy of his *A Bible-Reading for Schools,* which had just been issued. Arnold's central argument in the Preface is that Isaiah, as a text in the schools, will serve the cause of "letters," and not in any special sense *religion*: "If poetry, philosophy, and eloquence, if what we call in one word *letters*, are a power, and a beneficent wonder-working power, in education, through the Bible only have the people much chance of getting at poetry, philosophy and eloquence."[14] He justifies this view by a distinc-

---

[13] The "family trouble" alluded to was the death of "Budge," Arnold's second son, Trevenen William, age eighteen, on February 16 (*L*, II, 90).

[14] Matthew Arnold, *A Bible-Reading for Schools: The Great Prophecy of Israel's Restoration* (*Isaiah: Chapters 40–66*), p. x.

tion; he insists that "the Bible's application and edification" is separable from "its literary and historical substance."[15] The former unleashes Arnold's bête noire, "religious differences," a point he explains by referring to an "application" Newman makes of a text from Isaiah in "The Protestant Idea of Antichrist" (1840), one of the pieces reprinted in *Essays Critical and Historical*:

To take an example which will come home to all Protestants: Dr. Newman, in one of those charming Essays which he has of late rescued for us, quotes from the 54th chapter of Isaiah the passage beginning, *I will lay thy stones with fair colours and thy foundations with sapphires,* as a prophecy and authorisation of the sumptuosities of the Church of Rome. This is evidently to use the passage in the way of application. Protestants will say that it is a wrong use of it; but to Dr. Newman their similar use of passages about the beast, and the scarlet woman, and Antichrist, will seem equally wrong; and in these cases of application who shall decide? But as to the historical substratum, the primary sense of the passage Dr. Newman quotes, what dissension can there be?[16]

Thus Arnold had invoked Newman in a characteristically ambiguous way—as, for all the "charm" of his writings, the mistaken promulgator of religious "dissension." It is not surprising, then, that Newman, though polite ("The idea of your book is excellent"), takes exception to Arnold's thesis. He salutes Arnold as a "champion of 'letters' in popular education, as against science," and admits, "doubtless the Old Testament is the only book . . . which can serve as literary matter in popular schools." Nevertheless, he cannot accept Arnold's program for the use of the Bible as primarily literature for younger readers:

On the other hand, I should dread to view it as literature in the first place— and there will be no time, in the years available for the education of the masses, to read it over a second time, viz. in its literary aspect. A devout mind, which loves the objects which are its ultimate scope, and which instinctively sees our Lord moving along the successive prophetical announcements, may and will (if cultivated) go on to admire its wonderful poetry, and will bear safely, in a critical and scholarlike way, to investigate its literal and first meaning. But how few children are devout! As things

15 *Ibid.*, p. xxx.
16 *Ibid.*, pp. xxx–xxi; *ECH*, II, 184.

are, the prophecies of Isaiah come to the young as their Creed in the garb of poetry. The great dogmatic truths of the Gospel are inculcated on them in the medium of the imagination and the affections. If the duty of mastering the literal text and its historical and geographical circumstances is put upon young minds, who have not learned to be devout, nor have the subtlety necessary for being at home with the method of type and antitype, either they will be perplexed and put out to find (e.g.) Isai liii means at once Jeremiah or an abstract prophet and our Lord, or they will never learn the secret sense of the sacred text at all. (*UL*, pp. 63–64)

Without apparent irony, however, Newman ends: "I must not conclude without taking grateful notice of the kindness with which, as on former occasions, you introduce my name at p. xxx" (*UL*, pp. 64–65).

Arnold's reply of May 28 is curious. He begins by speaking of the great pleasure Newman's letter has given him, and this at once leads to his most explicit acknowledgment of Newman's influence on him:

There are four people, in especial, from whom I am conscious of having *learnt*—a very different thing from merely receiving a strong impression—learnt habits, methods, ruling ideas, which are constantly with me; and the four are—Goethe, Wordsworth, Sainte-Beuve and yourself. You will smile and say I have made an odd mixture and that the result must be a jumble: however that may be as to the whole, I am sure in details you must recognise your own influence often, and perhaps this inclines you to indulgence. (*UL*, pp. 65–66)[17]

[17] Though the relationship between Arnold and Sainte-Beuve has not yet been satisfactorily worked out, the influence would seem clearly one of "habits" and "methods," as opposed to the larger "ruling ideas" of Arnold's career—a distinction borne out by the existing documents (see Louis Bonnerot, *Matthew Arnold: Poète*, pp. 517–539, and R. H. Super, "Documents in the Matthew Arnold–Sainte-Beuve Relationship," *Modern Philology*, LX [February 1963], 206–210). Ruth Zabriskie Temple (*The Critic's Alchemy: A Study of the Introduction of French Symbolism into England*, pp. 53–61) vigorously argues that "Arnold's criticism has no real resemblance in theory, in spirit, or in practice" to that of Sainte-Beuve. At any rate, he can hardly be said to have figured in Arnold's "development" in nearly so substantive a way as did the other three figures cited here. In an unpublished letter to his mother dated October 16, 1869 (in the possession of Arnold Whitridge), Arnold comments on the recent death of Sainte-Beuve: "I have learnt a great deal from him, and the news of his death struck me as if it had been that of some one very near to me. When George Sand and Newman go, there will be no writers left living from whom I have received a strong influence: they will all have departed."

Thus the profound "impression" of 1868 and the "general disposition of mind" of 1871, have become "habits, methods, ruling ideas." The reason for this strong acknowledgment here, on the heels of a letter in which Newman clearly does *not* endorse the central argument of the Preface to Arnold's *Bible-Reading*, is not at first apparent. The most likely keys are the date and the word "details." In May 1872 Arnold was undoubtedly deep in the composition of *Literature and Dogma,* which, in its numerous references to Newman, reveals that Arnold was reading rather heavily in Newman's works at this period. Whether these references support Arnold's view that the "habits, methods, ruling ideas" of even the religious works are indebted to Newman remains to be seen.

CHAPTER SIX   Literature and Dogma

The chapters of *Literature and Dogma* were probably not composed in the order in which they appeared in book form in February 1873. The only two installments to appear in periodical form, comprising what is now the short Introduction and Chapter I, and Chapters II–IV, were published in the *Cornhill* for July and October 1871. Arnold's letter of November 29, 1871 (*UL,* p. 57), indicates that Arnold was then working on material later included in Chapter X. Professor Townsend argues convincingly that Arnold's original intention was to conclude his series with what are now Chapters V and X. Chapters VI–IX would then have filled out and clarified these original ideas, and Chapters XI–XII brought the whole to a conclusion.[1] Newman is referred to by name in only three chapters, VII, IX, and X, with one reference repeated in the Preface written for the book. Newman does not figure at all in the

[1] Francis G. Townsend, "The Third Instalment of Arnold's *Literature and Dogma,*" *Modern Philology,* L (February 1953), 200.

two periodical installments, and by far the heaviest preoccupation with his ideas occurs in Chapter X, presumably being written in November and December of 1871. Moreover, all explicit references to Newman in *Literature and Dogma* are to two works only, the *Essay on Development of Doctrine* and the two volumes of the *Essays Critical and Historical*. These facts coupled with that of Arnold's acquiring the two volumes of the *Essays* in November, suggest it was the latter work that stimulated Arnold to a fresh consideration of Newman's ideas as they might be seen to affect this central effort of his campaign to transform English religion and to deepen his own humanism.

It is best, then, to consider Arnold's treatment of Newman in *Literature and Dogma* in the order in which he presumably wrote the chapters now extant. Arnold begins Chapter X by summarizing the points he made in the opening chapter: the *people* for the first time are rejecting the characteristic tenets of orthodox Christianity, both the Catholic "story of the divine authority of the Church," as well as the general Christian theology of the Trinity ("the fairy-tale of the three Lord Shaftesburys"), on the grounds, which Arnold accepts, that none of this belief can be "verified." On the other hand, Arnold also rejects the extreme alternatives offered by "our philosophical Liberal friends," who propose a secular morality quite apart from the Bible and historical Christian experience. Arnold's own position, characteristically, is mediatorial: he accepts the rationalist position that even the existence of God—"a great Personal First Cause, who thinks and loves, the moral and intelligent Governor of the Universe; a sort of elder Lord Shaftesbury . . . infinitely magnified"—is unverified and unverifiable; but he equally deplores giving up the use of the Bible as the source of religion and morality, "the true religion of the Bible: righteousness, and the method and secret of Jesus" (*LD*, pp. 281–283). His object will be to develop a religious position, *for the masses*, which is nontheistic and yet draws upon the imaginative and emotional fullness of specifically Christian and hence Biblical sources.

Arnold's concern here, as in *St. Paul and Protestantism*, is to shape an argumentative tool that will go to the root of Christian theology and undercut all present positions. He at once admits that if "the Great Personal First Cause, the God of both natural and revealed religion," *could* be verified, we might then be warranted in admitting the rest of Christian doctrine, which follows from this root belief. Hence Arnold is impatient with those half-hearted rationalizers of Christian doctrine who will not go all the way at once with him in asserting what seems to Arnold self-evident, the unverifiability of God's existence. These people

set to work to make religion more pure and rational, as they suppose, by pointing out that this or that of these doctrines is false. . . . The Unitarians are, perhaps, the great people for this sort of partial and local rationalising of religion; for taking what here and there on the surface seems to conflict most with common sense, arguing that it cannot be in the Bible and getting rid of it, and professing to have thus relieved religion of its difficulties. And now, when there is much loosening of authority and tradition, much impatience of what conflicts with common sense, the Unitarians are beginning confidently to give themselves out as the Church of the Future. (*LD*, p. 284)

Arnold replies by citing the argument of "antecedent probability" used by Butler and Newman:

But in all this there is in reality a good deal of what we must call intellectual shallowness. For, granted that there are things in a system that are puzzling, yet they belong to a *system*; and it is childish to pick them out by themselves and reproach them with error, when you leave untouched the basis of the system where they occur, and indeed admit it for sound yourself. . . . Now, with the One Supreme Governor, and miracles, given to start with, it may fairly be urged that that construction put by common theology on the Bible-data . . . is the natural and legitimate construction to put on them, and not unscriptural at all. Neither is it unreasonable; in a system of things, that is, where the Supreme Governor and miracles, or even where the Supreme Governor without miracles, are already given. (*LD*, pp. 284–285)

This, as Arnold says, is Butler's argument in the *Analogy* against the Deists and Socinians, "that in your and my admitted system of nature there are just as great difficulties as in the system of revelation" (*LD*, pp. 285–286).

At this point Arnold invokes Newman and does something very daring; in effect, he reconsiders and now endorses Newman's arguments from the *Essay on Development* on probability which Arnold had re-fused to concede in "Puritanism and the Church of England." In that earlier essay, it will be recalled, Arnold had accepted Newman's formu-lation of an inherent power of "development" in Christian doctrine but had abruptly, on a priori grounds, censured as "arbitrary and con-demned by the idea itself" Newman's extension of that idea "in sup-port of the pretensions of the Church of Rome to an infallible authority on points of doctrine" (*SPP*, p. 124). But now, for purposes that soon become evident, Arnold is willing to follow Newman's idea *à outrance* and accept at least the *logical validity* of his (formerly "arbitrary" and patently impossible) line of argument:

The only question, perhaps, is, whether Butler, as an Anglican bishop, puts an adequate construction upon what Bible-revelation, this basis of the Supreme Governor being supposed, may be allowed to be; whether Catholic dogma is not the truer construction to be put upon it. Dr. Newman urges, fairly enough: Butler admits, analogy is in some sort violated by the fact of revelation; only, with the precedent of natural religion given, we have to own that the difficulties against revelation are not greater than against this precedent, and therefore the admission of this precedent of natural religion may well be taken to clear them. And must we not go further in the same way, says Dr. Newman, and own that the precedent of revelation, too, may be taken to cover more than itself; and that as, the Supreme Governor being given, it is credible that the Incarnation is true, so, the Incarnation being true, it is credible that God should not have left the world to itself after Christ and his Apostles disappeared, but should have lodged divine insight in the Church and its visible head? So pleads Dr. Newman; and if it be said that facts are against the infallibility of the Church, or that Scripture is against it, yet to wide, immense things like facts and Scripture, a turn may easily be given which makes them favour it; and so an endless field of dis-cussion is opened, and no certain conclusion possible. . . .

Only, there may come some one, who says that the basis of all our infer-ence, the Supreme Governor, is *not* the order of nature, is an assumption, and not a fact; and then, if this is so, our whole superstructure falls to pieces like a house of cards. And this is just what is happening at present. (*LD*, pp. 286–287)

Newman's argument, involving the passage Arnold inquired about in the letter of November 29, is of course central to the *Essay on Development*,[2] and by now it is not surprising to see Arnold granting Newman's case for "the oneness of Catholicism" in order, paradoxically, to burke all "partial and local rationalising" of theology, on the ground that the first principle of theistic metaphysics is "an assumption which cannot possibly be verified" (*LD*, p. 299). Arnold insists: "It is no use beginning lower down, and amending this or that ramification, such as the Atonement, or the Real Presence, or Eternal Punishment, when the root from which all springs is unsound" (*LD*, p. 294). His chief concern has been, and remains, the fear that the masses will reject the Bible in favor of a purely secular and utilitarian morality like that of Bentham or Spencer, in the general overthrow not only of characteristic Christian doctrines like the Atonement and the Real Presence but also of metaphysical notions like the personality and unity of God (*LD*, pp. 299, 287, 290, 294).

Arnold's strategy is complex. Against orthodox Christians he argues that the notion of a Personal God is unintelligible and unverifiable— according to a special notion of verification. Against the rationalizing philosophical Liberals (whose positivism he accepts) he argues, nevertheless, that the masses need emotional and imaginative support for the practice of morality, and that this can only come from the Bible, considered as a comforting and uplifting poetic testimony to *righteous-*

---

[2] See *EDD*, pp. 122–123. As to "the extent of that violation," Newman maintains, "Supposing the order of nature once broken by the introduction of a revelation, the continuance of that revelation is but a question of degree" (*EDD*, p. 123). On pages 135 ff., Newman develops the thesis, "Christianity being one, all its doctrines are necessarily developments of one, and, if so, are of necessity consistent with each other, or form a whole." The compelling quality of the argument, which Arnold acknowledges, is clear on pages 154–155: "You must accept the whole or reject the whole; reduction does but enfeeble, and amputation mutilate. It is trifling to receive all but something which is as integral as any other portion; and, on the other hand, it is a solemn thing to receive any part, for, before you know where you are, you may be carried on by a stern logical necessity to accept the whole." See also *D&A*, p. 398, and *Apologia*, p. 180.

T. H. Huxley, in "Agnosticism and Christianity" (1889), in effect inverts Newman's arguments in a similar way. Where Newman insisted that Biblical miracles have no stronger basis than the miracles of Christian history and concluded that Christian miracles can be accepted, Huxley inferred that *no* miracles could be accepted (see *Collected Essays of Thomas Henry Huxley*, ed. Leonard Huxley, V, 309–365).

ness ("that mighty *not outselves* which is in us and around us") as verified through the whole of man's history. Finally, against what Arnold sees as the compromising non-Christian but theistic devotees of Unitarianism, he argues that their logic is unsound, since they reject individual Christian doctrines as incredible or irrational but fail to recognize that Christian theology is a logically valid concatenation of probabilities and that only by striking at the very root of all theology can individual Christian tenets be cast down. This last argument, on the logical and systematic coherence of theology, though not of course its application, Arnold adapted from Newman. It is not directly to the purpose here to point out that, logically and rhetorically, Arnold has probably granted too much in accepting Newman's "fairly" argued case. That is, to accept the coherence of Newman's linked probabilities is to raise the strong possibility that the Bible does in fact support *his* view of a dogmatic system and not Arnold's rationalized collection of natural moral truths—quite apart from the metaphysical question of the existence of a Personal First Cause. For present purposes, however, it is enough to note that again Arnold appreciatively reproduces and accepts a central and specifically Catholic theory of Newman's—the idea, in fact, on which Newman's conversion to Rome hinged—which he abruptly turns against Newman's intentions.

Arnold's confrontation with Newman in Chapter X was not yet over. Arnold ends by approvingly repeating a notion he had attributed to Newman and Hooker in "Puritanism and the Church of England," but which he now ascribes to Hooker and Butler, that "the Bible does not and cannot tell us itself, in black and white, what is the right construction to put upon it," and that for this we need (in Hooker's words) "reasoning and collection" (*LD,* pp. 301–302). But Arnold, in a now familiar manner, simply throws this doctrine back against the orthodox theologians by arguing, "Now it is simply from experience of the human spirit and its productions, from observing as widely as we can the manner in which men have thought, their way of using words and what they mean by them, and from reasoning upon this observation and experience, that we conclude the construction theologians put upon the Bible to be false, and ours to be the truer one" (*LD,* p. 302). In other words, Arnold claims to "collect" his version of Israel's conception of

God as the "not ourselves" and the Eternal Power that makes for righteousness, "because the more we come to know how ideas and terms arise, and what is their character, the more this explanation of Israel's use of the word 'God' seems the true and natural one" (*LD*, pp. 302–303). Similarly, his version of Jesus' doctrine and work, collected by comparing the Biblical data with "the history of ideas and expressions," will increasingly be seen as "the true and natural one." Jesus' teaching was misunderstood by his disciples: "only time gradually brings its lines out more clear" (*LD*, p. 303). "Time," here, is a heuristic agency; Arnold has returned to the realm of the *Zeitgeist,* whose claims he had urged against the dogmatists in "Puritanism and the Church of England."

Thus, although Arnold may invoke a Hooker, a Newman, or a Butler in support of the notion that reasoning and collection are the means for ascertaining the true drift of the Bible's meaning, Arnold's sense of this process—involving, it seems, a superior knowledge of "how ideas and terms arise, and what is their character"—is somehow richer than theirs and is sanctioned by nothing less than the vast tides of history. This tendentious argument is pursued as Arnold turns to Newman once again. He rejects "the theologians' notion of dogmas presupposed in the Bible, and of a constant latent reference to them," on the vague grounds that somehow "experience" and our increasing knowledge "of the history of ideas and expressions" make it less convincing. He then quotes from Newman's "Prospects of the Anglican Church" (1839): "The Fathers *recognised* a certain truth lying hid under the tenor of the sacred text as a whole, and showing itself more or less in this verse or that, as it might be. The Fathers *might have traditionary information* of the general drift of the inspired text which we have not" (*LD*, p. 303; citing *ECH*, I, 286). Arnold's comment on this passage marks a moment when seemingly all the elements of his complex reaction to Newman's personality and thought are fused:

Born into the world twenty years later, and touched with the breath of the "Zeit-Geist," how would this exquisite and delicate genius have been himself the first to feel the unsoundness of all this! that we have heard the like about other books before, and that it always turns out to be not so, that a right interpretation of a document, such as the Bible, is *not* in this fashion.

Homer's poetry was the Bible of the Greeks, however strange a one; and just in the same way there grew up the notion of a mystical and inner sense in the poetry of Homer, underlying the apparent sense, but brought to light by the commentators; perhaps, even, they might have traditionary information of the drift of the Homeric poetry which we have not;—who knows? But, once for all, as our literary experience widens, this notion of a secret sense in Homer proves to be a mere dream. So, too, is the notion of a secret sense in the Bible, and of the Fathers' disengagement of it. (*LD*, pp. 303–304)

Newman is still an "exquisite and delicate genius," but born twenty years too early to be intellectually transformed by the *Zeitgeist*. Arnold seems to be saying that his own generation, which came to maturity in the forties, was the first that could dispense with "mere dreams" like an allegorical sense in Scripture—dreams dispersed, presumably, by such channels of the newly active Time-Spirit as the Higher Criticism of the Bible and advances in the geological and biological sciences.

It was of the utmost strategic value to cite Newman on so abstruse a point as "a secret sense" in the Bible, a subject of some concern to Newman, especially in his Anglican years. Of course Arnold knew that there were other possible views, as his next words indicate:

Demonstration in these matters is impossible. It is a maintainable thesis that the allegorising of the Fathers is right, and that this is the true sense of the Bible. It is a maintainable thesis that the theological dogmas of the Trinity, the Incarnation, and the Atonement, underlie the whole Bible. It is a maintainable thesis, on the other hand, that Jesus was himself immersed in the *Aberglaube* of his nation and time, and that his disciples have reported him with absolute fidelity; in this case we should have, in our estimate of Jesus, to make deductions for his *Aberglaube,* and to admire him for the insight he displayed in spite of it. (*LD*, p. 304)

Clearly, the implicit dogmatic substructure of the Bible was a point of far greater and more continuous concern to Newman than the allegorical reading of Scripture. Nevertheless, perhaps Arnold was correct in choosing to discuss Newman in relation to one of his most antirationalistic views; for here Arnold confronts Newman directly as the supreme nineteenth-century expositor of the *mystery* inherent in religious truths who conceived of the universe of supernatural truth and reality as a realm on the edges of man's ordinary consciousness the shadowy outlines of which were fragmentarily revealed to him by Scripture. In Arnold, for all the Biblical quality of his religiously tinged moralism, one feels that mystery in Newman's sense has been torn away or, more accurately, gently brushed aside by a disenchanted Time-Spirit here identified with man's widening "literary experience." On the other hand, one ought not to minimize the cosmic, quasi-Providential functions of the Time-Spirit itself as it sponsors the progress of the modern critical intellect and, in particular, Arnold's emergent reading of Scripture through the rough waters of the nineteenth century. In fact, as he says later in a daring passage in the Preface, the Roman Catholic notion of an infallible interpreting authority is a kind of blundering forecast of the *Zeitgeist*'s role: "The infallible Catholic Church is, really, *the prophetic soul of the wide world dreaming of things to come*; the whole human race, in its onward progress, discovering truth more complete than the parcel of truth any momentary individual can seize . . . The Pope himself is, in his idea, the very Time-Spirit taking flesh, the incarnate '*Zeit-Geist*'!" (*LD*, p. xxvi). Supported by such a power, Arnold need not argue:

Absolute demonstration is impossible, and the only question is: Does experience, as it widens and deepens, make for this or that thesis, or make against it? And the great thing against any such thesis as either of the two we have just mentioned is, that the more we know of the history of the human spirit and its deliverances, the more we have reason to think such a thesis improbable, and it loses hold on our assent more and more. On the other hand, the great thing, as we believe, in favour of such a construction as we put upon the Bible is, that experience, as it increases, constantly affirms it; and that, though it cannot *command* assent, it will be found to *win* assent more and more. (*LD*, p. 305)

Arnold is speaking here, implicitly, in the name of that "criticism" and "culture," an ideal of perfected human consciousness, which he had developed in the *Essays in Criticism* and *Culture and Anarchy*. In the Introduction Arnold had promised "a literary treatment of religious history and ideas" and a discussion "of the relation of letters to religion . . . of their effect upon dogma, and of the consequences

of this to religion" (*LD*, pp. 4, 5). As he was to explain in the
Preface of 1873, Arnold rejects the "infelicitous" and "blunt-edged"
methods of the German Biblical critics in favor of his own literary
method, that of culture, which leads to "justness of perception" (*LD*,
p. xxi). The reading of the Bible involves, says Arnold, crucial matters of conduct and morality; hence, all the more urgent is the need
we have for culture, which is the true interpreter of the Bible and
which "implies not only knowledge, but right tact and justness of
judgment, forming themselves by and with knowledge" (*LD*, pp.
xxvi–xxvii). This, then, is what Arnold means by our widening "literary experience," "the history of the human spirit and its deliverances"; for culture, knowing the best that has been known and said
in the world, necessarily includes "the history of the human spirit"
(*LD*, p. xi). Thus, in reading the Bible, to the knowledge of scientific textual study must be joined the tact and the multifaceted literary
consciousness of *culture*. Presumably, neither the German textual
methods nor Arnold's historically oriented "culture" were possible to
men before Arnold's generation, before *criticism*, which had come to
life again at the Renaissance, had so far advanced as to provide a
method by which Bible and Creeds could be read and judged (*LD*,
pp. xxv, xviii). The Time-Spirit, in whose hands Arnold trustingly
places himself, has now for the first time "turned his light" fully upon
the inner structure of Christian belief.

How does Newman figure in this argument? Not merely, I think,
as an "adversary." Instead, Newman as an "exquisite and delicate
genius" is recalled to our attention precisely as the supreme representative of urbanity, intellectual delicacy, the Oxford spirit, and culture. A note of calculated pathos and regret is evident in this later
reference to Newman. By every natural quality of mind and temperament, as well as by the quality and tone of his writings, Newman represented to Arnold the ideal of culture. Added to this was the aesthetic
appeal of Newman as an apparently tragic failure, in this case a man
born out of his time. Arnold's regret seems to be that the man who
stood for all that he associated with the Oxford temper could not,
through the accidents of time and circumstance, join him in applying

that temper to the vexing religious problems of the age. The *Zeitgeist* itself, now seemingly enfranchised permanently by modern "criticism," operates, despite its German name, not by the asperities of argument but precisely by the Oxford suavity and urbanity Arnold had so admired in Newman's *Apologia*. For when Arnold says his reading of the Bible does not *command* but *wins* assent, he means this:

> But the valuable thing in letters,—that is, in the acquainting oneself with the best which has been thought and said in the world,—is, as we have often remarked, the judgment that forms itself insensibly in a fair mind along with fresh knowledge; and this judgment almost any one with a fair mind, who will but trouble himself to try and make acquaintance with the best which has been thought and uttered in the world, may, if he is lucky, hope to attain to. For this judgment comes almost of itself; and what it displaces it displaces easily and naturally, and without any turmoil of controversial reasonings. The thing comes to look differently to us, as we look at it by the light of fresh knowledge. We are not beaten from our old opinion by logic, we are not driven off our ground;—our ground itself changes with us. (*LD*, p. 7)

In rejecting Newman's reading of the Bible, Arnold is implicitly rejecting the old Oxford, the theological "Oxford of the past" (*CPW*, V, 105), at least for its inability to absorb and, with its characteristic tone, somehow master the complex new components of the religious situation.

The question at issue throughout *Literature and Dogma* had been, what does it mean to "verify" a proposition, whether, say, Arnold's view of the Bible or Newman's? Arnold argues that the first principle of "metaphysical theology," the existence of a Great Personal First Cause, is unverified and unverifiable. His own moralism, however— the principle that *righteousness leads to happiness*—has a "scientific basis of fact"; it can be proved, as directly and experimentally as the fact that fire burns, in our own experience and by knowing the moral history of the human race.[3] On the other hand, in the statements cited, he hints at a rather different process of intellectual and spiritual per-

---

[3] See *Literature and Dogma*, Chapter I, "Religion Given"; and both parts of "St. Paul and Protestantism."

suasion; continually reinforced by modern knowledge of total human history, the *Zeitgeist*'s version of truth establishes itself and wins our assent by eschewing logic and the "turmoil of controversial reasonings" in favor of an undefined but subtle movement of the whole psyche working insensibly, easily, naturally. Newman had described a process very similar to this in the *Apologia*, where he says that "It is the concrete being that reasons; pass a number of years, and I find my mind in a new place; how? the whole man moves; paper logic is but the record of it" (*Apologia*, p. 153). This line anticipates the central argument, that "the whole mind reasons," of Newman's last major work, *The Grammar of Assent*. Strangely, there is no evidence that Arnold ever took note of this treatise on "the logical cogency of faith" and the psychology of belief, although he had no doubt read reviews on the appearance of the book in February 1870, just as he concluded *St. Paul and Protestantism*, his own major exposition of the nature and grounds of "faith."

For complex reasons, some of them already discussed in this study, Arnold was unable to respond to the totality of Newman's thinking on the psychology of faith, despite the fact that this central line in Newman's thought, stretching from the Oxford University Sermons to the *Grammar of Assent*, may be justly described as the most remarkable example of the "literary treatment of religious history and ideas" published in England during Arnold's lifetime. Newman's thought was almost a working model for Arnold's prescription to apply "culture" to religious matters; moreover, it was an authoritative precedent for Arnold's conviction that the mind in religion moves not by "logic" and the "turmoil of controversial reasonings," but "insensibly." Some of the reason for Arnold's incomprehension was suggested long ago by R. H. Hutton. Seeming almost to have in mind Arnold's passage on Newman and to be answering the condescension and complacency that mar Arnold's tone, Hutton reversed the premises of the argument. It was, he counters, precisely because twenty years separated Arnold from Newman and because Arnold came to maturity in the eighteen-forties that "certain premature scientific assumptions, . . . in vogue before the limits of the region in which the uniformity of nature has been verified, had been at all carefully defined, run through all his theoretical writings."[4] Hutton argues:

Undoubtedly the twenty years or so by which he is Cardinal Newman's junior made an extraordinary difference in the intellectual atmosphere of Oxford, and of the English world of letters outside Oxford, during the time at which a thoughtful man's mind matures. Mr. Arnold was not too late at Oxford to feel the spell of Dr. Newman, but his mind was hardly one to feel the whole force of that spell, belonging as it does, I think, rather to the stoical than to the religious school—the school which magnifies self-dependence, and regards serene calm, not passionate worship, as the highest type of the moral life. And he was at Oxford too early, I think, for a full understanding of the limits within which alone the scientific conception of life can be said to be true. A little later, men came to see that scientific methods are really quite inapplicable to the sphere of moral truth, that the scientific assumption that whatever is true can be verified is, in the sense of the word "verification" which science applies, a very serious blunder, and that such verification as we can get of moral truth is of a very different though I will not scruple to say no less satisfactory, kind from that which we expect to get of scientific truth. Mr. Arnold seems to me to have imbibed the prejudices of the scientific season of blossom, when the uniformity of nature first became a kind of gospel, when the *Vestiges of Nature* was the book in vogue, when Emerson's and Carlyle's imaginative scepticism first took hold of cultivated Englishmen, and when Mr. Froude published the sceptical tales by which his name was first known amongst us. Mr. Arnold betrays the immovable prejudices by which his intellectual life is overridden in a hundred forms; for example, by the persistency with which he remarks that the objection to miracles is that they do not happen, the one criticism which I venture to say no one who had taken pains to study evidence in the best accredited individual cases, not only in ancient but in modern times, would choose to repeat. And again, he betrays it by the pertinacity with which he assumes that you can verify the secret of self-renunciation, the secret of Jesus, in the same sense in which you can verify the law of gravitation, one of the most astounding and, I think, false assumptions of our day.[5]

[4] Richard Holt Hutton, *Essays on Some of the Modern Guides to English Thought in Matters of Faith*, p. 133.

[5] *Ibid.*, pp. 131–132.

Newman enters *Literature and Dogma* by name only four more times. In Chapter VII, Arnold attempts to define the essential matter of what "faith" in Jesus means. He had earlier explained his view of faith, in *St. Paul and Protestantism*, as "to die with Christ to the law of the flesh, to live with Christ to the law of the mind" (*SPP*, p. 64), a process accomplished by such psychological mechanisms as "grace," "influence," and "sympathy." Faith, then, is a self-induced moral transformation, with Jesus as an "aid" and "model." Here again, in *Literature and Dogma*, faith is described as an "attachment," "influence," "intuition," a new "power of [moral] insight" which comes to our help (*LD*, pp. 208, 216). This translation of familiar theological terms is essential to Arnold's two-part program to "spiritualize" Christianity: he will, on the one hand, avoid the "materialising mythology" of traditional theology in favor of the "lofty spiritualism" (*LD*, pp. 218, 224) of his own Christianized morality; on the other, he will establish the "natural" and "simple" character of this exalted morality, dependent on neither metaphysics nor appeals to truths that transcend reason. Arnold's quarrel is with the orthodox view that faith and reason are opposed, that the essence of faith is "to take on trust what perplexes the reason," and that to believe in Jesus is "to receive a doctrine puzzling to the reason, but which, if adopted, will gradually become clear" (*LD*, pp. 209–210). Arnold will now have none of this traditional opposition, seen to be of common interest to Newman and to the Arnold of the sixties, for the simple reason that religion, for him, is an imaginatively elevated moralism in a universe without metaphysics.

Almost by instinct Arnold turns to Newman for the orthodox view. Citing Tract 73 (1835), Arnold deals out "respect" and "deference" with one hand and a kind of brusque exasperation with the other:

No one has more insisted on this opposition between faith and reason than a writer whom we can never name but with respect,—Dr. Newman. "The moral trial involved in faith," he says, "lies in the *submission of the reason* to external realities partially disclosed." And again: "Faith is, in its very nature, the acceptance of what our *reason* cannot reach, simply and absolutely upon testimony." But surely faith is in its very nature (with all deference be it spoken!) nothing of the kind. (*LD*, p. 211; *ECH*, pp. 35, 31)

Perhaps nowhere is Arnold more directly impatient with Newman, as is clear in his emphatic repetition of Newman's words and the strong hint that Newman is one who "sophisticates" religion:

But *attention, cleaving, attaching oneself fast* to what is undeniably true,— this is what the faith of Scripture, "in its very nature," is; and not the submission of the reason to what puzzles it, or the acceptance, simply and absolutely upon testimony, of what our reason cannot reach. And all that the Bible says of bringing to nought the wisdom of the wise, and of receiving the kingdom of God as a little child, has nothing whatever to do with the believer's acceptance of some dogma that perplexes the reason; it is aimed at those who sophisticate a very simple thing, religion, by importing into it a so-called science with which it has nothing to do. (*LD*, pp. 211–212)

Newman somehow seems caught up, whether or not intentionally, in Arnold's moral indignation at the "clever" people who attend "to the difficult *science* of matters where the plain *practice* they quite let slip" (*LD*, p. 212). At any rate, Arnold ends the section continuing his rough handling of Newman by flatly negating his now twice-repeated words:

The only right contrast, therefore, to set up between faith and reason is, not that faith grasps what is too hard for reason, but that reason does not, like faith, attend to what is at once so great and so simple. The *difficulty* about faith is, to attend to what is very simple and very important, but liable to be pushed by more showy or tempting matters out of sight. The *marvel* about faith is, that what is so simple should be so all-sufficing, so necessary, and so often neglected. And faith is neither the submission of the reason, nor is it the acceptance simply and absolutely upon testimony of what reason cannot reach. Faith is: *the being able to cleave to a power of goodness appealing to our high and real self, not to our lower and apparent self.* (*LD*, pp. 214–215)

(It should be remarked that Arnold's rejection of an "opposition between faith and reason" need not imply the retreat, which it might at first seem, from his position of the early sixties which links him with

Newman. For what Arnold rejects here is the notion that by faith a man gets to some *truth* or "dogma" beyond simple reason, whereas Newman's emphasis is that faith submits to realities *beyond* reason. Thus the two are still joined, at least to the extent that, for both, the act of faith is not essentially intellectual; for Newman it is a complex assent of the whole personality, reason being only one factor; for Arnold it is a "simple" act of the moral will, "practice" being its essence and reason irrelevant. The "opposition between faith and reason" thus remains substantially intact in both men.)

References to Newman appear twice in Chapter IX. A superficial glance makes the first allusion to him seem incidental. In attacking *Aberglaube*—"*extra-belief,* belief beyond what is certain and verifiable" (*LD*, p. 70)—Arnold repeats and expands his attack in *St. Paul and Protestantism* on the entire edifice of Christian theology. The three chief creeds of Christendom attempt to make religion into "abstruse metaphysical conceptions" at "a time when the possibility of true scientific criticism, in any direction whatever, was lessening rather than increasing" (*LD*, p. 251). Moreover, Arnold sweepingly claims, by examining the internal quality of the expressions of Jesus according to somewhat murky literary criteria, to judge "that our three creeds, and with them the whole of our so-called orthodox theology, are founded upon words which Jesus in all probability never uttered" (*LD*, p. 255). Arnold is repeating the argument he had urged in "Puritanism and the Church of England" against Newman's application of the doctrine of development. That is, in the post-Apostolic age "the world and society presented conditions constantly less and less favourable to sane criticism. . . . For dogmatic theology is, in fact, an attempt at both literary and scientific criticism of the highest order; and the age which developed dogma had neither the resources nor the faculty for such a criticism" (*LD*, 256–257). Since all such efforts draw on "a very wide experience from comparative observation in many directions" and employ "a very slowly acquired habit of mind," the Christian metaphysics of the Middle Age is on a par with their efforts in natural philosophy—geography, history, physiology, and cosmology (*LD*, pp. 257–258).

Further, "as one part of their scientific Bible-criticism, so the rest"

(*LD*, p. 258). Arnold attemps to call into question the dogmatic reading of Scripture in the creeds by putting it on a par with the view that
the Bible holds "a secret allegorical sense, . . . higher than the natural
sense" (*LD*, p. 258). This, it will be remembered, was Arnold's strategy in Chapter X, where Newman is made to seem to hold that "the
allegorising of the Fathers" as to the true sense of the Bible is as trust-
worthy as their deriving Christian dogma from it (*LD*, p. 304). The
strategy now is identical: "The worth of all the productions of such
a critical faculty is easy to estimate, for the worth is nearly uniform"
(*LD*, pp. 258–259). He continues: "The moment we think seriously
and fairly, we must see that the Patristic interpretations of prophecy
give, in like manner, their author's measure as interpreters of the true
sense of the Bible. Yet this is what the dogma of the Nicene and
Athanasian Creeds professes to be, and must be if it is to be worth
anything,—*the true sense extracted from the Bible*; for, 'the Bible is
the record of the whole revealed faith,' says Dr. Newman. But we
see how impossible it is that this true sense the dogma of these creeds
should be" (*LD*, p. 259; *ECH*, I, 90). In the earlier reference, in Chapter X, Newman had been made to endorse patristic allegorizing in order to undermine his authority as a Biblical critic. Here again, Newman's "*whole* revealed faith" is made to seem to cover the entire range
of medieval extravagance in interpretation. (In fact, Newman in this
essay of 1838 was only parenthetically conceding a point; his chief
purpose, against ultra-Protestant Biblicism, was to press his Anglican
case for "Tradition" and the "Church Catholic" as the "divinely-ap-
pointed guide" in religious truth.)

All must go: every aspect of patristic and medieval criticism is
marked by "nullity" and "futility," and "The Schoolmen themselves
are but the same false criticism developed, and clad in an apparatus of
logic and system" (*LD*, pp. 259–260). Hence the whole of Christian
thought is "an illusion," an "utter blunder" (*LD*, pp. 271, 313).
Arnold's line of argument, then, is to fuse every aspect of historic
Christian thought—patristic allegory, the Creeds, Scholasticism—into
a single indistinguishable lump of absurdity on the grounds that *no* medieval statement can be said to be either critically sound in itself, because of the age in which it was made, or, therefore, the true interpre-

tation of the Bible. True interpretation was, indeed, reserved for the
nineteenth century—and not for heavy-handed German textual scholars but for a few men of wide culture like Matthew Arnold, who, not by
hard reasoning but by paying attention to the whispers of the *Zeitgeist*,
would clear away the lumber of Christian thought as if so many cob-
webs. Arnold's "plain," "simple" moralism lies intellectually "on the
surface of the Bible"; "righteousness and the God of righteousness, the
God of the Bible, are in truth quite independent of the God of ecclesiastical dogma, the work of critics of the Bible" (*LD*, pp. 263, 265).
Christian dogma, that "grotesque mixture," is all of a piece: "The best
way is to throw it aside altogether, and forget it as fast as possible"
(*LD*, pp. 262, 314). As he had done in Chapter X, Arnold strikes to
the root, his well-advised instinct being always to bring *every* aspect of
Christian thought into question, lest any loophole be opened through
which the concept of the supernatural or of a personal God could be
smuggled back. There can be no compromise; no orthodox Christian
must be allowed to make futile adjustments or distinctions.

It is at this point in Chapter IX that the second reference to Newman is made:

Catholic dogma itself is true, urges, however, Dr. Newman, because intelligent Catholics have dropped errors and absurdities like the False Decretals
or the works of the pretended Dionysius the Areopagite, but have not
dropped dogma. This is only saying that men drop the more palpable
blunder before the less palpable. The adequate criticism of the Bible is
extremely difficult, and slowly does the "Zeit-Geist" unveil it. Meanwhile,
of the premature and false criticism to which we are accustomed, we drop
the evidently weak parts first; we retain the rest, to drop it gradually and
piece by piece as it loosens and breaks up. But it is all of one order, and in
time it will all go. Not the Athanasian Creed's damnatory clauses only, but
the whole Creed; not this one Creed only, but the three Creeds,—our whole
received application of *science,* popular or learned, to the Bible. For it was
an inadequate and false science, and could not, from the nature of the case,
be otherwise. (*LD,* p. 261)

What is not clear to the casual reader is that the passage alluded to in
Newman's *Essay on Development* is the key to the intention and

method of the whole book, and indeed, to much of his polemical writing.

Not only have the relative situation of controversies and theologies altered, but infidelity itself is in a different, I am obliged to say, in a more hopeful position, as regards Christianity. The facts of revealed religion, though in their substance unaltered, present a less compact and orderly front to the attacks of its enemies, and allow of the introduction of new conjectures and theories concerning its sources and its rise. The state of things is not as it was, when an appeal lay to the supposed works of the Areopagite, or to the primitive Decretals, or to St. Dionysius's answers to Paul, or to the Coena Domini of St. Cyprian. The assailants of dogmatic truth have got the start of its adherents of whatever Creed; philosophy is completing what criticism has begun; and apprehensions are not unreasonably excited lest we should have a new world to conquer before we have weapons for the warfare. (*EDD*, pp. 28–29)

Newman sought to give Catholic orthodoxy weapons appropriate to the nineteenth century. Much of what Christianity had casually accreted to itself—errors in cosmology, science, history, or metaphysics—was distinguishable from a core of dogma. But Arnold steadfastly refused to follow any such logic: "it is all of one order, and in time it will all go." Just as, in *St. Paul and Protestantism*, Arnold could concede that the whole Bible was written on the principle of development, but would not follow Newman's argument as to the probability of an external authority empowered to distinguish true from false developments, so, here and in Chapter X, Newman must be made to endorse the *whole* history of Christian theology, without any possible mechanism for distinguishing between fundamental dogma and the scientific errors of the past.

Arnold's final direct reference to Newman in *Literature and Dogma* occurs near the beginning of the Preface. Sensing the revolutionary situation that traditional religion was facing, Arnold's concern is primarily with "the spread of scepticism" and the "contemptuous rejection of the Bible" on the part of the masses (*LD*, pp. v–vii) because his religion is above all the religion of the Bible, whose prospects all the churches so lament. To testify that Catholics and Protestants agree on this point, he gives more of a quotation from Newman than he had given in Chapter IX: "What the religion of the Bible is, how it is to be got at, they may not agree; but that it is the religion of the Bible for which they contend they all aver. 'The Bible,' says Dr. Newman, 'is the record of the whole revealed faith; so far all parties agree' " (*LD*, pp. vii–viii; *ECH*, I, 190). Why Arnold invokes Newman here, in this Anglican statement of 1838, is not clear, beyond the fact that by bringing in "Catholic" testimony Arnold can proceed on the assumption that *all Christians* (even Catholics, commonly thought to be non-Biblicists) are agreed on the role of the Bible in religion. This discussion of Newman's place in *Literature and Dogma* can be concluded in no better way than by noting that in another work of 1838, Number 85 of the *Tracts for the Times,* Newman had showed himself acutely alive to this process whereby growing skepticism regarding Christian doctrine leads to the rejection of the Bible. He expresses the fear that "men ought, if consistent, to proceed from opposing Church doctrine to oppose the authority of Scripture. . . . a battle for the canon of Scripture is but the next step after a battle for the Creed. . . . Nay, I would predict as a coming event that minds *are to be* unsettled as to what is Scripture and what is not" (*D&A*, pp. 198–199). This statement recalls that, although Newman and Arnold held markedly different versions of "what the religion of the Bible is," they were both centrally concerned with a striking number of similar problems that they saw as the heart of the religious crisis of the age—for example, the psychological basis of the act of faith, the fate of the Bible in a skeptical age, the need for proofs of religious belief adequate to the nineteenth century's concept of vertification, the sense of a vast, cosmically sponsored "development" in religious doctrine, and the integral and systematic character of Christian theology, to be accepted or rejected as a whole.[6]

[6] From a number of other passages in *Literature and Dogma* which recall Newman strongly, the following may be cited. On the antecedent probability of a Revelation, see *LD*, p. 158, and *OUS*, p. 195. On the idea that no one aspect can be called the sum of Christianity, see *LD*, p. 193, and *EDD*, pp. 33–34. On the Kingdom of God as a kingdom of righteousness that endures *because* of righteousness, see *LD*, pp. 337–339, and *Sermons*, pp. 241–242—the latter in close conjunction with the text, "many are called, few chosen." Finally, it seems more than likely that Arnold's quotation from Erskine of Linlathen (*LD*, p. 312) is derived from the same Tract (*ECH*, I, 59)

CHAPTER SEVEN Catholicism and the Future
of Religion

It is not known whether Arnold sent Newman a copy of *Literature and Dogma* when
it was issued in February 1873, and his en-
gagement with Newman's thought is never again as prolonged or intense. Nevertheless, Arnold's interest in Newman remains strong during the remainder of the eighteen-seventies; the two chief foci of the
interest are his concern for the future of the Roman Catholic Church—
its religious character, its dogmatic claims, and its public role—and his
concern for the Catholic position on the education question, especially
in Ireland. Conversely, Newman's return of interest in Arnold is based
on "that sympathy you have for what you do not believe"—for supernatural Christianity, and specifically for the Roman Catholic Church.

Nowhere in the seven articles appearing from October 1874 to
September 1875 in the *Contemporary* as a "Review of Objections to
'Literature and Dogma'," and reprinted late in 1875 as *God and the
Bible,* does Newman's name appear. However, Arnold seems to allude
to him in the Preface written for the book. Arnold's rhetorical stance,
in repeating the arguments of *Literature and Dogma* against dogma, is
that of contempt for "the want of intellectual seriousness" among the
dogmatists. As an example, he gives Cardinal Manning's defense of
"the miraculous resuscitation of the Virgin Mary" on the grounds that
the story is "beautiful" and "a comfort and help to pious souls" (*GB*,
p. xix). Later, he adopts a similar attitude toward Papal Infallibility:
"But the same levity is shown by more cautious Catholics discussing the
Pope's infallibility, seeking to limit its extent, to lay down in what
sense he is really infallible and in what sense he is not; for in no sense
whatever is or can he be infallible, and to debate the thing at all shows
a want of intellectual seriousness." Characteristically, Arnold's retort

---

from which Arnold quotes Newman on the "moral trial involved in faith" (*LD*, p.
211; *ECH*, I, 35).

is more petulant than logical: "there is plainly no such thing existing as the said infallible Church" (*GB*, p. xxvi). It seems likely that Arnold is referring to Newman's *Letter to the Duke of Norfolk*, issued in January 1875, which was a careful and qualified defense of infallibility against the pretensions of the ultramontanes like Cardinal Manning, W. G. Ward, and Edward Talbot in England, and Louis Veuillot in France. Also of interest to Arnold in Newman's letter would have been the discussion of the Catholic Church and "Liberalism," at least in the Continental sense of the term. Newman accepts the collapse of "the whole theory of Toryism" (defined as "loyalty to persons") as a *fait accompli*:

> The Pope has denounced the sentiment that he ought to come to terms with "progress, liberalism, and the new civilization." I have no thought at all of disputing his words. I leave the great problem to the future. God will guide other Popes to act when Pius goes, as He has guided him. No one can dislike the democratic principles more than I do. No one mourns, for instance, more than I, over the state of Oxford, given up, alas! to "liberalism and progress," to the forfeiture of her great medieval motto, "Dominus illuminatio mea." (*DofA*, II, 268)

And yet as if further answering the question put to him in Arnold's letter of November 29, 1871, Newman sees a distant hope of reconciliation: "in centuries to come, there may be found out some way of uniting what is free in the new structure of society with what is authoritative in the old, without any base compromise with 'Progress' and 'Liberalism'" (*DofA*, II, 268). This is Newman's mature "conservative" stand on the future of the Catholic Church in a democratic, pluralistic society.

Early in 1874 Arnold issued selected chapters of an earlier volume, *Schools and Universities on the Continent* (1868), under the title of *Higher Schools and Universities in Germany*. For it, he wrote a long and important introduction on his educational, religious, and social views. Late in 1875 he issued an augmented version of *A Bible-reading for Schools* (1872) under the new title, *Isaiah XL–LXVI, With the Shorter Prophecies allied to it,* with a rewritten Preface from which the original reference to Newman had been expunged. Both of these volumes were sent to Newman at different times before January 3, 1876, the date of Newman's acknowledgment, his longest known letter to Arnold. (I have numbered paragraphs in order to facilitate annotation.)[1]

The Oratory

Jany 3. 1876

P.S. A happy
New Year to you.

Dear Mr Arnold

[1]   I owe you thanks for two of your books, the former of which I ought to have acknowledged long, long ago, but it did not require an acknowledgment any particular day and other things did, and so I put it off from day to day.

[2]   The volume on Prussian Schools is of standard value, and does not admit of nor call for any remark from readers like myself. But what specially interested and pleased me was your Preface, advocating the claims of the Irish Catholic University on State recognition. Your argument, as deduced from the Prussian policy and system, is clear and good, if it really is the fact, as I understand you to say, that Catholics have in Prussia two State-recognized Universities. I suppose they are Munster and Braunsburg. And if this really is the case, the hardship of obliging Seminarists to receive University Education before they are instituted as Parish Priests, is much diminished.

[3]   It must be recollected, however, that the present strict Seminary System, as existing among Catholics, has been a reaction from the license of ecclesiastical education before the Council of Trent, which, being mainly in Universities, had filled the Church with a lax and disreputable clergy. Ever since, the Holy See has been suspicious of a University life, as dangerous to the priestly character. And I cannot help thinking that the education of men for any profession, legal, medical, as well as clerical, must in a certain sense be narrow, if it is to be effective for the purposes of that profession, and that absolute freedom of word and deed in religious matters, is as inconsistent with the duties of a parish priest as a like liberty in military matters with the duties of a soldier, or in parliamentary action with those of a

---

[1] This letter and Arnold's reply of January 10, below, are presented through the assistance of Father Dessain.

member of the Cabinet. It may be well to have also a class of clergy who receive a liberal education, but I doubt whether they would (on a large scale) answer, whether as parochi or as regulars.

[4]   And then, moreover, there are difficulties inherent in your plan, though I do not mean to say that they are insurmountable.

[5]   For instance, allowing that the Government might be allowed the appointment of Professors, still I do not see how, in a University formally Catholic, the ecclesiastical authorities can surrender their claim to possess a standing Veto on Professors. Surely the Government cannot be allowed the liberty of appointing whom they wish, provided he calls himself a Catholic;—of appointing or upholding a man, who, like Arius or Apollinaris, is, or becomes, unfaithful to the Catholic Creed. Not only the theory, but the philosophical and historical teaching of such men, as Arius or Apollinaris, would be un-Catholic.

[6]   As to what the Catholic Bishops claimed of Lord Mayo, I do not see why they might not have asked, in your words, "the *government* of their University," for it is only what Oxford has on the whole, though some Visitors of Colleges are laymen, and some Professors are appointed by the Crown. We used to say that the Archbishop of Canterbury was Visitor of the University.

[7]   Nor can I follow you in thinking that by the Church "ought to be meant the laity," any more than the word is equivalent to "the clergy." I think the people are the *matter,* and the hierarchy the *form,* and that both together make up the Church. If you object that this virtually throws the initiative and the decision of questions into the hands of the clergy, this is but an internal peculiarity of the Catholic religion. The Anglican Church is also made up of a like form and matter; though here, in consequence of the genius of Anglicanism, the power of the matter predominates. But if you attempt to destroy the existing relation between form and matter, whether in Anglicanism or Catholicism, you change the religion; it is more honest to refuse to recognize Catholicism, than to refuse to take it as it is.

[8]   By the bye, I don't acquiesce in your definition of a truism, which I conceive to be a truth too true for proof or for insistence. Triteness is at best an accident of it. If this be so, a falsism is a falsehood too false for refutation, not a trite falsehood.

[9]   Now is it not ungracious in me to have said all this, when I am really grateful for your advocacy of us?

[10]   As to your other Volume, your Edition of Isaiah, I will only say that it is a most attractive book—and your (excuse me) standing aloof from Revelation does not mar its beauty. It is that sympathy you have for what you do not believe, which so affects me about your future. It is one of my standing prayers that you and your brother may become good Catholics.

Very Sincerely yours
John H Newman

NOTES:

Par. 2. Arnold refers to Bismarck's Catholic policy on pages ix and following. The two Catholic Universities are Münster and Braunsberg, which Newman misspells.[2] As early as 1860 Newman had expressed nearly the same reservations as to the possibilities for a wide training in general culture in the Seminaries.[3]

Pars. 5 and 6. Discussed by Arnold (pp. xviii ff.): "The Irish bishops claimed from Lord Mayo the government of their Irish university, the right to veto on the appointment of professors, the right of dismissing professors. This would make the university simply a continuation of the seminary with a State payment. But what is the object of of a university? To diffuse the best culture by means of the best professor" (p. xviii). Arnold grants that Catholics are correct in demanding Catholics to teach theology, philosophy, history; he insists, however, that this is best done "by the whole nation in its collective and corporate character, by the State acting through a responsible minister" (p. xix). (On page xvi of his copy, at Arnold's comment on "the best culture which the nation has to give," Newman sharply queries in the margin: "*What* culture? is it best *because* infidel?")

Par. 7. Arnold asks (p. lii): "But who are interested in the Church, that is, in the society formed of those concerned about religion? The clergy only? No, as we have seen, the whole people. And who are

---

[2] Matthew Arnold, *Higher Schools and Universities in Germany*, p. 147. Hereafter cited in text by page numbers alone.

[3] Wilfrid Ward, *The Life of John Henry Cardinal Newman*, I, 512–518.

really the Church? Evidently the whole religious society, and not its ministers only. The ministers exist for the sake of the community to which they minister; the clergy are for the people, not the people for the clergy. A national church is what is wanted." This is stated even more unambiguously at page liii, where Arnold denies the view that "the clergy are the Church and the community are the State"; instead, "the community . . . is the Church." Newman's citation, then, seems a rough paraphrase of Arnold's argument; he had written in the margin of page liv in his copy: "The Church is not mere matter, but *form* and matter, clergy *as well* as laity."

Par. 8. "A truism, as is well known, is something true and trite. Now, the principle in question ["that the State ought to have nothing to do with religion"] is not exactly a truism, but it is next door to it; it is what Archbishop Whately used to call a *falsism*. A truism is something true and trite, and a falsism is something trite and false" (p. xx).

Par. 10. As for Arnold's "sympathy" for what he does not believe, his tone in *Higher Schools* is generally sympathetic to religion, and especially to Roman Catholicism. Religion, he says, "is a natural human need which will manage to satisfy itself" (p. xxiii). "All forms of religion are but approximations of the truth. Your own [Protestantism] is but an approximation. It is true, one approximation may be better off than another. But all great forms of Christianity are aimed at the truth" (p. xxxv). Roman Catholicism is "that form of Christianity which has most penetrated the societies where it lived, most laid hold on the multitude and been reacted on by the multitude" (p. xxiii). "The Roman Catholic religion is the religion which has most reached the people. The bulk of its superstitions come from its having really plunged so far down into the multitude, and spread so wide among them. The two great ideas of religion are the idea of conduct and the idea of happiness; and no religion has equalled Catholicism in giving on a great scale publicity to the first and reality to the second" (p. xxxv). Also, although the two great disadvantages in Roman Catholicism are said to be "its load of popular error" and "its Ultramontanism," Arnold concedes: "Long before the Reformation serious and intelligent

Catholics could, for their single selves, separate these accretions ["the accretions and superstitions inseparable" from "the great popular religion of Christendom"] from their religion . . . Serious and intelligent Catholics can do for their single selves the same thing still" (p. xliii). (It should be noted that this last is an about-face of the position developed in *Literature and Dogma* [*LD*, p. 261], that the Catholic system was "all of one order" and must be jettisoned as a whole.) Of course it should be borne in mind that Arnold desired for the future a Catholicism of a very special cast; as he put it in a letter of April 1874: "My ideal would be, for Catholic countries, the development of something like old Catholicism, retaining as much as possible of old religious services and usages, but becoming more and more liberal in spirit" (*L*, II, 132). The reference to Arnold's brother Tom recalls that 1876 was the year of his return, after a decade, to the Catholic Church; Newman may at this time have received some intimation of the change. In a letter of July 1876, Arnold refers to Tom and immediately repeats "what I often say to Liberals, that Catholicism cannot be extirpated; that it is too great and too attaching a thing for that; that it can only be transformed, and that very gradually. It is easy for me to say this who look at Catholicism from a distance and see chiefly its grandeurs and sentimental side" (*L*, II, 154). Arnold knew of course that the process would not be rapid; just a month before, in June, he remarked: ". . . it is curious how utterly the religiously disposed people in Catholic countries are without belief in Catholicism's power to transform itself. I, however, believe that it will transform itself" (*L*, II, 151).

As further background to this letter, it may be remarked that Newman had discussed the defeat of Gladstone's Irish University Bill of February 1873 in his *Letter to the Duke of Norfolk* (*DofA*, II, 181 ff.). Lord Eversley explains Gladstone's intentions:[4]

He proposed to constitute a single great University for Ireland, for teaching as well as examining purposes, on a purely unsectarian basis, to which

[4] Lord Eversley [George John Shaw Lefevre], *Gladstone and Ireland: The Irish Policy of Parliament from 1850–1894*, p. 53.

colleges of either sectarian or unsectarian character were to be affiliated. . . .
No endowment or grant was to be given to the Catholic College, but the
University was to be endowed with £50,000 a year from Trinity College,
and partly by a State grant. . . . Professorships were to be provided by the
University, subject to a proviso, which came to be described as "a gagging
proposal," that there were to be no Professors of Religion, Morals, or History. These subjects were to be left to the Colleges to deal with, in any manner that they might think best.

Archbishop Cullen opposed the University, while Manning favored it;
the Presbyterians of the North of Ireland denounced it, as did the Governing Board of Trinity College.[5] Arnold's letter to *The Times* of
July 31, 1879 (*ELR*, pp. 212–215), concerns the Irish University Act
of that year, which "substituted for the Queen's University an examining University on the model of that of London."[6]

Arnold replied to Newman's letter within a week:

> Pains Hill Cottage.
> Cobham, Surrey.
>
> Jan. 10th 1876
>
> My dear Dr Newman
>
>   It gives me the most sincere gratification to send you my books, whenever
> I feel that I can do so without impropriety, and my sending them is in no
> wise meant to put you to the trouble of writing an acknowledgment. But of
> course I feel always pleased and honoured at receiving a letter from you. All
> that you say on the subject of a Catholic University is valuable and interest-
> ing to me. The difficulty about conceding to a Catholic University in Ire-
> land the same amount of self-government that Oxford and Cambridge have,
> comes, I suppose, from the Irish University needing to be supported by
> direct grant from the State. However, I would gladly, for my part, see a
> Catholic University established in Ireland with the same kind of independ-
> ence which the English Universities have, if Catholics could be brought to
> demand no more and the British Parliament to concede as much. But the
> matter is one where, unhappily, reason has even far less part in determining
> the settlement, than it has in our politics generally.
>
>   I will do no more than express my grateful thanks for the tone of kind-

---

[5] *Ibid.*, p. 54.
[6] *Ibid.*, p. 90.

ness in which your letter concludes, and I beg you to believe me, with a deep sense of esteem and obligation,

ever most sincerely yours,
Matthew Arnold.—

Arnold's list of books to read in 1876 includes "Newman's Discussions" (*NB*, p. 591)—the *Discussions and Arguments*, which Newman had sent him in 1872, including above all, "The Tamworth Reading Room." The only explicit reference to Newman in *Last Essays on Church and Religion*, published early in 1877, occurs in "A Psychological Parallel" (November 1876), and the source is a surprising one. Arnold has been asked whether a man who holds the view of religion set forth in *Literature and Dogma* can justifiably take orders in the Church of England. His answer is that since ordination requires at least "a general consent" to the Thirty-nine Articles, and since the view of *Literature and Dogma* is that the Prayer Book's claim —that the Creeds are "science" and the true formulation of Christianity—is false, such a man cannot "at present" be ordained. Arnold goes on to attack subscription to the Articles as a condition of Church of England orders, and in fact to *any* "test which lies outside the Ordination Service itself":

The Ordination Service itself, on a man's entrance into orders, and the use of the Church services afterwards, are a sufficient engagement. Things were put into the Ordination Service which one might have wished otherwise. Some of them are gone. The introduction of the Oath of Supremacy was a part, no doubt, of all that *lion and unicorn* business which is too plentiful in our Prayer Book, on which Dr. Newman has showered such exquisite raillery, and of which only the Philistine element in our race prevents our seeing the ridiculousness. (*LECR*, p. 211)

Arnold is referring to the first of Newman's lectures on *The Present Position of Catholics in England*, published in 1851.[7] In what was perhaps the finest sustained comic performance in his writings, New-

---

[7] John Henry Newman, *Lectures on the Present Position of Catholics in England*, pp. 30, 41. In addition to the books already mentioned, inscribed copies of both *Last Essays on Church and Religion* and *Mixed Essays* (1879) are in Newman's room in Birmingham as is—surprisingly—an unmarked copy of *Cromwell* (1843), Arnold's Oxford prize poem.

man illustrated the difference between "knowing what is said and thought of Catholics" in the traditional English Protestant view, and "what they really are," by showing that hyperpatriotic "Anglo-mania" and "John Bull-ism" might be treated by the Czar of Russia as a dangerous secret society. Here, again, Newman is Arnold's model in his conflicts with "modern Liberalism and Dissent," for the religious prejudices of the British middle-class Philistine were of a piece with his social and political prejudices. Moreover, the closing remark of Newman's lecture[8] might have been made by Arnold himself: "Such is the consequence of having looked at things all on one side, and shutting the eyes to the others."

One other passage in *Last Essays*, on the future of the Catholic Church, calls Newman to mind. In the Preface, Arnold argues his now-familiar case, "that Christianity will survive because of its natural truth," and that the historic forms of Christian worship will not be "extinguished by the growth of a truer conception of their essential contents" (*LECR*, p. 177). These forms, he explains,

will survive as poetry. Above all, among the Catholic nations will this be the case. And, indeed, one must wonder at the fatuity of the Roman Catholic Church, that she should not herself see what a future there is for her here. Will there never arise among Catholics some great soul, to perceive that the eternity and universality, which is vainly claimed for Catholic dogma and the ultramontane system, might really be possible for Catholic worship? But to rule over the moment and the credulous has more attraction than to work for the future and the sane. (*LECR*, p. 178)

Is it not justifiable to suggest that Arnold's scarcely concealed impatience with Newman in the religious writings springs from his sense that Newman, perhaps the supreme "great soul" of Arnold's experience and very likely the most large-visioned Catholic of the nineteenth century, had somehow culpably failed to see the future with Arnold's own clarity and had in fact enlisted his extraordinary powers of mind, style, and personality in support of an "impossible" and scarcely "sane" system?

After the publication of *Last Essays*, Arnold turned again to the

---

[8] Newman, *Present Position of Catholics*, p. 41.

consideration of the social and literary issues that had engaged him in the sixties, though his social views were permanently enriched by his wrestling with the religious perplexities of the age. In July 1878 appeared "Irish Catholicism and British Liberalism," in which Arnold once again takes up the question of the State endowment of a Catholic University in Ireland which he had discussed in the Preface to *Higher Schools and Universities in Germany* (1874). Almost certainly Arnold would have had Newman, and their 1876 exchange of letters, in mind through much of the essay. Arnold speaks of the desire of Irish Catholics for a University: "The Protestants of Ireland have in Trinity College, Dublin, a university where the teachers in all these matters which afford debatable ground between Catholic and Protestant are Protestant. The Protestants of Scotland have universities of a like character. In England the members of the English Church have in Oxford and Cambridge universities where the teachers are almost wholly Anglican. Well, the Irish Catholics ask to be allowed the same thing" (*MxE*, p. 76). And Arnold approves the Irish rejection of Gladstone's former offer of "a university without theology, philosophy, or history" (*MxE*, p. 76). Of course, what lies in the way of real State endowment is "the deep-rooted prejudices of the middle-class against Catholicism": "All they [Irish Catholics] feel is that they are kept from having what they want, and what is fair, and what we have ourselves, because the British middle class, being such as we have described it, pronounces their religion to be *a lie* and *heathenish superstition*" (*MxE*, p. 96). Newman had put the case in very similar terms as early as 1851, in the *Present Position of Catholics* (which Arnold was reading late in 1876). As an illustration of the "narrow and one-sided condition of the Protestant intellect" toward Catholicism, Newman says:

For instance, as regards the subject of Education. It has lately been forcibly shown that the point which the Catholic Church is maintaining against the British Government in Ireland, as respects the Queen's Colleges for the education of the middle and upper classes, is precisely that which Protestantism maintains, and successfully maintains, against the same Government in England—viz., that secular instruction should not be separated from religious. The Catholics of Ireland are asserting the very same principle as the Protestants of England; however, the Minister does not feel the logical force of the fact; and the same persons who think it is so tolerable to indulge Protestantism in the one country, are irritated and incensed at a Catholic people for asking to be similarly indulged in the other.[9]

Arnold repeats his own solution, which the Irish would be unreasonable to reject: "The professors should be nominated and removed, not by the bishops, but by a responsible minister of State acting for the Irish nation itself" (*MxE*, p. 93).

Interestingly, Arnold here repeats and expands his very sympathetic view of the historic Roman Catholic Church which had appeared in *Higher Schools*. Catholicism is "the religion which has most reached the people," "the great popular religion of Christendom" (*MxE*, pp. 86–87). Hence, his impatience with advanced Liberals "who have no conception of the Christian religion as of a real need of the community": "whoever treats Catholicism as a nuisance, to be helped to die out as soon as possible, has the heart, the imagination, and the conscience of Catholics, in just revolt against them" (*MxE*, pp. 85, 87). Of course, "Ultramontanism, sacerdotalism, and superstition" (that is, dogma, Papal claims, and so on) must be given up; but then the Church "is left with the beauty, the richness, the poetry, the infinite charm for the imagination, of its own age-long growth, . . . unconscious, popular, profoundly rooted, all-enveloping" (*MxE*, pp. 88–89). It would be an error to view this panegyric as mere aesthetic sentimentality; at stake is Arnold's precise conception of "the Christianity of the future." His vision of man's future demands, for its integrity, a religious and specifically Catholic form of religious ritual and poetry: "The need for beauty is a real and now rapidly growing need in man; Puritanism cannot satisfy it; Catholicism and the English Church can. The need for intellect and knowledge in him, indeed, neither Puritanism, nor Catholicism, nor the English Church can at present satisfy. That need has to seek satisfaction nowadays elsewhere,—through the modern spirit, science, literature" (*MxE*, pp. 101–102). Thus the Catholic Church—along with the Church of England, which "kept in great measure the traditional form of Catholicism and thus preserved

9 *Ibid.*, p. 179.

its link with the past, its share in the beauty and the poetry and the charm for the imagination of Catholicism" (*MxE*, pp. 99–100)— alone succeeds in "investing" with beauty those "elementary truths of inescapable depth and value, yet of extreme simplicity," which are the center of Arnold's Christianized humanism (*MxE*, p. 102). *This* then will be the function of religion in the future:

> I persist in thinking that Catholicism has, from this superiority, a great future before it; that it will endure while all the Protestant sects (in which I do not include the Church of England) dissolve and perish. I persist in thinking that the prevailing form for the Christianity of the future will be the form of Catholicism; but a Catholicism purged, opening itself to the light and air, having the consciousness of its own poetry, freed from its sacerdotal despotism and freed from its pseudo-scientific apparatus of superannuated dogma. (*MxE*, p. 90)

Thus, too, Arnold's separation of morality and reason, first evident in the sixties, remains intact, with morality and aesthetic experience linked on the one hand, and "the modern spirit, science, literature" unreconciled and unassimilated on the other. The essence of Arnold's view of religion in the religious works—as a small body of "elementary truths" of morality "lighted up" with Biblical poetry and incapable of metaphysical formulation—remains similarly intact.

The change lies in the fact that Arnold's view of religion, and especially the religion of the future, is now embodied historically and concretely in the Catholic Church. Of course this highly aestheticized Christianity of the future (which "invests" morality with charm, richness, imagination, poetry, beauty) will be *conscious* of being "purged," "opening itself to the light," "freed" from its own dogmatic pretensions—presumably it *will* have acknowleged the claims of the "modern spirit" and "science." But it is equally true that here, as in Arnold's peculiar theory of development, one cannot properly speak of reconciliation or assimilation but merely of the sweeping away of pseudo science. This decapitated Catholic Church (its long history of religious speculation lopped off as incapable of verification by the standards of the modern critical intellect) would remain as the external, institutional expression of a complex of aesthetic and moral experience which, *even in its reduced form,* cannot be reconciled with contemporary views of man's place in the universe. Arnold is here on the way to the impasse of "Literature and Science" (1882). His discussion of the Catholic Church in this earlier essay (which he called "my argument for the Catholics" [*L,* II, 186; May 25, 1879]) is summarized here because it is developed in conjunction with practical matters of Irish educational policy on which he had communicated with Newman and which had long been of special interest to Newman, and because it helps the reader understand the precise tone of Arnold's treatment of Newman in the religious works. Arnold was convinced that "the Catholics are to be mended . . . by gradually inducing them to admit the influences of the time against them, and to feel their penetrative effect" (*L,* II, 184 [Easter, 1879]). His impatience with, and sometimes near contempt for, Newman's dogmatic views, in *St. Paul and Protestantism* and *Literature and Dogma,* are all the more intense because Newman, despite the range of his gifts, was born a generation too soon to lead the Catholic Church into the "light and air" that is the medium of "the modern spirit."

It should be evident now that Arnold's claim of 1871, that Newman was a model in his conflicts "with modern Liberalism and Dissent, and with their pretensions and shortcomings," is true only with important qualifications. Of course Liberalism and Dissent were coupled as an object of attack in Arnold's mind as they could never quite be in Newman's. Arnold analyzes both forces in essentially aesthetic terms, since both are enemies of the complete human development he is sponsoring. It was the Oxford Movement's sentiment for "beauty and sweetness" which subtly undermined "the hardness and vulgarity of middle-class liberalism" and "the hideous and grotesque illusions of middle-class Protestantism" (*CPW,* V, 105–157); similarly, in the seventies, "The need for beauty is a real and now rapidly growing need in man; Puritanism cannot satisfy it, Catholicism and the English Church can" (*MxE,* pp. 101–102). A passage in an essay of February 1879 (*"Ecce, Convertimur ad Gentes"*), clearly deriving from "The Tamworth Reading Room" (1841), suggests, nevertheless, that this important early attack of Newman's on Liberal pretensions very likely had lain behind Arnold's treatment of Liberalism in the religious writings. For example, in Chapter X of *Literature and Dogma* Arnold's first concern is with "the special moral feature" of the day; he sees that for the first time the *people* are losing religion and the Bible and cannot be counted on to counteract the antireligious propaganda of "cultivated wits":

When our philosophical Liberal friends say, that by universal suffrage, public meetings, Church-disestablishment, marrying one's deceased wife's sister, secular schools, industrial development, man can live very well; and that if he studies the writings, say, of Mr. Herbert Spencer into the bargain, he will be perfect, he will have "in modern and congenial language the truisms common to all systems of morality," and the Bible is become quite old-fashioned and superfluous for him;—when our philosophical friends now say this, the masses, far from checking them, are disposed to applaud them to the echo. (*LD*, p. 282)

The question Arnold puts to destructive religious critics in the Preface to *God and the Bible* is this: when the "illusions" of the Christian past are forsaken what will we give men in their place (*GB*, p. xi)? However much "the voice of modern liberalism" may foretell the extinction of Christian belief, a popular reaction in favor of American revivalists is the answer: "It is so, because throughout the world there is a growing feeling, that whatever may have been amiss with the old religion, modern liberalism, though it confidently professed to have perfect and sufficient substitutes for it, has not" (*GB*, p. xii). In the body of his text, Arnold argues against the growing popularity of "a kind of revolutionary Deism, hostile to all which is old, traditional, established and secure" (*GB*, p. 6).

This line of thought is very close to the argument of "The Tamworth Reading Room," where Newman is concerned about precisely the Liberal attempt to find a new source of unity for society: "The old bond . . . was Religion; Lord Brougham's is Knowledge" (*D&A*, p. 285). The passage from "*Ecce, Convertimur*" not only draws from "The Tamworth Reading Room," which Arnold was reading in 1879 (*NB*, pp. 326–327), but comments on it and qualifies it:

But above all, we are on our guard against expecting too much from institutions like this Working Men's College. We are reminded what grand expectations Lord Brougham and other friends of knowledge cheap and popular, the founders of the Mechanics' Institutes, held out; what tall talk they indulged in; and we are told to look and see how little has come of it all. Nature herself fights against them and their designs, we are told. At the end of his day, tired with his labour, the working man in general cannot well have the power, even if he have the will, to make any very serious and fruitful efforts in the pursuit of knowledge. Whatever high professions these institutions may start with, inevitably their members will come, it is said, to decline upon a lower range of claim and endeavour. They will come to content themselves with seeking more amusement and relaxation from their Institute. They will visit its reading-rooms merely to read the newspapers, to read novels; and they are not to be blamed for it.

No, perhaps they are not to be blamed for it, even if this does happen. And yet the original lofty aspiration, the aspiration after the satisfactions, solace, and power which are only to be got from true knowledge, may have been right after all. In spite of the frequent disappointment, the constant difficulty, it may have been right. For to arrive at a full and right conception of things, to know one's self and the world,—which is knowledge; then to act firmly and manfully on that knowledge,—which is virtue; this is the native, the indestructible impulse of the spirit of man. All the high-flown commonplaces about the power of knowledge, and about the mind's instinctive desire of it, have their great use, whenever we can so put them as to feel them animating and inspiriting to us. For they are true in themselves; only they are discredited by being so often used insincerely. (*IEO,* pp. 358–359)

The reference to Brougham and to reading rooms, the phrases "we are reminded" and "we are told," and the expressions "tall talk" and "high-flown commonplaces," all suggest Newman's scornful attack on Brougham and the "Knowledge School" in "The Tamworth Reading Room." Arnold's "mere amusement and relaxation" is a reference to Newman's denial of Brougham's and Peel's argument that curiosity, diversion, recreation, "utility and amusement," will somehow improve a man morally by putting "him above the indulgence of sensual appetite" (*D&A,* p. 276). Newman answers that knowledge "never healed a wounded heart, nor changed a sinful one; but the Divine Word is with power" (*D&A,* p. 270)—from the very passage Arnold cited in his notebooks.

Arnold's response is complex. He is not only putting a higher value on "the original, lofty aspiration"; he is actually adopting, in a less blatant and "insincere" form, the view of the Knowledge School that knowledge leads to virtue. No doubt Newman's supernaturalist argument was severe, especially for the purposes of the occasion;[10] but Arnold here is implicitly marking the distance between Newman's religious position and his own naturalistic humanism. Arnold follows Newman, in his conflicts with Liberalism and Dissent, more in method and tone than in ultimate philosophical presuppositions.

Arnold's most elaborate comment on Newman's view of Liberalism occurs in his *Quarterly* review of "De Maistre's Lettres et opuscules inédits" (October 1879). Arnold considers a fictional M. Cherchemot, an extreme Liberal theorist, whose failing is not to recognize that "Things grow slowly, and in a gradual correspondence with human needs." Arnold proceeds, carefully dealing out approval and disapproval of Newman (who had been made a Cardinal in May):

Only, in their aversion to M. Cherchemot and his shallowness, Burke and Joseph de Maistre do not enough consider the amount of misinformation, hamper, and stoppage, coming at last to be intolerable, to which human things in their slow process of natural growth are undoubtedly liable. They do not enough consider it; they banish it out of their thoughts altogether. Another trenchant and characteristic maxim of Joseph de Maistre, which Burke, too, might have uttered, is this: "Il faut absolument tuer l'esprit du dixhuitième siècle"—"The spirit of the eighteenth century must be stamped out utterly." One is reminded of Cardinal Newman's antipathy to "Liberalism." And in a serious man a strong sense of the insufficiency of Liberal nostrums, of the charlatanism of Liberal practitioners, as also of the real truth, beauty, power, and conformity to nature of much in the past of which these practitioners are intolerant, is abundantly permissible. Still, when one has granted all that serious men like Joseph de Maistre and Cardinal Newman may fairly say against the eighteenth century and Liberalism, when one

[10] Arnold may also have had in mind Newman's more balanced discussion of the Mechanics' Institutes in "Discipline of Mind" (*Idea*, p. 360–362). There he acknowledged that they have "provided a fund of innocent amusement and information for the leisure hours of those who might otherwise have been exposed to the temptation of corrupt reading or bad company." But his point, although no longer theological, is that this "mere diversion of the mind" is not to be mistaken for "real education."

has admired the force, the vigour, the acumen, the sentiment, the grace with which it is all said, one inquires innocently for that better thing which they themselves have in store for us, and then comes the disappointment. Joseph de Maistre and Cardinal Newman have nothing but the old, sterile, impossible assumption of their "infallible Church;" at which a plain man can only shake his head and say with Shakespeare, "There is no such thing!"

It cannot be too often repeated: these eminent individualities, men like Burke, or Joseph de Maistre, or Cardinal Newman, are by no means to be taken as guides absolutely. Yet they are full of stimulus and instruction for us. We may find it impossible to accept their main positions. But the resoluteness with which they understand the prevailing ideas of their time, the certainty with which they predict the apparition of something different, are often a proof of their insight. Whatever we may think of Ritualism, its growth and power prove Cardinal Newman's insight in perceiving that what he called Liberalism, but what we may perhaps better describe as the mind of Lord Brougham, was in general, and in the sphere of religion more particularly, quite inadequate, and was not destined to have things for ever its own way. (*ELR,* p. 218)

The reference to Brougham indicates that this is a further qualification of Newman's severe position in "The Tamworth Reading Room." Arnold is acknowledging that his discipleship is fundamentally negative: as he had also said in *Culture and Anarchy,* the meaning and long-range success of the Oxford Movement was its indictment of Liberalism as, especially in religion, "inadequate"; but at bottom "Tory" thinkers like Burke, de Maistre, and Newman have unacceptable main positions, their chief positive virtue being their ability to stand against the triumphant Liberalism of the age and to project a faint vision of the future beyond Liberalism—presumably a reconciling vision, and presumably extending beyond their actual rather negative Toryism and traditionalism. Whatever that future may be, it cannot be given to us by men who, almost perversely, continue to press the "old, sterile, impossible" claims of the Catholic system.

CHAPTER EIGHT Newman and the Future of Poetry

Decades of intellectual and (at long distance) personal engagement had passed when Arnold finally met Newman at the reception in mid-May 1880. At the meeting, arranged by the new Cardinal, Arnold reported, "Newman took my hand in both of his and was charming" (*L*, II, 196). This brief encounter may have reactivated Arnold's interest in Newman's thought. Certainly Newman is very likely at the heart of the key opening passage of "The Study of Poetry," written late in 1880, which is Arnold's most important statement on the quasi-religious function of poetry in the modern world:

"The future of poetry is immense, because in poetry, where it is worthy of its high destinies, our race, as time goes on, will find an ever surer and surer stay. There is not a creed which is not shaken, not an accredited dogma which is not shown to be questionable, not a received tradition which does not threaten to dissolve. Our religion has materialised itself in the fact, in the supposed fact; it has attached its emotion to the fact, and now the fact is failing it. But for poetry the idea is everything; the rest is a world of illusion, of divine illusion. Poetry attaches its emotion to the idea; the idea *is* the fact. The strongest part of our religion to-day is its unconscious poetry." (*EC-2*, pp. 1–2)[1]

Denis Butts argues convincingly[2] that this view of poetry and religion was "anticipated" in Newman's "Prospects of the Anglican Church" (1839), reprinted in *Essays Critical and Historical*:

How, then, in our age are those wants and feelings of our common nature satisfied, which were formerly supplied by symbols, now that symbolical language and symbolical rites have almost perished? Were we disposed to

---

[1] This passage is a transposition and alteration of remarks in the final paragraph of Arnold's introduction to *The Hundred Greatest Men*, written earlier in 1880 (*ELR*, pp. 237–239).

[2] Denis Butts, "Newman's Influence on Matthew Arnold's Theory of Poetry," *Notes and Queries*, N.S. V (June 1958), 255–256.

theorize, we might perhaps say, that the taste for poetry of a religious kind has in modern times in a certain sense taken the place of the deep contemplative spirit of the early Church. At any rate it is a curious circumstance, considering how much our active and businesslike habits take us the other way, that the taste for poetry should have been developed so much more strongly amongst ourselves than it seems to have been in the earlier times of the Church; as if our character required such an element to counterbalance the firmer and more dominant properties in it. . . . It may appear to some far-fetched, of course, to draw any comparison between the mysticism of the ancients, and the poetry or romance of the moderns, as to the religious tendencies of each; yet it can hardly be doubted, that, in matter of fact, poetry has been cultivated and cherished in our later times by the Cavaliers and Tories in a peculiar way, and looked coldly on by Puritans and their modern representatives. . . . Poetry then is our mysticism; and so far as any two characters of mind tend to penetrate below the surface of things, and to draw men away from the material to the invisible world, so far they may certainly be said to answer the same end; and that too a religious one. (*ECH*, I, 290–291)

Butts comments: "Newman, then, sees poetry as providing something for mankind which even the harsher aspects of society cannot destroy, although the Church at Newman's time appeared to neglect it"; and so, despite Newman's special pleading and the difference of his approach to religion (and, it may be added, the unrepresentative character of this passage, in Newman's writings), "it is more than likely that here were the origins of Arnold's own lofty conception of the high destiny of poetry. He has, as it were, merely extended Newman's vision."[3] Butts's linkage is confirmed, not only by Arnold's numerous references to the *Essays* in *Literature and Dogma*, but more specifically by the fact that one of those references—to the "truth lying hid under the tenor" of the text of the Bible (*LD*, p. 303)—occurs only four pages earlier in this same essay on "Prospects of the Anglican Church."

Arnold's involvement with Newman reaches a final high pitch of intensity in 1882 and 1883. These were important years for the revaluation of the Oxford Movement. The men of Newman's and Arnold's generations, now in later life, were summing up their im-

[3] *Ibid.*, p. 256.

pressions of the prodigious movement in which they had had a stake as young men. In 1881 J. A. Froude published his lengthy "The Oxford Counter-Reformation," which Arnold would almost certainly have known of; and in 1882 came the *Reminiscences* of Thomas Mozley, Newman's brother-in-law, which Arnold had read by the time of his "Liverpool Address" late in September.[4] Both accounts were highly autobiographical, and both had included detailed evaluations of Newman's personality and influence. Moreover, there occurred, apparently sometime in 1882 or early 1883, a second and more protracted meeting with Newman. This generally overlooked second encounter took place at the London home of Chief Justice Coleridge, a friend of Arnold's from his Oxford days. As told by Coleridge's son (who mistakenly refers to it as a first meeting) :

They had each expressed a wish to meet the other, so my father arranged it apparently by accident. With perfect taste and by common consent they talked together as a pair of ripe scholars, and no one would have supposed they were not old and familiar friends. They even with great urbanity quizzed each other, though Matthew Arnold never for a moment departed from the sort of attitude of a favourite pupil discoursing with an honoured master.

Each parted manifestly pleased with the other and subsequently they each in turn expressed the pleasure they had found in the society of the other.[5]

It was inevitable, in these circumstances, that Arnold's interest in Newman should suddenly intensify and that he too should attempt a personal revaluation of that extraordinary historical and spiritual movement which had affected the lives of so many men of talent and genius and which by now could be seen in something like historical perspective.

The shadow of Newman falls heavily across all three of the lectures Arnold delivered on his American tour of 1883–1884 (later col-

---

[4] See *Five Uncollected Essays of Matthew Arnold*, p. 92. For Newman's annoyance with Mozley's "seriously inaccurate" account, see Wilfrid Ward, *The Life of John Henry Cardinal Newman*, II, 513.

[5] Stephen Coleridge, *Memories*, p. 55. The terminal date is fixed by Coleridge's remark (*Famous Victorians I Have Known*, p. 46) that Newman's last visit to 1, Sussex Square, was on May 29, 1883.

lected as *Discourses in America,* 1885), but his role is largest in "Literature and Science," which Arnold first gave as the Rede Lecture at Cambridge in May 1882. This, Arnold's carefully considered answer to T. H. Huxley's attack on classical studies in "Science and Culture" (1880), is like Huxley's lecture in being ostensibly about the curriculum of the schools but actually a statement of its author's central humanist position. That Arnold considered himself to be speaking in the name of that Oxford tradition of theological humanism which he had in the past identified with the person and writings of Newman is clear from the substance of his lecture. But the original opening of the Rede lecture, printed in August in the *Nineteenth Century* but excluded from the book version, shows Arnold explicitly in a mood to analyze the nature of the Oxford tradition. Speaking before a Cambridge audience, Arnold contrasted the characteristic traditions of the two great universities:

the University of Oxford . . . has produced great men, indeed, but has above all been the source or the centre of great movements. . . . within the range of what is called modern history . . . we have the great movements of Royalism, Wesleyanism, Tractarianism, Ritualism. . . . You have nothing of the kind. . . . Yours is a University not of great movements, but of great men.[6]

Newman's presence is felt especially in the opening and closing pages of "Literature and Science," where Arnold defends the specifically classical character of literary humanism. With some irony Arnold states the contemporary objection that liberal education has traditionally been fitted for persons of leisure, and that it is absurd "to inflict this education upon an industrious modern community, where very few indeed are persons of leisure, and the mass to be considered has not leisure, but is bound, for its own great good, and for the great good of the world at large, to plain labour and to industrial pursuits, and the education in question tends necessarily to make men dissatisfied with these pursuits and unfitted for them!" (*DA*, p. 77). This is of course a version of the very same utilitarian objection to which Newman had

[6] Matthew Arnold, "Literature and Science," *Nineteenth Century,* XII (August 1882), 218.

addressed himself in the *Idea of a University*. The Newmanesque character of Arnold's ideal is further underscored when it is presented as a living tradition deriving from Plato and the Greeks: this educational ideal "is still mainly governed by the ideas of men like Plato," and "passed from Greece to Rome to the feudal communities of Europe" (*DA*, p. 76). Newman had argued that we "recur to Greece and Athens with pleasure and affection, and recognize in that famous land the source and the school of intellectual culture" (*Idea*, p. 230). This passage is from Newman's "Christianity and Letters," and the indebtedness is emphasized by the fact that Arnold soon thereafter (*DA*, p. 83) cites the climactic passage, from "The Function of Criticism," on the unity and continuity of European culture, which probably derived from this same lecture.

In the body of the essay, Arnold has no difficulty in overthrowing a main objection of Huxley's. Arnold agrees that knowing the best that has been thought and said in the world means, historically, the best of modern societies as well as of ancient, and, substantively, the matter of modern scientific discoveries and not mere *belles lettres*. But he goes on to argue a highly complex case for the emotional and moral function of "letters" in the formation and sustaining of human character—a function that letters, as opposed to science, are pre-eminently fitted to perform. Finally, he restricts his scope even further at the end by arguing once more for the unique and permanent claim of the classics, especially Greek, to the central position in the educational scheme. Characteristically, Arnold defends this view with deceptive simplicity by appealing to "the instinct of self-preservation in humanity. The instinct for beauty is set in human nature, as surely as the instinct for knowledge is set there, or the instinct for conduct. If the instinct for beauty is served by Greek literature and art as it is served by no other literature and art, we may trust to the instinct of self-preservation in humanity for keeping Greek as part of our culture" (*DA*, p. 131). Arnold's educational ideal is at once more aesthetic and more moralistic than Newman's characteristically intellectualist position but "Christianity and Letters" had made almost identical points. For example, Newman says, "The simple question to be considered is, how best to strengthen, refine, and enrich the intellectual powers; the perusal of the poets, historians, and philosophers of Greece and Rome will accomplish this purpose, as long experience has shown; but that the study of the experimental sciences will do the like, is proved to us as yet by no experience whatever" (*Idea*, p. 229). Concerning the "instinct" that preserves Greek, Newman states: "though there were times when the old traditions seemed to be on the point of failing, somehow it has happened that they have never failed; for the instinct of Civilization and the common sense of Society prevailed, and the danger passed away, and studies which seemed to be going out gained their ancient place, and were acknowledged, as before, to be the best instruments of mental cultivation, and the best guarantees for intellectual progress" (*Idea*, p. 229).

Clearly Arnold's debt to Newman in formulating a classicist literary position, above mere utility, which sees the Western tradition as "carrying on those august methods of enlarging the mind, and cultivating the intellect, and refining the feelings, in which the process of Civilization has ever consisted" (*Idea*, p. 223), remains strong to the end. What may not be so evident at first glance is that a major strategy that Arnold adopts in minimizing Huxley's claims in the body of the essay is borrowed from "The Tamworth Reading Room"—which Arnold seems to have been reading again in 1881 (*NB*, p. 350), and which has cropped up again and again in Arnold's attacks on Liberal pretensions. Arnold readily conceded to Huxley that "knowing the great results of the modern scientific study of nature" (Arnold gives as examples such crucial and controversial matters as Darwin's theories on the origin of the human body and Huxley's views of nature as a "definite order" [*DA*, pp. 109–110]) is as important a part of education as are literature and art. But he entirely dissociates himself from the view of "the friends of physical science" that "to follow the processes by which those results are reached, ought . . . to be made the staple of education for the bulk of mankind" (*DA*, p. 95). The question is, in one respect, a very practical one, that of the actual distribution of the student's time in the school. In resisting the admission of these detailed scientific "processes" to the central position in education, Arnold adopts a superior and even mocking tone toward these absorbing trivia: "It is very interesting to know, that, from the albuminous white of the egg, the chick in the egg gets the materials for its flesh, bones, blood, and feathers; while, from the fatty yolk of the egg, it gets the heat and energy which enable it at length to break its shell and begin the world. It is less interesting, perhaps, but still it is interesting, to know that when a taper burns, the wax is converted into carbonic acid and water" (*DA*, pp. 96–97). Is not this the very point and something of the tone of Newman's citing a self-parodying passage attributed to Brougham: "Is there anything in all the idle books of tales and horrors, more truly astonishing than the fact, that a few pounds of water may, by more pressure, without any machinery, by merely being placed in one particular way, produce very irresistible force? What can be more strange, than that an ounce weight should balance hundreds of pounds by the intervention of a few bars of thin iron? Can anything surprise us more than to find that the colour white is a mixture of all the others? that water should be chiefly composed of an inflammable substance?" (*D&A*, pp. 271–272). Newman's more intense scorn reaches a peak when he refers to Peel's talking of "improved modes of draining, and the chemical properties of manure" (*D&A*, p. 263).

Even the development of Arnold's argument from this point parallels Newman's. Arnold argues that the very "constitution of human nature" works against making physical science the center of education. There are, he repeats, four powers that "build up" human life—"the power of conduct, the power of intellect and knowledge, the power of beauty, and the power of social life and manners" (*DA*, p. 101). "When we have rightly met and adjusted the claims of them all, we shall then be in a fair way for getting soberness and righteousness, with wisdom" (*DA*, p. 102). Newman, too, had said, for all the obvious differences of emphasis, "I have no fanatical wish to deny to any whatever subject of thought or method of reason a place altogether, if it chooses to claim it, in the cultivation of the mind . . . the great and true maxim is to sacrifice none—to combine, and therefore to adjust, all" (*D&A*, p. 274). Similarly, Newman contemptuously asserts that the implicit argument of the Knowledge School, that the art of life "consists, or in any essential manner is placed, in the cultivation of Knowledge, that the mind is changed by a discovery, or saved by a diversion, and can thus be amused into immortality,—that grief, anger, cowardice, self-conceit, pride, or passion, can be subdued by an examination of shells or grasses, or inhaling of gases, or chipping of rocks, or calculating the longtitude, is the veriest of pretenses which sophist or mountebank ever professed to a gaping auditory" (*D&A*, p. 268). Arnold's chief concern is with the unification of the human faculties, in particular with the relation of "these pieces of knowledge to our sense for conduct, our sense for beauty" (*DA*, p. 103). This is a process that proceeds not only from outside of "the sphere of our knowledge," but from within that sphere itself: "every one knows how we seek naturally to combine the pieces of our knowledge together, to bring them under general rules, to relate them to principles; and how unsatisfactory and tiresome it would be to go on for ever learning lists of exceptions, or accumulating items of fact which must stand isolated" (*DA*, pp. 104–105). This is of course the central idea of Discourse VI ("Knowledge viewed in Relation to Learning") in the *Idea*: "we cannot gain real knowledge on the level; we must generalize, we must reduce to method, we must have a grasp of principles, and group and shape our acquisitions by means of them" (*Idea*, p. 123).

In developing his complex and revealing argument, only briefly summarized here, Arnold goes on to admit in effect that the new conceptions of the universe *cannot*, at least yet, be "related" to our old "instincts." However, a religiously elevated poetry can provide in satisfactory aesthetic form those emotional supports once supplied by supernatural religion. Poetry refreshes, fortifies, elevates, quickens, solaces, relieves, and rejoices (*DA*, pp. 123, 114, 115); and thus it satisfies man's deepest needs, both moral and aesthetic, even in the absence of the metaphysical system that once seemed to buttress these emotions. Arnold admits that men will have to forego a meaningful synthesis of natural science and their religious and aesthetic experience; and thus the two "spheres" of the sixties, that of "knowledge and intellect" and that of "religion and poetry," remain as mutually exclusive as ever. If in the education of "the great majority of mankind" there must be a choice between humane letters and the natural sciences, Arnold will choose letters, because they "will call out their being at more points, will make them live more" (*DA*, p. 129). That is to say, I think, that the satisfaction of the perennial claims of our aesthetic and moral instincts must be the center of education and that letters best provide what can only be called an *illusion* of a Providential order and a human destiny beyond this life. (The examples that Arnold gives from the Bible and Homer [*DA*, pp. 120–121] obviously suggest this religious structure in the universe, but Arnold, with calculated innocence, claims to be unable to explain their effect.) What is of importance here is the fact that Arnold, in this ultimate statement of his mature humanistic goals, makes a religious, and specifically Christian, moral-aesthetic formation the center of education. I think there is no question that, at bottom and by his own lights, Arnold felt that, as against a Huxley, he stood beside Newman in this crucial debate of the nineteenth century—beside the Newman who never wavered from the principle that "Christianity, and nothing short of it, must be made the element and principle of all education" (*D&A*, p. 274). Thus, in appropriating Newman's tone and arguments from the *Idea* and "The Tamworth Reading Room," Arnold was not merely raiding a foreign country for weapons and strategies; he considered, rather, that he was here in the very line of the Oxford literary-religious humanist tradition. Metaphysically, and in the light of subsequent history, Arnold's position may be judged to be chimerical or, at best, a noble but confused failure. But to judge his intentions, as must also be done, is to see his religiously colored humanism as far closer to Newman's than a coarse theological calculus can reveal.[7]

The two other lectures of Arnold's American tour both refer to Newman directly, and both reveal that he was rereading *Parochial and Plain Sermons*, which had been reissued in 1869. "Numbers; or, The Majority and the Remnant" was written by early October 1883, just

[7] Surely William Robbins' comment (*The Ethical Idealism of Matthew Arnold*, p. 222, n. 2) on Arnold's analysis of the four powers in "Literature and Science," though roughly accurate and expressing the received opinion, requires, in the light of the present analysis, some further discriminations: "His discussion of three of them (beauty, intellect, social life and manners) closely parallels the point of view of Newman in the *Idea of a University*. The unbridgeable gulf between the two men is apparent, however, in Arnold's including of the fourth power, conduct, in his broadly cultural approach. However Newman influenced Arnold, it was not as a Catholic theologian."

before Arnold embarked (*L*, II, 253). He was urging on his American auditors the unpopular thesis that majorities are not likely to be all good: " 'The majority are bad,' said one of the wise men of Greece; but he was a pagan. Much to the same effect, however, is the famous sentence of the New Testament: 'Many are called, few chosen.' This appears a hard saying; frequent are the endeavours to elude it, to attenuate its severity. But turn it how you will, manipulate it as you will, the few, as Cardinal Newman well says, can never mean the many" (*DA*, p. 6). This is of course another reference to Newman's sermon, "Many Called, Few Chosen," of 1837 (*PPS*, V, 268). As early as 1863 Arnold had used this quotation, with its characteristically Calvinist coloring, in support of a double thesis on the prerogatives and immunities of an intellectual elite and on the need to protect "the many" from theological arguments that do not "edify." Why Newman should have been invoked once again is not fully clear, unless it was to give a kind of religious sanction to Arnold's political reflections; but in this same sermon Newman had also discussed the notion of a "remnant," a word that is "frequent with the prophets," including Isaiah (*PPS*, V, 255). This may have suggested Arnold's dwelling on Isaiah: "*The remnant!*—it is the word of the Hebrew prophets also, and especially is it the word of the greatest of them all, Isaiah" (*DA*, p. 15).[8]

Arnold's last sustained treatment of Newman comes in the third lecture, "Emerson," first given late in November of 1883. It was a "horrid lecture" (*L*, II, 260), written under difficulties in October and November while amidst the actual confusions of the American tour. Arnold portrays Newman as one of the four "voices" heard at Oxford forty years before by undergraduates of Arnold's generation. Certainly, as the evidence assembled here has shown, of the four voices mentioned—those of Newman, Carlyle, Goethe, and Emerson—only Goethe's can begin to rival Newman's for the clarity and frequency

---

[8] The idea of an "elect remnant" is also developed at length in Sermon XIV (*Sermons* [1898], pp. 193 ff.). Moreover, in the *Apologia* (p. 31), the paragraph following that on Dr. Arnold's orthodoxy ("But is *he* a Christian?") discusses Newman's growing conviction, during the Mediterranean tour of 1833, that he had a "mission," a conviction supported by the thought that "deliverance is wrought, not by the many but by the few, not by bodies but by persons."

with which it had been heard in Arnold's writings through the intervening decades. (Similarly, of the four men from whom Arnold claimed in 1872 to have learned "'habits, methods, ruling ideas"—Goethe, Wordsworth, Sainte-Beuve, and Newman—surely not even Goethe can be seen to have penetrated Arnold's characteristic modes of thought and expression as deeply as Newman did.) Newman is introduced here in one of the most highly wrought passages in all of Arnold's prose writings:

The name of Cardinal Newman is a great name to the imagination still; his genius and his style are still things of power. But he is over eighty years old; he is in the Oratory at Birmingham; he has adopted, for the doubts and difficulties which beset men's minds to-day, a solution which, to speak frankly, is impossible. Forty years ago he was in the very prime of life; he was close at hand to us at Oxford; he was preaching in St. Mary's pulpit every Sunday; he seemed about to transform and to renew what was for us the most national and natural institution in the world, the Church of England. Who could resist the charm of that spiritual apparition, gliding in the dim afternoon light through the aisles of St. Mary's, rising into the pulpit, and then, in the most entrancing of voices, breaking the silence with words and thoughts which were a religious music,—subtle, sweet, mournful? (DA, pp. 139–140)

The terms of this analysis are by now familiar: Newman's religious position is "impossible," but his essential power as a force both aesthetic (imagination, genius, style) and religious (spiritual apparition, religious music) remains unimpaired and somehow beyond mere positions.

Arnold goes on: "I seem to hear him still, saying: 'After the fever of life, after wearinesses and sicknesses, fightings and despondings, languor and fretfulness, struggling and succeeding; after all the changes and chances of this troubled, unhealthy state,—at length comes death, at length the white throne of God, at length the beatific vision'" (DA, p. 140). The words "I seem to hear him still" are misleading or at least ambiguous, since the sermon from which Arnold is quoting ("Peace in Believing," PPS, VI, 369–370) was preached in May 1839, and again in June 1841, presumably well before Arnold could have heard Newman. Arnold continues:

Or, if we followed him back to his seclusion at Littlemore, that dreary village by the London road, and to the house of retreat and the church which he built there,—a mean house such as Paul might have lived in when he was tent-making at Ephesus, a church plain and thinly sown with worshippers,— who could resist him there either, welcoming back to the severe joys of church-fellowship, and of daily worship and prayer, the firstlings of a generation which had well-nigh forgotten them? Again I seem to hear him: "The season is chill and dark, and the breath of the morning is damp, and worshippers are few; but all this befits those who are by their profession penitents and mourners, watchers and pilgrims. More dear to them that loneliness, more cheerful that severity, and more bright that gloom, than all those aids and appliances of luxury by which men nowadays attempt to make prayer less disagreeable to them. True faith does not covet comforts; they who realize that awful day, when they shall see Him face to face whose eyes are as a flame of fire, will as little bargain to pray pleasantly now as they will think of doing so then." (*DA*, pp. 140–142)

Arnold's comments here are doubly ambiguous, because this Advent sermon (*PPS*, V, 2–3) was preached in December 1838, long before Arnold's coming up to Oxford in the autumn of 1841, and because Newman did not go down to Littlemore for good and set up his "house of retreat" until early in 1842. Arnold ends: "Somewhere or other I have spoken of those 'last enchantments of the Middle Age' which Oxford sheds around us, and here they were!" (*DA*, p. 142; see also *CPW*, III, 290).

Most important are the rich, impressionistic details—almost Paterian in their suggestiveness and elusiveness—with which Arnold invokes Newman's qualities: imagination, genius, style, charm, spiritual apparition, gliding in the dim afternoon light, entrancing voice, "religious music,—subtle, sweet, mournful," enchantments of the Middle Age. This is among the rhetorically most effective passages in Arnold. The "medieval" effect here is to make Newman a kind of exalted, slightly theatrical, Merlin-like magician (charm, entrancing, enchantments) in a pre-Raphaelite mural. The passage achieves two purposes at once: it suggests the rather superficial and picturesque "charm" of Newman's *person* and *style*—that minimal source of Arnold's perennial interest—while it subtly reinforces his judgment of Newman's "impossible" position, for here Newman is simply the priest of that divine "illusion" that Arnold often saw Christian history and thought to be. The preceding chapters have made clear that Newman's influence on Arnold's writings extended to substantive matters of social, educational, and religious interest, far beyond (as Arnold himself said in 1872) a mere "strong impression," but the passage in the Emerson lecture, usually read apart from the larger scope of the relations existing between the two men, is almost invariably taken as expressing the sum of Arnold's indebtedness to Newman. Undoubtedly this suggestion of a limited range of appeal—as a stimulant to the imagination and a model of style—is part of Arnold's intention here. Publicly, and as a kind of last testimonial, Arnold carefully restricts Newman's power to the practice of a rather suspicious imaginative wizardry. Arnold was either unaware of, or unable or unwilling to acknowledge in public, the full extent of his engagement with Newman's thought and personality.

The remaining references to Newman are scattered and incidental. In December 1885 Arnold writes from Berlin that he had talked with Mommsen: "he is quite white, and older than I expected;—in manner, mode of speech, and intellectual quality something between Voltaire and Newman" (L, II, 362). In such a violent yoking of opposites, Arnold's intention remains unclear. In "The Nadir of Liberalism," which appeared in the Nineteenth Century for May 1886, Arnold introduced Newman's name in discussing the qualifications of a Liberal leader:

A Liberal leader here in England is . . . a man of movement and change, called expressly to the task of bringing about a modern organisation of society. To do this, he should see clearly how the world is going, what our modern tendencies and needs really are, and what is routine and fiction in that which we have inherited from the past. But of how few men of Mr. Gladstone's age can it be said that they see this: Certainly not of Mr. Gladstone. Some of whom it cannot be said may be more interesting figures than those of whom it can; Cardinal Newman is a more interesting figure, Mr. Gladstone himself is a more interesting figure, than John Stuart Mill. But a Liberal leader of whom it cannot be said that he sees how the world is really going is in a false situation. (ELR, p. 269)

Newman, then, remained to the end for Arnold a symbol of resistance to change; he is a permanently "interesting" figure, but he does
not "see clearly how the world is going, what our modern tendencies
and needs really are." And yet Newman's larger function (as also stated in the 1879 review of de Maistre) remains still intact, for Arnold also describes a Conservative leader's "business" as being, "to
procure stability and prominence for that which already exists, much
of it undeniably precious" (*ELR*, p. 269). Finally there is the unexpected reference to Newman in Arnold's posthumously published review of Dowden's life of Shelley (July 1888); Arnold appeals to
Newman—"if perchance he does me the honour to read these words"
—to judge, for no very clear reason, the Shelley-Godwin circle and
"the clerical and respectable Oxford of those old times, the Oxford
of Copleston and the Kebles and Hawkins, and a hundred more"
(EC-2, p. 238). By a curious justice Arnold ends where he began, as
the conscious inheritor of the dual Oriel tradition in which Copleston
and Hawkins (and implicitly Dr. Arnold) are as much at home as
the Kebles and Newman.[9]

CHAPTER NINE   Newman and the Center of the
                Arnoldian Vision

O ne of the main objectives of these pages
has been to explore the sheer mass of direct
and indirect references linking Arnold to
Newman. Arnold's interest in Newman the man and the thinker is
intense at every period of his life. There is no other relationship quite
like it in Arnold's career: no other man of the nineteenth century—

---

[9] "W.M." (Wilfrid Meynell?) published in the *Athenaeum* of August 23, 1890,
pp. 257–258, a letter (written sometime after May 1879) from Arnold, who had been
asked to settle a quibble concerning Newman's grammar.

neither Goethe, nor Sainte-Beuve, nor Emerson, nor Carlyle, nor Wordsworth—evoked from Arnold such a continuous and detailed intellectual response combined with such an intense personal veneration. Yet the reaction is often curiously mixed and inconclusive—especially from the period of the religious writings onward. Stephen Coleridge caught one side of the response when he spoke of Arnold's attitude in the interview with Newman in the eighties as that of "a favourite pupil discoursing playfully with an honoured master." Of course the reverence could often be mixed with disappointment and impatience, too.

It is not the purpose of these pages to treat the similarities of "style" which link the two men, except in so far as Arnold can be said to borrow recognizable phrases and argumentative strategies and in so far as style indicates similarities of outlook and temperament. Richard Holt Hutton long ago established the major terms of this comparison when he spoke of the "curious 'distinction' " that marked both styles, their delight in irony, their ability to indulge in extravagance and ridicule without arousing displeasure. "Both styles are styles of white light rather than of the lurid or glowing, or even rainbow order," and "Both have something in them of the older Oxford suavity, though in very different forms."[1] John Holloway more recently has extended the similarities to matters of general strategy:

Arnold's chief purpose is to recommend one temper of mind, and condemn another, and such things are more readily sensed through contact than understood through description. No author, of course, can give a favourable impression of his own temper of mind, except obliquely and discreetly. When Arnold writes of himself at length, it is usually in a deprecatory vein; but he causes us to glimpse his personality through various devices, and of these as with Newman, perhaps the most conspicuous is tone. Indeed he adopts a tone not unlike Newman's, save that it is usually less grave and calm, more whimsical and apologetic. Newman, after all, thought he had a powerful silent ally as Arnold did not.[2]

[1] Hutton, *Essays on Some of the Modern Guides to English Thought in Matters of Faith*, pp. 55–56. See also his comparison, p. 61. "Both are luminous, but Arnold's prose is luminous like a steel mirror, Newman's like a clear atmosphere or lake. Arnold's prose style is crystal, Newman's liquid."

[2] John Holloway, *The Victorian Sage: Studies in Argument*, pp. 207–208.

It should be added that Arnold sees the "temper of mind," which his critical career was designed to recommend, as *embodied* to a great extent in Newman the man and controversialist. As *Essays in Criticism* and *Culture and Anarchy* had abundantly revealed, the ideal was that of highest development of the older Oxford manner, which Arnold tended habitually to identify with Newman. As Gerard Manley Hopkins wrote to Coventry Patmore in 1887: "Newman does not follow the common tradition—of writing. His tradition is that of cultured, the most highly educated, conversation; the flower of the best Oxford life."[3]

In that shared Oxford tradition lies, I believe, the corrective to the still commonly accepted belief that Newman affected only Arnold's ideal of criticism and culture in the sixties and that the influence did not extend to the religious concerns of the seventies.[4] The fact is that Arnold's developing vision of human perfection, though always under the watchful eye of the suave humanistic intellectualism of the sixties, extended along an unbroken continuum into social and religious problems. Equally important is the fact that Arnold's vision is not detachable from the theologically oriented classicism of his Oxford inheritance. At issue is Arnold's essentially "mediatorial" position in nineteenth-century thought. Whatever his skepticism as to the alleged metaphysical basis of the traditional classical-Christian synthesis of European civilization, Arnold's chief concern was to provide a means by which men in future might keep the imaginative and emotional supports and safeguards of inherited patterns of thought, feeling, and morality. Put negatively, this was the view that Jacobinism, or even "liberalism" after the pattern of the younger Mill—with their optimistic and secularist faith in reason and their systematic programs of reform—were insufficiently equipped to provide the fullness of life which Arnold increasingly predicted for the masses.

As a first basis for questioning the received opinion, one should note that Newman was, as Arnold feelingly acknowledged, his model in his attacks on *both* Liberalism and Dissent. The juxtaposition of so-

---

[3] *Further Letters of Gerard Manley Hopkins*, ed. Claude Colleer Abbott, p. 380.

[4] J. D. Jump, *Matthew Arnold*, p. 24; and William Robbins, *The Ethical Idealism of Matthew Arnold*, discussed in Chapter 8, note 7 above.

ciety and religion is significant; and Newman's own practice had to a large extent justified the extension of the term "Liberalism." Moreover, attacks on both "modern liberalism" and "revolutionary Deism" were as characteristic of Arnold's religious works as of the social writings before and after. In defending both "culture" and his "religion of the Bible" Arnold was countering the demand of nineteenth-century radicalism for a *total* revision of human character and human destiny. Second, Arnold's use of Newman in the religious works is far more complicated than has been assumed. For all the ultimate incompatibility of the two men's positions, Newman is cited as an authority almost as often as he is cited as an adversary. In *St. Paul and Protestantism*, for example, Arnold can quote long passages from Newman on the development of doctrine and find them applicable to his own sense of the term, while refusing to follow Newman's arguments on the need for an external interpreter. More incidentally, he can in one place dismiss Newman's sense of *securus judicat orbis terrarum* and yet within a few pages cite Newman on the need for inference and collection in interpreting the Bible. The process in *Literature and Dogma* is, admittedly, more consistently negative. Arnold flatly rejects Newman's view on the opposition between faith and reason, as well as on an allegorical sense in Scripture. More ambivalently, Arnold concedes Newman's complex Catholic argument for the "systematic" character of the Christian religion, only to scuttle the whole by denying the first premise out of hand. Even more strangely, Arnold at one point scoffs at Newman's argument that Catholics can separate dogma from "errors and absurdities," and yet within a year he calmly admits that "serious and intelligent Catholics" can and should separate "accretions and superstitions" from the essence of their religion. Twice, moreover, Arnold approvingly cites Newman's authority on the Bible as the record of the whole revealed faith. Further, in *Last Essays on Church and Religion* Newman is introduced with relish as having exposed with "exquisite raillery" the British Philistine's combined patriotic and anti-Catholic prejudices. It should be added that Newman himself, "this exquisite and delicate genius," an "incomparable" and "sagacious" formulator of religious truths, is almost invariably handled with great tact. Even in disagreeing, Arnold speaks "with all deference" and refers to Newman as "a writer whom we can never name but with respect." The effect of all this is, at the very least, complex. Certainly, Newman seems almost half an ally in the religious writings—as the attacker of Liberal and Dissenting pretensions, as the fully adequate expositor of certain important religious ideas, and as a spokesman for certain acceptable Christian views of the Bible; and over all there hovers the image of the "exquisite and delicate genius," the very embodiment of Arnold's ideals of the sixties, who should have been—and might have been, Arnold feels, but for an accident of history—Arnold's natural partner and model in *every* aspect of his wide-ranging scrutiny of English civilization.

The customary view is too simple, finally, because it does not take into account Newman's focal position in the totality of Arnold's humanism. Arnold's characteristic mode of thought is dialectical, and history itself he saw as a long series of often violent oscillations between man's polarized impulses—all of them necessary to the total man. What Arnold projected in *Culture and Anarchy*, and again after the deepening of his thought in the religious writings, was the vision of a possible permanent future reconciliation of the warring impulses within societies and within individual men. This increasingly optimistic and purposive vision was of course deeply Platonic; it is well summed up in words that Arnold admiringly quotes from Benjamin Jowett: "The moral and intellectual are always dividing, yet they must be reunited, and in the highest conception of them are inseparable" (*LECR*, p. 179). The question for Arnold, then, as for a whole line of critics of culture from whom he stemmed, was how much of man's past was available to the new man of the future and how much of it was desirable. In defining what of the past was essential for man's future, Newman's example was of central importance. For Arnold the mediator, Newman is perhaps the most adequate and acceptable representative of conservative thought after Burke. The review of de Maistre (1879) sets the precise terms of Arnold's acceptance and rejection of Newman's testimony. Arnold is perfectly clear that the "main positions" of Burke, de Maistre, and Newman are unacceptable—especially "the old, sterile, impossible assumption" of an infallible Church on the part of the latter two. But equally clear is Arnold's

approval of Newman's "antipathy to 'liberalism' ": "in a serious man
a strong sense of the insufficiency of Liberal nostrums, of the charlatanism of Liberal practitioners, as also of the real truth, beauty, power,
and conformity to nature of much in the past of which these practitioners are intolerant, is abundantly permissible." For all his disappointment at the "Tory" positions of these three men, Arnold repeats
a judgment he had applied in *Culture and Anarchy* to the Oxford
Movement which suggests that conservatism may not be entirely
incompatible with a *vision* of future possibility: "the resoluteness with
which they withstand the prevailing ideas of their time, the certainty
with which they predict the apparition of something different, are often
a proof of their insight." Above all, I would stress that Newman's
"impossible" dogmatic stance did not disqualify him, in Arnold's
mind, for the deepest sort of religious insight: "Whatever we may
think of Ritualism, its growth and power prove Cardinal Newman's
insight in perceiving that what he called Liberalism . . . was in general,
and in the sphere of religion more particularly, quite inadequate, and
was not destined to have things for ever its own way" (*ELR*, p. 218).

Ultimately, Arnold took Newman for a teacher and model in both
crucial areas of his religiously colored humanism—in the establishment of a high, complex ideal of intellectual culture and in a central
and religious orientation in life in which man's historical experience
would be both his burden and his glory, and a norm by which he could
continue to seek his definition of himself. Dwight Culler has remarked
that Arnold's ideal of culture in the sixties and Newman's in the *Idea*
both sought to establish a "source of value, larger than the self and
perfectly distinct from it"; and he extends the remark to say that
Arnold's effort "is of the same character in the field of humanism as
Newman's was in the more decisive sphere of religion."[5] I would
correct this by extending the analogy further to the quest for "detachment" and "catholicity" in the religious efforts of *both* men. R. H.
Hutton long ago provided the terms for this analogy: "both, with all

[5] A. Dwight Culler, *The Imperial Intellect: A Study of Cardinal Newman's Educational Ideal*, p. 235; *Apologia* (ed. A. Dwight Culler), p. xviii. Culler mentions
(*Apologia*, p. xvii) that Arnold's objective ideal "would serve as 'a power not ourselves which makes for righteousness'," but does not explore the idea.

their richness of insight, have had that strong desire to rest on something beyond that insight, something they can regard as independent of themselves, which led Newman first to preach against the principle of private judgment, and to yearn after an infallible Church, while it led Matthew Arnold to preach what he calls his doctrine of verification —namely, that no religious or moral instinct is to be trusted unless it can obtain the endorsement on a large scale of the common consent of the best human experience."[6] Nor should one forget Arnold's characteristic hankering after the absolute, in his positing an "Eternal Power, not ourselves, by which *all things* fulfil the law of their being," "The Eternal who makes for righteousness." For the ground of Arnold's persistent attention to Newman was his conviction that his own critical and religious career was "an attempt conservative, and an attempt religious" (*GB*, p. xli).

This analysis has been unable so far to consider the large residue of intense, virtually unparalleled "feeling" that permeates both Arnold's correspondence and his public references to Newman and that energizes the entire course of what is surely one of the most complex and important relationships of the nineteenth century. The letters, for example, are suffused with "an inexpressible sense of gratitude and attachment," "a deep sense of esteem and obligation" (January 20, 1868; January 10, 1876). The intensity is only comparable to Arnold's almost Hamlet-like affection for his dead father, revealed continually in the letters to his mother. It is almost as if Arnold thought of Newman as a kind of second—and perhaps even more adequate—spiritual father. If Dr. Arnold can be seen as one of the authors of Arnold's latitudinarianism and of his historical sense, Newman is clearly Arnold's model for delicate intellectual and spiritual perception, and for the correct mode of public dispute. Certainly the Oxford tutor-student relationship, which Newman described as "a bond of union" or "intercommunion" built on "mutual sympathies" (*Idea*, p. 130), is one of the paradigms of their friendship.

Perhaps the best way to suggest both the emotional ambiance of Arnold's attitudes toward Newman and some of the possible causes of

6 Hutton, *Essays*, pp. 50–51.

it, is to note that Newman is habitually conceived in terms that parallel Arnold's conception of Jesus. A duality runs through both images. Jesus is both the sponsor of a certain "temper," and a tragic failure. In *Literature and Dogma,* for example, Arnold claims that the "charm and power" of Jesus lay in "the mild, uncontentious, winning, inward mode of working . . . which was his true characteristic" (*LD,* p. xiv). And at the very end of his life Arnold repeats: "Not less important than the teachings given by Jesus is the *temper* of their giver, his temper of sweetness and reasonableness, of *epieikeia*" (*EC-2,* p. 296). But the world was not ready then to accept the full meaning of Jesus. As Arnold put it in 1876, he is unwilling to reject "the poetry of popular religion," because "it is an aim which may well indeed be pursued with enthusiasm, to make the true meaning of Jesus, in using that poetry, emerge and prevail. For the immense pathos, so perpetually enlarged upon, of his life and death, does really culminate here: that Christians have so profoundly misunderstood him" (*LECR,* p. 228). And at the very end of *God and the Bible,* Arnold solemnly repeats the Biblical phrase he more than once had associated with Newman, "Many are called, few chosen," and comments: "In the severity of this sentence, Jesus marks how utterly those who are gathered to his feast may fail to know him" (*GB,* p. 342).

That Newman was similarly both the exemplar of a subtle "temper" and a tragic failure was a view not unknown in Arnold's time. Oscar Wilde, for example, who picked up many of his critical notions from Arnold, expressed the duality in his letters. In 1876 he writes: "His [Newman's] life is a terrible tragedy. I fear he is a very unhappy man"; and on the occasion of Newman's death in 1890, he remarks: "In what a fine 'temper' Newman always wrote! the temper of a scholar. But how subtle was his simple mind!"[7] Evidence of Arnold's idea of Newman's Christ-like "temper" is abundant: the "charm," "mildness," "sweetness," and "reasonableness" he attributes to Jesus are paralleled in the words Arnold again and again associates with Newman—"charm," "genius," "delicacy," and the adjective "exquisite" (used three times)—and in his identification of Newman with "the senti-

---

[7] *The Letters of Oscar Wilde,* ed. Rupert Hart-Davis, pp. 20, 274.

ment of Oxford for beauty and sweetness." Presumably Jesus' "uncontentious" manner is paralleled in Newman's acclaimed "urbanity";
likewise, Jesus' characteristic "inward mode of working" strongly recalls the "inward qualities and excellences" Arnold found in Newman's "influence and writings" (letter of January 1868). As for the
pathos of Newman's life, the precise tone of the "sympathy" with
which Arnold bade "any son of Oxford" to look on Newman in 1864
(*CPW*, III, 244) became clear two years later in the first of the Celtic
lectures, when Arnold, no doubt thinking of Newman's Catholic al-
legiances, spoke of him as "the champion of a cause more interesting
than prosperous,—one of those causes which please noble spirits, but
do not please destiny, which have Cato's adherence, but not Heaven's"
(*CPW,* III, 305). In considering Newman in the farewell lecture of
1867 Arnold speaks of the failure of the Oxford Movement and the
Oxford "attachment to so many beaten causes" (*CPW, V,* 106).
Literature and Dogma presents Newman, "this exquisite and delicate
genius," as a man born sadly out of his time, twenty years too early to
be "touched with the breath of the *'Zeit-Geist'* " (*LD,* pp. 303–304).
The Emerson lecture of 1883, finally, clearly presents Newman as old,
personally isolated ("in the Oratory at Birmingham"), and deprived
of intellectual influence and power by a commitment irrelevant to the
"doubts and difficulties" of the day. The hope men attached to him in
earlier years that he would "transform and renew . . . the Church of
England" was dashed and, I think it is implied, Newman's career made
pointless. Through all of this runs Arnold's slight condescension and
the self-consciously picturesque and literary effect of portraying Newman as a man of consummate imaginative and spiritual power whose
influence was frustrated and made ineffectual by accidents of history
and failures of understanding.

Nevertheless, because Arnold's portrait of Newman is very close
to his highly aesthetic reading of the character of Jesus, Newman comes
to occupy a startlingly central position in Arnold's idea of human perfection; he is at once the embodiment of intellectual refinement and a
model for the conduct of public debate, as well as perhaps the clearest
exemplar Arnold knew of the temper of Jesus, which he recommended,
and the tragedy of Jesus, which he found so affecting. Newman could

be all of these for Arnold because the intellectual ideal of the sixties was so closely allied with the spiritual temper recommended centrally in the religious writings. Almost all aspects of Arnold's mature thought can be seen as derived from his deeply felt role as continuator of the line of Oxford humanism, while many of his major themes center in the person of Newman, the supreme Oxford humanist. No other figure in Arnold's development—not Goethe, or Wordsworth—is so frequently found at the center of Arnold's total humanistic vision.

Arnold, Pater and the
Dialectic of Hebraism and Hellenism

ᛙᚱ

PART I

THE SCARCE

REMEDIABLE CLEAVAGE

CHAPTER TEN The Dialectical Impulse

In the mid-seventeen-nineties, in his work *On Naive and Sentimental Poetry,* Friedrich Schiller, like other German Hellenists before and after, proclaimed the failure of modern society and religion and appealed to the ancient Greeks as examples of perfect humanity. The Greeks were still part of Nature; only later came a humanity divided within itself. "Feeling and thought," he declared, "were not yet split in pieces, that scarce remediable cleavage in the healthy nature of man had not yet taken place."[1] Later in the same decade, Goethe, who found in Schiller's critical writings the very expression of the "Greek" ideal he himself aspired to in this period, added: "The highest idea of man can be attained only through manysidedness, liberality. The Greek was capable of this in his day. The European is still capable of it."[2] Seventy years later, Matthew Arnold in *Culture and Anarchy,* his most "Hellenizing" work, declared that human perfection as culture defined it and as the Greeks lived it goes *beyond* religion, that is, beyond Christianity, by listening to "*all* the voices of human experience" in working toward the ideal of "a harmonious expansion of *all* the powers

[1] Cited in Humphry Trevelyan, *Goethe and the Greeks,* p. 198.
[2] *Ibid.,* p. 199.

which make the worth of human nature" (*CPW,* V, 93, 94). In his own "mechanical and external" civilization, the appeal must constantly be to the "best art and poetry of the Greeks, in which religion and poetry are one, in which the idea of beauty and of a human nature perfect on all sides adds to itself a religious and devout energy" (*CPW,* V, 100). And in 1877, in the concluding words of the Preface to *Last Essays on Church and Religion,* his final attempt to salvage Christianity by reestablishing it on a "natural" basis, Arnold cited Benjamin Jowett's words on the Socratic notion of "the inter-dependence of virtue and knowledge": "The moral and intellectual are always dividing, yet they must be reunited, and in the highest concep-tion of them are inseparable" (*LECR,* p. 179).

For Walter Pater, in one of his first published essays, on Johann Winckelmann (1867), the founder of "aesthetic paganism" in Ger-many, the crucial problem of the modern world was whether Goethe's Hellenic ideal of "*Heiterkeit,* blitheness or repose, and *Allgemeinheit,* generality or breadth," can be made operative in "the gaudy, perplexed light of modern life" (*Ren-1,* pp. 186, 201). Even more specifically, can the ideal "in which man is at unity with himself, with his physical nature, with the outward world," be "communicated to artistic pro-ductions which contain the fulness of the experience of the modern world" (*Ren-1,* pp. 196, 204)? Nearly twenty years later, Pater's autobiographical spokesman, Marius, speculates on the unity of human activity, and takes deep satisfaction in the notion that morality may be, "in effect, one mode of comeliness in things—as it were music, or a kind of artistic order, in life" (*ME,* II, 4).

These characteristic utterances are gathered here to suggest that a set of antitheses and proposed reconciliations, which provided the unity of German Hellenism in the late eighteenth century, are at the heart of the line of continuity from Arnold, through Pater, to the nineties in late nineteenth-century England. A complex and highly dialectical process, worked out in the thought of the major German figures and every-where related to the cult and "myth" of Greece first effectively formu-lated by Winckelmann, enjoys an extraordinary recrudescence in the careers of Arnold and Pater. Put simply, the problem is that of the transcendence, whether through rejection or synthesis, of the dualisms with which the Western tradition, especially in Platonism and Christianity, was seen to have burdened man. In Goethe's time as in Arnold's there is a search for a new basis of life compatible with the exigencies of modern thought and experience, and yet ensuring fullness of consciousness, "fulness of being." In ethics, in human psychology, and especially in artistic production, the attempt to provide what Arnold, looking to Goethe, called in 1866 a new interpretation of human life and "a new spiritual basis" for European civilization (*CPW*, III, 381) involved as its major counters a special version of "Hellenic" values and a radical revaluation of the Christian tradition. The dualisms to be transcended might be within the individual—the psychological dualism of feeling and thought; the metaphysical split between matter and spirit, body and soul; the ethical rupture of morality and aesthetics, or morality and the intellect, or duty and desire; the artistic antagonism between the spiritual and the "sensible," the outward and the inward, form and essence, passion and order. Or the dichotomy might be broadly cultural—northern "soul" and southern "form," the classical and the romantic, Christianity and paganism, individual self-development against humane "service" to mankind. Whatever the mode of transcendence, however, and there are often numerous resolutions even in a single career—a morality above morality, a return to the Greeks, a new Christianity—the norm, for many of the Germans as for Arnold and Pater and their successors, is increasingly the *aesthetic*.

It seems clear that the most critical factor in the complex cultural struggle was Christianity and the Christian tradition, a Christianity debilitated by internal division and increasingly isolated from the mainstream of modern culture. The way for modern "aestheticism," whether German or English, as for much of the heterodoxy of the nineteenth century, was prepared by the Enlightenment, which had thrown Christian theology on the defensive, a role for which it was to have no adequate weapons for generations. The major figures of the Enlightenment had appealed to *truth*, not *beauty*, as their standard, whereas the German Hellenists had more frankly sought a belief or myth "more beautiful, more in keeping with the dignity of man, than the Christian."[3] Nevertheless, the doctrines most objected to were very much the same for both groups: such matters as Original Sin, asceticism, the system of rewards and punishment, other-worldliness. Somewhat similarly, such first-generation Victorian agnostics as George Eliot, F. W. Newman, and J. A. Froude, prepared in part by eighteenth-century rationalism, rejected Christian theology because of an *ethical revulsion* against such doctrines of the "economy" of salvation as Original Sin, Reprobation, Baptismal Regeneration, Vicarious Atonement, and Eternal Punishment. Only later was their rejection confirmed by the Higher Criticism of the Bible and evolutionary theory.[4] Figures like Arnold and Pater, however, though their desertion of Christianity was nurtured in the same climate of opinion, appeal far more frankly to *aesthetic* criteria in rejecting Christian standards. Of course, the cultural climate, even when the sometimes amazing lag in the importation of Continental thought into England is considered, was by no means the same in Goethe's Weimar as in Arnold's Oxford and London. Above all, there hovers over much of Arnold's and Pater's work the intimidating specter of "Science," stern, unrelenting, equipped by Huxley and others with a superseding "morality" of its own. The solidifying orthodoxy of scientific naturalism now added its resounding "No" to the hope for any simple accommodation with historic, supernaturalist Christianity.

For all their sense of an obligation to jettison the metaphysical basis of much of the inherited Christian view of the world, Arnold and Pater are nonetheless both "conservative" in important senses of the word, both extraordinarily aware of the richness of the total cultural tradition endangered by the collapse of orthodox belief, and both persistently concerned to retain certain traditional modes of feeling, thought, and expession even in the straitened intellectual conditions of modern life. It seems true to say not only that Arnold and Pater were

[3] Henry Hatfield, *Aesthetic Paganism in German Literature: From Winckelmann to the Death of Goethe*, p. 1. As will be evident, much of my reference to the German background is indebted to Professor Hatfield's extraordinarily illuminating work.

[4] See Howard R. Murphy, "The Ethical Revolt against Christian Orthodoxy in Early Victorian England," *American Historical Review*, LX (July 1955), 800–817.

both "moralists" (as most readers would agree today), but also that they both, in different ways, conceived a certain "religious" mode of consciousness to be the crown of the perfected life. Here, their German predecessors, though few of them were simply "anti-Christian," were of less direct value to them. But inevitably Arnold and Pater looked back to the German Hellenists for terms in which to express the related cultural dilemma of their own age. Arnold, for example, is openly dissatisfied with the alternatives available to the Victorian mind. Puritanism, the Christianity sponsored by the Victorian middle class, had little sweetness and no light, while the new rationalism and utilitarianism employed reason, its own fierce light, without sweetness, without a consciousness of the richness of the human composite or the human past. In the German Hellenists Arnold, and Pater with him, found a deep concern with the ideal of totality and with the central tradition of the West in art and letters, combined with a frank rejection, or at least critical reexamination, of the Christian theology to which it had been historically attached. Arnold's and Pater's own relations with Christianity varied significantly through the years, and the precise relationship in their work between the classical deposit and "Christianity" fluctuates in important ways. However, three crucial themes provide much of the unity of each career and link the men indissolubly: the persistent merging of religious and aesthetic categories; the concern for the transcendence of human duality at the psychological and ethical levels; and culturally, the pitting of a "Greek" ideal of life, derived in large part from the German Hellenists, against a rejected "medieval" Christianity.

One purpose of the following chapters is to suggest the complexity and significance of Arnold's place in Pater's writings, especially in the dichotomy of Hebraism and Hellenism. The central motifs of Pater's intellectual development are not clear until it is seen that his long recognized dependence on Arnold—in a multitude of echoing phrases, themes, ideas, and attitudes—is part of a larger system of correspondences. Their relationship is a curious combination of open, implied, and perhaps concealed borrowing; and of modification and correction, often through amplification. Whether as a stimulus or sometimes as an irritant, Arnold is surprisingly often at the base of Pater's most important statements concerning art, religion, and the problems of modern life. In effect, this study becomes an attempt to define a central theme of the Aesthetic Movement in late nineteenth-century England, in two of its chief figures. Inevitably, some of the unity of nineteenth-century culture is also revealed, as well as the process by which the aesthetic paganism of German thought from Winckelmann to Hegel and Heine is adapted generations later to altered circumstances. Certainly the Aesthetic Movement itself, if not of first-class stature intellectually, resembles the vast effort of German thought in being a serious and respectable attempt to provide fullness of life to a society increasingly aware, as Arnold put it, that the immense inherited "system of institutions, established facts, accredited dogmas, customs, rules," fails to correspond to the wants of modern life. The awakening of this "sense of want of correspondence between the forms of modern Europe and its spirit, between the new wine of the eighteenth and nineteenth centuries, and the old bottles of the eleventh and twelfth centuries, or even of the sixteenth and seventeenth," says Arnold referring to Goethe, is "the awakening of the modern spirit" (*CPW*, III, 109). A hundred years of science, the Industrial Revolution, and a revitalized and triumphant rationalism had only made the problem of cultural integration the more pressing, though the hopes for success in that later venture were eventually and inevitably far less sanguine.

The decisive issues for both Arnold and Pater, as for the Germans, were the authority and viability of religion and religious experience, the spilt old wine of the past, in the modern synthesis, and the relation of religion to other aspects of life. That sustained critical effort entailed, as a result, a redefinition of human nature, the attempt to strike a new balance among the components of the human totality. The synthesis achieved by Arnold and Pater proved unstable for a number of reasons. Their varying responses to "ascetic," "medieval," otherworldly Christianity become a touchstone of their own development. The responses vary from a virtual rejection of Christianity in favor of a classical ideal to the positing of two Christianities, one life-destroying and illegitimate, the other life-bestowing and humane.

CHAPTER ELEVEN   The Hellenism of Arnold
and Pater

Arnold was never so deeply bitten by
Grecomania as was Pater. Arnold's "Hellenism"—as it emerges in the early poems,
the Preface of 1853, the Preface to *Merope*, the Homer lectures, the
Essays in Criticism, the Celtic lectures, and *Culture and Anarchy*—is a
decidedly tamed and refined version of German Hellenism, though
linked to it by a search for an alternative to Christianity. In place of
Titanism, or Prometheanism, or heroic struggles against the gods, there
is the slightly donnish Rugby and Balliol "classical" man, detached to
be sure from Christianity but never aggressively hostile to religion.
Culture and Anarchy is symptomatic in hesitating between synthesis
and a Hellenism *above* Christianity. The ideal is everywhere "moral"
and smacks more of Herder's ethical humanitarianism than of Goethe's
or Schiller's more aesthetic humanism. Above all, Arnold's Greece is
invested with a Winckelmannian calm and leans toward the statuesque,
a sunlit Apollonianism.[1] The "noble simplicity and tranquil grandeur"
of orthodox Hellenism is again and again at the center of Arnold's
view of high Greek culture: his key terms are "calm," "objectivity,"
"harmonious acquiescence of mind," "noble serenity," "repose," "radi-
ance," "harmony," "grace and serenity" (*CPW*, I, 1, 20, 28, 59; III,
378; V, 100, 125). Arnold's Hellenic ideal of "reason, ideas, light"
shines with a cold and rather academic clarity; most damagingly, it
was, even in his generation, uninformed. Pater was far more alive, both

[1] Warren D. Anderson, in *Matthew Arnold and the Classical Tradition*, usefully
surveys Arnold's treatment of classical figures and themes, suggesting, from the viewpoint of an informed twentieth-century classical scholar, the subjectivity and highly
variable authenticity in Arnold's Apollonian classicism. Anderson conveys less successfully the total context of Arnold's "Hellenism," its origin in German thought of
the eighteenth and nineteenth centuries, and its role as part of a larger modern culture
struggle between Christian and pagan values.

temperamentally and for dialectical reasons of his own, to the "other" tradition—roughly, the Dionysian—in Greek art and religion.

Arnold's idealized and simplified Hellenism was in part a product of personal need and temperamental affinity. As T. S. Eliot once put it, "The vision of the horror and the glory was denied to Arnold."[2] This statement is very similar to the charge of R. H. Hutton, an acute clerical critic of Arnold's own generation. Hutton's *Spectator* review of *Essays in Criticism* nettled Arnold, and provoked him to this response:

> the article has Hutton's fault of seeing so very far into a millstone. No one has a stronger and more abiding sense than I have of the "daemonic" element—as Goethe called it—which underlies and encompasses our life; but I think, as Goethe thought, that the right thing is, while conscious of this element, and of all that there is inexplicable round one, to keep pushing on one's posts into the darkness, and to establish no post that is not perfectly in light and firm. One gains nothing on the darkness by being, like Shelley, as incoherent as the darkness itself. (*L*, I, 289–90; March 1865)

At bottom, Arnold's Hellenism is cautious, and ultimately balanced, first, because of his uninterrupted involvement with Christianity in the sixties, and second, because his attitude is a unique blend of rationalization and conciliation. His Hellenic ideal of comprehensiveness, harmony, totality (in Sophocles Arnold finds human nature "in its completest and most harmonious development," politically, socially, religiously, morally; *CPW*, I, 28) easily becomes something like a diplomatic strategy in the ideal of "facing in every direction" and the hatred of "all over-preponderance of single elements" (*L*, I, 360, November 1865; I, 287, January 1865). Arnold's persistent concern with the role of Christianity joins with his rationalizing and conciliatory instincts in his fascination with the idea—endorsed by "the modern spirit" and "science," and associated with Wilhelm von Humboldt, Baron Bunsen, and Friedrich Schleiermacher—of a Christianity stripped of its "alien Semitic" features and brought into line with "the opener, more flexible Indo-European genius."[3]

---

[2] T. S. Eliot, *The Use of Poetry and the Use of Criticism*, p. 106.

[3] *On the Study of Celtic Literature* (December 1865) in *CPW*, III, 301. See *L*, I, 442 (Christmas 1867): "Bunsen used to say that our great business was to get rid of all that was purely Semitic in Christianity, and to make it Indo-Germanic, and

Arnold's most developed treatment of the relation of Greek values to Christianity came with his discussion of Hellenism and Hebraism, in *Culture and Anarchy*. Rarely was he so satisfied with a performance; in June 1869, he wrote his mother that the chapters on Hellenism and Hebraism are "so true that they will form a kind of centre for English thought and speculation on the matters treated in them" (*L*, II, 13). His point of view toward Christianity in *Culture and Anarchy* is inconclusive; and significantly, he immediately turned his attention to directly religious concerns for the next eight years. He wrote his mother in June 1870, shortly after the appearance of *St. Paul and Protestantism*: "I do hope that what influence I have may be of use in the troubled times which I see are before us as a healing and reconciling influence" (*L*, II, 41). Surely Arnold is nowhere more Goethean than in his adoption of this role as healer and reconciler; as Henry Hatfield explains, Goethe's nature, apart from the period of his most doctrinaire Hellenism, "was basically conciliatory, . . . and he repeatedly attempted to bring the Hellenic and the Judeo-Christian positions into harmony."[4] Arnold's writings are unquestionably open to T. S. Eliot's charge, "All his writing in the kind of *Literature and Dogma* seems to me a valiant attempt to dodge the issue, to mediate between Newman and Huxley."[5] But it may be urged as fairly and more sympathetically that Arnold's mediatorial and conciliatory impulse simply sought to recognize the results of and the limitations imposed by "science" while preserving the most precious modes of knowledge from the past. It seems to have gone unnoticed that Arnold himself acknowledged that the inconclusive treatment of his Hellenism sprang precisely from his dual fear of the new (and presumably pagan and amoral) aestheticism, to which Pater was already making notable contributions, and of the new "tyrannical" orthodoxy of scientific rationalism. Charles Kingsley wrote Arnold in 1870 praising *Culture and Anarchy*, and Arnold replied: "If I was to think only of the Dissenters, or if I were in your position, I

Schleiermacher that in the Christianity of us Western nations there was really much more of Plato and Socrates than of Joshua and David."

[4] Henry Hatfield, *Aesthetic Paganism in German Literature: From Winckelmann to the Death of Goethe*, p. 216.

[5] Eliot, *Use of Poetry*, pp. 105–106.

should press incessantly for more Hellenism; but, as it is, seeing the tendency of our young poetical litterateur (Swinburne), and, on the other hand, seeing much of Huxley (whom I thoroughly liked and admire [*sic*], but find very disposed to be tyrannical and unjust), I lean towards Hebraism, and try to prevent the balance from on this side flying up out of sight."[6] That a reaction against the arrogance of the new antiliterary promoters of scientific education was a prime motive for Arnold's religious writings is clear in the Preface to *Literature and Dogma*; that it also inspired the careful qualifications of his treatment of Hebraism and Hellenism should not be surprising. What is too little understood is that, even in the sixties, Arnold's insistence that his Hellenic "culture" be tempered by a moralized and untheological Christianity, and that his own program be one of "moderation," is in part his implicit response to an insurgent aestheticism.[7]

A good deal of the difference between Pater's version of Hellenism and Arnold's can be attributed to Pater's more unambiguous acceptance of the results and implications of contemporary science. It is very hard to accept one reader's view that Pater was less aware than Arnold of the importance of science.[8] On the contrary, Pater welcomed evolutionary theory—both Hegelian and Darwinian—as confirming what René Wellek calls his own fundamental, Heraclitean "experience of the flux of time."[9] Although Darwin could lead him to critical and metaphysical confusion,[10] a key to Pater's work is the acceptance, from the

[6] G. W. E. Russell, *Matthew Arnold*, p. 168.

[7] See a letter to his mother enclosing Kingsley's note (*L*, II, 50–51): "With Swinburne the favourite poet of the young men at Oxford and Cambridge, Huxley pounding away at the intelligent working man, and Newdigate applauding the German Education minister for his reactionary introduction of the narrowest Protestantism into the schools, and for thus sending psalm-singing soldiers into the field who win battles —between all these there is indeed much necessity for methods of insight and moderation."

[8] Edwin Berry Burgum, "Walter Pater and the Good Life," *Sewanee Review*, XL (July 1932), 276–293.

[9] René Wellek, *A History of Modern Criticism*, Vol. IV: *The Later Nineteenth Century*, p. 396.

[10] Wellek points out (*Later Nineteenth Century*, pp. 396–397) Pater's paradoxical willingness to see "progress" in the world, along with the reign of the flux. Philip Appleman, in "Darwin, Pater, and a Crisis in Criticism" (*1859: Entering an Age of Crisis*, eds. Philip Appleman, William A. Madden, Michael Wolff, pp. 81 ff.),

beginning, of the rigorous limitations imposed by the spokesmen of post-Kantian philosophy and evolutionary science.[11] For example, in "Winckelmann" the central problem is how to create an art that preserves "the sense of freedom" (which Pater associates with "Hellenic humanism") while remaining aware that "The chief factor in the thoughts of the modern mind concerning itself is the intricacy, the universality of natural law even in the moral order" (*Ren-1*, p. 205).[12] Moreover, the Preface to the *Renaissance* announces that metaphysical questions are everywhere simply "unprofitable" (*Ren-1*, p. viii). Elsewhere in the *Renaissance*, Pater speaks of medieval misconceptions of "the place in nature both of the earth and of man" (*Ren-1*, p. 28) in the very accents Huxley adopted in the sixties.[13]

---

correctly underscores Darwin's influence on Pater and views it as leading his criticism into two antithetical positions: relativism and impressionism (the "empirical, evolutionary view of art"), and historicism ("evolution" as enabling us to give a work its full historical setting).

[11] See J. Gordon Eaker, *Walter Pater: A Study in Methods and Effects*, p. 5.

[12] Pater's strategy here—calling for an art that preserves an "as-if" sense of freedom despite modern necessitarianism—strikingly anticipates the complex argument of Arnold's "Literature and Science" (1882), in which he defends a religiously colored poetry that gives us the momentary *impression* of living in a providential universe, even while accepting without demur the naturalistic deductions of Darwin and Huxley.

[13] Pater is discussing the fact that Pico's medieval emphasis on "the dignity of human nature" is based on the equally medieval "misconception of the place in nature both of the earth and of man"—that is, the view of the earth as the center of the universe, a fixed point around which the sun and moon and stars revolve: "And in the midst of all is placed man, . . . the bond or copula of the world" (*Ren-1*, p. 28). He continues (p. 30): "That whole conception of nature is so different from our own. . . . How different from this childish dream is our own conception of nature, with its unlimited space, its innumerable suns, and the earth but a mote in a beam; how different the strange new awe and superstition with which it fills our mind!" In Thomas Henry Huxley's *Collected Essays*, see "On Improving Natural Knowledge" (1866), I, 37: "the naturalists find man to be no centre of the living world, but one amidst endless modifications of life"; "Man's Place in Nature" (1863), VII, 154: the righteous are unable "to appreciate the grandeur of the place Man occupies" now in the "visible world"; and VII, 155: evolution will provide "a reasonable ground of faith in [man's] attainment of a nobler Future," a view that is far from "diminishing our reverence and our wonder." Moreover, a "poetic" passage like the following from an essay of 1860—"Harmonious order governing eternally continuous progress—the web and woof of matter and force interweaving by slow degrees, without a broken thread, that veil that lies between us and the Infinite—that universe which alone we

This limitation to immediate experience is precisely the one accepted by Matthew Arnold, part of whose confusion in *Literature and Dogma* derives from his attempt to establish a kind of devout Christian agnosticism by a capricious "literary" method that is somehow only an extension of empirical methods of "verification." The extreme example of the marriage of aestheticism and scientific observation occurs in the Preface to the *Renaissance,* where Pater declares that the end of the "analytical" aesthetic critic is reached when he has "disengaged" "the virtue by which a picture, a landscape, a fair personality in life or in a book, produces this special impression of beauty or pleasure," and "noted it, as a chemist notes some natural element, for himself and others" (*Ren-1*, p. ix). Robert Shafer's unsympathetic remarks about Pater apply equally to Arnold: "Pater's life-long attempt was, in substance, to save and find some valid sanction for the rewards and fruits of culture on the terms imposed by scientific naturalism. His effort was, accepting to the full conclusions of the natural science of his time, still to provide a sure basis for the personal life of the individual particularly in its highest aspects." Shafer's implication, that to accept the supposedly scientific "purely empiric method" as the sole path to truth was in effect to make "culture" impossible, seems beyond dispute.[14]

What then differentiates the attitudes of Arnold and Pater toward science, and how does the difference affect their view of Hebraism and Hellenism? Arnold certainly accepted at every stage of his critical career the metaphysical enunciations of the Huxleyan dispensation. But he deplores the larger cultural consequences of the new propaganda for science, the effects on belief among the working class (a mixed re-

---

know and can know; such is the picture which science draws of the world" (II, 59)—seems to lie behind the passage on freedom and determinism in "Winckelmann": "The chief factor in the thoughts of the modern mind concerning itself is the intricacy, the universality of natural law, even in the moral order. . . . necessity . . . is a magic web woven through and through us, like that magnetic system of which modern science speaks, penetrating us with a network subtler than our subtlest nerves, yet bearing in it the central forces of the world."

[14] Robert Shafer "Walter Pater Redivivus," *The Open Court,* XXXIV (April 1920), 225, 226. Shafer ends (p. 230) with the paradox that the Paterian "sensationalist" is inevitably the "bosom-friend" of "the popularizer of natural science."

ligious and political fear) and on the content of the broadening base
of popular education. Moreover, science seemed contemptuously to
reject Arnold's assertion that a "Christian" religious consciousness was
still possible even while accepting the emerging synthesis concerning
man and the universe. Pater, by contrast, seems more at home with the
new world view from the beginning, and although he sees modern
necessitarianism as destructive of essential elements in art, he works
far more singlemindedly in his early career for a "modern" culture
that is frankly pagan after the model of Goethe in his most Hellenic
phase, a culture that does not need for its crown a specifically Christian
coloring. Even the sense of "freedom," which the modern artist must
strive to suggest in a "tragic" art, is in no special sense Christian.
Nevertheless, it is religious, in the broadest sense, and religious in a
way consciously opposed to Arnold's views. Pater's Hellenism was a
deliberate response to, and modification of, Arnold's view of the
Greeks. Pater adopts the fervor, the sensuousness, some of the implicit
sexuality, and a good deal of the anti-Christian tone of certain parts of
German Hellenism. His view of Greece is considerably more complex
than Arnold's, rather better informed, and more historically authentic.
By adding the Dionysian tradition to the Apollonian, Pater was able,
for polemical purposes, to advance his "enriched" view of Greek
religion as a conscious alternative to a played-out Christianity. Pater's
greater knowledge allowed him to challenge Arnold's occasional high
evaluation of medieval Christianity by suggesting that Greek popular
religion, undervalued by Arnold, had permanent elements of depth
and complexity which simply reappear in the Middle Ages. In the
process, Periclean Athens, which had been Arnold's supreme exem-
plum, tends to lose its uniqueness, is less detached from a complex
historical background, and is reduced in interest to a level with other
examples of high productive culture, above all the Italian Renaissance.
This is not to suggest that the attempt to integrate Christianity into some
higher synthesis—part of the nineteenth century's great attempt to
come to terms with its "medieval" past—was ever entirely absent from
Pater's successive attempts at reconciliation. In a sense Pater's religious
development, from the paganism of the mid-sixties to some approxi-

mation of historic Christianity twenty years later, seems clearer than Arnold's.

The man Pater, however, is neither simple nor easily analyzed. His deep need for synthesis is matched by a deep dualism running through his career and noticed by many readers. Ferris Greenslet speaks of "two conflicting mental dispositions" in Pater: "There was an abstracting, idealising, centripetal motive, tending to Puritanism or Pantheism in religion, counterbalanced by a more materialistic centrifugal force that found its natural religious affinities in very diverse quarters, in polytheistic Paganism, in Catholicism, or even in agnosticism."[15] Edwin Burgum found that this conflict between sensuality and a "religious" impulse had a psychological parallel in the struggle between spontaneity and control.[16] No doubt, in general the pagan impulse, "the Greek point of view," dominated: his naturalism caused Pater to define Christianity "as nearly as possible in Greek terms."[17] Certainly the Preface to the *Renaissance* proposes a life of precisely annotating sense impressions, while it disparages as unprofitable all metaphysical speculation. Pater's last work, *Plato and Platonism*, defines the Platonic dialectic in two senses—the one as a method in the search after transcendental truth, the other as a "temper," an inward-turning process of "tentative thinking and suspended judgment," valuable as maintaining receptivity to the many-sidedness of truth—and clearly opts for the second. But there is a good deal more to be said about the authenticity of Pater's Christianity and the place of religion in Pater's various attempts at synthesis. It is simply not true to say that Pater "Hellenized purely," and did not even pay lip service to Hebraism.[18]

The deeper unifying pattern of Pater's career is provided by these

[15] Ferris Greenslet, *Walter Pater*, p. 105. A. C. Benson (*Walter Pater*, pp. 11–12) speaks of "two distinct strains in Pater's mind": "a strong impulse towards transcendental philosophy, a desire to discern as far as possible the absolute principles of life and being," and "a strong attraction to precise and definite types of beauty."

[16] Burgum, "Walter Pater and the Good Life," pp. 283–284.

[17] *Ibid.* See Edward Thomas, *Walter Pater: A Critical Study*, p. 222: Pater "aspired to be what he conceived to be a Christian, a Greek with Christianity added to his Hellenism, but by instinct and natural piety he was a Greek."

[18] T. S. Eliot, *Selected Essays*, p. 441; Iain Fletcher, *Walter Pater*, p. 17.

repeated attempts at synthesis. As Graham Hough has pointed out, Pater, for all his Victorian timidity and donnishness, "had an immense appreciation of the variety and multitudinousness of the world, and what is peculiar to his creed is not its sensationalism, but its unwillingness to sacrifice any of this variety."[19] This may be his strength, but Pater's unwillingness to countenance "renunciations" may also have been the tragic flaw in his central line of endeavor. The key words of the *Renaissance* are indicative: unity, inclusiveness, many-sidedness, adjustment, and the harmony of intellect, heart, and senses. Unacceptable are system, exclusion, fanaticism. Perhaps a dream of some universal "compatibility" is the key to the writings and to the projected personality behind them. But as Hough puts it, in Pater's habitual tendency toward fusion and unity, "it is not always easy to see whether he is merely blurring outlines, or really transcending dualities in a higher synthesis."[20] The tendency is evident in such diverse matters as his preference for periods of transition when cultural forces can be pictured as moving in a dialectical advance, his vision of the accommodation of a "religious phase possible for the modern mind" to contemporary naturalism, and even his willingness to go against his own instincts in seeking out the best in the Philistine world of the Spartans.[21] The reasons for Pater's ultimate failure at synthesis and transcendence are not far to seek. Certainly his criticism conveys a far weaker sense than does Arnold's of the social function of the arts and of criticism.[22] Yet most readers today agree that Pater's aestheticism, for all its confusion of ethics and aesthetics, is essentially a special *morality*—not art for art's sake but art for the sake of a special conception of the perfected life.[23] If the crisis in this ethic can be detected, it comes, at least by the time of *Marius* in the eighties, with the realization that self-

[19] Graham Hough, *The Last Romantics*, p. 143.

[20] *Ibid.*, p. 163.

[21] Greenslet (*Walter Pater*, pp. 53–54) speaks of Pater's choice of "fluid, romantic periods of transition foreshadowing the complexity of his own time." C. M. Bowra ("Walter Pater," *Sewanee Review*, LVII [Summer 1949], 396) remarks on Pater's unexpected generosity toward the Lacedaemonians in *Plato and Platonism*.

[22] Louise Rosenblatt, *L'Idée de l'Art pour l'Art dans la Littérature Anglaise pendant la Période Victorienne*, p. 172; Fletcher, *Walter Pater*, p. 31.

[23] See Fletcher, *Walter Pater*, p. 20; Eliot, *Selected Essays*, pp. 438, 440.

cultivation is incomplete in isolation from others. This is the crisis of "sympathy" in *Marius*, involving certain "renunciations" and self-sacrifice. Marcus Aurelius, indifferent to the effect of his activities on others, stands in sharp contrast to the Christian Cornelius, who is outward-turning, superior to self-indulgence. The dilemma, obviously autobiographical in basis, is clear again in another late tale, "Apollo in Picardy," in which "Greek" indifference to pity and sympathy is the issue.[24] Put simply, Pater did not always, in Burgum's words, "remain satisfied with the natural morality of the Greeks."[25]

Perhaps Graham Hough is correct in his reading of the 1888 review of *Robert Elsmere* (*EG*, pp. 55–70) when he claims that Pater implies there can be no reconciliation, only the necessity of choice, between the "two estimates of life," the scientific and the Augustinian. The tragedy may be that Pater is finally unable to make the choice. He seems to endorse Marius' painful discovery that the newly revaluated higher morality of Cornelius is possible only on the condition of accepting Christian dogma.[26] Neither Marius nor Pater, once they had seen the inadequacy of the Greek morality of "adjustment" and "accommodation," could unambiguously make that final synthesis and exclusion, a dialectic of transcendence beyond the dialectic of the "elusive, provisional, contingent," in which, "as Lessing suggests, the search for truth is a better thing for us than its possession" (*PP*, pp. 186–187).

Matthew Arnold's own ethical crisis came earlier but in remarkably similar terms. The doctrine of criticism and culture in *Essays in Criticism* opened him to a variety of charges, especially those of hedonism, ethical self-centeredness, and indifference to the needs of the world. *Culture and Anarchy* is quite explicitly an attempt to defend culture against the charge of being "frivolous and useless," and to establish "the love of our neighbour" as in fact its "main and pre-eminent" motive (*CPW*, V, 95, 91). And the religious writings of the seventies with their emphasis on "dying to self" are unintelligible unless seen as a further strengthening of the ethical substrate of his evolving humanism. Certainly in the reassertion of his ideal of culture, after his return

[24] See Burgum, "Walter Pater," pp. 290–291.
[25] *Ibid.,* p. 290.
[26] Hough, *Last Romantics,* p. 155; see Burgum, "Walter Pater," p. 290.

to politics and literature in 1877, Arnold never again adopts quite the supremely self-confident "Greek" air of the sixties.[27] Like Pater after him, Arnold exhibits a traditional dualism in a variety of ways. Arnold and Pater remain for us figures of permanent interest and significance precisely because both are "moralists" who assign a high role to art and intelligence in modern life. The crises of their careers, their various attempts to synthesize the scarcely remediable divisions in the modern inheritance, throw light on some of the profound and often overlooked running issues of modern life. In the final accounting, neither was able to be simply Greek or Christian; instead, they are both "modern," in a sense each had endorsed.[28] Beyond the inevitably inhibiting Victorian timidity and fear of paganism, the two interrelated careers—each an example of the great "critical effort" that Arnold called for in England, almost unparalleled for fullness, sustained power, honesty, and "adequacy"—are immensely significant attempts, even in their failure, to provide a new spiritual basis for modern life which incorporates nothing less than a "comprehensive" view of the totality of man's past.

CHAPTER TWELVE   The Sources

The sources of Arnold's Hellenism in German thought from Winckelmann to Heine are complex and not easily arranged in a meaningful pattern. Certainly he, no more than Pater, shows wide knowledge of the prime original texts of German aesthetic

[27] The measure of Arnold's change of tone can be caught in "A Speech at Eton" (1879; *IEO*, pp. 409–429), which defends classical education and harmonious self-development in the words of *Culture and Anarchy*, but with a much deepened awareness of the "moral inadequacy" of both ancient and modern attempts to transform life.

[28] Burgum, "Walter Pater," p. 293. Burgum's otherwise admirable study of Pater reduces the scope and significance of his career to a mere example of Victorian spiritual palsy.

thought. The evidence of Arnold's essays, notebooks, and reading lists is scattered and fragmentary, and not until recently was it known that Arnold undertook an extensive course of philosophical readings in the mid-forties.[1] He read Victor Cousin's history of eighteenth-century thought, apparently as a guide. Immanuel Kant's *Critique of Pure Reason* appears twice in the list, along with Herder's *Metakritik*. Schelling's *Bruno* and his *Philosophy of Art* share room with Creuzer's *Symbolik und Mythologie der Alten Völker, besonders der Griechen.* Arnold read Humboldt's essay on the *Bhagavad-Gita*, which would have appealed to him on several counts. Also listed are Carlyle's *Critical and Miscellaneous Essays*, which we know Arnold read carefully.[2] But a survey of Carlyle's numerous essays on German literature reveals, not unexpectedly, that he is remarkably indifferent to the Hellenizing side of German thought. The essay on Jean Paul brings up, without referring to either Herder or Goethe or Humboldt, the idea of a harmonious comprehensive culture: "For the great law of culture is: Let each become all that he was created capable of being; expand, if possible, to his full growth"; "A harmonious development of being, the first and last object of all true culture, has been obtained."[3] In the essay on Schiller Carlyle cites a passage from the *Aesthetic Letters* on the freedom of poetry from moral and political restraints.[4] But that is nearly all.

Arnold says that he came to Goethe through his reading of Carlyle. It is known that he read *Wilhelm Meister* in Carlyle's translation (*DA*, p. 143) and that he bought Goethe's *Werke* in the mid-forties.[5] What Arnold found in Goethe at this period is too broad a speculation for the present study, but certainly in a late work like the *Wanderjahre* (1821), Goethe's "most nearly Christian work," Arnold found a

[1] Kenneth Allott, "Matthew Arnold's Reading-Lists in Three Early Diaries," *Victorian Studies,* II (March 1959), 254–266.

[2] *Ibid.*, p. 264; Kathleen Tillotson, "Matthew Arnold and Carlyle" (Warton Lecture on English Poetry), *Proceedings of the British Academy,* XLII (1956), 133–153.

[3] Thomas Carlyle, *The Works of Thomas Carlyle,* ed. H. D. Traill, XXVI, 19, 20.

[4] *Ibid.,* XXVII, 213.

[5] Allott, "Matthew Arnold's Reading-Lists," p. 257.

Goethe who, as Henry Hatfield says, had gone well beyond "the doctrinaire classicism of his middle years."[6] The emphasis on "renunciation " and service to others, even at the expense of the universal cultivation of the individual,[7] suggests Arnold's religious writings of the seventies. Above all, the Pedagogic Province (Chapters X and XI), with its "religion of Sorrow"—which was to occupy the center of Arnold's 1863 essay "Pagan and Mediaeval Religious Sentiment" and was to be the exciting cause of Pater's "Winckelmann"—presents a Goethe far from paganism. His Christianity, though it averts its gaze from "blood and wounds," is authentic enough to recognize "humility and poverty, mockery and despite, disgrace and wretchedness, suffering and death," as somehow "divine." Moreover, "the Christian religion having once appeared, cannot again vanish; having once assumed its divine shape, can be subject to no dissolution."[8] Goethe's religion of "suffering" and "renunciation" remains, to be sure, highly aesthetic, and its practice is largely elaborate play-acting; but Arnold's version of Christianity was demonstrably influenced by it.

Arnold's knowledge of the major German figures seems to have been largely derived from articles in the English and French periodicals by means of which he sustained his intellectual life, especially with regard to current Continental thought. In the mid and late sixties, the years of the Celtic lectures and *Culture and Anarchy,* there appear in the notebooks a number of suggestive references to the German Hellenist tradition. In 1866 Arnold quotes three substantial passages from the review of a life of Winckelmann in the *Revue Moderne.* Clearly Arnold, though he could not subscribe to Winckelmann's extreme anti-Christian sentiments, found congenial the emphasis on "the harmonious and free development of human nature," and on those virtues "which raise the dignity of man," since these are key ideas in the farewell lecture of 1867, where culture is said to place perfection "in the ever-increasing efficacy and in the general harmonious expansion

---

[6] Henry Hatfield, *Aesthetic Paganism in German Literature: From Winckelmann to the Death of Goethe,* p. 217.

[7] *Ibid.,* p. 224.

[8] Carlyle's translation of *Wilhelm Meister,* II, 267 (Vol. XXIV of the *Works*).

of those gifts of thought and feeling which make the peculiar dignity, wealth, and happiness of human nature" (*CPW*, V, 94).[9]

Arnold accords Lessing and Herder special honor by linking them with Abelard as "great men of culture," for having attempted to "humanise" knowledge and diffuse it "outside the clique of the cultivated and the learned" (*CPW*, V, 113). The Preface to *Merope* (1858) refers several times to "the great Lessing," "the great German critic," and to the *Hamburgische Dramaturgie* (*CPW*, I, 42 ff.). In 1863 Arnold ranks Lessing with Goethe and Voltaire as one of the three great sources of "intellectual influence" in Europe of the past century and a half and shows his acquaintance with the *Erziehung des Menschengeschlechts* (*CPW*, III, 41, 53).[10] In 1868 Arnold obviously read with considerable attention a lengthy two-part article on Lessing by Victor Cherbuliez, the French critic, in the *Revue des Deux Mondes*. Among the several ideas of interest to Arnold were the modern view of universal explication through history and the dis-

---

[9] The following three extracts appear in *NB*, pp. 41–42: "Cette âme antique, on la reconnaît chez Winkelmann dans sa joie d'être au monde, à la fois vive et mesurée, dans cette pleine confiance en soi-même et en sa propre industrie, dans son amour de la gloire, heureux du succès et pourtant si eloigné de la vanité et de la suffisance, dans cette façon de s'abandonner joyeusement à l'heure présente, sans regarder très-loin ni en avant ni en arrière, dans cette franchise abrupte et entière que met W. à confesser sans fard et sans ambages tout ce qui le concerne, conduite, sentiments et pensées."

"W. n'accepte rien qui puisse contrarier en quoi que ce soit l'harmonieux et libre développement de la nature humaine. Il dit qu'il s'occupe peu de la religion, ayant à s'occuper d'autres choses plus agréables, pour ne pas dire plus importantes."

"Ailleurs W. ne craint pas d'opposer à la doctrine et à la morale chrétienne la manière de penser et de vivre des anciens, et il donne à celle-ci l'avantage: 'Chez les anciens, dans les meilleurs temps on n'estimait que les vertus héroïques, j'entends celles qui élèvent la dignité de l'homme; celles, au contraire, dont l'exercice abaisse nos idées, n'étaient ni enseignées ni recherchées. Car l'éducation des anciens était entièrement opposée à la nôtre; celui-ci, quand elle est bonne, vise par-dessus tout à la pureté des moeurs et à la pratique des devoirs extérieurs de la religion; celle des anciens était faite pour rendre le coeur et l'esprit sensible au véritable honneur, pour accoutumer la jeunesse à une vertu mâle et magnanime qui méprisât tous les buts subalternes et la vie même, pour peu qu'une entreprise lui parût conforme à la grandeur de ses idées. Chez nous on étouffe toute noble ambition et on nourrit un orgueil hypocrite'."

[10] Lessing is praised in the Celtic lectures (*CPW*, III, 359) for his intense perception of "the incongruous and absurd."

tinction between Christianity and the accounts of the Evangelists and Apostles (*NB,* pp. 71, 75).[11]

In 1864 Arnold shows interest in Herder by copying a passage on the French background of Herder's "sentiment de la sympathie humaine," his "passion de l'humanité" (*NB,* pp. 26–27). Moreover, "Herder's Ideen" appears in the list of reading each year from 1866 to 1869 (*NB,* pp. 579, 581, 584, 586). The subject of Arnold's obvious affinity for Herder's optimistic view of the progressive movement of God through history again goes beyond the scope of the present work; but certainly the Hellenism of *Culture and Anarchy* is centrally indebted to the ideal of *Humanität* in the *Ideen* and elsewhere, an ideal of total human realization through the development of all of man's powers which Herder associated with the Greeks. Herder's ideal involved, as Hatfield explains, "the reconciliation of the ethical with the aesthetic, and the humane with the humanistic."[12] In the eighteen-sixties Arnold would not have endorsed the detachment from the Bible and Christianity implied in the phrase he quotes from Lessing, "la Bible n'est pas la religion" (*NB,* p. 75). But what would have interested Arnold, as well as Pater, was the notion advanced by both Lessing and Herder of two Christianities, medieval Christianity as opposed to a "reasonable Christianity" acceptable to the eighteenth century. Lessing explicitly opposed a barbarous, "superstitious" Christianity to a Christianity of reason.[13] Herder, less explicitly, distinguishes superstitious, medieval, "decayed" Christianty, which was fearful of the flesh and fit for the vulgar and which had no part in the great synthesis, from his own higher, humane Christianity, which is the original religion of Christ.[14] This notion is echoed in Arnold's distinction in *Literature and Dogma* between the religion of Christ and the *Aberglaube,* both popular and learned, attached to it during the benighted Christian centuries. The idea is even more emphatically used in Chapter XXI (" 'The Minor Peace of the Church' ")

[11] See also *NB,* pp. 76, 90. Arnold also read an essay on Lessing in the *North American,* in 1867 (*NB,* p. 56).

[12] Hatfield, *Aesthetic Paganism,* p. 58.

[13] *Ibid.,* p. 28.

[14] *Ibid.,* pp. 54, 59.

of Pater's *Marius*, in the distinction between the authentic "humane" Christianity of the second century and the monastic and ascetic Christianity of later times. This also seems in effect much the same distinction made in the *Greek Studies*, where the crude and earthy religion of the many is several times contrasted to the refined religious consciousness of the few, the "special souls." For Arnold at least, Herder's *Humanität* would have appealed because of its insistence on the need for beauty balanced by its deeply ethical strain. At times Arnold's Hellenism—and certainly his Hebraism—sound closer to Herder's ideal than to Goethe's.

Perhaps Arnold's rather academic Hellenism is best described as a synthesis of Herder and Goethe, mediated by Wilhelm von Humboldt. In *Culture and Anarchy*, against a reviewer who had invoked Humboldt's name in support of keeping governmental action within the strictest limits, Arnold argued:

Wilhelm von Humboldt, one of the most beautiful souls that have ever existed, used to say that one's business in life was first to perfect oneself by all the means in one's power, and secondly to try and create in the world around one an aristocracy, the most numerous that one possibly could, of talents and characters. He saw, of course, that, in the end, everything comes to this,—that the individual must act for himself, and must be perfect in himself; and he lived in a country, Germany, where people were disposed to act too little for themselves, and to rely too much on the Government. But even thus, such was his flexibility, so little was he in bondage to a mere abstract maxim, that he saw very well that for his purpose itself, of enabling the individual to stand perfect on his own foundations and to do without the State, the action of the State would for long, long years be necessary. (*CPW*, V, 161)

This notion of going beyond self-cultivation to the creation of an effective aristocracy of talents was of course a paramount goal of Arnold's mature Hellenism. He had copied out these ideas from the *Revue Germanique* as early as November 1864.[15] In the same year, he read a long

15 "Wilhelm von Humboldt—un des exemples les plus parfaits de ce besoin d'accroître sans cesse sa valeur intime et ses richesses intérieures qui fut aussi, pour un homme tel que Goethe, la préoccupation de toute la vie. Une telle disposition a pour origine quelque haute idée de la nature humaine, de sa dignité, de sa grandeur. In

earlier three-part article on Humboldt, also in the *Revue Germanique*, and thus was aware of the full scope of Humboldt's career (*NB*, p. 630). This reading is reflected in the first of the Celtic lectures (delivered in December 1865) in a passage cited above on removing the "Semitic" elements from Christianity (*CPW*, III, 301). Arnold is clearly a little uncomfortable with this "genuine Teuton," and even apologizes a little: "Humboldt's is an extreme case of Indo-Europeanism." It seems likely, however, that Humboldt confirmed the social implications of Arnold's doctrine of culture which were present to some degree even in the "Function of Criticism" where they were seen as the idea of *propagating* the best that is known and thought in the world and thereby *creating* and *establishing* a current of true and fresh ideas (*CPW*, III, 271, 282). Above all, Humboldt would have reinforced the essentially *educational* character of culture, and Arnold shows himself especially alive to Humboldt's reforming activities as Prussian Minister of Education and as the founder of the University of Berlin (*CPW*, V, 161). Arnold would have found substantially congenial the new humanism of the German schools, described in Friedrich Paulsen's words: "In the Greek ideal the new age found the image of perfection, instead of in Christianity: the image of the perfect man instead of the God who became man. . . . Hellenizing humanism is a new religion, the philologists are its priests, the universities and schools its temples."[16] Arnold was never, however, as icily detached from Christianity as was this formidable, remote "Teuton," and immediately after *Culture and Anarchy* he turned his attention to establishing his own "religion of the Bible," which would profoundly alter the Hellenic quality of his humanism.

The notebooks reveal that, almost by a reflex action, the rather self-regarding Germanic Hellenism that attracted Arnold until the mid-sixties was being superseded by an outward-turning, social, ethical, and educational doctrine involving some inevitable, if reluctantly acknowledged, straitening of the idea of self-perfection. In 1866 Arnold copied

---

Humboldt's eyes—after individual perfection the great thing to be aimed at de créer, par l'instruction, une aristocratie, la plus nombreuse possible, d'intelligences et de caractères" (*NB*, p. 26).

[16] Cited in Hatfield, *Aesthetic Paganism*, p. 210.

the following orthodox statement of German Hellenic aestheticism,
attributed to Friedrich Wolf the great philologist:

> The Greek ideal is this; a purely human education, and elevation of all
> the powers of mind and soul to a beautiful harmony of the inner and outer
> man. . . . As long as there exists in the world a generation who make this
> elevation their aim, so long they will turn to the ancients for instruction and
> encouragement in prosecuting it. The simplicity, the dignity, the grand
> comprehensive spirit of their works, will ever make them a source from
> which the human soul will draw perpetual youth. (*NB*, p. 40)

This statement, one half of the doctrine of "Sweetness and Light," is
echoed as late as 1868 in a citation from a French source on the Sophoclean model of the ideal man: "la plénitude et l'élévation du développement intellectuel, la noblesse inaltérable de la beauté virile" (*NB*,
p. 75).[17] But even within the classical context, other currents were in
motion. In 1866 Arnold cites the following: "We must sacrifice, says
Plato, all individual will to reason, to that higher nature which is incapable of being the object of selfish impulse" (*NB*, p. 40). Two
years later Arnold shows himself interested in the notion that "Les
Grâces étaient chez les Grecs le symbole de cette harmonie sociale
qu'établissent la bienveillance et la mutuelle sympathie" (*NB*, p. 81).
The religious character of this social harmony and mutual sympathy is
indicated in a quotation of the same year from Edmond Scherer, a
favorite critic of Arnold's: "L'oeuvre de notre perfectionnement est
une oeuvre collective et éternelle" (*NB*, p. 73). This is of course a
statement of the reflex side of Arnold's doctrine of "culture"—that
the individual, if his own culture is to be perfect, is obliged "to carry
others along with him in his march towards perfection, . . . to enlarge

---

[17] This quotation, and the one following it—"Sophocles chante l'humanité à l'heure
où elle se dégage des fatalités sombres et se dirige librement vers la lumière. On
trouve dans lui un mélange de vigeur et de sérénité" (*NB*, p. 75)—would also have
attracted Arnold because they strikingly echo the very phrasing of Arnold's view of
Sophocles in the Inaugural Lecture of 1857. Fullness of development, nobility, "light,"
the mixture of "vigor" and "serenity"—these are the notes Arnold stresses in his
earlier, more uncomplicated Hellenism. The poetry of Sophocles represents human
nature "in its completest and most harmonious development" in all directions; it
displays both "noble serenity" and "energy"; and all is suffused by "grace and light"
(*CPW*, I, 28).

and increase the volume of the human stream sweeping thitherward"
(*CPW*, V, 94). This evolution of ideas prepared the way for the ethical doctrine of *Literature and Dogma*. Arnold's was never a thoroughgoing "pagan" Hellenism; his demand for beauty is always balanced
by a deeply ethical view of what the Greeks can provide for both the
intellectual and moral "deliverance" of the nineteenth century. It is
significant, however, that his own ethical crisis is played out *within*
the context of what may broadly be called German Hellenism and
aestheticism and only then transferred to an explicitly Christian context.

Goethe's total impact on Arnold is very complex indeed.[18] We
know that Arnold read him continually from the forties onward;
Goethe's name appears again and again in the reading lists of the fifties.
But Arnold, whose moralized view of Goethe as "a strong tower into
which the doubter and the despairer might run and be safe" (*MxE*, p.
213) was derived from Carlyle, cites surprisingly little from Goethe
in the notebooks of the fifties, often only maxims, almost Carlylean
in tone, on the need for work and discipline. The obvious conclusion
to be drawn is that Goethe played a notably small part in the development of Arnold's Hellenism in the sixties. Admittedly, Goethe's view
of the classical culture and classical art had important effects on Arnold's literary judgments. The Preface to *Merope*, for instance, approves Goethe's idea of "repose" in Greek tragedy (*CPW*, I, 59); and
in the Homer lectures, Arnold approvingly cites, in defense of a "noble
poetry," the implicitly Promethean definition of "the noble or powerful
nature—the *bedeutendes Individuum* of Goethe" (*CPW*, I, 189).

---

[18] On Goethe's influence see James Bentley Orrick, "Matthew Arnold and Goethe,"
Publications of the English Goethe Society, N.S. IV (1928), 5–54; Charles D. Wright,
"Matthew Arnold's Response to German Culture." W. H. Bruford in *Culture and
Society in Classical Weimar, 1775–1806*, makes several glancing but suggestive references to the English scene. He is illuminating on the post- and anti-Christian character
of the German "culture" ideal, its ethical and social dimensions, its political conservatism, its parallels with Bloomsbury attitudes, and the sinister direction it later
took as a result of detachment from larger political and social realities (see pp. 2–3,
199, 395–396, 399, 401, 406 ff., 410, 423). Bruford, in "Goethe and Some Victorian
Humanists" (*Papers of the English Goethe Society*, N.S. XVIII [1949], 34–67),
mentions the influence of Goethe's "secular humanism" on several figures, including
Arnold and Pater, but concludes that his influence over Victorian England "was never
really fundamental" (p. 64).

Moreover, Arnold cites Goethe's severe view of the Homeric mood ("in our life here above ground we have . . . to enact Hell") as pre- ferable to "the tender pantheism" of Ruskin (*CPW*, I, 102). Goethe's influence on Arnold is limited by Arnold's reservations concerning his poetic achievement, which is not, in his view, "in the true grand style" (*CPW*, I, 144). Although Goethe remains a man of "strongest head and widest culture" (*CPW*, I, 14), his major poetry is not what Arnold sought in his own special critical mission: works like *Faust* and *Her- mann und Dorothea* are regularly disparaged as lacking in the Goethe- an *Architectonicè* recommended in 1853. However, Goethe's own intense Hellenism from 1785 to about 1805 and its formulation in Schiller at the same period did not directly mold Arnold's critical Hel- lenism of the sixties. Instead, Goethe's role in the shaping of Arnold's Hellenism was, I think, as the sponsor of the "complete culture and unfettered thinking" Arnold found in Goethe's Germany (*CPW*, III, 263). In the essays of 1863, it is Goethe's "profound, imperturbable naturalism," his "mind profoundly impartial and passionately aspiring after the science, not of men only, but of universal nature" (*CPW*, III, 110, 176), which provide the climate for Arnold's "great intel- lectual effort" of that and the following years. The presentation of the Hellenism of *Culture and Anarchy* is a crucial episode in a longer and sustained effort to deepen and "Christianize" the ethical and social basis of Arnold's humanism. In that effort Goethe's Hellenism, anti-Christian and focused almost exclusively on problems of art and the artist, was already irrelevant. More important to Arnold's view of the Greeks was the fact that, as the notebooks show, all during the fifties and sixties he was acquiring, in connection with works like *Merope* and the Homer lectures, a wide knowledge of ancient culture (no doubt more accurate than Goethe's could have been) through reading some of the best products of German historical and literary scholarship—though the degree to which the spirit of nineteenth-century classical studies was itself indebted to the German Hellenists is not to be disregarded.[19]

---

[19] The extravagant praise Arnold extends to Hegel, linking his name in dignity with those of Parmenides, Spinoza, and Plato (*CPW*, III, 65, 181), and the levity of the reference to "Hegel's 'Phenomenology of *Geist*'," in *Friendship's Garland* (*CPW*, V, 76), suggest that Arnold was both overawed and (British empiricist that he was

Heinrich Heine, whose name appears frequently in the reading lists from 1852 on, is a special case in the development of Arnold's Hellenism. He and Goethe figure as the great heroes of the "modern spirit." Arnold's essay on Heine remains probably the finest and most influential in English, and Heine's treatment of the Greeks, though profoundly revaluated by Arnold, provides a springboard for Arnold's first contrast of the Greek and Christian, in the seminal "Pagan and Medieval Religious Sentiment." It should also be borne in mind that not only in Pater, but in Robert Buchanan, James Thomson, Charles Algernon Swinburne, and others, Heine is repeatedly invoked in the seventies and later in the resurgence of "paganism" in England.[20] The present study should be placed within this larger cultural context, a context created and shaped to an important extent by Arnold and Pater.

---

after all) annoyed and amused by this last of the heroic system-makers. The vagueness of all references to Hegel indicates that Arnold knew only as much as he could glean from the article on Hegel in the *Biographie universelle ancienne et moderne* in 1864 (*NB*, p. 568). Certainly he displays no detailed knowledge of Hegel's historical scheme of the evolution of art which encumbers Pater's "Winckelmann,"

[20] Sol Liptzin, *The English Legend of Heinrich Heine.*

PART II

ARNOLD, PATER, AND

THE REINSTATEMENT OF MAN

CHAPTER THIRTEEN "Coleridge" and the Higher
Morality

That Pater knew Arnold's work intimately, and absorbed great amounts
of his spirit into his own writings, is
a critical commonplace. But the extraordinary extent and significance
of the influence, even at the verbal level, has never been documented.
Pater liked "The Scholar-Gipsy," which had thrown a romantic haze
over the Oxford countryside, and after he went up to Oxford in October 1858 he "eagerly" attended Arnold's lectures, enjoying the "im-
pudence" and the "onslaught of the Philistines."[1] From the beginning

---

[1] Thomas Wright, *The Life of Walter Pater,* I, 173. Although some of Pater's
letters are now available (see Lawrence G. Evans, "Some Letters of Walter Pater,"
Ph.D. dissertation, Harvard University, 1961), very few of Pater's attitudes toward
Arnold are recorded. He once, apparently in the seventies, spoke of "the six men then
living who were certain to be famous—Tennyson, Browning, Ruskin, Matthew
Arnold, Swinburne, and Rossetti," and declared that Arnold "has exercised the most
potent influence on intellectual manners" (*ibid.,* II, 23). William Sharp (*Papers
Critical and Reminiscent,* p. 203) reported that Pater showed him, around 1880, an
"original, or first copy, of the first three stanzas of [Arnold's] *Morality,*" evidently
given him by Arnold. One would very much like to know if this implies a meeting, or
at least a correspondence. Walter E. Houghton (*The Victorian Frame of Mind,
1830–1870,* pp. 14–18, 281) offers suggestive but perhaps overly polarized contrasts
between Arnold and Pater.

the influence was very deep, almost crippling at times. A first exercise, "Diaphanéitè," dated July 1864 and understandably never printed by Pater, is to a large extent a pastiche of Arnold's phrases, already subtly and characteristically twisted to new ends Pater's evocation (probably autobiographical in intention) of a special temperament, prophetic of the next generation, is a study in "perfect intellectual culture," an advocacy of coming "nearer and nearer to perfection," a call "to value everything at its eternal worth," and the establishment of an ideal of "just equipoise" in which no gift or virtue or idea "has an unmusical predominance" (*MS*, pp. 249, 248, 252). But this is only the small change of the Arnoldian rhetoric. Even more unmistakable is the reference to the "intellectual throne" (*MS*, p. 249), a phrase in "The Scholar-Gipsy" (l. 184). Arnold's definition of religion as that which "has *lighted up* morality" (*CPW*, III, 234) occurs twice, in the phrase "a mind lighted up by some spiritual ray within" and in the description of Raphael as one who was "lighted up" by the Renaissance and the Reformation, yet "yielded himself to neither" (*MS*, pp. 250, 253). But what Pater is saying, and what he implies, is by no means a carbon copy of Arnold. Pater's disturbing "sexless beauty," "a moral sexlessness, a kind of impotence, an ineffectual wholeness of nature" (*MS*, p. 253), is a world away in tone and import from the moralism and puritanism of Arnold's own ideal of wholeness.

Pater's critical career was properly inaugurated with the essay on Samuel Taylor Coleridge of January 1866. This is Pater's impressive, if not yet fully coherent, attempt to define the function of "criticism" and "culture" in modern life and to suggest the role of the "modern spirit" in shaping a mode of quasi-religious "spirituality" available to the few. Pater is clearly on the highroad to the *Renaissance*. In this full-dress rehearsal, Arnold's *Essays in Criticism* are frequently the point of departure, but everywhere there appears the reshaping pressure of a unique, emerging review of life. Despite the Arnoldian aura created by references to "Forms of intellectual and spiritual culture," "the human spirit on its way to perfection," "complete culture,"disinterestedness, and a personified "critical spirit," Pater at once announces a new frontier in the advancement of the modern spirit. He redefines Arnold's "modern spirit" as the "relative spirit," and what it is relativizing is, precisely, *morality.* "Modern thought is distinguished from ancient by its cultivation of the 'relative' spirit in place of the 'absolute.' . . . To the modern spirit nothing is or can be rightly known except relatively under conditions. . . . Hard and abstract moralities are yielding to a more exact estimate of the subtlety and complexity of our life."[2] The scope of the "critical intellect" is radically reduced to "a world of fine gradations and subtly linked conditions, shifting intricately as we ourselves change" (p. 108). The literary life of Coleridge, who is everywhere "restlessly scheming to apprehend the absolute," was "a disinterested struggle against the application of the relative spirit to moral and religious questions"; happily, Coleridge failed, for his "was a struggle against the increasing life of the mind itself" (p. 108).

If "criticism" is redefined and restricted, "culture" is even more drastically diminished from Arnold's comprehensive assessment of the modern world to the establishment of a new "higher morality of the few." The problem of the relation of religion to culture becomes that of how to retain "the religious graces" for those who "have passed out of Christianity." Pater scoffs at Coleridge's fear that in the rejection of the supernatural "the spiritual element in life will evaporate also, that we shall have to accept a life with narrow horizons, without disinterestedness, harshly cut off from the springs of life in the past." But the "narrowness," Pater retorts, is all the other way. This spiritual element in life is simply "the passion for inward perfection with its sorrows, its aspirations, its joy," and these mental states are "the delicacies of the higher morality of the few." These states are "only the permanent characteristics of the higher life," expressed by great religious spirits like Augustine and the author of the *Imitation* in the limited metaphysical and theological terms of their own culture—such ideas as "the doctrines of sin and grace, the fluctuations of the union of the soul and its unseen friend." The mental states are permanent, the intellectual framework is variable: the states exist for "those who are capable of a passion for perfection," although "that religious expression of them is no longer congruous with the culture of the age."

2 [Walter Pater], "Coleridge's Writings," *Westminster Review,* N.S. **XXIX** (January 1866), 107. Cited by page number in text throughout this chapter.

But since inwardness continues to appear only in a few forms, "culture cannot go very far before the religious graces reappear in it in a subtilized intellectual shape." For example, certain aspects of the religious character—"Longing, a chastened temper, spiritual joy"—"have an artistic worth distinct from their religious import." They are valuable, "not because they are part of man's duty or because God has commanded them, still less because they are means of obtaining a reward, but because like culture itself they are remote, refined, intense, existing only by the triumph of a few over a dead world of routine in which there is no lifting of the soul at all." Our culture, then, is incomplete, "we fail of the intellectual throne," if it is not crowned by these religious qualities of "inward longing, inward chastening, inward joy." "Religious belief, the craving for objects of belief, may be refined out of our hearts, but they must leave their sacred perfume, their spiritual sweetness, behind." The defenders of "the older and narrower forms of religious life against the claims of culture" cannot understand this "law of the highest intellectual life," but they "are often embarrassed at finding the intellectual life heated through with the very graces to which they will sacrifice it." Thus, "the modern aspirant to perfect culture" finds "in the higher class of theological writings . . . the expression of the inmost delicacies of his own life, the same yet different!" Just as the "spiritualities of the Christian life" have in the past drawn men into "the broader spiritualities" of other systems, so, many of this generation who, "through religion, have become dead to religion," find "some feature of the ancient religious life, not in a modern saint, but in a modern artist or philoshopher! For those who have passed out of Christianity, perhaps its most precious souvenir is the ideal of a transcendental disinterestedness. Where shall we look for this ideal? In Spinoza; or perhaps in Bentham or in Austin" (pp. 126–127).

I have summarized this remarkable argument at length because it is not readily available[3] and because it is the most explicit rationale for what may be called a "religious aestheticism," not only in Pater but perhaps in the English language. The whole essay breathes a total and almost contemptuous detachment from Christianity and Christian

---

[3] The theological portions that had not been reprinted were issued in Walter Pater, *Sketches and Reviews*, ed. Albert Mordell.

belief which Arnold never displayed and which Pater himself, even in the years of the Renaissance studies, never again revealed so uncompromisingly. The tone is rather openly autobiographical and this may account for Pater's reluctance to reprint it. That Arnold's concepts of criticism and culture lay behind this new "religious" reading of life is evident in references to "inward perfection," the "passion for perfection," and "disinterestedness"—all of which are themselves clearly enough derived from religious contexts—and in the reiterated allusion, in "the intellectual throne," to "The Scholar-Gipsy." But the essential relation of this argument to Arnold's thought lies in the fact that the essay is largely the logical extension of the premises of Arnold's culture. It represents the basis for Pater's search for a "sort of religious phase possible for the modern mind." For Pater perfect culture strives for the preservation of a permanent spiritual element in life; this element survives in a small number of mental states or religious graces (longing, chastening, joy) even in the absence of the objects that formerly excited these states and of the systems to which they were erroneously attached. Now freed permanently from the need for *any* metaphysical or theological rationale, these modes of consciousness can be cultivated for their own sake, no longer justified on ethical grounds (duty, love of God, rewards) but discriminated simply by the remoteness, refinement, and intensity of the states themselves. The experience of the residuary perfume and sweetness of older erroneous beliefs in this new higher morality or broader spirituality will be evoked by a wide acquaintance with the best art or philosophy or theology, and will no longer be claimed exclusively by the older narrow and untenable forms of religious life.

In this expression of Pater's early thought lies the explicit basis for the morality that readers have long detected in the *Renaissance*. Pater regards a certain kind of religious consciousness as the permanent summit of the most worthy human striving; it may be achieved without belief in a transcendent object of consciousness, indeed without any detectable object at all save certain evocative intellectual and aesthetic stimuli. Pater's essay presents a first statement of the "counsel to get all the emotional kick out of Christianity, without the bother of believing it," the basis for which T. S. Eliot attributes to a more innocent

Arnold.[4] Certainly Arnold provided the elements for Pater's confusion of religion and aesthetic experience, especially in claiming, as he was to do in *Culture and Anarchy*, that culture "goes beyond religion" (*CPW*, V, 94) in striving for "perfection" through the harmonious expansion of *all* human powers. But the passage Eliot most likely has in mind is the famous opening of "The Study of Poetry," not written until 1880. There, Arnold argues that in the collapse of creeds, dogmas, and traditions, poetry has an immense future: " 'Our religion has materialised itself in the fact, in the supposed fact; it has attached its emotion to the fact, and now the fact is failing it. But for poetry the idea is everything; the rest is a world of illusion, of divine illusion. Poetry attaches its emotion to the idea; the idea *is* the fact. The strongest part of our religion to-day is its unconscious poetry' " (*EC-2*, pp. 1–2). However, Pater had anticipated this attitude as early as the Coleridge essay, when he says, "Dogmas are precious as memorials of a class of sincere and beautiful spirits, who in a past age of humanity struggled with many tears, if not for true knowledge, yet for a noble and elevated happiness. That struggle is the substance, the dogma only the shadowy expression" (p. 129). The point is that Pater seized on the logical implications of the Arnoldian view of culture from the first, well before Arnold himself more cautiously drew out the "aesthetic" consequences of his doctrines.

What is lacking from Pater's synthesis, and what frees him from some of the hesitancies and illogicalities of Arnold's view of the relation of religion to culture, is Arnold's "strong and irrational moral prejudice."[5] For what unmistakably divides Pater from Arnold in 1866 is Pater's astonishingly unruffled aloofness in the face of the supersession of traditional morality. In the notorious Conclusion to the *Renaissance*—written as early as 1868—Pater was to shock and disturb many by the implications of his advice, "The theory, or idea, or system, which requires of us the sacrifice of any part of this experience, in consideration of some interest into which we cannot enter, or some abstract morality we have not identified with ourselves, or what is only conven-

---

[4] T. S. Eliot, *Selected Essays*, p. 434.
[5] *Ibid.*, p. 441.

tional, has no real claim upon us" (*Ren-1*, pp. 211–212). Even more explicit and systematic was the anarchic moralism of the Coleridge essay, which began with the enunciation, "Hard and abstract moralities are yielding to a more exact estimate of the subtlety and complexity of our life," and ended with a protest against "every formula less living and flexible than life itself":

> What the moralist asks is, Shall we gain or lose by surrendering human life to the relative spirit? Experience answers, that the dominant tendency of life is to turn ascertained truth into a dead letter—to make us all the phlegmatic servants of routine. The relative spirit, by dwelling constantly on the more fugitive conditions or circumstances of things, breaking through a thousand rough and brutal classifications, and giving elasticity to inflexible principles, begets an intellectual finesse, of which the ethical result is a delicate and tender justness in the criticism of human life. (pp. 131–132)[6]

This statement represents nothing less than the transference to the moral realm of the qualities Arnold had required of the critical spirit. Pater approves of *subtlety, complexity*, the *relative* spirit, *elasticity*, a *delicate* and *tender* justness in "the criticism of human life," in opposition to *hard* and *abstract* moralities, *rough* and *brutal* classifications, *inflexible* principles. In "The Function of Criticism" and "The Literary Influence of Academies," Arnold had demanded that criticism proceed by way of charm, graciousness, urbanity, felicity, and patience, that it be a thing of "quick, flexible intelligence," of "intellectual delicacy"; what he opposes is narrowness and crudeness, and his maxim is: "never to let oneself become abstract." In the Homer lectures Arnold had asked of the critic of poetry, that he should have "the finest tact, the nicest moderation, the most free, flexible, and elastic spirit imaginable; he should be indeed the 'ondoyant et divers.' the *undulating and diverse* being of Montaigne" (*CPW*, I, 174). Pater then has simply drawn out the essentially moral implications of Arnold's view of the function of art as "*a criticism of life*" (*CPW*, III,

---

[6] It may throw light on Pater's later career that, as late as 1889, both these passages were allowed to appear in the extensively revised Coleridge essay in *Appreciations*. Nevertheless, Pater said in 1882 that with much of the original Coleridge essay, "both as to matter and manner, I should now be greatly dissatisfied" (Evans, "Some Letters of Walter Pater," p. 53).

209), and asks of morality that it be no less "ondoyant et divers" than the exercise of the modern critical intellect, its guiding genius. Again, of course, all is changed in transit. Even in the two major essays on criticism, Arnold's major object is to establish "a fixed standard, an authority," outside the willful and eccentric self, much as did Coleridge himself. Certainly Arnold never wavered in his defense of an "absolute" morality. Pater's competent continuation of the "degradation of philosophy and religion, skilfully initiated by Arnold," as Eliot describes it,[7] begins full-blown in Pater's first published essay. Pater, in short, had developed the full implications of Arnold's view of religion and culture before Arnold had presented his own more cautious extensions of it in works like *Culture and Anarchy* and "The Study of Poetry."

A further decisively important theme in the rather haphazard structure of "Coleridge" demands attention. Pater initiates his extended series of confrontations and adjustments of classical culture and Christianity, in a breath-taking one-paragraph sketch of European intellectual history. His ostensible purpose is to ridicule the vanity of Coleridge's attempt to "reconcile" the conflict between reason and faith which has existed since the dawn of the Renaissance. Early Christianity had recognized the conflict, he explains, and "based its plea upon its own weakness" in the confrontation with classical culture. Christianity frankly asserted claims that had no appeal to "any genuinely human principle." Paradoxically, this was its strength: the medieval Church's appearance of having reconciled faith and philosophy was only illusory; faith triumphed only through the unnatural "worship of sorrow and weakness" on the part of the weak, who were then the whole of Europe. Far from reconciling faith and reason, the Middle Ages were simply "a strange suspension of life" for "the classical culture which is only the human reason in its most trenchant form" (pp. 114–115). As knowledge of "that pagan culture" spread again, the conflict was resumed. The two elements, faith and that which is approved "in a sincerely scientific sphere," have never since really mixed. Writers as different as John Locke and Jeremy Taylor, each with a liberal philos-

[7] Eliot, *Selected Essays*, p. 437.

ophy and a defense of orthodox belief, exhibit "a divided mind"; the inability of the two elements to fuse in a single mind reveals "their radical contrariety."

The Catholic church and humanity are two powers that divide the intellect and spirit of man. On the Catholic side is faith, rigidly logical as Ultramontanism, with a proportion of the facts of life, that is, all that is despairing in life coming naturally under its formula. On the side of humanity is all that is desirable in the world, all that is sympathetic with its laws, and succeeds through that sympathy. Doubtless, for an individual, there are a thousand intermediate shades of opinion, a thousand resting-places for the religious spirit; still, . . . fine distinctions are not for the majority; and this makes time eventually a dogmatist, working out the opposition in its most trenchant form, and fixing the horns of the dilemma; until, in the present day, we have on one side Pius IX., the true descendant of the fisherman, issuing the Encyclical, pleading the old promise against the world with a special kind of justice; and on the other side, the irresistible modern culture, which, as religious men often remind us, is only Christian accidentally. (p. 115)

Thus Pater's career begins at the low watermark of his sympathetic regard for Christianity, especially Catholic Christianity. This passage, significantly unreprinted, assumes a crudely belligerent rationalist point of view, that of an optimistic morality play in which orthodox Christianity and the "irresistible" modern spirit stand opposed in "radical contrariety." After going underground during the Middle Ages, the classical spirit, or reason, has steadily reemerged since the Renaissance, and Christianity will evidently have no place in the modern view of life. Pater's surprising hostility to any accommodation between the two "elements" is not at all characteristic of his later statements on the subject, though he will never quite give up the notion that Christianity is somehow antihuman and appeals to what is "despairing in life." Significantly, this is also Arnold's view of the history of the modern spirit and its permanent enfranchisement in the nineteenth century after sporadic appearances in ancient Greece, the Renaissance, and the Enlightenment. But despite his contempt for medieval theology, which was to rise to a crescendo in *St. Paul and Protestantism* and *Literature and Dogma,* Arnold speaks everywhere in the early essays with great sympathy for actual medieval religious life and repeatedly shows his interest in the "fascinating Middle Age." Indeed, Pater's mention of "the worship of sorrow and weakness" may be a first reference to Arnold's "Pagan and Medieval Religious Sentiment," in which Arnold defends medieval Christianity against Heine's attacks. Certainly, in the following year Arnold's essay was to lie at the center of Pater's next venture in criticism. At the very least, Pater's *magna instauratio* displays a "paganism" matching that of Heine.

The very last words of "Coleridge," however, show Pater struggling for a more complex view of the modern situation. He declares Coleridge to be "the perfect flower of the romantic type":

More than Childe Harold, more than Werther, more than René, Coleridge, by what he did, what he was, and what he failed to do, represents that inexhaustible discontent, languor, and home-sickness, the chords of which ring all through our modern literature. Criticism may still discuss the claims of classical and romantic art, or literature, or sentiment; and perhaps one day we may come to forget the horizon, with full knowledge to be content with what is here and now; and that is the essence of classical feeling. But by us of the present moment, by us for whom the Greek spirit, with its engaging naturalness, simple, chastened, debonair, . . . is itself the Sangraal of an endless pilgrimage, Coleridge, with his passion for the absolute, for something fixed where all is moving, his faintness, his broken memory, his intellectual disquiet, may still be ranked among the interpreters of one of the constituent elements of our life. (p. 132)

In itself, the passage simply reflects a commonplace of German aestheticism—for example, Schiller's contrast of "naive" (classical) and "sentimental" (medieval and romantic) literature, *both* of which modern man needs for totality and harmony.[8] For the purposes of this study, this statement suggests that Pater, even in 1866, saw that "the Greek spirit" was not to have everything its own way in the coming years.

[8] Henry Hatfield, *Aesthetic Paganism in German Literature: From Winckelmann to the Death of Goethe*, p. 140; Humphrey Trevelyan, *Goethe and the Greeks*, p. 200.

CHAPTER FOURTEEN   "Winckelmann" and Pagan
Religious Sentiment

The union of the Greek and the romantic spirits is the central clue to
Pater's important essay on Winckel-
mann, published a year later. If not always fully coherent, the essay
remains a remarkable display of knowledge and judgment by a man
of twenty-seven. It first established the Paterian view of life and
stated with some subtlety the complex of issues put under a harsher
light in "Coleridge." The dialectic of "Winckelmann" is so complex
that some of its central focus and its polemical matrix seem to have
escaped detection. "Wincklemann" asks whether there is a "Hellenism" possible in the modern world and seeks to establish the relation
of such a "Hellenism" to medieval Christianity, the romantic spirit,
and nineteenth-century science. In answering, Pater carefully selects
certain aspects of Hegel's theory and history of the arts, in order to
define a special mode and morality of existence possible to a small
number of exceptional souls. What has not been seen is that Pater
so shapes the course of his argument as to make it a rejection and correction of Matthew Arnold's views of Christian and classical culture.

The presence of the Arnold of *Essays in Criticism* is very marked
in a number of ways. There is, first of all, in the 1867 essay a paragraph, never reprinted, mentioning "Maurice de Guérin's 'Centaure,'
now so well known to English readers through Mr. Arnold's essay."[1]
Moreover, the lofty judicial impartiality of Arnold's "criticism" sets
the tone of Pater's essay: Pater's "at the bar of the highest criticism"
(*Ren-1*, p. 157) has the very accent of Arnold's "at the tribunal of
literary criticism" (*CPW*, III, 54). Pater, speaking of the "aim of a
right criticism" (*Ren-1*, p. 200), is the echo of Arnold defining "criticism, real criticism" (*CPW*, III, 268). Especially Arnoldian is the

[1] Walter Pater, "Winckelmann," *Westminster Review*, N.S. XXXI (January
1867), 105.

personification of criticism. Arnold's criticism that "may and must remind it [Protestantism]" or that "must maintain its independence" is also Pater's active protagonist: "criticism can reject neither, because . . ." or "criticism entertains consideration of him . . ." (*CPW*, pp. 281, 280; *Ren-1*, pp. 158, 200). But Pater's essay is most centrally preoccupied with Arnold because it sets out to recast the balance of Greek, Christian, and modern established in Arnold's "Pagan and Medieval Religious Sentiment" (1864; *CPW*, III, 212–231). Arnold's essay is directly alluded to in Pater's description of the Renaissance as a return to "the life of the senses and the understanding," in his reference to the medieval "worship of sorrow," and in his twice appealing to "the imaginative intellect," which turns out to be the double of the "imaginative reason," the dialectical culmination of Arnold's essay.

The dialectical structure of Arnold's essay, which Pater very likely heard on its delivery at Oxford in March 1864, is very subtle, and the neat juxtapositions and oppositions, followed by a brilliant and provocative conclusion deftly tying up complex materials in a simple phrase, make it the natural focus that it became in Pater's thought for some years. It begins with the apparently academic topic, to give "a near, distinct sense of the real difference in spirit and sentiment between paganism and Christianity, and of the natural effect of this difference upon people in general"; actually the question becomes the far less disinterested one of what the elements of "the modern spirit's life" are—precisely the question Pater was to ask in "Winckelmann." Arnold opens with a surprisingly long section in praise of the "wide-embracing" quality of the Catholic Church of history, if not "the Church of the future," then "indisputably the Church of the past, . . . the Church of the multitude." This religious appeal to the multitude becomes the essay's criterion of religious authenticity—that is, until the great bravura solution of the ending. Prepared by this long, even affectionate praise of the medieval spirit, the reader is not surprised that the bulk of the essay is concerned to award the prize to Christianity rather than to paganism. Arnold's "representative religious poem of paganism," the Fifteenth Idyll of Theocritus, despite "a certain grace and beauty," shows none of the religious emotion that a symbolic treatment of the Adonis story would reveal and has nothing that is elevating, consoling, or "in our sense of the word religious." The hymn to Adonis is exactly adapted to "the tone and temper of a gay and pleasure-loving multitude: "The ideal, cheerful, sensuous, pagan life is not sick or sorry." But "by the very intensity and un-remittingness of its appeal to the senses and the understanding, by its stimulating a single side of us too absolutely," this pagan life finally fatigues and revolts us.

By neat antithesis, St. Francis is seen to have fitted religion for pop-ular use, consoling men through his marriage with poverty: "Poverty and suffering are the condition of the people, the multitude." Men naturally take pleasure in the senses, but medieval Christianity offered a refuge from misery in man's "heart and imagination." Theocritus' hymn "takes the world by its outward, sensible side"; St. Francis' Canticle, "by its inward, symbolical side." The first admits only the pleasure-giving; "the second admits the whole world, . . . but all trans-figured by the power of a spiritual emotion, all brought under a law of supersensual love, having its seat in the soul." At this moment, Christianity is clearly a more powerful religious force than paganism. But the antithesis has not yet been worked out to its logical end. For if the life of Pompeii was an extreme of sensualism, St. Francis' asceti-cism was the extreme of spiritualism. "Human nature is neither all senses and understanding nor all heart and imagination." The Renais-sance is then described as a return to this "pagan spirit," to the life of the senses and the understanding. The Reformation, in turn, was like St. Francis' revival in being "a reaction of the moral and spiritual sense against the carnal and pagan sense." But the "grand reaction" against spiritualism and the return to the senses and understanding, came with the eighteenth century. Arnold now turns to Heine, as a champion of the new paganism, who divided the whole world into "barbarians and Greeks." Arnold quotes from a passage of *The History of Religion and Philosophy in Germany* attacking the "fever" and "over-tension" and melancholy asceticism of the Middle Ages and looking to the reign of the "religion of pleasure" in which "the body and soul shall have made their peace together." In "the old, ideal, limited, pagan world," which was never sick or sorry, answers Arnold, reflecting a knowledge of German aesthetics, this ideal may have been possible; but in "the new, real, immense, post-pagan world" when "the shock of accident is unceasing, the serenity of existence is perpetually troubled," not even Heine can live the pagan ideal. This is proved by a grotesque passage of Heine's written on his deathbed, entirely lacking in "the clear, positive, happy, pagan character"; the "religion of pleasure" is thus a failure as "a comfort for the mass of mankind, under the pressure of calamity, to live by." The strength of the religion of sorrow is that it provides "a stay for the mass of mankind, whose lives are full of hardship." Above all, it actually conveys more *joy* than the pagan religious sentiment, "actual enjoyment of the world." Medieval Christianity, far from being characterized by gloom and austerities, drew much greater delight from the natural world than paganism did: gladness, not sorrow, made the fortune of Christianity, "not its assigning the spiritual world to Christ, and the material world to the devil, but its drawing from the spiritual world a source of joy so abundant that it ran over upon the natural world and transfigured it."

If the essay had ended here, the original problem, a contrast of two religious attitudes, would have been worked out, and Christianity would be the victor; but the dialectic would have been incomplete. In a sudden reversion to an earlier statement of opposite deficiencies in the two religious spirits, Arnold resolves the problem with a stroke: "the main element of the modern spirit's life is neither the senses and understanding, nor the heart and imagination; it is the imaginative reason." In Greece from 530 to 430 B. C., the Greece of Simonides, Pindar, Aeschylus, and Sophocles, Arnold claims that poetry made "the noblest, the most successful effort she has ever made as the priestess of the imaginative reason, of the element by which the modern spirit, if it would live right, has chiefly to live." Arnold protects himself by suggesting that the effort was not perfect, that even in Pindar's time the fatal movement toward Pompeii was implicit. Moreover, Greece may not have provided poets with the necessary "fulness of varied experience." "Perhaps in Sophocles the thinking-power a little overbalances the religious sense, as in Dante the religious sense overbalances the thinking power." Arnold has obviously abandoned his earlier criterion, the "consoling" power of a religion *for the multitude.*

The problem of the creation of an "adequate" modern poetry, which occupied Arnold from the Preface of 1853 onward, is now his real concern. The Greek poets from Pindar to Sophocles are not to be blindly imitated, "But no other poets so well show to the poetry of the present day the way it must take; no other poets have lived so much by the imaginative reason; no other poets have made their work so well balanced; no other poets, who have so well satisfied the thinking-power, have so well satisfied the religious sense." And in a startling reversal of his previous tender regard for Christianity, Arnold finishes by commenting on a passage of the Oedipus Rex, "Let St. Francis,—nay, or Luther either,—beat that!"

The attempt in "Pagan and Mediaeval Religious Sentiment" to suggest the place of the religious spirit in modern life is Arnold's most ambitious historical effort before his account of Hebraism and Hellenism in 1868. That it both stimulated and nettled Pater is shown in the numerous allusions to it in the Renaissance studies and later. What is at stake is Arnold's and Pater's differentiated readings of the needs of the modern spirit, and of the "religious" quality of that new consciousness. In substance, Pater accepts Arnold's reading of history and his ideal of "imaginative reason": what he cannot swallow is Arnold's high (if qualified) praise of medieval Christianity, its having "elements" to contribute to the modern synthesis, its "joyful" character. In the sixties Pater fundamentally accepted Heine's, not Arnold's, view of medieval religion: ascetic Christianity *had* created the fictitious and morbid quarrel between the body and soul. Arnold's 1864 essay becomes the background for a surprising number of historical judgments in Pater's career.

Pater's Winckelmann essay is so centrally a response to Arnold's "Pagan and Mediaeval Religious Sentiment" that, after the opening pages in review of Winckelmann's career, the very structure of his argument parallels Arnold's. By rejecting the uniqueness and value of the medieval religion of sorrow, by qualifying Arnold's views on the alleged superficiality of Greek popular religion, and finally by proposing a version of Arnold's Hellenic solution in a larger historical perspective, Pater consciously sets out to readjust the relations among the major factors in Arnold's own complex equation. The opening section is devoted to Winckelmann's interpretation of "the Hellenic spirit." First, he experiences the freedom of the imagination which the Renaissance itself felt. "How facile and direct," this Renaissance sentiment is made to say, using Arnold's phrase, "is this life of the senses and understanding when once we have apprehended it! This is the more liberal life we have been seeking so long, so near to us all the while. How mistaken and roundabout have been our efforts to reach it by mystic passion and religious reverie; how they have deflowered the flesh; how little they have emancipated us! . . . the lost proportions of life right themselves" (*Ren-1,* pp. 153–154). The antagonism of Hellenism and medievalism is thus at once established as the essential crux of Pater's study and, though with a new evaluation, is put very much in Arnold's terms. The viewpoint, verbally and philosophically, is frankly that of Heine as given in Arnold's essay. Pater maintains that Winckelmann's perfection is a narrow one and that it cannot compare with the "elasticity, wholeness, [and] intellectual integrity" of Goethe, "with his universal culture." But Goethe learned from Winckelmann the "integrity" of this intense sort of perfection for which Winckelmann was willing to cast away from himself other interests, religious, moral, political.[2] This is a conflict of ideals—between a "complete" and a "selective" culture— which will persist in Pater until *Marius.* "There have been," says Pater, "instances of culture developed by every high motive in turn, and yet intense at every point; and the aim of our culture should be to attain not only as intense but as complete a life as possible. But often the higher life is only possible at all on condition of a selection of that in which one's motive is native and strong; and this selection involves the renunciation of a crown reserved for others" (*Ren-1,* pp. 157–

[2] At this point (*Ren-1,* p. 157) Pater discusses Winckelmann's conversion: "Casting the dust of Protestantism off his feet—Protestantism which at best had been one of the *ennuis* of his youth—he might reflect that while Rome had reconciled itself to the Renaissance, the Protestant principle in art had cut off Germany from the supreme tradition of beauty." This seems to reflect Arnold's discussion (*CPW,* III, 226) of the Reformation as "a reaction of the moral and spiritual sense against the carnal and pagan sense; it was a religious revival like St. Francis's, but this time against the Church of Rome, not within her; for the carnal and pagan sense had now, in the government of the Church of Rome itself, its prime representative."

158). In 1867 it awaits a temporary solution in the final pages of the essay.

The argument proper begins with Pater's surprisingly Arnoldian (and Newmanesque) discussion of "the classical tradition, the orthodoxy of taste." This Hellenic tradition provides the unity of Western culture, and its authority is proved not only in Winckelmann's life but in the general history of culture:

The spiritual forces of the past, which have prompted and informed the culture of a succeeding age, live, indeed, within that culture, but with an absorbed, underground life. The Hellenic element alone has not been so absorbed or content with this underground life; from time to time it has started to the surface; culture has been drawn back to its sources to be clarified and corrected. Hellenism is not merely an element in our intellectual life; it is a conscious tradition in it. (*Ren-1*, p. 169)[3]

This is the "element of permanence, a standard of taste" in art, which Pater will later subordinate more to the special "conditions of time and place" which he here deprecates (*Ren-1*, pp. 169–170). He reminds us that "this standard of artistic orthodoxy" arose in Greece "at a definite historical period"—the century from 530 to 430 B. C. which Arnold had selected. Pater undertakes to explain the conditions under which this standard arose. "Greek art," he begins, "when we first catch sight of it, is entangled with Greek religion" (*Ren-1*, p. 170). The relation of art to religion is the subject of Pater's essay as it was of Arnold's. Pater's major purpose, now, is to attack medieval Christianity and its influence upon art; this he does in two stages. First, he redefines Greek religion anthropologically by asserting a ritual basis common to *all* religions, including those of Greece and the Middle Ages; through the special conditions of Greek life, its religion was

---

[3] This passage seems to follow rather closely, in tone and language, a passage in Arnold's Preface to *Merope* concerning the "classical school": "Greek art—the antique —classical beauty—a nameless hope and interest attaches, I can often see, to these words, even in the minds of those who have been brought up among the productions of the romantic school. . . . So immortal, so indestructible is the power of true beauty, of consummate form: it may be submerged, but the tradition of it survives: nations arise which know it not, which hardly believe in the report of it; but they, too, are haunted with an indefinable interest in its name, with an inexplicable curiosity as to its nature" (*CPW*, I, 38–39).

able to give rise to a high art, as medieval Christianity was not; as a result, medieval Christianity loses any unique religious or artistic claims it might seem to have upon us. Second, retaining the production of art as his criterion, Pater adopts enough of Hegel's scheme of art history to explain why the medieval conception of life prohibited the use of an independent tradition in art and was in fact the enemy of the artist. Using Winckelmann as a model, Pater focuses upon the conditions favorable to the life of the artist and to the "artistically" conceived life in a broader sense.

Pater's first strategy is to challenge the familiar academic notion of Greek religion as "gay and graceful," as "the religion of art and beauty," of Zeus and Athena, and of Homer, and to provide in effect a rich prehistory for what Arnold was soon to call the Greece of "grace and serenity" (*CPW*, V, 125). This customary view is partial because it fixes on "the sharp bright edge of high Hellenic culture, but loses sight of the sombre world across which it strikes." Relying on Hermann's *Gottesdienstliche Alterthümer der Griechen*, he distinguishes between a ritualistic system and a cycle of poetic conceptions in Greek religion. At the base of *all* religions is an ineradicable "universal pagan sentiment, . . . which existed before the Greek religion, and has lingered far onward into the Christian world" and which takes account of the "sadness" of the mind when it wanders from the here and now. This eternal, indestructible pagan basis of all religions fixes itself in ritual: "It is the anodyne which the religious principle, like one administering opiates to the incurable, has added to the law which makes life sombre for the vast majority of mankind" (*Ren-1*, pp. 172–173). (This is in effect to give an unpleasant twist to Arnold's favorable conception of religion as a "refuge" and "consolation" for the misery and suffering that are "the condition of . . . the immense majority of mankind"; *CPW*, III, 223.) Other sources—with the Greeks, mythology—add more definite religious ideas to the "unprogressive ritual element." The cult, the religious observance, remains fixed; the myth, the religious conception, is fluid with the freedom of the intellect. This religious mythology is itself pagan and has "the pagan sadness": "It does not at once and for the majority become the higher Hellenic religion" (*Ren-1*, p. 174). This primeval pagan sentiment, "against which the higher Hellenic culture is in relief," is found not only in the common world of Greek religion but also in Christian countries "least adulterated by modern ideas." In Catholic Bavaria, as well as in the common world of ancient Greece, where moral and theological ideas imperfectly adjust to the permanent ritual basis with its unknown origin and half understood meaning, religious life has its popular "worship of sorrow, . . . its mournful mysteries" (*Ren-1,* p. 175).

The supreme Hellenic culture is a sharp edge of light across this gloom. The Dorian cult of Apollo, rational, chastened, debonair, with his unbroken daylight, always opposed to the sad Chthonian divinities, is the aspiring element, by force and spring of which Greek religion sublimes itself. . . . Out of Greek religion under happy conditions arises Greek art, *das Einzige, das Unerwartete,* to minister to human culture. The claim of Greek religion is that it was able to transform itself into an artistic ideal. (*Ren-1,* pp. 175–176)

The polemical force of this line of argument should now be evident. By insisting, on the authority of "science," that the "anodyne" element is common to *all* religions, Pater implies that the primeval Greek religion is as satisfactory as the medieval "religion of sorrow." Above all, it is Greek religion that has the unique claim upon us, in its having transformed itself into an artistic ideal.

For this second stage of his argument, Pater borrows just enough of Hegel to attack medieval art and to establish his own "sensuous" view of life. The polemical intention becomes clear as Pater informs us that the thoughts of the Greeks about themselves and their relations to the world were readily turned into "an object for the senses": This is "the main distinction between Greek art and the mystical art of the Christian middle age, which is always struggling to express thoughts beyond itself" (*Ren-1,* p. 176).[4] He explains the distinction

---

[4] These words are first used in 1873; the 1867 version (Walter Pater, "Winckelmann," p. 94) attributes directly to Hegel the concept of the "ideal" as "the idea turned into an object of sense." Pater then applies this standard to art: does the work "express in terms of sense . . . man's knowledge about himself and his relation to the world?" The Hegelian origins of many of the ideas in "Winckelmann," and thus of the Hegelian basis of Pater's view of life and art, is obscured as Hegel's name is

by comparing two actual art works. Just as Arnold had chosen a "representative religious poem of paganism," Pater selects a "characteristic work of the middle age," Fra Angelico's "Coronation of the Virgin." His object is to castigate the "exaggerated inwardness" of medieval art: what is outward and sensible in Angelico's work "is only the symbol or type of an inexpressible world to which he wishes to direct the thoughts" (*Ren-1*, p. 177). But a work of Greek art, the Venus de Milo, is "in no sense a symbol, a suggestion of anything beyond it own victorious fairness. The mind begins and ends with the finite image, yet loses no part of the spiritual motive. That motive is not lightly and loosely attached to the sensuous form, as the meaning to the allegory, but saturates and is identical with it" (*Ren-1*, p. 178). Here Pater echoes the Hegelian "concrete universal," with its identification of "motive" and "sensuous form"; and in this passage appears the proximate source of Pater's lifelong interest in the artistic unity of form and matter in the art work.

The Greek mind, Pater explains, was fortunate in having paused at a certain limited stage of self-reflectiveness: "it has not yet become too inward; the mind has not begun to boast of its independence of the flesh; the spirit has not yet absorbed everything with its emotions, nor reflected its own colour everywhere." Self-reflection itself will end eventually, says Pater in a fervor of anti-Platonism, "in a defiance of form, of all that is outward, in an exaggerated idealism. But that end is still distant; it has not yet plunged into the depths of Christian mysticism" (*Ren-1*, pp. 178–179). The rhetorical force of this passage is

---

progressively eliminated from revisions of the essay between 1867 and the third edition of the *Renaissance* in 1888. Germain d'Hangest (*Walter Pater: l'Homme et l'Oeuvre*, I, 348 n and 352–353 n) points out that, although Pater followed Hegel in asserting the "nostalgic dream" of an ideal Greece, the two men differ radically on the ultimate nature of art. Pater in effect identifies the sensible and the spiritual, whereas in Hegel the two spheres confront each other. Art for Hegel is only a partial reconciliation and will give way to the abstractions of pure thought; for Pater, in obvious contrast, art is a "mystical absolute" and will not undergo a Hegelian obsolescence. This, I suggest, explains what would otherwise be an inexplicable change of tone less than two years later, when Pater declares: "What we have to do is to be for ever curiously testing new opinions and courting new impressions, never acquiescing in a facile orthodoxy of Comte or of Hegel, or of our own" (*Ren-1*, p. 211).

unusually strong for Pater; it not only provides the aesthetic grounds of his anti-Christian sentiment at this period but also suggests the personal force behind his rejection of Christianity. This ideal Greek art, in which thought does not outstrip sensuous embodiment, comes as the product of two conditions: first, the "pause" in self-reflectiveness, and second, the Greek emphasis on physical beauty, especially in the human form (*Ren-1,* pp. 179 ff.). One should not regret that this "unperplexed youth of humanity" passed into a "mournful maturity"; for after the medieval death of the senses, great joy was in store for those who found the ideal still alive.[5] Following Hegel's classification, Pater places sculpture at the center as the supreme expression of "the Greek spirit, the humanistic spirit," between architecture, which is lacking in self-awareness, and painting, music, and poetry ("the special arts of the romantic and modern ages"), which are excessively "self-analytical." Sculpture deals most exclusively with the human form, which is somehow also "pure form," and in this way becomes "a perfect medium of expression for one peculiar motive of the imaginative intellect" (*Ren-1,* p. 184). The phrase "imaginative intellect" points in the direction of a fusion of the sensuous and the "ideal"—precisely the Hegelian "concrete universal." Surely it also suggests the "imaginative reason" by which Arnold attempted to synthesize the senses and the understanding, and the heart and the imagination—or in a different and equally problematic formula, the thinking power and the religious sense. At any rate, Pater's "supreme Hellenic culture," with its "blitheness or repose" and "generality or breadth," involves the *choice* of the "imaginative intellect" as it refracts, selects, transforms, and recombines images (*Ren-1,* p. 186).

Significantly, the qualities that Winckelmann's criticism discerned in Greek sculpture are transferred to Winckelmann himself, who then

---

[5] This is my reading of this rather oblique passage (*Ren-1,* pp. 181–182): "The worshipper was to recommend himself to the gods by becoming fleet and serpentining, and white and red, like them. . . . That is the form in which one age of the world chose 'the better part'—a perfect world, if our gods could have seemed for ever only fleet and serpentining, and white and red—not white and red as in Francia's 'Golgotha.' Let us not say, would that unperplexed youth of humanity, seeing itself and satisfied, had never passed into a mournful maturity; for already the deep joy was in store for the spirit of finding the ideal of that youth still red with life in its grave."

becomes the supreme representative of a special kind of temperament and character. Form in the Hellenic ideal has a "central impassivity," a "depth and repose": the motion in Greek sculpture is "ever kept in reserve," is "very seldom committed to any definite action"; the "colourless unclassified purity of life, with its blending and interpenetration of intellectual, spiritual, and physical elements," is "the highest expression of that indifference which is beyond all that is relative or partial," an indifference rejecting "any one-sided experience"; and finally, Greek art tends even to merge distinctions of sex (*Ren-1*, pp. 189–192). Winckelmann's temperament is declared to possess the same characteristics. In the "well-rounded unity of his life," he is undisturbed by political, moral, and religious interests alien to his nature. In morals as in criticism, "he enunciates no formal principles, always hard and one-sided" (*Ren-1*, pp. 193–194). Never "onesidedly self-analytical," Winckelmann displayed (in phrases repeated from "Diaphanéitè")[6] "a moral sexlessness, a kind of impotence, an ineffectual wholeness of nature." The serenity of this temperament is shown in Winckelmann's handling the sensuous side of Greek art in the pagan manner, with no sense of "want, or corruption, or shame" (*Ren-1*, p. 194). Shifting back to the production of arts, Pater declares this to be possible because supreme works of art remove some of the "turbid fever" of the senses; for the artist "has gradually sunk his intellectual and spiritual ideas in sensuous form," until, "more and more immersed in sense," it alone has interest for him (*Ren-1*, p. 195). This extraordinary set of qualities, which somehow inheres in *artists*, in *art works*, and in the *life* of the supreme "Hellenic" critic, and which is a development of the autobiographically tinged portrait of the special "nature" in "Diaphanéitè," is then made the occasion for an unexpected fling at the Christian attitude toward art:

How could such an one ever again endure the greyness of the ideal or spiritual world? The spiritualist is satisfied in seeing the sensuous elements escape from his conceptions; his interest grows, as the dyed garment bleaches in the keener air. But the artist steeps his thought again and again into the

[6]Francis X. Roellinger ("Intimations of Winckelmann in Pater's Diaphanéitè," *English Language Notes*, II [June 1965], 277–282) shows that important portions of the earlier essay were carried over, almost verbatim, into "Winckelmann."

fire of colour. To the Greek this immersion in the sensuous was indifferent. Greek sensuousness, therefore, does not fever the blood; it is shameless and childlike. But Christianity, with its uncompromising idealism, discrediting the slightest touch of sense, has lighted up for the artistic life, with its inevitable sensuousness a background of flame. . . . It is hard to pursue that life without something of conscious disavowal of a spiritual world; and this imparts to genuine artistic interests a kind of intoxication. From this intoxication Winckelmann is free; he fingers those pagan marbles with unsinged hands, with no sense of shame or loss. That is to deal with the sensuous side of art in the pagan manner. (*Ren-1,* pp. 195–196)

Pater, perhaps more from fidelity to the Hegelian scheme than from personal inclination, immediately sets about countering any regret that man should have passed beyond the Hellenic ideal, "in which man is at unity with himself, with his physical nature, with the outward world," to attempt a perfection "that makes the blood turbid, and frets the flesh, and discredits the actual world about us" (*Ren-1,* p. 196). This statement exactly matches the description of the "spiritual-ist" Christian world for which Pater has several times expressed disapproval. What makes it possible for him to justify this later "perfection," obviously, is the fact that it is realized best *within* the history of Greece. That is, in Greek tragedy there occurs the note of conflict which saves man from the ennui of perfection and finally provides "a broader and profounder music." What Pater seizes upon, even in Hegel's schematic view, is the "dignity" within conflict which tragedy displays and the "joy," "a blithe and steady poise," which the Greek spirit was able to win even from discouragements (*Ren-1,* pp. 196–197).[7]

---

[7] Pater must have known that Arnold shared this by no means original view of tragedy. See the Preface of 1853 (*CPW,* I, 2): "In presence of the most tragic circumstances, represented in a work of art, the feeling of enjoyment, as is well known, may still subsist; the representation of the most utter calamity, of the liveliest anguish, is not sufficient to destroy it; the more tragic the situation, the deeper becomes the enjoyment; and the situation is more tragic in proportion as it becomes more terrible." In the Preface to *Merope,* Arnold declares (*CPW,* I, 58–59) that Greek tragedy provides "a lofty sense of the mastery of the human spirit over its own stormiest agitations; and this, again, conducts us to a state of feeling which it is the highest aim of

As Pater notes, Winckelmann did not penetrate into that later stage of Greek achievement. Pater's rhetoric here becomes very difficult to penetrate. The elements of his attitude are complex: clearly he feels a temperamental affinity for Winckelmann's rather immobile "sculpturesque" classicism, even for its sexual ambiguities; moreover, he had repeatedly expressed contempt for Christian "spiritualism" as hostile to art; but, finally, the "progressive" Hegelian standpoint, not to speak of Goethe's example, drove him to acknowledge the *necessity* of a "turbid" and even a "grotesque" art—and this in turn forced an accommodation not only with the romantic temperament, but, more reluctantly, with its historical prototype, the "spectral" Middle Ages. Pater admits that Winckelmann's supreme insight into "the typical unity and repose of the sculpturesque" blinded him to that bolder art "which deals confidently and serenely with life, conflict, evil. Living in a world of exquisite but abstract and colourless form, he could hardly have conceived of the subtle and penetrative, but somewhat grotesque art of the modern world" (*Ren-1*, p. 197). Winckelmann inevitably failed to see what Hegel detected, that there is "even a sort of preparation for the romantic temper within the limits of the Greek ideal itself."

For Greek religion has not merely its mournful mysteries of Adonis, of Hyacinthus, of Ceres, but it is conscious also of the fall of earlier divine dynasties. . . . Around the feet of that tranquil Olympian family still crowd the weary shadows of an earlier, more formless, divine world. Even their still minds are troubled with thoughts of a limit to duration, of inevitable decay, of dispossession. Again, the supreme and colourless abstraction of those divine forms, which is the secret of their repose, is also a premonition of the fleshless consumptive refinements of the pale mediaeval artists. That high indifference to the outward, that impassivity, has already a touch of the corpse in it; we see already Angelico and the 'Master of the Passion' in the artistic future. The crushing of the sensuous, the shutting of the door upon it, the flesh-outstripping interest, is already traceable. Those ab-

---

tragedy to produce, to *a sentiment of sublime acquiescence in the course of fate, and in the dispensations of human life."* "This sentiment of acquiescence is, no doubt, a sentiment of *repose."*

stracted gods . . . seem already to feel that bleak air in which, like Helen of Troy herself, they wander as the spectres of the middle age. (*Ren-1,* pp. 197–198)

Pater's uneasiness with romantic art, but far more with Christian art and asceticism, is here very marked. The admired impassivity and indifference of Winckelmann's Greek gods, which Pater found so temperamentally congenial, is, by a cruel paradox that Pater is honest enough to confess, akin to the art-destroying asceticism of the Middle Ages.

In a paragraph not reprinted after 1867, including the mention of Arnold's essay on Maurice de Guérin cited above, Pater goes on: "In this way there is imported into Hellenism something not plastic, not sculpturesque. . . . So some of the most romantic motives of modern poetry have been borrowed from the Greek." For example, in the tale of the Centaur, Guérin "found a vehicle for all that romantic longing which the modern temper has inherited from mediaeval asceticism."[8] Pater seems caught in a certain logical dilemma. Evidently, he has seized on the notion of a double tradition in Greek religion and Greek art partly in order to disprove the uniqueness of the Christian "religion of sorrow"; moreover, the dream of a perfect Greece in the Hegelian history and theory of art provided authority for the dismissal of a "spiritualist" Christian art. But Hegel's theory of tragedy and of a progressive art and Pater's own admirable sense of the richness of modern literature forced Pater to legitimatize and emphasize the counter tradition and thus to affirm the medieval ancestry of romantic art. The "romantic element" in Greek art had furthered, though it did not cause, the decay of Hellenic art: "but it shows how delicate, how rare were the conditions under which the Hellenic ideal existed."[9] The question then becomes: "Did Christianity quicken that decline?" Pater's basic viewpoint is clear: "The worship of sorrow, the crucifixion of the senses, the expectation of the end of the world, are not in themselves principles of artistic rejuvenescence." He answers that early Christianity did quicken that decay by accepting only the poorest forms of

---

[8] Pater, "Winckelmann," p. 105. [9] *Ibid.,* p. 105.

a moribund classical art.[10] "Gradually," however, "as the world came into the church, as Christianity compromised its earlier severities, the native artistic interest reasserted its claims." With this increasing secularization the "delicate problem" that Christian art faced was that of the "sensuous expression of conceptions which unreservedly discredit the world of sense" (*Ren-1*, p. 198):

If we think of mediaeval painting as it ranges from the early German schools, still with the air of a charnel-house about them, to the clear loveliness of Perugino, we shall see that the problem was met. Even in the worship of sorrow the native blitheness of art asserted itself; the religious spirit, as Hegel says, 'smiled through its tears.' . . . But in proportion as this power of smiling was refound, there came also an aspiration towards that lost antique art, some relics of which Christian art had buried in itself, ready to work wonders when their day came. (*Ren-1*, pp. 198–199)

Pater's statement appears to be a very ambiguous answer: somehow the "native blitheness" of art asserted itself *in* the worship of sorrow; but the genuine article, "that lost antique art," was still buried, awaiting a resurrection. That ambiguity is strongly marked in a "reconciling" paragraph, one of Pater's very first attempts to align pagan and Christian motifs:

The history of art has suffered as much as any history by trenchant and absolute divisions. Pagan and Christian art are sometimes harshly opposed, and the Renaissance is represented as a fashion which set in at a definite period. That is the superficial view; the deeper view is that which preserves the identity of European culture. The two are really continuous: and there is a sense in which it may be said that the Renaissance was an uninterrupted effort of the middle age, that it was ever taking place. When the actual relics of the antique were restored to the world, it was to Christian eyes as if an ancient plague-pit had been opened: all the world took the contagion of the life of nature and the senses.[11] Christian art allying itself with that restored antiquity which it had ever emulated, soon ceased to exist. For a time art

[10] *Ibid.*, p. 106.

[11] Arnold has defined the Renaissance as "a return towards the life of the senses and the understanding" (*CPW*, III, 226). In 1868 he referred to it as "that irresistible return of humanity to nature and to seeing things as they are" (*CPW*, V, 173).

dealt with Christian subjects as its patrons required; but its true freedom
was in the life of the senses and the blood—blood no longer dropping from
the hands in sacrifice, as with Angelico, but, as with Titian, burning in the
face for desire and love. And now it was seen that the mediaeval spirit too
had done something for the destiny of the antique. By hastening the decline of art, by withdrawing interest from it, and yet keeping the thread of
its traditions, it had suffered the human mind to repose, that it might awake
when day came, with eyes refreshed, to those antique forms. (*Ren-1*, pp.
199–200)

The alleged identity of European culture is only precariously defended
here; at least, it has little to do with Christianity itself. Christians opposed "the life of nature and the senses" which they detected in the
new-found ancient art; in fact Christian art itself died of its new al-
liance with the restored antiquity that, somehow, "it had ever emulated." The new spirit had the true freedom of "the life of the senses
and the blood," of "desire and love," and so transformed the Christian
subjects it treated. But this is simply to assert that in medieval art there
was an unassimilated "antique" or pagan element waiting to be re-
vived. Pater's dubious defense of the medieval spirit is symptomatic.
Clearly, that spirit, by withdrawing interest from the visible world, is
essentially incompatible with art; yet medieval art had somehow "ever
emulated" ancient art and even kept "the thread of its traditions." As
the later essays of the *Renaissance* will make much clearer, this thread
of Hellenic tradition leading to the Renaissance is in itself unassimil-
able to the Christian spirit. Christianity, it is evident, has little to offer
to art or to the artistic life. The identity of European culture is defined
by the persistence, even if at times underground, of the self-sufficient
Hellenic tradition.

After this highly qualified statement of a double basis for modern
culture, Pater turns for the supreme synthesis to Goethe, who "illustrates that union of the Romantic spirit, its adventure, its variety, its
deep subjectivity, with Hellenism, its transparency, its rationality,
its desire for beauty";[12] Winckelmann is important only for having
made known to Goethe the Hellenic element, which has the pre-

[12] This is a passage recorded by Arnold in 1879 (*NB*, p. 321).

ponderance in the Goethean synthesis (*Ren-1*, p. 201). This is, then, a more developed assertion of the union of the two "constituent elements of our life," the romantic and the Greek spirits, which Pater threw out at the end of the Coleridge essay. The question for Goethe, as Pater poses it, is whether the "breadth, centrality, with blitheness and repose," of the Hellenic ideal can be brought into "the gaudy, perplexed light of modern life." As usual, Pater has an answer for the aesthetic critic or observer and one for the artist. "Culture-balance" can no longer be achieved by the simple Greek "perfection of bodily form, or any joyful union with the world without"; instead, Goethe's Hellenism has "the completeness and serenity of a watchful, exigent intellectualism" (*Ren-1*, pp. 201–203). What then does Goethe mean by "life in the whole, *im Ganzen*"? Those seeking this supreme self-culture are met by many forms of the "one-sided development of some special talent"; but instead of weighing the claims of these various "alien" (and partial) forms, or even of "reaping" what these forms can give them, their instinct is to find in the various forms their own strength. The intellect does indeed discover "the laws, the operation, the intellectual reward of every divided [specialized, partial] form of culture"; "but only that it may measure the relation between itself and them. It struggles with those forms till its secret is won from each, and then lets each fall back into its place in the supreme, artistic view of life." These elevated natures rejoice, "with a kind of passionate coldness, . . . to be away from and past their former selves"; they especially resist "that abandonment to one special gift which really limits their capabilities" (*Ren-1*, p. 203). Sensuous experience, religious insight, "the commonplace metaphysical instinct": as men of "large vision" we must renounce all these "if we mean to mould our lives to artistic perfection." Philosophy, for example, serves culture not by some illusory insight into truth, but by helping us "detect the passion and strangeness and dramatic contrasts of life" (*Ren-1*, p. 204). So much for a self-culture *above* all divided forms of culture; in the "supreme artistic view of life," in which we "mould our lives to artistic perfection," we draw strength from all the actual activities of life, in order to have a totally unlimited "capability." The only suggested *object* of that "exigent," coldly detached and observant intellectualism is a *view* of "the passion and strangeness and dramatic contrasts of life."[13]

These statements reveal the central focus of the Paterian view of life. It is tempting to declare, as some readers have, that Pater's behest to "mould our lives to artistic perfection" means that the life of the supreme aesthete is to be somehow aesthetically patterned after the art object itself; but a closer examination shows that "the supreme artistic *view* of life" is a call to seek out, with the help of high art and by taking into oneself the power of insight of a supreme artist like Goethe, as much as possible of the passion and strangeness and drama of life. The life observed will be the life of others, the lives of people *engaged* in the necessarily "divided" forms of human "enthusiasm"; the culture-observer has no proper life of his own except detached observation, the detection of aesthetic patterning in the life of the world about him. All of human thought and activity—now that history, Hegel, and science have freed man from the need for concerning himself with a chimerical "truth" or conventional moral perfection—is simply grist for the very fine-grinding mills of a small class of emancipated aesthetic observers. Pater's "culture" was, then, never intended as a creed for the many—otherwise, it would be destroying the raw material of its own self-development, the passionate and engaged narrower forms of human activity. For certain "natures," for the "few," it offered, as the Coleridge essay put it, the "perfume" and "sweetness" of what is "remote, refined, intense"—offered an aesthetically satisfying arrangement distilled from the life around us. Pater is in effect defining his own role in life and that of a few others who aim at the life of culture. Even if one lacks the productive powers of the great artist, he is allowed to participate in the "supreme artistic view of life"; he is by implication in a better position to do so than the necessarily engaged artist himself.

In a final paragraph, however, Pater suggests that this culture he associates with Goethe was directly in touch with "the practical functions of art, . . . actual production." The problem now is more special: how can breadth, centrality, with blitheness and repose, be communicated to

---

[13] I have explored the Arnoldian matrix of Pater's ideal aesthetic "type" in "The 'Wordsworth' of Pater and Arnold: 'The Supreme, Artistic View of Life'," *Studies in English Literature,* VI (Autumn 1966), 651–667.

art works "which contain the fulness of the experience of the modern world" (*Ren-1*, p. 204)?[14] Only poetry—defined as "all literary production which attains the power of giving pleasure by its form as distinct from its matter"—can "command that width, variety, delicacy of resources, which will enable it to deal with the conditions of modern life. What modern art has to do in the service of culture is so to arrange the details of modern life, so to reflect it, that it may satisfy the spirit." What the spirit needs in the face of modern life is the "sense of freedom": modern science tells us of "the intricacy, the universality of natural law even in the moral order"; it locates in each individual a web of necessity related to "the central forces of the world" (*Ren-1*, p. 205). That arrangement of details, satisfying to the spirit, becomes a demand that art "represent men and women in these bewildering toils so as to give the spirit at least an equivalent for the sense of freedom" (*Ren-1*, pp. 205–206). Goethe's *Elective Affinities* succeeds in dealing with modern life but reflecting upon it blitheness and repose. Though we cannot modify natural laws, "there is still something in the nobler or less noble attitude with which we watch their fatal combinations"; in Goethe's novel, the network of law "becomes a tragic situation, in which a group of noble men and women work out a supreme *dénouement.*" "Who," Pater asks at length, "if he foresaw all, would fret against circumstances which endow one at the end with so high an experience?" (*Ren-1*, p. 206). Pater is not, however, asking men and women to refrain from fretting against the circumstances of their own lives in order to gain some insight into them. For the cherished "experience" is precisely that gained from the *art object*, or at most from the observation of the life situations of *others*, and not from any insight into the circumstances of the observer's own situation. Properly speaking, Pater's ideal observer has no "life" of his own, and art's

[14] Arnold had noted in "Pagan and Mediaeval Religious Sentiment" (*CPW*, III, 231) that an inherent limitation of his admired Greek poets was the fact that "the life of their beautiful Greece could not afford to its poets all that fulness of varied experience, all that power of emotion, which

'. . . the heavy and the weary weight
Of all this unintelligible world'

affords the poet of after-times."

service to modern culture, in giving to the spirit a make-believe "equivalent for the sense of freedom," is exclusively a service to Pater's "observer"-culture of intense and refined experiences. We are invited to *watch* the noble or less noble attitudes of men and women, caught in the entanglement of necessity, working out a supreme dénouement *as if they were free.* Goethe's—or Arnold's—culture has been radically reduced to providing for specially qualified sensibilities glimpses of passion and strangeness and dramatic contrast in the life of others; the special requirement of that state of perceptiveness is that it must detach itself from, must in a sense "renounce," participation in the life from which it extracts the experience. Art no longer exists even to enhance "life" in any ordinary sense of the term. It may be said that Pater's early aestheticism is in effect a program addressed to a special class of souls for transcending the human condition.

CHAPTER FIFTEEN   Arnold, Pater, and the Supreme,
Artistic View of Life

Pater placed the seal upon his extraordinary effort at critical self-definition (all done before the age of thirty) in a review of Morris' poems in October 1868, the final paragraphs of which became the notorious Conclusion to the *Renaissance.* The central intention of the review is a further attempt to suggest the exact place of classical and medieval motifs in "modern" literature. The romantic reaction against the neoclassicism of the eighteenth century was for Pater as much "a return to true Hellenism" as a "pre-occupation with things mediaeval." Pater distinguishes various elements in medieval poetry. The superficial kinds—used by Scott and Goethe—are simply "adventure, romance in the poorest sense, grotesque individualism." The "stricter, imaginative mediaevalism"—found in Hugo and Heine—drew in two other elements of the medieval spirit: "its mystic religion at its apex in Dante and St. Louis, and its mystic passion, passing here and there into the great romantic loves of rebellious flesh, of Lancelot and Abelard." This distinction leads Pater into a discussion of "the strange suggestion of a deliberate choice between Christ and a rival lover": "religion shades into sensuous love, and sensuous love into religion." Daringly, he suggests that only because the Latin hymn writers had a "beautiful idol," presumably Christ, did medieval Christianity make its way "among a people whose loss was in the life of the senses."[1] Provençal poetry creates a rival religion, deeply colored by Christian sentiment; the mood of the cloister takes a new direction and wins an unlooked-for new life. In fact, may not our "most cherished sacred writings," once belief in them has gone, "exercise their highest influence as the most delicate amorous poetry in the world"? Provençal poetry learned from religion "the art of directing towards an imaginary object sentiments whose natural direction is towards objects of sense." Religion gave to that poetry "reverie, illusion, delirium," for after all, "That whole religion of the middle age was but a beautiful disease or disorder of the senses" (p. 302). The "wild, convulsed sensuousness" of medieval poetry is attributable to a "tension of nerve" created by sealing up all the outlets of passion (p. 303). Pater is interested in the change of manner from Morris' *The Defence of Guenevere* (1858) to that of *The Life and Death of Jason* (1867) as explaining the difference between the Hellenic and the medieval spirit. The later work has no medieval delirium or illusion, "no experiences of mere soul while the body and bodily senses sleep or wake with convulsed intensity at the prompting of imaginative love"; instead, there are "the great primary passions under broad daylight." This simplification explains "a transition which, under many

[1] [Walter Pater], "Poems by William Morris," *The Westminster Review,* N.S. XXXIV (October 1868), 301. Cited by page number in text throughout this chapter. This, like a number of other statements, is considerably mitigated in the first edition of *Appreciations* (1889); "Aesthetic Poetry" was dropped in later editions. That these changes indicate the extent of Pater's movement from an anti-Christian position in the sixties, was suggested by E. K. Brown ("Pater's Appreciations: A Bibliographical Note," *MLN,* LXV [April 1950], 247–249).

forms, is one law of the life of the human spirit, and of which the Renaissance is only a supreme instance." Even the monk in his cloister, his vision open only to the spirit, "divined, aspired to and at last apprehended a better daylight, but earthly, open only to the senses" (p. 305). It is reasonable to conclude that the Hellenic tradition has a central, if not exclusive, claim to the title "the life of the human spirit." Thus the Renaissance remains a movement from "the overwrought spiritualities of the middle age to the earlier, more ancient life of the senses," and the classical tales of a late medieval like Chaucer are interesting because they communicate a sense of escape from the somber cloister to "that true light," while at the same time their mood will add to the story of Cupid and Psyche "that passionate stress of spirit which the world owes to Christianity." Art, at certain times and in special moods, can, it seems, combine the "grace of Hellenism" and "the sorrow of the middle age" (pp. 307–308).[2]

The setting of the famous Conclusion seems never to have been explained. Pater notes that part of the pagan spirit of Morris' poetry is the sharp contrast between "the sense of death and the desire of beauty." A Philistine observer is made to protest: " 'The modern world is in possession of truth; what but a passing smile can it have for a kind of poetry which, assuming artistic beauty of form to be an end in itself, passes by those truths and the living interests which are connected with them, to spend a thousand cares in telling once more these pagan fables as if it had but to choose between a more and a less beautiful shadow?' " Pater accepts the assumed challenge: "let us see what modern philosophy, when it is sincere, really does say about human life and the truth we can attain in it, and the relation of this to the desire

---

[2] Pater on Dante's "mystic religion" or "mystic passion," which passes "into the great romantic loves of rebellious flesh," and on "the overwrought spiritualities of the middle age" is suggestively close to Arnold's "Dante and Beatrice" (1863), one of his most antimedieval performances (*CPW*, III, 3–11). Arnold states that "the vital impulse of Dante's soul is towards reverie and spiritual vision"; Dante sets himself "the task of sacrificing the world to the spirit, of making the spirit all in all, of effacing the world in presence of the spirit" (p. 4). Moreover, "the followers of the spiritual life tend to be antinomian in what belongs to the outward life: . . . it is the fault of the spiritual life, as a complete life, that it allows this tendency: by dint of despising the outward life, it loses the control of this life, and of itself when in contact with it" (p. 9).

for beauty" (p. 309). *The relation of the attainment of truth to the desire for beauty*: this is the express subject of Pater's immensely influential paragraphs. His first sentence, "To regard all things and principles of things as inconstant modes or fashions has more and more become the tendency of modern thought," is the prejudicial and skeptical summary of modern epistemology which is illustrated in three paragraphs of images of flux, first in our physical life, then in "the inward world of thought and feeling." "Such thoughts," Pater comments in a paragraph that was never reprinted, "seem desolate at first; at times all the bitterness of life seems concentrated in them"; clearly the point of the last three paragraphs of the Conclusion is to show that a life attuned to modern "solipsism" need not be desolating.

Those paragraphs (pp. 311–312), among the best known in the language, are simply a summary of the doctrine of the Coleridge and Winckelmann essays. Pater's ideal is still his observer-culture: "The service of philosophy, and of religion and culture as well, to the human spirit, is to startle it into a sharp and eager observation."[3] To those who correctly argue that "Not the fruit of experience but experience itself is the end" is a doctrine of *life* and not of *art*, I would further discriminate by pointing out that that "life" is precisely the shadow-life of the detached aesthetic *observer* of ordinary life. For the invitation "to discriminate every moment some passionate attitude in those about us and in the brilliance of their gifts some tragic dividing of forces on their ways" recalls the demand for a "tragic" vision in modern art at the end of "Winckelmann." The idea that "Theories, religious or philosophical ideas, as points of view, instruments of criticism, may help us to gather up what might otherwise pass unregarded by us" had appeared almost verbatim in "Winckelmann"; and "The theory or idea or system which requires of us the sacrifice of any part of this experience, in consideration of some interest into which we cannot

[3] Geoffrey Tillotson (*Criticism and the Nineteenth Century*, pp. 135–136), points out the significant softening undergone by the key sentences, especially those concerning religion, between 1867 and 1888. One of the most interesting is the transformation of "High passions, . . . ecstasy and sorrow of love, political or religious enthusiasm, or 'the enthusiasm of humanity' " into "Great passions, . . . ecstasy and sorrow of love, the various forms of enthusiastic activity, disinterested or otherwise" (*Ren-3*, p. 238).

enter, or some abstract morality we have not identified with ourselves, or what is only conventional, has no real claim upon us," recalls both of the earlier essays.[4] Is this, then, a philosophy of "life"? Pater's criterion of success in life is "getting as many pulsations as possible into the given time" allotted us. He explicitly warns those who choose the path of "high passions"—"ecstasy and sorrow of love, political or religious enthusiasm, or the 'enthusiasm of humanity' ": "Only, be sure it is passion, that it does yield you this fruit of a quickened, multiplied consciousness. Of this wisdom, the poetic passion, the desire of beauty, the love of art for art's sake, has most; for art comes to you professing frankly to give nothing but the highest quality to your moments as they pass, and simply for those moments' sake."

"A quickened, multiplied consciousness" remains the immobile and rather parasitical Paterian ideal. This is not "art for art's sake"—that is an ideal for the artist only; nor is it life for the living's sake: it is intense self-stimulation through visual perception, for the moment's sake. Geoffrey Tillotson has remarked that Pater's "languor" is matched by a certain intensity and energy, "strongly" experiencing: "Pater's power of modifying impressions was a power like that of lust."[5] The precise kind and object of that experience is evident in Pater's key words. He uses a swarm of words suggesting refined, passive, sensuous, largely visual experience—observation, mood, insight, variegated, dramatic, see, senses, eye, lifted horizon, strange dyes and flowers, curious odors, art works, the face of one's friend, discriminate, splendor of experience, see and touch, curiously test new opinions, new impressions, regard—which beget a second swarm of terms suggesting intense momentary thrills, frissons: delicious recoil, race, drift, flight, tremulous, dissolution, pulsations, rouse, startle, ecstasy, ex-

---

[4] "Philosophy serves culture not by the fancied gift of absolute or transcendental knowledge, but by suggesting questions which help one to detect the passion and strangeness and dramatic contrasts of life" (*Ren-1*, p. 204). [Walter Pater], "Coleridge's Writings," *Westminster Review*, N.S. XXIX, (January 1866) 107: "Hard and abstract moralities are yielding to a more exact estimate of the subtlety and complexity of our life." And *Ren-1*, p. 203: "They do not care to weigh the claims which this or that alien form of culture makes upon them"; and *Ren-1*, p. 193: "Interests not his, nor meant for him, political, moral, religious, never disturbed him."

[5] Geoffrey Tillotson, *Criticism*, pp. 112, 113.

quisite passion, excitement, irresistibly real and attractive, the focus of
"vital forces," melts, grasp, stirring, desperate effort, "courting" impressions. Pater's impressions were those of "an individual in his isolation," a mind "keeping as a solitary prisoner its own dream of a world";
that world is one of fugitive, solitary self-gratifications, almost vo-
yeuristic in tone and intensity.

All of this seems sufficiently distant from Matthew Arnold, whose
critical career was designed to free the individual from the caprice and
isolation of his "ordinary self," and restore him to an objective order—
socially, politically, religiously—where men are "united, impersonal,
at harmony" (CPW, V, 134). But Professor Tillotson is right in noting that Arnold had already to some extent sanctioned much of Pater's
Conclusion.[6] He cites Arnold's detailed analysis of Maurice de Guérin's
special gift for interpreting the natural world, a faculty based on "a
peculiar temperament, an extraordinary delicacy of organisation and
susceptibility to impressions." Such a poet is largely "passive and ineffectual": "he resists being riveted and held stationary by any single
impression, but would be borne on for ever down an enchanted stream.
He goes into religion and out of religion, into society and out of society, not from motives which impel men in general, but to feel what it
is all like; he is thus hardly a moral agent. . . . He hovers over the tumult
of life, but does not really put his hand to it" (CPW, III, 30–31). "As-
suredly," Arnold adds, "it is not in this temperament that the active
virtues have their rise"(CPW, III, 32). This description of a special
temperament—with its emphasis on passivity—is strikingly close to
the attempt at character description which unifies Pater's emerging view
of the perfected life from "Diaphanéitè" in 1864 to the Morris review
in 1868.[7]

---

[6] *Ibid.,* p. 140.

[7] Clyde de L. Ryals has considered "The Nineteenth-Century Cult of Inaction"
(*Tennessee Studies in Literature,* IV [1959], 51–60), which he attributes to "the
Romantic overemphasis on the individual and the individual imagination, which
sought to create a world of make-believe and fancy and, in turn, tended to undermine
the will and the ability to act," and to "a commercial society's overemphasis on
practical values, causing the sensitive writer of the period to invert those values into
a mode of philosophy which stressed the life of contemplation as opposed to the life
of action" (p. 51). He finds Pater the "philosopher" of the Victorian phase of the

Above all, it is hard to resist the impression that Pater's "diaphanous" temperament is in fact the moral equivalent of Arnold's ideal of "disinterested" criticism. In "Diaphanéitè," this special character "crosses . . . the main current of the world's life" and has no "service" to perform for the world (*MS*, p. 248); and the Coleridge essay shows a full awareness of the "disinterested" ideal.[8] It is in "Winckelmann," however, that Pater especially shares with the Arnold of "The Function of Criticism" (*CPW*, III, 258–285) an emphasis on renunciation, detachment, and indifference. Arnold's criticism values knowledge and thought "without the intrusion of any other considerations whatever." "Disinterestedness" means "keeping aloof from what is called 'the practical view of things' "; it must resolutely follow "the law of its own nature, which is to be a free play of the mind on all subjects." It steadily refuses to lend itself to "ulterior, political, practical considerations." It must keep in "the pure intellectual sphere," "detached . . . from practice." Criticism is a "subtle and indirect action," embracing "detachment" and "abandoning the sphere of practical life," and will inevitably be the work of "a very small circle." The secret of this "disinterested endeavour" is "never to let oneself become abstract." "Winckelmann" likewise speaks centrally of the "archaic immobility" of the Greek statues, what motion they have being "a motion ever kept in reserve, which is very seldom committed to any definite action." When Pater speaks of an "indifference which is beyond what is relative and partial," he repeats Arnold's direction that criticism must refuse to remain in the sphere of "narrow and relative conceptions." Winckelmann was undisturbed by "interests not his, nor meant for him, political, moral, religious." High Hellenic form exhibits an "indifference to the outward," an "impassivity." Forbidding any "one-sided development," the supreme artistic view of life, held by the few, with its "passionate coldness," forbids "abandonment to one special gift." Finally, Goethe's culture requires that "we must renounce" the

---

cult (p. 56), but though he speaks of Arnold's "ambivalence" (p. 58) on the matter, he draws no line from Arnold to Pater.

[8] [Pater], "Coleridge's Writings," pp. 108, 126–127, 131.

actual activities of the world. Again, what is in Arnold confined to the literary and critical sphere, Pater eagerly applied directly to morals and to his special version of "life." If Pater has not yet suggested (as he will in 1874) that by "moulding our lives to artistic perfection" he means us to shape our lives almost as if they were actual art objects, he *is* suggesting that the detachment of the ideal critical intellect is indeed the paradigm for the higher life available for the "few" of extraordinary receptivity.

The dissimilarity of their thought goes beyond a confusion of categories; even in "The Function of Criticism" the ultimate goal of Arnold's indifference and detachment was to provide a climate for creative activity, by giving currency to "adequate ideas." By the time of *Culture and Anarchy* the "social" motive had changed the entire ethical complexion of Arnold's ideal. Professor Tillotson's notion that Pater's twice-used phrase about rendering a "service to culture"—once in "Winckelmann" and once in the Conclusion to the *Renaissance*— somehow aligns him with Arnold's goal of "making the middle-class mind more lovely"[9] obscures the inward-turning character of Pater's "self-culture" in these early essays. Even the final paragraph of "Winckelmann" concerned with "the practical functions of art, . . . actual production," deals not with the energetic encouragement of a climate favorable to creation but with the "high experience" of tragic involvement which certain modern artists—Goethe and, by 1888, Hugo —could provide for the isolated, febrile sensibility. To the correct observation that Pater extended a friendlier welcome to contemporary literature than did Arnold[10] must be added the fact that Pater—caught in the "web" of science, industrialism, and democracy a generation later than Arnold—at bottom *despaired* of changing society as the mature Arnold never did. Both were possessed of "the desire of beauty" (*Ren-1*, p. 213; *CPW*, V, 107), but Arnold's "desire after the things of the mind simply for their own sakes" (*CPW*, V, 91) is finally a world away from Pater's "art for art's sake" (*Ren-1*, p. 213). For Arnold's disinterestedness envisaged nothing less than the reshaping

[9] Geoffrey Tillotson, *Criticism*, p. 140.
[10] *Ibid.*, p. 146.

and elevating of the Victorian mind, whereas Pater's renunciation and indifference seek to retain an inherited fullness of "experience," in detachment from the vulgar actualities of Victorian life, for a small band of elite "Oxonian" souls. These men will be "artists," too, though with a diminished vitality or closeness to the raw materials of art; but they will above all seek to make their own the supreme, artistic *view of life*. If there is a "moment" when the Keatsian artist announces an ultimate severance from the hope of affecting nineteenth-century life, it may be in Pater's first essays of the late sixties, as Matthew Arnold's great "critical effort" is systematically reshaped into the catchwords of the new aestheticism. Aestheticism, with roots in the Romantics, Ruskin, the Pre-Raphaelites, and Swinburne, found an adequate rhetoric only in Pater: the terms were in Arnold, but where they reappear, they are "the same yet different." Arnold is a father of Aestheticism but only in an oblique and problematical way.

CHAPTER SIXTEEN The Renaissance

The first of Pater's actual Renaissance studies was the essay on Leonardo da Vinci, published in November 1869. Within the more technical context of poetry and the fine arts, Pater continues to search for new and more adequate formulas of human "wholeness" and "completeness," especially in the "engaging personalities" of his Renaissance hero-artists. Everywhere in these studies occurs the theme of the abandonment, or modification, or "use" of the "old religion." In the search for formulas for his "strange," "singular," "curious," "subtle," "exotic," "remote" souls, Christianity, or at least medieval Christian art, becomes the supplier of the "inwardness" that Pater demands as a supplement to Greek "form." But Pater's succes-

sive formulas for the place of Christianity in Western culture, some
of them more conciliatory than in the earliest essays, to some extent
reflect, in their mutual incompatibility, the accretive and random development of the *Renaissance* volume.

It is no exaggeration to say that in his Leonardo essay Pater continues to take his basic definitions and evaluations from Matthew
Arnold. Arnoldian phrasing is at the very heart of the essay. "Curiosity
and the desire of beauty—these are the two elementary forces in Leonardo's genius; curiosity often in conflict with the desire of beauty,
but generating, in union with it, a type of subtle and curious grace"
(*Ren-1*, p. 102). Arnold's *Culture and Anarchy,* which had appeared
in book form in January 1869, makes "curiosity" (or "a desire after
the things of the mind simply for their own sakes and for the pleasure
of seeing them as they are") and the "keen desire for beauty"—the
"sweetness and light" of the farewell lecture—the essential components of culture or the Greek spirit (*CPW*, V, 91, 107, 98–100). Moreover the next words of Pater's essay confirm the Arnoldian matrix:
"The movement of the fifteenth century was two-fold: partly the
Renaissance, partly also the coming of what is called the 'modern spirit,' with its realism, its appeal to experience; it comprehended a return
to antiquity, a return to nature" (*Ren-1*, p. 102). Arnold's Inaugural
Lecture at Oxford, "On the Modern Element in Literature" (1857),
finally published in February 1869, had discussed the characteristics of
"modern" periods like Periclean Athens: great energy, great freedom,
"the most unprejudiced and intelligent observation of human affairs,"
and "intellectual maturity" or the "critical spirit" (*CPW*, I, 23–25).
Arnold's full analysis of the "modern spirit" came in "Heinrich
Heine" (1863) where he underlines the lack of correspondence between the spirit and the needs of the eighteenth and nineteenth centuries and the vast inherited system of institutions and dogmas. "Pagan
and Mediaeval Religious Sentiment" also conceives the Renaissance as
"a return towards the pagan spirit, . . . towards the life of the senses
and the understanding," a "reaction against the rule of the heart and
and the imagination" (*CPW*, III, 226). Finally, in *Culture and Anarchy* Arnold had spoken of the Renaissance as "that great re-awaken-

ing of Hellenism, that irresistible return of humanity to nature and to seeing things as they are" (*CPW*, V, 173).[1]

The central motif of Pater's volume, that of an enlarged and enriched version of human nature at the heart of the Italian Renaissance, is sounded in the Leonardo essay. The agitation and restlessness of Leonardo's "sinister" art, essentially a conflict between the reason and the senses, come from his "divinations of a humanity too wide" for the earlier Florentine style, "that larger vision of the opening world which is only not too much for the great, irregular art of Shakespeare" (*Ren-1*, p. 105). The holistic and inclusive quality of Pater's vision of an expanding human nature is apparent when he makes the Mona Lisa, in what is perhaps the most notorious passage in his writings, the embodiment of the old fancy of "a perpetual life, sweeping together ten thousand experiences," or the symbol of the modern idea of "humanity as wrought upon, and summing up in itself, all modes of thought and life" (*Ren-1*, p. 119). Moreover, Leonardo becomes a hero of Arnoldian disinterestedness applied to the life of the artist. Setting the ends of art above "moral or political ends," for him "the novel impression conveyed, the exquisite effect woven, counted as an end in itself—a perfect end" (*Ren-1*, pp. 110–111). The line of the other essays is set when Pater ends by dismissing the question of Leonardo's religion as irrelevant in one who set beauty before all else (*Ren-1*, p. 122).

Pater's view of the role of religion in life becomes even clearer in "Botticelli" (August 1870). Botticelli's art gives "a more direct inlet into the Greek temper" than even the best of ancient Greek art, because we are familiar with Greek art while Botticelli's art is the record of the first impression made by the Hellenic spirit "on minds turned back towards it in almost painful aspiration from a world in which it had been ignored so long" (*Ren-1*, p. 48). Of especial interest here is

---

[1] One senses Arnold's "Modern Element" behind Pater's analysis of Leonardo. The "key" to Leonardo's life is a "struggle between the reason and its ideas, and the senses, the desire of beauty": "This agitation, this perpetual delay, give him an air of weariness and ennui." He struggles not to be overwhelmed by "science" and "ideas" (*Ren-1*, pp. 105–106). Arnold's Lucretius, through the "predominance of thought, of reflection," becomes a martyr of the modern conflict of thought and feeling, filled with "depression and ennui" (*CPW*, I, 32).

Pater's use of this "Greek" Botticelli as a pre-eminent example of Winckelmannian detachment; he makes the supreme "refusal": he is "one of those who are neither for God nor for his enemies" (*Ren-1*, p. 44). "So just what Dante scorns as unworthy alike of heaven and hell, Botticelli accepts, that middle world in which men take no side in great conflicts, and decide no great causes, and make great refusals. He thus set for himself the limits within which art, undisturbed by any moral ambition, does its most sincere and surest work" (*Ren-1*, p. 45).

Dialectically, the central essay of Pater's *Renaissance* is that on Pico della Mirandola (October 1871). The tone is conciliatory, and the central question is methodological: how to find a true method for the "reconciliation of the gods of Greece with the Christian religion." In that quest, Pater, while still accepting Arnold's reading of the Greek spirit and its "reassertion" in the Renaissance, readjusts the proportions of Arnold's estimate of the place of religion in life. Behind this essay is not only "Heinrich Heine" but also, for the first time, Arnold's "reconciling" discussion of Hebraism and Hellenism, in *Culture and Anarchy*. The overt subject is the syncretism of the Florentine Platonists: "To reconcile forms of sentiment which at first sight seem incompatible, to adjust the various products of the human mind to each other in one many-sided type of intellectual culture, to give the human spirit for the heart and imagination to feed upon, as much as it could possibly receive, belonged to the generous instincts of that age" (*Ren-1*, p. 18). They asked "whether the religion of Greece was indeed a rival of the religion of Christ; for the older gods had rehabilitated themselves, and men's allegiance was divided" (*Ren-1*, p. 19). "Reconciliation," "adjustment": these were also the central terms of Arnold's treatment: the Greeks arrived at the "idea of a comprehensive adjustment of the claims of both the sides in man, the moral as well as the intellectual, of a full estimate of both, of a reconciliation of both" (*CPW*, V, 179). Arnold's rhetorical strategy is to urge this adjustment and reconciliation of Christian moralism and Greek intellectualism with evenhanded impartiality: the tone of his discussion and of his humanism is shown in phrases like "reconciling force," "mutual understanding and balance," "connecting and harmonising," "proportion" (*CPW*, V, 157, 177, 184, 190). But the startling, and not untypical, final ploy is to award the palm to Hellenism. Much earlier Arnold had stated that culture goes *beyond* religion as "generally conceived by us" in being "a harmonious expansion of *all* the powers which make the beauty and worth of human nature" (*CPW*, V, 94); now he shows that Hellenism is in fact superior to Hebraism by opposing "the notion of cutting our being in two, of attributing to one part the dignity of dealing with the one thing needful, and leaving the other part to take its chance" (*CPW*, V, 184). If indeed Hellenism is not "always for everybody more wanted than Hebraism," still "at this particular moment, and for the great majority" of Arnold's countrymen, it is more needed (*CPW*, V, 181). Arnold's provocative display of dialectics deeply influenced Pater.

As if matching strategies with the Arnold of "Pagan and Mediaeval Religious Sentiment," Pater quotes a passage from Heine's *Gods in Exile* (first published in French in 1853), concerning the reappearance, in the Middle Ages, of the ancient gods in disguised form; this theme was to occupy Pater intermittently until the end of his career.[2] The Renaissance, Pater says, could not explain this "reconciliation of the religion of antiquity with the religion of Christ"; but a "modern scholar" would hold that "every intellectual product must be judged from the point of view of the age and people in which it was produced." Thus each religion "has contributed something to the development of the religious sense," and they all can be justified "as so many stages in the gradual education of the human mind" (*Ren-1*, pp. 21–22). This incompatible amalgam of a progressive "education" of the race, after the manner of Lessing, and a total historical relativism seems not to trouble Pater; forgetting the purposiveness, he serenely announces: "The basis of the reconciliation of the religions of the world would thus be the inexhaustible activity and creativeness of the human mind itself, in which all religions alike have their root, and in which all alike are laid to rest." Or he will simply use "historic sense" in two different meanings: the scholars of the fifteenth century "lacked the very rudiments of the historic sense, which by an imaginative act throws itself back into a world unlike one's own, and judges each intellectual product

[2] See John Smith Harrison, "Pater, Heine, and the Old Gods of Greece," *PMLA,* XXXIX (September 1924), 655–686.

in connection with the age which produced it; they had no idea of development, of the differences of ages, of the gradual education of the human race" (*Ren-1*, p. 22). Like many another nineteenth-century "relativist," Pater obviously draws heavily on the rationalist assumption of purposiveness and meaning in history, itself a hang-over from the Christian eschatological view of history. For rationalist and relativist alike, nineteenth-century "science" has brought about a kind of millennium, a decisive end to illusory metaphysical readings of history and human destiny. All such speculations are finally "laid to rest" in a series that is somehow also a "development," and the "religious sense" remains, as it did in the Coleridge essay, a permanently accessible distillation made from all the ignorant dogmas of the past. For the moment, Pater would seem to rest in the implication that, in the "successive stages in a gradual development of the religious sense" (*Ren-1*, pp. 22–23), history itself—or at least the historical point of view of the nineteenth century—is the great reconciler of the apparent incompatibilities among religious positions. All of history converges on that more broadly diffused religious sense described in the Coleridge essay.

Of course the allegorical interpretation on which these Florentine scholars were thrown back, forcing various religions to subsist side by side and "substantially in agreement with each other," is merely a curiosity, "an element in the local colour of a great age." But it does illustrate "the faith of that age in all oracles, its desire to hear all voices, its generous belief that nothing which had ever interested the human mind could wholly lose its vitality" (*Ren-1*, p. 23)—which is not only a view Pater finds sympathetic, but also one that probably sums up his preceding exercises in literary and religious anthropology. More successful is the "practical truce and reconciliation of the gods of Greece with the Christian religion" achieved in fifteenth-century art; Pico, like numerous others in Pater's hall of notables, is of interest because his own life "is a sort of analogue or visible equivalent to the expression of this purpose in his writings" (*Ren-1*, pp. 23–24). Even Pico's outward appearance is an image of an almost Winckelmannian "inward harmony and completeness of which he is so perfect an example" (*Ren-1*, p. 25). The place of religion in Pico's life, as well as Pater's view of a possible reconciliation, remains ambiguous. Pico's enormous, if uncritical, erudition led to "the generous hope, so often disabused, of reconciling the philosophers with each other, and all alike with the Church"; but Pico ends up in orthodox Christianity, "an early instance of those who, after following the vain hope of an impossible reconciliation from system to system, have at last fallen back unsatisfied on the simplicities of their childhood's belief" (*Ren-1*, pp. 27–28).

The sharpest confrontation of the medieval and Renaissance spirits comes with a discussion of Pico's insistence on "the dignity of human nature, the greatness of man." In itself, this is a medieval theme, and it shares the medieval misconception of man's place in nature. But false as was its basis, the theory, when reiterated by a man like Pico, has its use:

For this high dignity of man thus bringing the dust under his feet into sensible communion with the thoughts and affections of the angels was supposed to belong to him not as renewed by a religious system, but by his own natural right; and it was a counterpoise to the increasing tendency of mediaeval religion to depreciate man's nature, to sacrifice this or that element in it, to make it ashamed of itself, to keep the degrading or painful accidents of it always in view. It helped man onward to that reassertion of himself, that rehabilitation of human nature, the body, the senses, the heart, the intelligence, which the Renaissance fulfills. (*Ren-1*, p. 29)

This is, it seems apparent, conflated Arnold. Pater's "reassertion" and "rehabilitation of human nature" are very close to Arnold's definition in *Culture and Anarchy* of the Renaissance as "an uprising and reinstatement of man's intellectual impulses and Hellenism" (*CPW*, V, 172). Moreover, Pater's four-part division of human nature—"the body, the senses, the heart, the intelligence"—is so close to the final formula of Arnold's "Pagan and Mediaeval Religious Sentiment," "the senses and understanding, . . . the heart and imagination," as to suggest that Pater is consciously countering Arnold's assignment to the Renaissance of the senses and understanding alone. Pater is in effect asserting that the Renaissance is as adequate an expression of the "imaginative reason," as adequate a servant of the "modern spirit," as Arnold's great Greek century.[3]

[3] That Arnold is very much on Pater's mind here is confirmed by the appearance of

Pater's final statement of the problem adds a new element: "It remained for a later age to conceive the true method of effecting a scientific reconciliation of Christian sentiment with the imagery, the legends, the theories about the world, of pagan poetry and philosophy" (*Ren-1*, p. 36). Apparently, Pater's "historic sense" is really science in action: for him nineteenth-century "developmental" biology and perhaps an emergent anthropology both endorse a historical relativism judging each intellectual product in connection with its own age. How the religious sense "develops" within this scheme is left unexplained. One suspects Pater was unwilling to pursue these themes at length in 1871. What elements in Christianity attracted the men of the Renaissance is not fully clear. Pater only says that the "imaginative" reconciliation effected by Christian artists working with pagan subjects created a new mythology "which grew up from the mixture of two traditions, two sentiments, the sacred and the profane"; the Renaissance did not "ask curiously of science concerning its origin, its primary form and import, its meaning for those who projected it" (*Ren-1*, pp. 36–37). This tantalizingly undeveloped hint opens the highroad to the *Greek Studies*. For the moment Pater merely claims that Pico is "a true *humanist*," one who believed that "nothing which has ever interested living men and women can wholly lose its vitality" (*Ren-1*, p. 38).

The following month (November 1871), in his study "The Poetry of Michelangelo," Pater makes two important statements concerning Catholic Christianity which indicate new lines of thought. Until this point Pater had usually aligned medieval Christianity with Platonism as forms of "exaggerated idealism," "discrediting the slightest touch of sense," and hence antagonistic to the very principle of art. But now he asserts: "Dante's belief in the resurrection of the body, through which even in heaven Beatrice loses for him no tinge of flesh-colour or fold of raiment even, and the Platonic dream of the passage of the soul through one form of life after another, with its passionate haste to escape from the burden of bodily form altogether, are, for all effects of art or poetry, principles diametrically opposite" (*Ren-1*, p. 76). This

---

the following passage, scarcely two pages later: " 'It is not hard to know God, provided one will not force oneself to define him' has been thought a great saying of Joubert's" (*Ren-1*, p. 32). It was thought so by Arnold (*CPW*, III, 197).

statement is a significant qualification of Pater's view of orthodox medieval Christianity as an unbroken "dark age" of asceticism; but he goes on to welcome "the catholic church" into a highly ambiguous religious synthesis of his own. Michelangelo lived on into a time when "neo-catholicism," the Counter Reformation, had taken the place of the Renaissance. He was now a stranger to a church opposed to art and fixed in "a frozen orthodoxy":

In earlier days, when its beliefs had been in a fluid state, he too might have been drawn into the controversy; he might have been for spiritualising the papal sovereignty, like Savonarola; or for adjusting the dreams of Plato and Homer with the words of Christ, like Pico of Mirandula. But things had moved onward, and such adjustments were no longer possible. For himself, he had long since fallen back on that divine ideal which, above the wear and tear of creeds, has been forming itself for ages as the possession of nobler souls. And now be began to feel the soothing influence which since that time the catholic church has often exerted over spirits too noble to be its subjects, yet brought within the neighbourhood of its action; consoled and tranquillised, as a traveller might be, resting for one evening in a strange city, by its stately aspect and the sentiment of its many fortunes, just because with those fortunes he has nothing to do. (*Ren-1*, p. 81)

This "divine ideal" for "nobler souls," presented with obvious sympathy by Pater, represents, at least for the moment, an appeal to a special religious ideal *above* "reconciliations" and "adjustments." It looks very much like one of those "broader spiritualities" broached in the Coleridge essay: the creeds are gone, but the "religious graces" derived from "the older and narrower forms of religious life" are still possible. At this point the outlines of *Marius the Epicurean* appear in the distance, though the patronizing tone suggests there were still miles to travel.[4]

---

[4] [Walter Pater], "Coleridge's Writings," *Westminster Review*, N.S. XXIX (January 1866), 129: "Dogmas are precious as memorials of a class of sincere and beautiful spirits, who, in a past age of humanity struggled with many tears, if not for true knowledge, yet for a noble and elevated happiness. That struggle is the substance, the dogma only its shadowy expression." This passage anticipates not only the famous opening of "The Study of Poetry" and certain passages in "Literature and Science," but also a number of Arnold's attitudes toward the Roman Catholic Church in the seventies (see above, Chapter 7).

"Luca della Robbia," first published in 1873, is important for the purposes of this study because in it, for the first time, Pater suggests and concedes that the "mystical" Christian Middle Ages did in fact have a vital element to contribute to art. Further, Pater explains "that profound expressiveness, that intimate impress of an indwelling soul," found in Italian sculpture of the earlier fifteenth century. The low relief of Luca and others of his school helped overcome an inherent limitation of sculpture, a tendency to "a hard realism, a one-sided presentment of mere form, that solid material frame which only motion can relieve, a thing of heavy shadows and an individuality of expression pushed to caricature" (*Ren-1*, p. 54). The three great styles in sculpture have expanded this "too fixed individuality of pure unrelieved uncoloured form" in different ways. The way of Phidias and the Greeks is that which Winckelmann and Goethe called "breadth, generality, universality": seeking the type in the individual, abstracting and expressing only the permanent, the structural, the abiding (*Ren-1*, p. 55). The price of this was "the sacrifice of what we call *expression*." Michelangelo, suffused with medieval feeling, reacted against this abstraction:

when Michelangelo came, with a genius spiritualised by the reverie of the middle age, penetrated by its spirit of inwardness and introspection, living not a mere outward life like the Greek, but a life full of inward experiences, sorrows, consolations, a system which sacrificed what was inward could not satisfy him. To him, lover and student of Greek sculpture as he was, work which did not bring what was inward to the surface, which was not concerned with individual expression, character, feeling, the special history of the special soul, was not worth doing at all. . . . he secured for his work individuality and intensity of expression, while he avoided a too hard realism. . . . (*Ren-1*, p. 56)

What time has done to the Venus de Milo, "fraying its surface and softening its lines, so that some spirit in the thing seems always on the point of breaking out of it, as if in it classical sculpture had advanced already one step into the mystical Christian age," Michelangelo achieves by his characteristic "incompleteness, which suggests rather than realises actual form" (*Ren-1*, p. 57). This incompleteness relieves any hard realism and gives the effect of life: through it, "he combines the utmost of passion and intensity with the expression of a yielding and flexible life" (*Ren-1*, p. 58). This, combined with the preceding essay on Michelangelo, is Pater's most developed and most sympathetic discussion of "Catholic" Christianity and medieval religious feeling before *Marius*.

Pater had promised a third solution to the problems of sculpture. With his love of dialectical conciliations, he discusses the system of low relief of the Tuscan sculptors, midway between the abstracted "pure form" of the Greeks and the "studied incompleteness" of Michelangelo, "relieving that expression of intensity, passion, energy, which would otherwise have hardened into caricature" (*Ren-1*, p. 58). This subtle and skillful conventionalism of the fifteenth century, with its "profound expressiveness" and "subtler sense of originality," conveying the artist's most "inward and peculiar" moods, is temperamentally more appealing to Pater than the Titanism of Michelangelo. However, once he had fully acknowledged, through the figure of Michelangelo, that "inwardness and introspection," which were essential elements of romantic and modern artistic "expressiveness," had roots in the spiritual "reverie" of the Middle Ages, Pater's earlier intransigence concerning medieval religion was fundamentally compromised. The essays on Michelangelo and Luca della Robbia mark an important if partial turning of Pater's antireligious "sensuous" ideal of art toward a reconsideration of Christian "spiritualism."

Another essay published in 1873, "Aucassin and Nicolette," further attempts to heal the exaggerated "rupture between the middle age and the Renaissance"—but fundamentally in the ambiguous Arnoldian terms Pater had used in the earliest essays. His subject is a Renaissance, discussed by French historians, at the end of the twelfth and the beginning of the thirteenth century, "a Renaissance within the limits of the middle age itself, a brilliant but in part abortive effort to do for human life and the human mind what was afterwards done in the fifteenth" (*Ren-1*, pp. 1–2). The Renaissance was not simply the revival of classical antiquity; rather, it was "a many-sided but united movement, in which the love of the things of the intellect and the imagination for their own sake, the desire for a more liberal and comely

way of conceiving life, make themselves felt" and which leads to new
sources of intellectual and imaginative enjoyment (*Ren-1*, p. 2). There
was a "great outbreak" of such feeling in this medieval period—evident
in pointed architecture, the doctrines of romantic love, and Provençal
poetry; medieval strength turns to sweetness, and sweetness prompts
men "to seek after the springs of perfect sweetness in the Hellenic
world" (*Ren-1*, pp. 2–3). It is a Renaissance because for so long
a "dark age" these intellectual and imaginative instincts had been
"crushed." This theory "seeks to establish a continuity between the
most characteristic work of the middle age . . . and the work of the
later Renaissance, . . . and thus heals that rupture between the middle
age and the Renaissance which has so often been exaggerated" (*Ren-1*,
p. 3).

But Pater is not offering here a view of the medieval "inwardness"
he detected in Michelangelo; instead, he presents the familiar view that
this proto-Renaissance has no *essential* connection with medieval spirituality at all:

But it is not so much the ecclesiastical art of the middle age, its sculpture
and painting,—work certainly done in a great measure for pleasure's sake,
in which even a secular, a rebellious spirit often betrays itself,—but rather
the profane poetry of the middle age, the poetry of Provence, and the
magnificent aftergrowth of that poetry in Italy and France, which those
French writers have in view when they speak of this Renaissance within the
middle age. In that poetry, earthly passion, in its intimacy, its freedom, its
variety—the liberty of the heart—makes itself felt; and the name of Abelard,
the great clerk and the great lover, connects the expression of this liberty
of heart with the free play of human intelligence round all subjects presented to it. . . . (*Ren-1*, pp. 3–4)[5]

At the very end of the essay the explicit "antinomianism" of Pater's
ideal Renaissance is made clear, clearer ever than in the sloughing off
of "hard and abstract moralities" in the Coleridge essay of 1866, or
of the "abstract morality we have not identified with ourselves" of the
Conclusion of 1868:

[5] The connection of the story of Abelard and Heloise with the Tannhäuser legend
(*Ren-1*, pp. 4–6, 15) is an allusion to Heine's "Gods in Exile." See Harrison, "Pater,
Heine, and the Old Gods," pp. 658–659.

One of the strongest characteristics of that outbreak of the reason and the imagination, of that assertion of the liberty of the heart in the middle age, which I have termed a mediaeval Renaissance, was its antinomianism, its spirit of rebellion and revolt against the moral and religious ideas of the age. In their search after the pleasures of the senses and the imagination, in their care for beauty, in their worship of the body, people were impelled beyond the bounds of the primitive Christian ideal; and their love became a strange idolatry, a strange rival religion. It was the return of that ancient Venus, not dead, but only hidden for a time in the caves of the Venusberg, of those old pagan gods still going to and fro on the earth, under all sorts of disguises. The perfection of culture is not rebellion but peace; only when it has realised a deep moral stillness has it really reached its end. But often on the way to that end there is room for a noble antinomianism. (*Ren-1,* p. 15)[6]

Pater retreats a step and speaks of "this rebellious element, this *sinister* claim for liberty of heart and thought" (*Ren-1,* p. 16; my italics), as found in the Albigensian movement or the millenarian speculations of Joachim of Floris; but the final quotation from Pater's medieval tale, "perhaps the most famous expression" of this spirit, is designed to leave the "languid sweetness" of this cult of beauty and of the body deliciously in the reader's mind.

Thus this healing of the rupture of medieval and Renaissance ideals is quite illusory. It seems clear that in this reassertion of Pater's earlier views of the Renaissance and of Christianity, essentially in Arnoldian terms, he is pointedly expanding and reshaping Arnold's much more intellectualist and moralistic view of the Renaissance—and of "the modern spirit" itself. For example, Pater's "the love of the things of the intellect and the imagination for their own sake, the desire for a more liberal and comely way of conceiving life," is simply a variation of Arnold's formula in *Culture and Anarchy,* "a desire after the things of the mind simply for their own sakes"; and the addition of "imagination" and "sweetness" and a "liberal and comely" life was amply sanctioned by Arnold's opposing the ideal of beauty and sweetness to the "hideousness and rawness," the "hardness and vulgarity," of mid-

---

[6] These last two sentences, which also appear in 1877, were dropped from the edition of 1888.

dle-class English life (*CPW*, V, 106–107). Moreover, Pater's twice speaking of an "outbreak" of reason and imagination and once of an "assertion" of liberty of heart is plainly very close to Arnold's "uprising and reinstatement of man's intellectual impulses and of Hellenism" (*CPW*, V, 172). But the "liberal" quality of modern life for Pater obviously took to itself areas not envisaged by Matthew Arnold. A key sentence neatly embodies the process of adaptation: in the poetry of the Renaissance of the twelfth century, "earthy passion, in its intimacy, its freedom, its variety—the liberty of the heart—makes itself felt; and the name of Abelard, the great clerk and the great lover, connects the expression of this liberty of heart with the free play of human intelligence round all subjects presented to it." This statement in part echoes Arnold's Hellenic ideal of "letting a free play of thought live and flow around all our activity," and his view that Abelard, "in spite of all his imperfections," had been one of the heroes of culture (*CPW*, V, 158, 70). But passion, intimacy, the liberty of the heart—not to speak of the "worship of the body"—were emphatically no part of Arnold's proposed pattern of human life. In fact, Pater's praise of Abelard, in the connection Heine made with the Venus of the Tannhäuser legend, endorses Heine's hedonistic version of Renaissance values which Arnold had firmly rejected in "Pagan and Mediaeval Religious Sentiment." Similarly, Pater's repeated pairs, "reason and imagination," "the senses and the imagination," "heart and thought," clearly imply once again that Arnold's sought-for reconciliation of "the senses and understanding," and "the heart and imagination," *was* realized in the Renaissance. What could be a more direct denial of Arnold's praise of the Middle Ages as the supreme era of "the heart and imagination" than Pater's description, in the Preface of 1873, of the Renaissance as a "breaking down of those limits which the religious system of the middle age imposed on the heart and imagination" (*Ren-1*, p. xii)?

Pater's "strange idolatry, a strange rival religion," beyond the bounds of the Christian ideal and reminiscent of the confusion of religious and amorous experience endorsed in the 1868 Morris review, hovers between a *noble* antinomianism and a *sinister* claim for liberty of heart and thought. In either case, however, the new ideal would be classed as *Aselgeia*, or *Lubricity*—the demand for "the free development of our senses"—which Arnold associated with Ernest Renan and the French and which was denied a role in the life of "our higher *real self*."[7] Admittedly, neither Arnold nor Pater is detached or clinical about sexuality or the life of the senses in the manner of a later generation. In 1873 the highest reach of Pater's view of the perfected life is antinomian and almost mystical in its "prophetic" and millenarian vision of a "final dispensation of a spirit of freedom, in which the law has passed away" (*Ren-1*, p. 16). In contrast, Arnold, in 1864, felt the "modern spirit" sponsored a balance precisely between "the thinking-power" and "the religious sense." Despite the apparent comprehensiveness of his ideal of the "imaginative reason," the "life of the senses" played a very restricted role in the Arnoldian vision of man's future. To the end he retains an unbreakable grip on the "strong and irrational moral prejudice" that Eliot sees as playing so decisive a role in his life: in 1884 he insists that The Eternal has guaranteed that the worship of Lubricity "is against nature, human nature, and that it is ruin" (*DA*, p. 57).[8]

[7] See *LD*, pp. 322 ff.; *DA*, pp. 37 ff.; and Lionel Trilling, *Matthew Arnold*, pp. 314 ff.

[8] On Arnold's presiding presence in the Preface of 1873—in Pater's citation of " 'To see the object as in itself it really is'," and the allusion to Arnold in "what is this song or picture to *me*" (*CPW*, I, 140; III, 258, 110)—see Ruth C. Child, *The Aesthetic of Walter Pater*, pp. 133–134; Geoffrey Tillotson, *Criticism and the Nineteenth Century*, pp. 107 ff. On the sources of Arnold's and Pater's views of the Renaissance, see Appendix II.

CHAPTER SEVENTEEN   Arnold, Pater, and the
Complete Religion
of the Greeks

Pater's "Wordsworth" (1874) marks a pause in his development. In his defense of "impassioned contemplation" as a higher ethic in which means and ends are identified and in which life is treated "in the spirit of art" (*Appr.*, pp. 60–62), he epitomized his view of the ideal aesthetic observer which he had been developing since the essay on Winckelmann. In its concern for the "sum of perfection," its rejection of the "machinery" of life, its opposition of *being* to *doing*, its near identification of morals and manners, and its advocacy of a detached witnessing of the spectacle of human life, "Wordsworth" draws heavily on Arnold's "Sweetness and Light" and other essays of the sixties. More important, the ideal of isolated immobile observation is clearly a simplification and extension of Arnold's ideal of disinterested criticism, now shorn of its social orientation though freely drawing on the religious ambiance of Arnold's ideal of culture and "perfection."[1]

Pater's chief work of the years 1875 through 1880 is the series of studies in Greek myth and art which became the bulk of the posthumously collected *Greek Studies*. The unifying theme is the elaboration and modification of the dialectically conceived classical-medieval antagonism, first developed in "Coleridge" and "Winckelmann." Once again, Arnold's "Pagan and Mediaeval Religious Sentiment" becomes both a source for Pater's ideal of life and the foil for his special reading of Greek culture. The new note of special interest is that Pater repeatedly implies that the Greek religious spirit is still somehow available today to at least the few, "those more elevated spirits" who, in the decline of the older religion, will "pick and choose and modify . . .

---

[1] See Chapter 14, note 13, above.

whatever in it may seem adapted to minister to their culture" (*GS*, p. 137). This series of essays—produced, surprisingly, in the years immediately before and during the first stages of the writing of *Marius* —thus becomes one of the most ambitious attempts in modern English letters to assert the viability in the present of a "pagan" religious ideal. Pater's technique again is to suggest that Greek religion is richer and more complex than Arnold and others suggest, that the later stages of Greek myth and the highest Greek sculpture with which it is allied incorporate the best features of the medieval religious spirit.

The contemporary relevance is immediately clear in the first of the two lectures titled "The Myth of Demeter and Persephone," delivered in 1875 and published in January and February 1876, which opens with the claim that by following the history of the myth of Demeter "we come across various phases of Greek culture, which are not without their likenesses in the modern mind." Moreover, Pater's characteristic elitist point of view is equally clear in the notion that the myth connects itself "with the picturesque superstitions of the many, and with the finer intuitions of the few" (*GS*, p. 81). He details three successive phases of the Demeter story: first, the "half-conscious, instinctive, or mystical, phase" of unwritten legend, expressing "certain primitive impressions of the phenomena of the natural world"; second, the conscious, or poetic and literary, phase, in which poets use "the vague instinctive product of the popular imagination . . . with a purely literary interest"; and third, the ethical phase, in which the persons and events of the narrative "are realised as abstract symbols, because intensely characteristic examples, of moral or spiritual conditions" (*GS*, p. 91). James Kissane has recently showed that Pater's approach to myth is typically Victorian in that his interest is humanistic and aesthetic and, inevitably, ethical, rather than anthropological.[2] Pater, like Ruskin and Symonds, looked for no truths in myths in the old manner, and, while aware of the new anthropology of the seventies, he does not look for patterns of primitive worship in myths. Instead, he is in the mainstream of Victorian mythology in his emphasis, as Kissane puts it, on "the primarily subjective origin of myths, their adaptability to

[2] See James Kissane, "Victorian Mythology," *Victorian Studies*, VI (September 1962), 5–28.

the conceptions of succeeding generations, and their resulting enrichment by this process of imaginative transformation and elaboration."[3] This flexible and organic concept, in which myth had no positive content but could never be outmoded,[4] proved admirably adaptable to Pater's polemical purposes.

Part of his strategy is to emphasize, even more than he had done in "Winckelmann," the "Biblical" and "medieval" quality of Greek myth, its "sacredness" and "mystery." For Greek religion to be, implicitly, an adequate rival to Christianity, Pater must demonstrate that it includes the now admittedly touching and picturesque and emotionally satisfying characteristics of medieval religion and yet *surpasses* medieval religion by its having given rise to high Greek art and thought. The Biblical and medieval parallels become labored and obtrusive. The modern reader finds the "spiritual element of Greek religion" in stories of the disguises and transformations of the gods: the apparition of Athene to Telemachus, for example, in Odyssey I, "has a quite biblical mysticity and solemnity" (*GS*, p. 119). The "mysteries," which are the expression of the worship of Demeter, "may or may not have been the vehicle of a secret doctrine, but were certainly an artistic spectacle, giving, like the mysteries of the middle age, a dramatic representation of the sacred story,—perhaps a detailed performance, perhaps only such a conventional representation, as was afforded for instance by the medieval ceremonies of Palm Sunday" (*GS*, p. 122). Moreover, Pater shows that "a parallel has sometimes been drawn between [the Eleusinian] festival and All Soul's Day," and says, concerning the hymn of Callimachus: "He developes, in something of the prosaic spirit of a medieval writer of 'mysteries,' one of the burlesque incidents of the story" (*GS*, pp. 123, 125).

The cutting edge of the argument is not felt until later, however, when discussing Ovid's treatment of the Demeter myth and his addition of "a pathos caught from homely things, not without a delightful, just perceptible, shade of humour even, so rare in such work. All the

---

[3] *Ibid.*, p. 19; Kissane is commenting on Pater's view that myth is "the projected expression of the ways and dreams of this primitive people, brooded over and harmonised by the energetic Greek imagination" (*GS*, p. 29).

[4] Kissane, "Victorian Mythology," p. 21.

mysticism has disappeared; but, instead, we trace something of that 'worship of sorrow,' which has been sometimes supposed to have had no place in classical religious sentiment" (*GS*, p. 134). Pater has, of course, gone back to the argument of "Winckelmann," where Newman's view of classical polytheism as "gay and graceful" had been sharply challenged by Pater's insistence on the immemorial and somber ritual prehistory of the high Hellenic culture. Similarly, Pater clearly recalls Arnold's polarized opposition of the medieval "religion of sorrow" and the allegedly superficial "religion of pleasure" of the Greeks, in "Pagan and Mediaeval Religious Sentiment." For it is essential to Pater's argument that the reader appreciate the deep ethical significance of the image of Demeter as "the divine sorrowing mother," or the image of her "enthroned, chastened by sorrow" (*GS*, p. 136):

The myth has now entered on the third phase of its life, in which it becomes the property of those more elevated spirits, who, in the decline of the Greek religion, pick and choose and modify, with perfect freedom of mind, whatever in it may seem adapted to minister to their culture. In this way, the myths of the Greek religion become parts of an ideal, visible embodiments of the susceptibilities and intuitions of the nobler kind of souls. (*GS*, pp. 136–137)

Here, again, Pater seems to be recalling that extraordinary passage in "Coleridge" on certain religious states of mind which remain, even "for those who have passed out of Christianity," "the delicacies of the higher morality of the few." For "the modern aspirant to perfect culture" finds in the best theological writings "the expression of the inmost delicacies of his own life, the same yet different!" One can only assume that in 1876 Pater is implicitly arguing that Greek myth more adequately conveys those religious graces than does Augustine, or Francis de Sales, or Newman, whom he had praised a decade earlier.

The ambitiousness of this, Pater's most developed defense of the power of a "pagan" religious ideal, and the seriousness with which he proposes it, are clear in a final paragraph, in which he explains his fundamental view of myth:

There is an attractiveness in these goddesses of the earth, akin to the influence of cool places, quiet houses, subdued light, tranquillising voices.

What is there in this phase of ancient religion for us, at the present day? The myth of Demeter and Persephone, then, illustrates the power of the Greek religion as a religion of pure ideas—of conceptions, which having no link on historical fact, yet, because they arose naturally out of the spirit of man, and embodied, in adequate symbols, his deepest thoughts concerning the conditions of his physical and spiritual life, maintained their hold through many changes, and are still not without a solemnising power even for the modern mind, which has once admitted them as recognised and habitual inhabitants; and, abiding thus for the elevation and purifying of our sentiments, long after the earlier and simpler races of their worshippers have passed away, they may be a pledge to us of the place in our culture, at once legitimate and possible, of the associations, the conceptions, the imagery, of Greek religious poetry in general, of the poetry of all religions. (*GS,* p. 151)

What does not appear in the version printed in *Greek Studies* is the virtually unheard of personal tone of the opening of this paragraph in the original periodical version of the lecture: "There is an attractiveness in these goddesses of the earth akin to the influence of cool places, quiet houses, subdued light, tranquillising voices; for me, at least, I know it has been good to be with Demeter and Persephone, all the time I have been reading and thinking of them; and all through this essay, I have been asking myself, what is there in this phase of ancient religion for us at the present day?"[5]

In "A Study of Dionysus" (December 1876) the polemical intention, if somewhat muted, is unmistakable: "the religion of Dionysus was, for those who lived in it, a complete religion, a complete sacred representation and interpretation of the whole of life" (*GS,* p. 18). In his stress upon the "energetic, imaginative intelligence" of the Greeks (*GS,* p. 11), Pater makes Greek religion the bearer of the religious holism that is at the basis of his humanism. The key is Pater's constantly renewed search for an adequate formula for the unification and harmonizing of the disparate forces of man's nature.

Dionysus, as we see him in art and poetry, is the projected expression of the ways and dreams of this primitive people, brooded over and harmonised

[5] Walter Pater, "The Myth of Demeter and Persephone," Part II, *Fortnightly Review,* N.S. XIX (February 1876), 276.

by the energetic Greek imagination; the religious imagination of the Greeks being, precisely, a unifying or identifying power, bringing together things naturally asunder, making, as it were, for the human body a soul of waters, for the human soul a body of flowers; welding into something like the identity of a human personality the whole range of man's experiences of a given object, or series of objects—all their outward qualities, and the visible facts regarding them—all the hidden ordinances by which those facts and qualities hold of unseen forces, and have their roots in purely visionary places. (*GS,* p. 29)

The dialectical nature of this historic process is equally characteristic. Pater discerns a "struggle" through the history of Greek art and drama "between the palpable and limited human form, and the floating essence it is to contain" (*GS,* p. 34). The world of the "old beliefs," a world of "Titanic vastness," is contrasted to "that limiting, controlling tendency, identified with the Dorian influence in the history of the Greek mind, the spirit of a severe and wholly self-conscious intelligence" (*GS,* pp. 34–35.). "These two tendencies . . . met and struggled and were harmonized in the supreme imagination, of Pheidias, in sculpture—of Aeschylus, in the drama" (*GS,* p. 35). So important to Pater has the presence of "sorrow" in a "complete" religion become, that he not only stresses that "It is out of the sorrows of Dionysus . . . that all Greek tragedy grows" (*GS* p. 40), but also makes sorrow an essential basis for the relevance of Greek religion to Pater's small band of elite souls. "If Dionysus, like Persephone, has his gloomy side, like her he has also a peculiar message for a certain number of refined minds, seeking, in the later days of Greek religion, such modifications of the old legend as may minister to ethical culture, to the perfecting of the moral nature" (*GS,* p. 49). When Pater declares this will be "the finer, mystical sentiment of the few, detached from the coarser and more material religion of the many" (*GS,* p. 50), he is again dealing with phases of Greek culture "which are not without their likenesses in the modern mind."

Sometime in 1878, according to C. L. Shadwell (*GS,* p. 2), Pater revised his four Greek studies with a view to publication, an intention he did not carry out. At that time he added to "Demeter and Persephone" an important passage that reveals it is still precisely Arnold's version of the "familiar view of Greek religion" which these studies are primarily directed against:

The "worship of sorrow," as Goethe called it, is sometimes supposed to have had almost no place in the religion of the Greeks. Their religion has been represented as a religion of mere cheerfulness, the worship by an untroubled, unreflecting humanity, conscious of no deeper needs, of the embodiments of its own joyous activity. It helped to hide out of their sight those traces of decay and weariness, of which the Greeks were continually shy, to keep them from peeping too curiously into certain shadowy places, appropriate enough to the gloomy imagination of the middle age; and it hardly proposed to itself to give consolation to people who, in truth, were never "sick or sorry." But this familiar view of Greek religion is based on a consideration of a part only of what is known concerning it, and really involves a misconception, akin to that which underestimates the influence of the romantic spirit generally, in Greek poetry and art; as if Greek art had dealt exclusively with human nature in its sanity, suppressing all motives of strangeness, all the beauty which is born of difficulty, permitting nothing but an Olympian, though perhaps somewhat wearisome calm. In effect, such a conception of Greek art and poetry leaves in the central expressions of Greek culture none but negative qualities; and the legend of Demeter and Persephone, perhaps the most popular of all Greek legends, is sufficient to show that the "worship of sorrow" was not without its function in Greek religion; their legend is a legend made by and for sorrowful, wistful, anxious people; while the most important artistic monuments of that legend sufficiently prove that the Romantic spirit was really at work in the minds of Greek artists, extracting by a kind of subtle alchemy, a beauty, not without the elements of tranquility, of dignity and order, out of a matter, at first sight painful and strange. (*GS,* pp. 110–111)

The clearly implied antagonist is Arnold, who had said, "The ideal, cheerful, sensuous, pagan life is not sick or sorry," and who had seen the superiority of the religion of sorrow to lie in its power to "console" and "to be a comfort for the mass of mankind, under the pressure of calamity, to live by" (*CPW,* III, 222, 228, 229). The upshot is that Pater's complete Greek religion and art are the dialectical harmony of the two polar tendencies of Greek life: they embody a full measure of the strangeness and beauty of the "romantic spirit" that remains even in the highest products of Greek art. This statement amplifies and slightly complicates the remarks of the Winckelmann essay: "Out of Greek religion under happy conditions arises Greek art, . . . to minister to human culture. The claim of Greek religion is that it was able to transform itself into an artistic ideal" (*Ren-1*, p. 176).

The two installments of "The Beginnings of Greek Sculpture" (February and March 1880) are of some importance in their implication that the "organic," "combining," "many-sided" early Greek religious *art* provides a pattern of *life* still available to the modern mind. Pater begins by protesting that because much is understood about the inner life of the Greeks from the poets and philosophers but very little is known about the craftsman's world, "students of antiquity have for the most part interpreted the creations of Greek sculpture, rather as elements in a sequence of abstract ideas, as embodiments, in a sort of petrified language, of pure thoughts, and as interesting mainly in connexion with the development of Greek intellect" (*GS*, p. 189). He readily acknowledges that the best works of Greek sculpture are "intellectualised" through "the profoundly reasonable spirit of design" in Greek art: "Yet, though the most abstract and intellectualised of sensuous objects, they are still sensuous and material, addressing themselves, in the first instance, not to the purely reflective faculty, but to the eye; and a complete criticism must have approached them from both sides" (*GS*, p. 190). This view (which anticipates Jacques Maritain's formula of art as "intelligentiated sense")[6] leads Pater to his most suggestive use of the organic analogy, which he had once criticized in Coleridge (*Appr.*, pp. 80–81). Greek art absorbs foreign sources in the way that physical organisms provide a "new cohering force" to already existing particles of matter (*GS*, p. 215). This is "a new, informing, combining spirit playing over all those mere elements" (*GS*, p. 216). This notion of the combining and cohesive power of early Greek art prepares for the implication that the religious matrix of Greek art provides the adequate synthesis of the sensuous and the

---

[6] Jacques Maritain (*Art and Scholasticism, and The Frontiers of Poetry*, pp. 163–165), speaks of the senses in glorified bodies as "intellectualized," and notes "that in the perception of the beautiful the intellect is, *through the means of the sensible intuition itself,* placed in the presence of a radiant intelligibility." He remarks that in art intellect and sense form "but one, or, if one may so speak, *intelligentiated sense,* which gives rise in the heart to aesthetic joy."

spiritual which Pater demands as an ideal of a many-sided culture. For instance, the "solemn images of the temple of Theseus are a perfect embodiment of the human ideal, of the reasonable soul and of a spiritual world; they are also the best *made* things of their kind, as an urn or a cup is well made." Even more explicitly: "A perfect, many-sided development of tectonic crafts, a state such as the art of some nations has ended in, becomes for the Greeks a mere opportunity, a mere starting-ground for their imaginative presentment of man, moral and inspired." The "informing, reasonable soul" enters a world of material splendor, and these two elements are continuously present in "Greek art after the heroic age" (*GS*, p. 223). Later, Pater maintains that Greek art was characterized by "an energetic striving after truth in organic form" (*GS*, p. 239). Moreover, in this age of the early Greek sculptors, which was still "simply religious, . . . this widespread artistic activity was a religious enthusiasm also" (*GS*, p. 241). The harmonizing process is evident, finally, in the idea that this impersonal early Greek art proved to be compatible with "types of art, fully impressed with the subjectivity, the intimacies of the artist" (*GS*, p. 242).

The culmination of this sustained series of arguments occurs in "The Marbles of Aegina" (April 1880), one of the most notable interpretative efforts of Pater's career. Having demonstrated in detail in his earlier studies the permanent presence of a darker and more profound background in his "complete" Greek religion, he turns his full attention to that misunderstood high Hellenic religion and art that he has now provided with a rich ancestry. The dialectical structure of his treatment is important, moreover, because it initiates the Apollonian-Dionysian dichotomy that was to provide the pattern of much of Pater's fiction.[7] His terms are not quite those of Nietzsche, however: the Ionian tendency is referred to as "Asiatic," and is opposed to the Dorian, or European, or "Apolline," or Hellenic. The Ionian influence, stressing the sensuous, was present from the beginning in Greek art. So was the emergent Dorian or European tendency, " a tendency to the realisation of a certain inward, abstract, intellectual ideal," directed toward "the impression of an order, a sanity, a proportion in all work,

[7] See R. T. Lenaghan, "Pattern in Walter Pater's Fiction," *Studies in Philology,* LVIII (January 1961), 69–91.

which shall reflect the inward order of human reason, now fully conscious of itself" (*GS*, p. 251). Greek sculpture not only undergoes the influence of these two opposing ideals but "by harmonising in itself their antagonism" reflects the larger pattern of Greek history in general (*GS*, p. 252).

The "centrifugal" Ionian or Asiatic tendency asserts itself in separatism and individualism in politics; despite its grace and freedom, its evident weakness prevented Greek unity. Against this force, Plato set the Dorian influence of "a severe simplification everywhere," "the ideal of a sort of Parmenidean abstractness and calm." This is, however, only the exaggeration of "that salutary European tendency, which, finding the human mind the most absolutely real and precious thing in the world, enforces everywhere the impress of its sanity, its profound reflexions upon things as they really are, its sense of proportion." This "centripetal" tendency links individuals and states and periods, "under the reign of a composed, rational, self-conscious order, in the universal light of the understanding" (*GS*, p. 253). This temper is best exemplified in "the religion of Apollo." Demeter and Dionysus remain throughout, as the "spiritual form" of life in grass and the green sap, almost entirely physical. But the physical element in Apollo is largely suppressed, and as "the 'spiritual form' of inward and intellectual light, in all its manifestations," he stands for those peculiarly European ideas, "of a reasonable, personal freedom . . .; of a reasonable polity; of the sanity of soul and body, through the cure of disease and of the sense of sin; of the perfecting of both by reasonable exercise or *ascésis*; his religion is a sort of embodied equity, its aim the realisation of fair reason and just consideration of the truth of things everywhere" (*GS*, p. 254). The same is true of Greek art, where the religion of Apollo sanctioned "the true valuation of humanity, in its sanity, its proportion, its knowledge of itself." This art expressed not only the highest and most ordered human intelligence but the great human passions as well (*GS*, p. 255). Thus the Apolline, the "true Hellenic influence," created Greek humanism with its permanent grasp of "the inward harmony and system of human personality" (*GS*, p. 256). This Apolline humanism—with its emphasis on an inward ideal, order, proportion, reason, harmony, reflecting on things as they really are, the universal light of the understanding, and consideration of the truth of things—is very close in tone and phrasing to the Arnoldian Hellenic ideal of criticism and culture in the sixties. Pointedly lacking is Arnold's persistent concern for morality, that wrestling with Christianity in the form of "Hebraism" which, by the time of *Culture and Anarchy*, had provided a chief dialectical pattern of his thought.

PART III

PATER AND THE THIRD

CONDITION OF HUMANITY

CHAPTER EIGHTEEN   Toward *Marius:*
Aesthetic Worship

Almost simultaneously with his impressive defense of the Greek ideal, Pater was, between 1876 and 1883, continuing that other series of statements concerning the Middle Ages and Christianity, in their relations to the Hellenic spirt and to modern literature, which had so occupied him in the essays of the Renaissance volume. As if with the other hemisphere of his brain and, in retrospect, as remote preparation for *Marius*, Pater again and again attempts, inconsistently and uncomfortably, to come to terms with the medieval inheritance of the modern world. The essay "Romanticism" (November 1876; later as Postscript to *Appreciations*, 1889) is illustrative. The subject is the definition of classicism and romanticism. Anticipating twentieth-century notions, Pater separates the view of romanticism and classicism as period concepts from the view that the romantic and classical spirits are two tendencies at work, in varying proportions, at all times (*Appr.*, pp. 247, 257). He does not deny that temperament has a role in the generation of the romantic spirit and that there are born romanticists and born classicists (*Appr.*, pp. 249, 257). Neither does he deny that romanticism in the limited sense is the product of "special epochs" (*Appr.*, p. 250). For example, one great period, that of German romanticism (Pater mentions Goethe and Tieck), is pictured as "listening in rapt inaction to the melodious, fascinating voices of the Middle Age," that other "romantic" age (*Appr.*, p. 249).[1] The problem becomes that of determining whether, as many German aestheticians had claimed, the Middle Ages are the special fount of the romantic spirit.

The answer is a carefully qualified affirmative. Pater again stresses the romantic element in Greek literature (*Appr.*, pp. 258–259), an idea he had used in the Greek studies and much earlier in "Winckelmann" to challenge the conventional view of the Middle Ages as the unique spiritual matrix of the romantic spirit in art and literature. Pater must, however, account for Dante and for Provençal love poetry. As he had done in the Morris review of 1868, Pater acknowledges that the "overcharged" spirituality of the Middle Ages provided the climate in which the intensities of the courtly love tradition flourished; but since romanticism crops up again and again in literary and spiritual history,

---

[1] Arnold and Oxford seem to suffuse parts of this essay. Pater makes the essential elements of the romantic spirit, "curiosity and the love of beauty," or as he puts it later, "the desire for beauty and sweetness" (*Appr.*, pp. 248–251). The "sweetness and light" of Arnold's farewell lecture at Oxford are defined precisely in these terms: light is "curiosity," the "desire to see things as they are"; and "sweetness" becomes "the keen desire for beauty and sweetness," "the sentiment of Oxford for beauty and sweetness" (*CPW*, V, 91, 107). When Pater comments on the "strange beauty" that the German Romantics found in the Middle Ages—"the idea of romanticism is still inseparably connected with Germany—that Germany which, in its quaint old towns, under the spire of Strasburg or the towers of Heidelberg, was always listening in rapt inaction to the melodious, fascinating voices of the Middle Age" (*Appr.*, p. 249)—we hear the echo of Arnold's famous (and ambiguous) apostrophe to Oxford in the Preface to *Essays in Criticism*: "Beautiful city! so venerable, so lovely, so unravaged by the fierce intellectual life of our century, so serene! . . . steeped in sentiment, . . . spreading her gardens to the moonlight, and whispering from her towers the last enchantments of the Middle Age . . . her ineffable charm. . . . Adorable dreamer, whose heart has been so romantic!" (*CPW*, III, 290). Moreover, Wolfgang Iser (*Walter Pater: Die Autonomie des Aesthetischen*, p. 110) points out the likeness of Pater's "*House Beautiful*, which the creative minds of all generations—the artists and those who have treated life in the spirit of art—are always building together" (*Appr.*, p. 241), to Arnold's two definitions of culture, "the acquainting ourselves with the best that has been known and said in the world, and thus with the history of the human spirit" (*LD*, p. xi), and as "a study of perfection, . . . which consists in becoming something rather than in having something, in an inward condition of mind and spirit" (*CPW*, V, 94–95).

he undercuts his concession by making the Middle Ages "only an illustration," even if the supreme illustration, of the romantic spirit. He
puts his argument this way: "The essential elements, then, of the
romantic spirit are curiosity and the love of beauty; and it is only as an
illustration of these qualities, that it seeks the Middle Age, because, in
the overcharged atmosphere of the Middle Age, there are unworked
sources of romantic effect, of a strange beauty, to be won, by strong
imagination, out of things unlikely or remote" (*Appr.*, p. 248). However, some ambiguity results from the following account of medieval
"romanticism":

Outbreaks of this spirit . . . come naturally with particular periods—times,
when, in men's approaches towards art and poetry, curiosity may be noticed
to take the lead, when men come to art and poetry, with a deep thirst for
intellectual excitement, after a long *ennui,* or in reaction against the strain
of outward, practical things: in the later Middle Age, for instance; so that
medieval poetry, centering in Dante, is often opposed to Greek and Roman
poetry, as romantic poetry to the classical. (*Appr.*, p. 250)

Romanticism is thus an "outbreak," "a reaction" of intellect against
ennui, presumably the *ennui* induced by *medieval* asceticism and ex-
cessive spirituality. Moreover, romanticism in "its true signification"
comes only with the literature of Provence, in which the desire for
beauty and sweetness is mingled with the "grotesque" and the almost
"insane": this is "a wholly new species of poetry, in which the *Renaissance* may be said to begin" (*Appr.*, pp. 205–251). Pater's essay
comes close to being an elaborate evasion of the question of the relation
of romanticism to medieval spirituality; it wavers between his two
earlier views—the first, that the Renaissance and the modern spirit,
even in the Middle Ages, are simply the antagonists of the medieval
spirit, or rather the insurrectionary outcropping of the suppressed Hellenic ideal; the second, that the unnatural rigors and intensities of the
medieval religious ideal provided precisely the atmosphere in which
an antinomian literature of the grotesque and the bizarre could flourish.

In 1877 Pater once again assayed the difficult relation of the Renaissance and the Middle Ages, in revising and expanding "Aucassin and
Nicolette" for its inclusion as "Two Early French Stories" in the sec-

ond edition of *The Renaissance*. The spirit of the additions is unexpectedly conciliatory toward Christianity: the principle on which Pater is operating is that of "the harmony of human interests." He develops the parallel between the legend of Tannhäuser and the story of Abelard:

When Abelard died, like Tannhäuser, he was on his way to Rome. What might have happened had he reached his journey's end is uncertain; and it is in this uncertain twilight that his relation to the general beliefs of his age has always remained. In this, as in other things, he prefigures the character of the Renaissance, that movement in which, in various ways, the human mind wins for itself a new kingdom of feeling and sensation and thought, not opposed to but only beyond and independent of the spiritual system then actually realised. The opposition into which Abelard is thrown, which gives its colour to his career, which breaks his soul to pieces, is a no less subtle opposition than that between the merely professional, official, hireling ministers of that system, with their ignorant worship of system for its own sake, and the true child of light, the humanist, with reason and heart and senses quick, while theirs were almost dead. He reaches out towards, he attains, modes of ideal living, beyond the prescribed limits of that system, though in essential germ, it may be, contained within it. As always happens, the adherents of the poorer and narrower culture had no sympathy with, because no understanding of, a culture richer and more ample than their own. After the discovery of wheat they would still live upon acorns . . . and would hear of no service to the higher needs of humanity with instruments not of their forging. (*Ren-3*, pp. 6–7)

This is a new Pater and a new solution to one of the most persistent problems of his intellectual career. The spirit of conciliation is evident in the first statement that the "new kingdom" won by the Renaissance is "not opposed to, but only beyond and independent of," the medieval religious system. Pater then makes the unprecedented announcement of the possibility that this new humanism of reason, heart, and senses may have been "contained in essential germ" within the medieval system itself. The only culprits now are the ignorant, inflexible priests.

Pater ends his considerably expanded essay by a significant qualification of that "sinister claim for liberty of heart and thought" which in 1873 he saw in the Renaissance *within* the Middle Ages:

But in the *House Beautiful* the saints too have their place; and the student of the Renaissance has this advantage over the student of the emancipation of the human mind in the Reformation, or the French Revolution, that in tracing the footsteps of humanity to higher levels, he is not beset at every turn by the inflexibilities and antagonisms of some well-recognised controversy, with rigidly defined opposites, exhausting the intelligence and limiting one's sympathies. The opposition of the professional defenders of a mere system to that more sincere and generous play of the forces of human mind and character, which I have noted as the secret of Abelard's struggle, is indeed always powerful. But the incompatibility with one another of souls really "fair" is not essential; and within the enchanted region of the Renaissance, one needs not be forever on one's guard. Here there are no fixed parties, no exclusions: all breathes of that unity of culture in which "whatsoever things are comely" are reconciled, for the elevation and adorning of our spirits. (*Ren-3*, pp. 26–27)

Presumably just because they exist in the subintellectual atmosphere of a "House" exclusively furnished with what is comely and thus have no part in doctrinal disputes such as marked the Reformation and the French Revolution, the most centrally representative figures of the Renaissance are aloof from "disputations" and "the spirit of controversy." Leonardo da Vinci, "with his kindred, live in a land where controversy has no breathing-place, and refuse to be classified." Pater acknowledges that in the antinomian literature of which *Aucassin and Nicolette* is a type, "the note of defiance, of the opposition of one system to another, is sometimes harsh"; but he begs leave to end with a morsel from the "saintly" tale of the friends Amis and Amile, "in which the harmony of human interests is still entire" (*Ren-*3, p. 27).

I think it evident that here, in 1877, Pater's career is at a critical dividing point. The mood of "Romanticism" (1876) had been one of reconcilement: he had asserted that, although *classical* and *romantic* have sometimes divided people of taste into opposing camps, in the House Beautiful "these oppositions cease" (*Appr.*, p. 241). With the additions of 1877, Pater has at last achieved a synthetic viewpoint sufficiently broad to include even the rigors of medieval Christianity, or at least "the saints," within that "harmony of human interests" which is the passkey to the House Beautiful. It can hardly be doubted that this intensified mood of reconciliation and harmony and the new welcome extended to Christianity reflect Pater's new religious interests in the later seventies. Never again does Pater produce the direct and unsubtle attacks on historic Christianity which marked his critical efforts as a young man. The central theme of Pater's writing, from this point until the appearance of *Marius*, is "unity of culture" and unity of personality in a subintellectual tradition of "fair souls" who live a life of "pure perception" analogous to the fusion of form and matter in a work of art. The saints are now admitted to this suddenly sunnier and totally inclusive structure of the House Beautiful because Christianity now proves adaptable to a culture of total perception by reason of its sacramentalism, its "aesthetic worship."

The most complete statement of Pater's aesthetics occurs in "The School of Giorgione" (October 1877), in which he insists on "the sensuous element in art": "art addresses not pure sense, still less the pure intellect, but the 'imaginative reason' through the senses" (*Ren-3*, p. 130). The famous statement, "*All art constantly aspires towards the condition of music*," is explained as meaning that music alone achieves the goal of obliterating the distinction between matter and form:

Art . . . is thus always striving to be independent of the mere intelligence, to become a matter of pure perception, to get rid of its responsibilities to its subject or material; the ideal examples of poetry and painting being those in which the constituent elements of the composition are so welded together, that the material or subject no longer strikes the intellect only; nor the form, the eye or the ear only; but form and matter, in their union or identity, present one single effect to the "imaginative reason," that complex faculty for which every thought and feeling is twin-born with its sensible analogue or symbol. (*Ren-3*, p. 138)

The unity of the art work thus corresponds to a complex faculty belonging to both artist and perceiver. The imaginative reason becomes the special instrument for the life of "pure perception," which is the individual's mode of participation in that larger "unity of culture" into which the child of light inserts himself. The phrase "imaginative reason" is of course Arnold's, and if Pater did not use it in precisely Arnold's sense,[2] it properly stood for Pater's version of the unity of consciousness and the modes of ideal living which had borrowed so heavily from Arnold.

Florian Deleal, the autobiographical hero of "The Child in the House" (August 1878), obviously a prototype of Marius, lives this life of pure perception with the aid of the imaginative reason. Pater notes the "predominance in his interests, of beautiful physical things, a kind of tyranny of the senses over him," and the fact that he placed little value on abstract thought and much on "its sensible vehicle or occasion" (*MS*, p. 186). The portrait of Florian is especially significant because it contains a statement of the grounds for the new admissibility of Christianity into the unity of culture. Florian "remembered gratefully how the Christian religion, hardly less than the religion of the ancient Greeks, translating so much of its spiritual verity into things that may be seen, condescends in part to sanction this infirmity, if so it be, of our human existence, wherein the world of sense is so much with us" (*MS*, p. 186).[3] This sensate religion is explained further in the study of Rossetti in 1883, when Pater was deep in the composition of *Marius*. There Christian sacramentalism, "aesthetic worship," is seen as canceling the distinction between spirit and matter, obviously on an analogy with the fusion of matter and form in art:

Spirit and matter, indeed, have been for the most part opposed, with a false contrast or antagonism by schoolmen, whose artificial creation those ab-

---

[2] Germain d'Hangest (*Walter Pater: l'Homme et l'Oeuvre*, I, 350, n. 24) sees the origin of the phrase in Arnold, but suggestively argues that the meaning is derived from Kant's "aesthetic judgment."

[3] Pater also comments that "religious sentiment, that system of Biblical ideas in which he had been brought up, presented itself to him as a thing that might soften and dignify, and light up as with a 'lively hope,' a melancholy already deeply settled in him" (*MS*, pp. 192–193). This suggests Arnold's definition of religion in *Literature and Dogma* as "ethics heightened, enkindled, lit up by feeling" (*LD*, p. 18) and, even more, the statement in "Marcus Aurelius" (1863) that Christianity, in contrast to the "constraint and melancholy" of Epictetus and Marcus Aurelius, "has *lighted up morality*" (*CPW*, III, 134).

stractions really are. In our actual concrete experience, the two trains of phenomena which the words *matter* and *spirit* do but roughly distinguish, play inextricably into each other. Practically, the church of the Middle Age by its aesthetic worship, its sacramentalism, its real faith in the resurrection of the flesh, had set itself against that Manichean opposition of spirit and matter, and its results in men's way of taking life; and in this, Dante is the central representative of its spirit. (*Appr.*, p. 212)

By about 1880, then, the Christian liturgy, to which Pater was so notoriously attached in private life, had become as successful an agent as Greek religion in providing man with an all-inclusive unity of consciousness and sympathy, above the antagonisms of spirit and matter and of fixed positions.

CHAPTER NINETEEN *Marius* and the Necessity of Religion

M*arius the Epicurean* (1885) is not only the supreme intellectual and artistic effort of Pater's career, but it represents the ultimate reach of the dialectical impulse that had governed so much of his earlier career. Moreover, the ethical and intellectual thrust of Pater's dialectic is closely parallel to the central line of Matthew Arnold's development in the sixties and seventies. *Marius* becomes a thoroughgoing revision or at least reshaping of Pater's characteristic positions in the *Renaissance* and elsewhere; and his basic dichotomy between culture and religion is worked out in terms strikingly close to Arnold's historical and ethical theory of the relations between Hebraism and Hellenism. That Arnold's Inaugural Lecture of 1857 and the essay on Marcus Aurelius (1863) had an important part in forming Pater's view in *Marius* of Marcus Aurelius and late

Roman civilization is now well established.[1] As readers have also seen,[2] the larger tissue of Arnoldian phrasing extends well beyond these two matters; my argument here is that the very structure of *Marius* reflects Pater's reading of *Culture and Anarchy* and Arnold's religious writings of the seventies.

The stages of Marius' progress have been carefully detailed, especially by R. V. Osbourn, who finds the pattern of the book in "the cycle of apparent stabilities recurrently failing": each alternative view of life is tested by death and each, except for the final Christian vision, found wanting.[3] *Marius* moves from the traditional religion and ethic, through a pleasurable paganism, to the apparent stability of Pater's partially hedonistic New Cyrenaicism; Stoicism then attracts him by its claim of a more complete life of "active serenity," and, after a stage in which he is prepared for the possibility of union with a transcendent power, he ends in the life of the Christian community.[4] That this move-

---

[1] See Kenneth Allott, "Pater and Arnold," *Essays in Criticism*, II (April 1952), 219–221. Louise M. Rosenblatt ("The Genesis of Pater's *Marius the Epicurean*," *Comparative Literature*, XIV [Summer 1962], 242–260) suggests a "pluralistic hypothesis," in which Lemaître's *Sérénus* is the most immediate "source," Renan's *Les Évangiles* provides the general philosophical attitudes, and Arnold's remains the "pervasive influence" that also led Pater to Renan. But Germain d'Hangest (*Walter Pater: l'Homme et l'Oeuvre*, I, 370, n. 20), convincingly argues that Pater's view of Marcus Aurelius, despite parallels with Renan, is in fact closer to Arnold's view. For example, Renan is completely satisfied with Aurelius' philosophy, whereas Pater has moral reservations and points out the Emperor's failure to see the future. Moreover, Pater sees Aurelius as faithful to the traditional polytheism, whereas Renan tends to make him a Renanian skeptic with no religion beyond the moral conscience. Pater's portrait is like Arnold's in putting at the center the fatigue and paralyzing sadness of Marcus Aurelius, and both men see his life, despite a certain beauty in it, as a failure. Federico Olivero (*Il Pensiero Religioso ed Estetico di Walter Pater*, p. 234) finds a foreshadowing of Marius' skepticism in Arnold's "In Utrumque Paratus" and "Empedocles."

[2] See Allott, "Pater and Arnold," pp. 219–221; and Graham Hough, *The Last Romantics*, p. 149.

[3] R. V. Osbourn, *"Marius the Epicurean,"* *Essays in Criticism*, I (October 1951), 398.

[4] *Ibid.*, pp. 397–398. The most careful charting of Marius' course appears in U. C. Knoepflmacher, *Religious Humanism and the Victorian Novel: George Eliot, Walter Pater, and Samuel Butler*, pp. 195–213. I have discussed the possible influence on *Marius* of George Eliot's version of "the 'agnostic' conversion novel" in "*Romola*

ment, hesitant as it may be concerning his ultimate commitment to Christianity, *is* intended to be a "progress," is obscured by the fact that the "Christian" Marius at the point of death seems temperamentally very similar to Marius at twelve years. As Billie Andrew Inman has shrewdly noted, "All of the themes introduced in the first three chapters can be traced throughout the work."[5] Apart from the numerous elements in the Christian community which are obviously not present in the inherited religion of Marius' childhood and which Mrs. Inman overlooks, the flaw in her argument is her neglect of the ambiguity into which Pater's double time scheme throws "that visionary idealism of the villa." As Osbourn puts it, "the historical setting is primarily of importance as a disguise for an autobiographical and philosophical progress in the nineteenth century, and not for its revelation of Antoine Rome."[6] The inherited religion will have close resemblances to the final Christian vision precisely because, in its nineteenth-century analogue, the inherited religion becomes the traditional Christianity abandoned by a sensitive young man of acute aesthetic susceptibilities; the later rapprochement with Christianity of such a man will inevitably bear certain resemblances to his boyhood faith, along with important additions and modifications.

The movement from stage to stage in Marius' progress is unified, moreover, by a persistent three-part conflict between Marius' intellectual and emotional impulses, a conflict manifested both in Roman society and in his own mind. As Mrs. Inman helpfully frames the oppositions,

Paganism, in his scheme, corresponds to the head and Christianity to the heart. Pater details three sides of this general conflict: (1) against the consuming concern of paganism for perfection in external display he places a Christian reverence for inner virtues; (2) against paganism's haunting sense of futility he places Christian hopefulness; (3) against paganism's

---

and the Origin of the Paterian View of Life," *Nineteenth-Century Fiction,* XXI (December 1966), 225–233.

[5] Billie Andrew Inman, "The Organic Structure of *Marius the Epicurean,*" *Philological Quarterly,* XLI (April 1962), 478.

[6] Osbourn, "*Marius the Epicurean,*" p. 392.

philosophic indifference to pain and its vulgar delight in brutality to animals he places Christian sympathy for all creatures. Each of these conflicts has a correspondent in the mind of Marius: (1) pure aesthetic judgment vies with moral concern; (2) a scepticism which engenders despair vies with a mysticism which engenders hope; (3) a tendency to develop the mind in detachment vies with a sympathy for the suffering of all creatures.[7]

Mrs. Inman finds this continuing oscillation between the aesthetic and skeptical view of life, and the moral and even mystical view, persisting to the very end and thus leaving unresolved the conflicts of Marius' life. But she does concede that in one aspect of this conflict of heart and head—"intellectual detachment *versus* sympathetic feeling"—the heart wins decisively.[8] It remains to suggest the implications of this complex dialectical structure in relation to Pater's earlier thought and to Arnold's sponsorship—in providing terms and ideas—of this new marriage of aestheticism and Christianity. Pater's opposition of head and heart becomes, in effect, a further set of variations in the prolonged struggle of Hebraism and Hellenism in the thought of both men.

The altered perspectives of Pater's view are evident early in the book in the sharp contrast of Flavian's rather sinister mobility, animation, and "eager capacity for various life" with the older "visionary idealism": "To Marius, at a later time, he counted for as it were an epitome of the whole pagan world, the depth of its corruption, and its perfection of form" (*ME*, I, 53). Pater is preparing for a thoroughgoing critique of his aestheticism as expressed in the *Renaissance*; indeed, *Marius* cannot be understood fully unless the reader is constantly alive to Pater's attempt to meet the charges of the critics of his first volume, perhaps above all W. H. Mallock. The basic opposition of the book between Hellenic culture and a "visionary" religion informs each stage of the dialetic. The early contrast between the childhood religion and the young man's new Epicureanism is presented in terms of Arnold's dichotomy between "culture" and traditional Christianity, Hellenism and Hebraism. The second dichotomy, that marked out between Marcus Aurelius' Stoicism and early Christianity, is drawn, as

[7] Inman, "Organic Structure of *Marius*," p. 484.
[8] *Ibid.*, pp. 487–488.

Kenneth Allott and others have shown, from Arnold's disparagement of Aurelius' melancholy in contrast to Christian "joy," in the essay of 1863 and elsewhere. The final reach of Pater's dichotomizing impulse is achieved when he introduced a new disjunction within Christianity, one between the "humanistic" Christianity of the second century and the unsatisfactory "ascetic" Christianity of the Middle Ages. The rejected ascetic Christianity plays the role assigned to English Puritanism in the interplay of Hebraism and Hellenism in *Culture and Anarchy*. His favored version of Christianity hovers between two related ideals: one, a Christianized version of Arnold's culture or Hellenism, with several dashes of the religion of *Literature and Dogma*; the other, a naturalistic, nondogmatic Christianity not unlike that moralized secular Christianity of Arnold's religious writings of the seventies, though Pater pointedly eschews the heavily *moral* emphasis Arnold imparts to his reading of religious history and psychology.

The point of especial importance here is that *Marius* recapitulates not only a number of stages in Pater's own development but also, with significant changes of tone and emphasis, the crucial struggles of Arnold's career. As Pater borrowed from Arnold's works the essential structure of his dilemmas, he now more systematically responds to a number of the very pressures that impelled Arnold continually to reshape the dilemmas and disjunctions of his own intellectual career.

To understand Pater's reliance on Arnold requires at least a synoptic view of the relations between culture and religion in Arnold's thought in the sixties and seventies. Arnold's straightforward contrast of Christian joy and the Stoic gloom of Marcus Aurelius in 1863 is undercut the next year in "Pagan and Mediaeval Religious Sentiment," where medieval religious joy is only temporarily awarded the palm over pagan sensuousness, and where the religiously tinged humanism of Periclean Athens and its "imaginative reason" offer a final aggressive challenge to Christianity: "Let St. Francis,—nay, or Luther either, —beat that!" (*CPW*, III, 231). Arnold's disinterested criticism in "The Function of Criticism at the Present Time," while having no direct relation to religion, derives a good deal of its power from the religious rhetoric in which it is swathed: Criticism inhabits the sphere of spiritual progression, its task is to lead men to the fullness of spiritual perfection, its subtle and indirect action works by the Indian virtue of detachment. The relation of religion to culture in *Culture and Anarchy* is more complex, partly because the book reflects Arnold's developing thought for a period of almost two years. In "Sweetness and Light" culture not only seeks to achieve what religion seeks—perfection, harmonious perfection, general perfection, an inward condition of mind and spirit—but it also engrosses and supersedes the functions of traditional religion: as the harmonious expansion of all the highest powers, avoiding the overdevelopment of any one faculty, "culture goes beyond religion, as religion is generally conceived by us" (*CPW*, V, 94). The model is Greek art and poetry, "in which religion and poetry are one"; the ideal of human life is the aesthetic one of "beauty, harmony, and complete human perfection" (*CPW*, V, 100). A year later, however, in "Hebraism and Hellenism," man's two impulses, intellectual and moral, are again said to have the same aim—"man's perfection or salvation"—but Arnold is at considerable pains to insist on the divergence of method by which they proceed. Arnold concedes that "the Hellenic conception of human nature" was unsound because late classical civilization lacked the "indispensable basis of conduct and self-control." But it is not "absolutely" unsound: it was simply not the "hour" for Hellenism. At another point Arnold assigns "the priority . . . to that discipline which braces all man's moral powers, and founds for him an indispensable basis of character" (*CPW*, V, 169–170). Arnold's most persistent posture of course is that of the reconciler, the sponsor of "the idea of a comprehensive adjustment of the claims of both the sides in man, the moral as well as the intellectual, of a full estimate of both, and a reconciliation of both" (*CPW*, V, 179). But the polemical mood breaks through as Arnold reminds the reader that for the Reverend W. Cattle and his fellow countrymen, "at this particular moment," Hellenism is more wanted (*CPW*, V, 181).

Literature and Dogma, the central statement of Arnold's religious position in the seventies, marks a retreat from both the easy merging of religious and aesthetic categories and the aggressive setting up of Hellenic inclusiveness over against Hebraic narrowness. Arnold speaks almost as if he were not the author of *Culture and Anarchy*:

Some people, indeed, are for calling all high thought and feeling by the name of religion; according to that saying of Goethe: "He who has art and science, has also religion." But let us use words as mankind generally use them. We may call art and science touched by emotion *religion,* if we will; as we may make the instinct of self-preservation . . . include the perfecting ourselves by the study of what is beautiful in art; and the reproductive instinct . . . include the perfecting mankind by political science. But men have not yet got to that stage; . . . neither do we yet think of religion as otherwise exercising itself. When mankind speak of religion, they have before their mind an activity engaged, not with the whole of life, but with that three-fourths of life which is *conduct.* (*LD,* pp. 18–19)

Arnold later explains this notion, which surely Pater would have read with considerable interest, when he says that the *"not ourselves,* by which things fulfil the real law of their being," extends greatly beyond the moral sphere and includes "art and science." This is not true in "the generality of men," however, because the moral side of that tendency includes so large a fraction of life: "Let us," Arnold pleads, "keep firm footing on this basis of plain fact, narrow though it may be" (*LD,* p. 40). But Arnold is not wholly comfortable, even in *Literature and Dogma,* with the restrictions that the special development of his Christian moralism places upon the totally engrossing tendency of his culture. He criticizes even his own definition of the God of Israel as "the Eternal Power, not ourselves, that makes for *righteousness,*" since it applies only to our moral side, and he bids us remember that "there is one-fourth of our being of which it does not strictly meet the wants, the part which is concerned with art and science" (*LD,* p. 308). "For the total man, therefore, the truer conception of God is as 'the Eternal Power, not ourselves, by which *all things* fulfil the law of their being;' by which, therefore, we fulfil the law of our being so far as our being is aesthetic and intellective, as well as so far as it is moral" (*LD,* pp. 348–349). Although it may be harsh, at present, to speak of pleasing or displeasing God in these two areas, nevertheless "as man makes progress, we shall surely come to doing this. For, the clearer our conceptions in science and art become, the more will they assimilate themselves to the conceptions of duty in conduct, will become practically stringent like rules of conduct, and will invite the same sort of language in dealing with them" (*LD*, p. 349). Arnold has prepared the way not only for his own return to the literary and political world with a much deepened, religiously colored doctrine of culture, but also for the special emphasis of the Paterian version of culture.

The ethical dynamic of this movement from the intellectualist position of disinterested criticism in the early sixties to the elevated and sometimes even mystical view of self-transcendence in the religious writings of ten years later is complex. It involves notions like service, the higher self, and as its culmination the "inspired self-sacrifice" of Jesus first developed in *Culture and Anarchy*. The deepening of the ethical substructure of Arnold's culture in the latter volume was, as already discussed, largely a response to the critics' charges of hedonism, aestheticism, uselessness, and self-centeredness. The argument of *Marius* was in large part shaped as an answer to the very similar charges directed against Pater's earlier writings; Pater understandably turned to Arnold's example for possible solutions to the ethical dilemmas that by 1880 evidently loomed large for him, too. Always in the background there is the mysterious matter, about which little will ever be known, of Pater's personal rapprochement with his own childhood religion.

A central thread of Arnold's ethical progress is the theme of the religious solidarity of mankind, based on sympathy, an idea related to the social utility of culture. Culture is a "moral, social, and beneficent" force, because the social motives—"love of our neighbour, the impulses towards action, help, and beneficence, the desire for removing human error, clearing human confusion, and diminishing human misery, the noble aspiration to leave the world better and happier than we found it"—are now "the main and pre-eminent" ground of culture. He explains the role of "sympathy" in this culture which seeks a "general" religious perfection:

And because men are all members of one great whole, and the sympathy which is in human nature will not allow one member to be indifferent to the rest or to have a perfect welfare independent of the rest, the expansion of our humanity, to suit the idea of perfection which culture forms, must be a *general* expansion. Perfection, as culture conceives it, is not possible while the individual remains isolated. The individual is required, under pain of being stunted and enfeebled in his own development if he disobeys, to carry others along with him in his march towards perfection, to be continually doing all he can to enlarge and increase the volume of the human stream sweeping thitherward. (*CPW*, V, 94)

This sympathy of the "one great whole," that best self by which "we are united, impersonal, at harmony," becomes in the Preface of 1869 a "*general* perfection, developing all parts of our society," and is explained in Pauline terms: "For if one member suffer, the other members must suffer with it; and the fewer there are that follow the true way of salvation, the harder that way is to find" (*CPW*, V, 235). Later in the same year, in "St. Paul and Protestantism," this is called Paul's "mystical conception" of identifying oneself with Christ and thus with Christ's "idea of the solidarity of men." The regenerate members of the human race, dying and rising with Christ, become "the mystical body of Christ." The life of Christ is incomplete if only this or that individual follows it: "The same law of emotion and sympathy, therefore, which prevails in our inward self-discipline, is to prevail in our dealings with others" (*SPP*, pp. 66–67). Thus what Mrs. Inman speaks of as Marius' movement from intellectual detachment to a Christian "sympathy for the suffering of all creatures," "sympathetic feeling," closely resembles the central movement of Arnold's intellectual career. The sympathy that Arnold places at the center both of his religiously conceived culture and his enlightened religion is the crown of Pater's new-found Christianity in *Marius*.

A review of Marius' career reveals that this ethical direction in Arnold's thought provides a pattern for the stages of Marius' spiritual progress. In tracing this movement, Pater not only revises a number of his earlier views but also subjects his own and Arnold's conception of culture to the kind of scrutiny given it by their critics; in this way, *Marius* becomes almost an epitome of the successive attempts by Arnold and Pater to shore up the assailable basis of culture. In the formation of Marius' Cyrenaicism, there are many echoes from *Culture and Anarchy* concerning mankind's deep yearning "towards ideal perfection," "completeness of life," "insight through culture," and culture as "a wide, a complete, education" and "the expansion and refinement of the power of reception" (*ME*, I, 98, 142, 157). Not only does Marius himself have a "poetic and inward temper," but he senses that his culture and "intellectual discipline" (referred to in Schiller's phrase as "an 'aesthetic' education") "might come even to seem a kind of religion—an inward, visionary, mystic piety, or religion" (*ME*, I, 147–148). Similarly, "the true aesthetic culture would be realisable as a new form of the contemplative life, founding its claim on the intrinsic 'blessedness' of 'vision,' " in a "world of perfected sensation, intelligence, emotion" (*ME*, I, 148). The first challenge to this ideal comes with the admission that culture may become "antinomian" by the standards of the received morality (*ME*, I, 149–150). Pater's first answer to criticism is that the charge of immoralism and hedonism is not applicable to Marius' form of Cyrenaic reflection: "Not pleasure, but fulness of life," was his goal (*ME*, I, 151). This phase of Marius' career even ends with a saving "inconsistency" in Marius, a note of limited selflessness. That is, despite his philosophy of the "mystic *now*," the moment, he wishes he could "arrest, for others also, certain clauses of experience, as the imaginative memory presented them to himself." This may merely be the literary impulse asserting itself, but it is connected with "his longing . . . for something to hold by amid the 'perpetual flux.' " (*ME*, I, 154–155).[9] The furthest reach of Marius' selfless feelings at this period is shown by his determination, not unconnected with the conscientious religion of his childhood, "to add nothing, not so much as a transient sigh, to the great total of men's unhappiness" (*ME*, I, 156)—which is a negative version of Arnold's "desire for . . . diminishing human misery," the "noble aspiration to leave the world better and happier than we found it" (*CA*, p. 44).

Much of volume II is preoccupied with the possibility, under the new Stoical influence, of an "adjustment" between "the old morality" and the Epicurean view of things. The old morality had been allowed no place in Marius' intellectual scheme because he feared its first principles might stand in the way of his goal of "a complete, many-sided

---

[9] This reference and a later one ("an inward need of something permanent in its character, to hold by"; *ME*, II, 18) indicate that Graham Hough's statement that Pater shows "none of Arnold's longing for certitude" (*The Last Romantics*, p. 137) requires some qualification.

existence." Now he fears that this dismissal reveals a "graceless 'anti-nomianism.' " Aware of "a strong tendency to moral assents," his concern becomes "to find a place for duty and righteousness in his house of thought" (*ME*, II, 6–7). In this "search after some principle of conduct," for some "theoretic equivalent to so large a proportion of the facts of life," Marius finds a temporary clue in Cornelius Fronto's defense of "the purely aesthetic beauty of the old morality" (*ME*, II, 7–9). Pater has now arrived almost exactly at the stage of culture indicated late in "Sweetness and Light," where Arnold speaks of the "best art and poetry of the Greeks, in which religion and poetry are one, in which the idea of beauty and of a human nature perfect on all sides adds to itself a religious and devout energy, and works in the strength of that" (*CPW*, V, 100). Pater's "adjustment" of morality and culture is precisely the point of a key passage in "Hebraism and Hellenism" which describes the Greek "idea of a comprehensive adjustment of the claims of both the sides in man, the moral as well as the intellectual, of a full estimate of both, and of a reconciliation of both" (*CPW*, V, 179). Of course Pater's "complete, many-sided existence" is reminiscent of a score of expressions in *Culture and Anarchy*—for example, the definition of Hellenism as "a many-sided perfecting of man's powers and activities," or the idea of "being complete at all points, the full and harmonious development of our humanity" (*CPW*, V, 185). Moreover, Pater's speaking of morality as "so large a proportion of the facts of life" has the ring of Arnold's famous definition of conduct, in *Literature and Dogma*, as "three-fourths, . . . at the very lowest computation, of human life," perhaps even four-fifths or five-sixths (*LD*, p. 13).

Chapter XVI, "Second Thoughts," is at once Pater's most poignant defense of his aestheticism and the most telling critique of its limitations. The argument breaks neatly in the middle, and each half implicitly acknowledges different kinds of critical challenges. The framework is the "isolating narrowness" that Marius now sees in his scheme of life, by contrast with the "wide prospect over the human, the spiritual, horizon" revealed in the discourse of the Stoic Fronto. Marius applies his own aesthetic criterion of "loss and gain," or the "economy" of life, to determine whether his Epicureanism "missed

something in the commerce of life, which some other theory of practice was able to include," and whether it "made a needless sacrifice"
(*ME*, II, 15). This fear of "sacrificing" some part of consciousness,
pervasive in *Marius*, seems clearly derived from Arnold's definition of
the bent of Hellenism, "to follow, with flexible activity, the whole play
of the universal order, to be apprehensive of missing any part of it, of
sacrificing one part to another, to slip away from resting in this or that
intimation of it, however capital" (*CPW*, V, 165). Ironically, however, where Arnold was in 1868 apprehensive of "resting" in the religious intimation of the universal order, Marius' new fear is that of
sacrificing the wider religious consciousness to his life of aesthetic perception. At any rate, Pater's limited defense of Cyrenaicism takes the
line that it is simply the philosophy of youth, ardent and sincere, but
one-sided and even fanatical, the "vivid, because limited, apprehension
of the truth of one aspect of experience" (*ME*, II, 15).

Although this "clear-eyed intellectual consistency" may indeed require the sacrifice of certain high convictions and first principles, Pater's chief point is that in the aesthetic devotee's "scrupulous idealism,
indeed, he too feels himself to be something of a priest, and that devotion of his days to the contemplation of what is beautiful, a sort of
perpetual religious service" (*ME*, II, 17). In short, the doctrine is that
of the idealistic young man and not of "the 'jaded Epicurean' " (*ME*,
II, 16). The very intensity of his self-development makes him especially open to the appeal of religion: "he has, beyond all others, an
inward need of something permanent in its character, to hold by"
(*ME*, II, 18). Although truth admittedly resides " 'in the whole'—
in harmonisings and adjustments" (almost Arnold's very prescription
of the "comprehensive adjustment" and harmonious "reconciliation"
of the two sides of man's nature), the "nobler form of Cyrenaicism—
Cyrenaicism cured of its faults" paradoxically merges with the religious temper:

If it starts with considerations opposed to the religious temper, which the
religious temper holds it a duty to repress, it is like it, nevertheless, and
very unlike any lower development of temper, in its stress and earnestness,
its serious application to the pursuit of a very unworldly type of perfection.
The saint, and the Cyrenaic lover of beauty, it may be thought, would at

least understand each other better than either would understand the mere man of the world. Carry their respective positions a point further, shift the terms a little, and they might actually touch. (*ME*, II, 20)

In this ultimate defense of a purified aestheticism, Pater can list the qualities of the nobler Cyrenaicism which approach those of the nobler phases of the traditional morality: "In the gravity of its conception of life, in its pursuit after nothing less than a perfection, in its apprehension of the value of time . . . it may be conceived, as regards its main drift, to be not so much opposed to the old morality, as an exaggeration of one special motive in it" (*ME*, II, 21). This rather strained performance, one of the most "synthesizing" in Pater, parallels Arnold's listing of the qualities in which culture is like religion—with the significant difference that Arnold's culture went *beyond* religion in inclusiveness, while Pater's aestheticism is somehow the extreme development of one aspect of religion itself.

Thus Pater refutes the charges of hedonism and antinomianism directed against the view of life expressed in the *Renaissance* by offering a purified and elevated aestheticism not only compatible with religion but actually especially conducive to religious vision. He goes on, in the second part of the argument, so far to acknowledge the charges of self-centeredness and narrowness as to shake the self-sufficiency of culture to its foundations. This new strategy takes the form of admitting that the older masters of Cyrenaic philosophy, though they experienced moments of almost "beatific" pleasure and knowledge, paid too high a price, "in the sacrifice of a thousand possible sympathies, of things only to be enjoyed through sympathy, from which they detached themselves, in intellectual pride" (*ME*, II, 21–22). By rejecting even the "higher view" of Greek religion available to the philosopher, these thinkers rejected a "whole comely system of manners or morals" which gracefully enveloped the whole of life and which would satisfy even the "merely aesthetic sense" (*ME*, II, 22–23). The failure of this Cyrenaic culture to profit by attention to Greek religion and Greek morality shows, Pater concludes, "their fierce, exclusive, tenacious hold on their own narrow apprehension" (*ME*, II, 24)—which is, by an amusing shift in rhetoric, the very terminology Arnold habitually employed to abuse English Puritans for their "rigidness and contentious-ness" and for their "narrow and mechanical conception" of salvation (*SPP*, p. 14; *CPW*, V, 187). But Marius, it is clear, must be carefully preserved from these harsher strictures: for it was perfection he had sought all along, even if a narrow perfection centered in "his capacities of feeling, of exquisite physical impressions, of an imaginative sympathy" (*ME*, II, 24). In his reawakened interest in the "venerable system of sentiment and idea," he found his old self again, as the pilgrim who had originally come to Rome, "with absolute sincerity, on the search for perfection" (*ME*, II, 26–27). This inherited order of sentiment and idea, first imparted to Marius by the Stoics, would indeed entail some curtailment of his liberty, but it "defined not so much a change of practice, as of sympathy—a new departure, an expansion, of sympathy" (*ME*, II, 27). He would be untrue to his own criterion of value "if he did not make that concession, if he did but remain just there" (*ME*, II, 28). Marius' own standards remain, for the while, "aesthetic"—there must be no "sacrifice" of any possible experience—but the phrase "the merely aesthetic sense" and references to sympathy, friendship, and patriotism prepare the reader for the advent of Pater's Hellenic Christianity.

Chapter XIX, "The Will as Vision," is crucial in presenting the growth of Marius' conscience and religious sense. His apprehensions of divinity are presented in some detail, and seem clearly to reflect Arnold's struggles with the idea of the transcendent in his writings of the seventies. Marius' speculation on a providential hand in his life and affairs, "an unfailing companion," brought him in the first place "an impulse of lively gratitude" (*ME*, II, 66–67). Under the direct influence of natural beauty, "he passed from mere fantasy of a self not himself, beside him in his coming and going, to those divinations of a living and companionable spirit at work in all things, of which he had become aware from time to time in his old philosophic readings," a "reasonable Ideal" known to the Greeks and to the Old and New Testaments (*ME*, II, 67–68). He saw that

his bodily frame . . . Nay! actually his very self—was yet determined by a far-reaching system of material forces external to it, a thousand combining currents from earth and sky. Its seemingly active powers of apprehension were, in fact, but susceptibilities to influence. The perfection of its capacity might be said to depend on its passive surrender, as a leaf on the wind, to the motions of the great stream of physical energy without it. And might not the intellectual frame also, still more intimately himself as in truth it was, after the analogy of the bodily life, be a moment only, an impulse or series of impulses, a single process, in an intellectual or spiritual system external to it, diffused through all time and place—that great stream of spiritual energy, of which his own imperfect thoughts, yesterday or to-day, would be but the remote, and therefore imperfect pulsations? (*ME*, II, 68–69)

Gratitude, a self not himself, the currents from earth and sky, susceptibilities to influence, passive surrender, the great stream of physical energy, the great stream of spiritual energy: these are some of the key terms and ideas of Arnold's theodicy and cosmology. Agnostic as to the "personality" of the transcendent element in things, Arnold prefers in *St. Paul and Protestantism* to define God as the *"stream of tendency by which all things strive to fulfil the law of their being"* (*SPP*, p. 8). This sense of God as "the source of life and breath and all things" is the "infinite element," the "element in which we live and move and have our being, which stretches around and beyond the strictly moral element in us, around and beyond the finite sphere of what is originated, measured, and controlled by our own understanding and will" (*SPP*, pp. 47, 49). "By this element," says Arnold, "we are receptive and influenced, not originative and influencing" (*SPP*, p. 49). The basic opposition remains that between the "voluntary, rational, and human world, of righteousness, moral choice, effort" and "the necessary, mystical and divine world of influence, sympathy, emotion" (*SPP*, p. 50). In *Literature and Dogma*, in discussing the origin of the religious impulse, Arnold again brings in those "facilities and felicities . . . suggestions and stimulations," to which visitations, he concludes, "we may well give ourselves, in grateful and devout self-surrender" (*LD*, pp. 25–26). The irrational "energy" and "power" in the world are amplified into "a tendency, which is *not ourselves*, but which appears in our consciousness, by which things fulfil the real law of their being" (*LD*, p. 39). This presumably corresponds to Pater's system of material forces, of which one's "very self" is a part. But there is for Arnold a more limited aspect, "the *not ourselves* by

which we get the sense for *righteousness*, and whence we find the help
to *do right*"; and, as shown above, this aspect of the not ourselves extends beyond this moral sphere to "art and science," thus including
the totality of man's spiritual operations (*LD*, pp. 27, 39). This more
limited view of the not ourselves would then correspond to Pater's intellectual or spiritual system, and great stream of spiritual energy.
When Pater says that this sense of companionship with a transcendent force "evoked the faculty of conscience, . . . in the form . . . of a
certain lively gratitude" (*ME*, II, 71), he echoes the Arnold who
speaks of "gratitude for righteousness," or put differently, who says
that with the happiness brought by morality, comes a "sense of gratitude" (*LD*, pp. 30, 41).

In Chapter XXI, "Two Curious Houses," Marius was reaching
"the critical turning-point in his days"; for he saw in "the blithe self-
expansion" of the Christians at worship the message of *peace* put forth
everywhere, "with images of hope, snatched sometimes from that faded
pagan world which had really afforded men so little of it from first
to last" (*ME*, II, 103). In effect, by allowing Marius to find in Christianity a "tranquil hope . . . heroic cheerfulness and grateful expansion
of heart," as well as "the solace or anodyne of his great sorrows," and
by disparaging the pagan world, Pater is quite openly reversing the
characteristic balance of cultural values presented in the Renaissance
and Greek studies and adopting the formerly rejected view of Arnold
in "Pagan and Medieval Religious Sentiment." Not until the following chapter, " 'The Minor Peace of the Church,' " does Pater present
his ultimate dialectical effort. Here Pater reasserts his Hellenic humanism, but now as one of the two traditions *within* historic Christianity and superior to Greek religion. The effect is to confound critics
of the allegedly antireligious tone regarding culture in the *Renaissance*
by showing it to be somehow the highest Christian ideal. Moreover,
the poles of Pater's dialectic—the familiar ones of culture and a puritan Christianity: in a word, Hellenism and Hebraism—are taken bodily from Arnold.

A prime characteristic of this brief period of the Minor Peace of the
Church was "the vision of a natural, a scrupulously natural, love,"
under the urgency of a "new motive," "a more effective sanction and

motive," than it had ever had before, though it was still unfathomable
to Marius (*ME*, II, 109 ff.). This is, presumably, the love of Christ.
This new motive and sanction of what Pater calls "the truth of nature"
in Christianity are important notes in Arnold's view of Christianity,
too. *Saint Paul and Protestantism*, as shown earlier, speaks of Christianity's new motive force, "the immense tidal wave of sympathy and
emotion" felt for Christ. *Literature and Dogma* refers to the new and
stronger motive as "personal devotion to Jesus Christ," a motive "full
of ardent affection and gratitude," and to "the sanction of joy and
peace" (*LD*, pp. 92, 172–173). Arnold asserts the identity of *natural*
and *revealed* religion (as opposed to the "artificial" religion of the
theologians) as being the product of a certain natural consciousness,
man's "experience of the power, the grandeur, the necessity of righteousness" (*LD*, p. 45). At any rate, the genius and power of Christianity, says Pater, are shown in the hope nurtured by Christian chastity. This chastity issued "in a certain debonair grace, and a certain
mystic attractiveness, a courtesy, which made Marius doubt whether
that famed Greek 'blitheness,' or gaiety, or grace, in the handling of
life, had been, after all, an unrivalled success" (*ME*, II, 111). Again
he adopts Arnold's previously rejected view that the Greek religion of
gaiety and pleasure (that of Gorgo and Praxinoe "chattering in their
blithe Doric") was a "manifest failure" as a religion for men to live
by (*CPW*, III, 228–229).

    This view of Christianity as a more successful sponsor of grace and
courtesy than pagan culture is the clue to Pater's remarkable development of what amounts to the idea of "two Christianities." Christian
belief had inspired chastity, which in turn rehabilitated "peaceful labour" after the pattern of Christ, "another of the natural instincts of
the catholic church, as being indeed the long-desired initiator of a religion of cheerfulness" (*ME*, II, 114). Pater offers his statement of a
theory of historical oscillation:

And this severe yet genial assertion of the ideal of woman, of the family, of
industry, of man's work in life, so close to the truth of nature, was also, in
that charmed hour of the minor "Peace of the church," realised as an
influence tending to beauty, to the adornment of life and the world. The
sword in the world, the right eye plucked out, the right hand cut off, the

spirit of reproach which those images express, and of which monasticism is
the fulfilment, reflect one side only of the nature of the divine missionary
of the New Testament. Opposed to, yet blent with, this ascetic or militant
character, is the function of the Good Shepherd, serene, blithe and debonair,
beyond the gentlest shepherd of Greek mythology; of a king under whom
the beatific vision is realised of a reign of peace—peace of heart—among
men. Such aspect of the divine character of Christ, rightly understood, is
indeed the final consummation of that bold and brilliant hopefulness in
man's nature, which had sustained him so far through his immense labors,
his immense sorrows, and of which pagan gaiety in the handling of life,
is but a minor achievement. Sometimes one, sometimes the other, of those
two contrasted aspects of its Founder, have, in different ages and under the
urgency of different human needs, been at work also in the Christian
Church. (*ME*, II, 114–115)

In Marius' mind, the favored version of "Christianity in its humanity,
or even its humanism, in its generous hopes for man, its common sense
and alacrity of cheerful service, its sympathy with all creatures, its appreciation of beauty and daylight," is sharply contrasted with Marcus
Aurelius' burden of "unrelieved melancholy" (*ME*, II, 115). The clue
to the nature of this humanistic Christianity lies in Pater's remark that
"so much of what Marius had valued most in the old world seemed
to be under renewal and further promotion" (*ME*, II, 116). At this
stage of its exposition, this Christianity is simply Pater's Arnoldian
culture and Hellenism taking to itself certain religious graces. For
example, Pater now explains what in 1883 he had called Christian
"sacramentalism" as the view that "the world of sense . . . set forth
the veritable unction and royalty of a certain priesthood and kingship of the soul within, among the prerogatives of which was a delightful sense of freedom" (*ME*, II, 116). The major part of Christian history, before and after this brief episode under the Antonines, was the
reign of the Christianity of "the dark ages," of an "austere *ascêsis*,"
of "exclusiveness, . . . puritanism, . . . ascetic gloom" and "tasteless
controversy." But this "gracious spirit" of the second century marked
a Christianity true to the "profound serenity" in the soul of Christ and
thus "conformable to the original tendency of its genius." It was the
spirit of this better Christianity—"Amiable, in its own nature, and full

of a reasonable gaiety"—which reasserted itself centuries later in St. Francis, Dante, and Giotto (*ME*, II, 117–119).

This theory of the two Christianities is only the prelude to an even more ambitious universal theory of ethical history:

In the history of the church, as throughout the moral history of mankind, there are two distinct ideals, either of which it is possible to maintain—two conceptions, under one or the other of which we may represent to ourselves men's efforts towards a better life—corresponding to those two contrasted aspects . . . discernible in the picture afforded by the New Testament itself of the character of Christ. The ideal of asceticism represents moral effort as essentially a sacrifice, the sacrifice of one part of human nature to another, that it may live the more completely in what survives of it; while the ideal of culture represents it as a harmonious development of all parts of human nature, in just proportion to each other. (*ME*, II, 120–121)

There can be little doubt that this contrast between asceticism with its "sacrifice" and culture with its "harmonious development" is precisely that which Arnold makes the center of his discussion of Hebraism and Hellenism. There, intelligence and morality are two "forces," "in some sense rivals, . . . as exhibited in man and his history," which the world is attracted to in alternation (*CPW*, V, 163). The passage that probably comes closest to Pater's words is one in which Arnold says of Hellenism that "it opposes itself to the notion of cutting our being in two, of attributing to one part the dignity of dealing with the one thing needful, and leaving the other part to take its chance" (*CPW*, V, 154). Pater had turned to Arnold's ethical and historical theory to explain the relations between Marius' Cyrenaicism and his broadening Stoic vision; here again, he draws on Arnold's definitions of Hebraism and Hellenism, but with a strikingly different balance of values. For it is evident that Pater's rather factitious Christianity as described in this chapter is in fact a blend of his own "comely" aestheticism and Arnold's Hellenism and culture, while the contentious kind of Christianity, militant, puritan, ascetic, exclusive, is parallel to Arnold's Hebraic English Protestantism. That the favored Christianity is indeed what "Marius had valued most in the old world" is confirmed by the characteristic vocabulary used concerning Christianity in this chapter—serene, blithe, debonair, sweetness, humanism, appreciation of beauty, freshness, grave and wholesome beauty, gracious spirit, amiable, reasonable gaiety, the grace of graciousness, tact, good sense, urbanity and moderation, cheerful liberty of heart, aesthetic charm, comely order, the graces of pagan feeling and pagan custom: the whole panoply of the Paterian rhetoric which had adorned, and given the characteristic resonance to, the often aggressively "pagan" Renaissance and Greek studies. The only potentially moral or mystical notions contained in the chapter are those of a cheerful service, a sympathy with all creatures, and the "priesthood and kingship" of the soul—all undeveloped at this stage. Pater cannot of course be accused of deception; certainly his emphasis on "the naturalness of Christianity" (*ME*, II, 122), Arnold's characteristic phrase in his later years,[10] indicates both some of the source of this religion, as well as its metaphysical status. At times the larger polemical thrust of Pater's argument comes to the surface, as when he mentions, apropos of the accommodation of pagan feelings and customs in this Antonine Christianity, "As if in anticipation of the sixteenth century, the church was becoming 'humanistic,' in an earlier, and unimpeachable *Renaissance*" (*ME*, II, 125). Pater was at once retreating from the antinomianism of the *Renaissance* volume while almost delightedly re-exhibiting his Hellenic ideal in sacerdotal robes.

Fairness demands, of course, that this crucial chapter on the "Minor Peace" be seen as only a stage, not the ultimate reach, of Marius' pilgrimage. There is more to the religion of this chapter than Winckelmannian or Goethean Hellenism in blasphemous disguise for this is not merely Arnold's culture in its more religious mood. I believe that when Pater makes "a cheerful temper" the special quality of Christian character (*ME*, II, 123), he is reflecting Arnold's more deeply moral conviction, in the religious writings, that "Christianity is, first and above all, a temper, a disposition" (*SPP*, p. xxii). In one of his most conciliatory moods, in *St. Paul and Protestantism*, Arnold insists that both Hebraism and Hellenism are "beauty and charm"; if Hellenism is "amiable grace and artless winning good-nature, born out of lucid-

---

[10] See, for example, Matthew Arnold, "A Comment on Christmas, "*Contemporary Review,* XLVII (April 1885), 457–472; reprinted in the Popular Edition of *St. Paul and Protestantism* (1887).

ity, simplicity, and natural truth," Christianity (not here, interestingly, Hebraism) is "grace and peace by the annulment of our ordinary self through the mildness and sweet reasonableness of Christ." Both, then, are "eminently *humane"* (*SPP*, p. xxxiii). *Literature and Dogma* repeatedly stresses that authentic Christianity—as opposed to the strange "aberrations" of medieval asceticism—consists in a spirit of "mercy and humbleness," "meekness, inwardness, patience, and self-denial," and "the exquisite, mild, winning felicity" of Jesus (*LD*, pp. 195, 74, 86, 194). Now Pater's Christ and his "amiable" Christianity are of the very same spiritual quality: Christ is "the Good Shepherd, serene, blithe and debonair," who announces "a reign of peace—peace of heart"; this "spirit of a pastoral security and happiness" reflects the "profound serenity," "the peaceful soul," of Jesus; and the Church is "a power of sweetness and patience" (*ME*, II, 119, 114, 115, 117, 121, 124).

It also seems likely that Pater's very favorable presentation of the "catholic church" and of Catholic ritual in this chapter is, at least in part, indebted to Arnold. Pater speaks, for example, of the "aesthetic charm of the catholic church, her evocative power over all that is eloquent and expressive in the better mind of man, her outward comeliness, her dignifying convictions about human nature" (*ME*, II, 123). He ends by commenting on the "generous eclecticism" of Catholic ritual: "It was thus the liturgy of the church came to be—full of consolations for the human soul, and destined, surely! one day, under the sanction of so many ages of human experience, to take exclusive possession of the religious consciousness" (*ME*, II, 127). Arnold's "Irish Catholicism and British Liberalism" (July 1878) appeared in the *Fortnightly,* where by far the greatest number of Pater's own essays of this period were first published. There, Arnold announced that when Catholicism is eventually stripped of its Ultramontanism, sacerdotalism, and superstition, "It is left with the beauty, the richness, the poetry, the infinite charm for the imagination, of its own agelong growth" (*MxE*, pp. 88–89). In this poetry and charm for the imagination lies the superiority of Catholicism to all the Protestant sects: "I persist in thinking that the prevailing form for the Christianity of the future will be the form of Catholicism" (*MxE*, p. 90). Published at the very time of Pater's first conception of the plan of *Marius*, Arnold's essay may well have confirmed a significant drift in Pater's religious thought.

I think it amply demonstrated that—even apart from the very important extent to which Arnold shaped Pater's view of Marcus Aurelius and his conception of the conditions of late classical civilization, a subject I have not gone into here—Pater looked to Arnold's writings of the sixties and seventies in elaborating Marius' dialectical advance from one alternative position to another; the religion of *Marius* represents, to a degree not hitherto recognized or detailed, a merger of Arnold's Hellenism and his Christianity of mildness and sweet reasonableness. Perhaps Arnold goes even further as Virgil to Pater's pilgrim. As explained earlier, Arnold's religious doctrine of "the solidarity of men" in "the mystical body of Christ," through the "law of sympathy and emotion," is the clue to his own highest religious perceptions in the religious writings. And *sympathy*, as Mrs. Inman and others have seen, is precisely the one area in which Pater's hero unequivocally achieves a triumph over aesthetic isolation and detachment. Especially in Chapter XXV, "Sunt Lacrimae Rerum," Marius' diary reveals that he is aware of the need for "an imaginative stimulus," to overcome his occasional "indifference . . . in regard to the sufferings of others." This "callousness," he realizes, is a failure in love (*ME*, II, 173 ff.). A "ready sympathy with the pain one actually sees" becomes the practical difference among men; the future lies with those who have the most of this "power of sympathy" (*ME*, II, 183). Through this power we may have intimations, even if only of "some mere general sense of goodwill—somewhere in the world perhaps"; as Marius puts it, in pity, even self-pity, " 'I seem to touch the eternal' " (*ME*, II, 183–184). (By this point in *Marius*, intriguingly, Pater has adopted for his needs Arnold's three chief periphrases for God: the not ourselves, the stream of tendency, and the Eternal.) The theme of sympathy is expanded in the final chapter, where Marius, at the point of death, feels "the link of general brotherhood, and feeling of human kinship" (*ME*, II, 217).

Pater parts company with Arnold precisely here, at the moment of Marius' rather abortive beautifying vision. Marius' point of view is curiously double: he retains the essential norm, and the phrases, of the "Wordsworth" essay, insisting on "vision" or *seeing* as the end of life, above *having* or *doing*. This vision of "beauty and energy" in things implies using life, "not as the means to some problematic end, but, as far as might be . . . an end in itself" (*ME*, II, 218–219). On the other hand, it is just this "elaborate and lifelong education of his receptive powers" which enables Marius to open himself, however tentatively, "towards possible further revelation some day—towards some ampler vision." Marius remains forever poised, the house of his soul "ready for the possible guest," buoyed up by "the great hope" (*ME*, II, 219–221). Both halves of this double vision fall outside the purview of Arnold's agnostic Christian moralism. The intense ethical strain in Arnold's religious writings strives for an active engagement with the world beyond even the highly qualified aesthetic views of *Essays in Criticism* and *Culture and Anarchy*; at the same time, despite certain hints of companionship with Christ and of a "mystical" self-surrender to the not ourselves, there emphatically will be no further revelation, no possible guest, in the cleanswept house of Arnold's religion of *joy in righteousness*.

CHAPTER TWENTY   Gaston and the Lower Pantheism

The conclusion of *Marius* is the furth-est reach of Pater's dialectical impulse, and thus the furthest and most satisfac-tory merger of religion and culture in his career. This merger remains a delicately poised dual vision: on the one hand, Marius at the point of death retains his essentially "aesthetic" point of view, his "un-clouded receptivity of soul"; on the other, this receptivity is now also an openness to the transcendent, the ample vision, the great hope or possibility of further revelation in life. The writings of the final decade do not retreat from this balance of skepticism and detachment on the one side, and religious feeling and the possibility of a submetaphysical "beatifying" vision on the other. Vision balances vision: one, the utmost "capacity" for the variety and flux of the world (the vision of life in the *Renaissance*), the other the near-apprehension of a possible absolute reality. This balance becomes the central argument of Pater's last major work, *Plato and Platonism*. The writings of Pater's final, rather inconclusive, decade attempt to define the psychological and spiritual climate of a "third condition" of humanity, the reconstructed human nature that is the ultimate goal of Pater's dialectical adjustments and reconciliations. But a deep and persistent dualism remains at the heart of Pater's vision of man; he was no more able than was Arnold to overcome a realistic perception of continuing divisions in the human psyche. The balance of Christian and pagan, body and soul, concrete and ideal, commitment and detachment—the whole range of Pater's opposites—is constantly reshifted as he looks for a formula adequate to his aspiration.

The place of Christianity in these final attempts at cultural synthesis remains ambiguous. As *Marius* and some of the later essays suggest, Pater favors a "mixed" culture. It will be Catholic in form (in art, ritual, emotional tone), corresponding to that mode of ideal vision which apprehends "the world as it should be, as we should be glad to find it." But the content of that culture would be a mixture of skepticism, pagan sensuousness, and aesthetic susceptibility, the vision of the world as a flux of vivid, incommunicable impressions that produce a specially privileged consciousness as the crown of life. This latter mode of vision would appeal to emergent evolutionary "science" for confirmation of a view of life as unending change, a Hegelian "secular process" without a transcendental sanction. By 1886 Pater's Christianity is, intellectually, so far orthodox that he can criticize Amiel for his inability "to see that the old-fashioned Christianity is itself but the proper historic development of the true 'essence' of the New Testament"; at fault is Amiel's "constitutional shrinking, through a kind of metaphysical prejudice, from the concrete—that fear of the actual—in this case, of the Church of history." It is not surprising that Pater adapts to his needs John Henry Newman's "sceptical" argument (discussed in Chapter 23, below) in favor of *assent*, "on probable evidence," as leading to "the large hopes of the Catholic Church" (*EG*, pp. 33–34).

The psychological conditions for Pater's "religious phase possible for the modern mind" become clearer in the important and evidently autobiographical review of *Robert Elsmere* in 1888. "Doubt" becomes the double-edged polemical weapon of a sort of devout agnosticism, to be used alternately against a blameably undoubting belief, and against a blameably certain unbelief. For "philosophy" and "science" now enforce doubt as the necessary condition of perception in the modern world; but "doubt," in Pater's double vision, also has the positive function of opening itself to the "possibility" of transcendence. Robert Elsmere, he argues, was right to leave the clergy, but he was wrong to perceive his doubts so late and to act so precipitately in such a complex question. "Had he possessed a perfectly philosophic or scientific temper, he would have hesitated. . . . [For,] one by one, Elsmere's objections may be met by considerations of the same *genus*, and not less weight, relatively to a world so obscure, in its origin and issues, as that in which we live" (*EG*, p. 67). Elsmere belongs to "a large class of minds which cannot be sure that the sacred story is true," and it may even have been his duty to act on his doubts.

But then there is also a large class of minds which cannot be sure it is false —minds of very different degrees of conscientiousness and intellectual power, up to the highest. They will think those who are quite sure it is false unphilosophical through lack of doubt. For their part, they make allowance in their scheme of life for a great possibility, and with some of them that bare concession of possibility (the subject of it being what it is) becomes the most important fact in the world. (*EG*, p. 68)

It seems clear that Pater felt he belonged to that class of minds which "cannot be sure it is false." This, along with a special preference for liturgy at once aesthetic and religious, may be said to be the essence of his religious position in his last years, as far as it can be understood.

The peculiar flavor of this position, aesthetic and "Catholic," is evident in, for example, "Art Notes in North Italy" (1890), where the "remarkable beauty" in the face of a saint painted by Romanino leads

to this observation: "Beauty and Holiness had 'kissed each other.' . . .
At the Renaissance the world might seem to have parted them again.
But here certainly, once more, Catholicism and the Renaissance, religion and culture, holiness and beauty, might seem reconciled. . . .
[This] reminds one how the great Apostle Saint Paul has made courtesy part of the content of the Divine charity itself" (*MS*, pp. 107–
108). A more problematical example of this wedding of religion and
culture is that of Raphael, the "seductively mixed manner" and "de-
lightfully blent effects" of whose early work are Pater's chief interest.
Raphael's painting of Apollo and Marsyas might stand as a parable of
"the contention between classic art and the romantic"; and Apollo "has
a touch . . . of Heine's fancied Apollo 'in exile,' who, Christianity now
triumphing, has served as a hired shepherd, or hidden himself under
the cowl in a cloister" (*MS*, pp. 47–48). Pater, perhaps referring to
the Pre-Raphaelites of his own century, discusses this "peculiar, tremulous, half-convinced, monkish treatment of that after all damnable
pagan world" as it affects his contemporaries: "And our own generation certainly, with kindred tastes, loving or wishing to love pagan art
as sincerely as did the people of the Renaissance, and medieval art as
well, would accept, of course, of work conceived in that so seductively
mixed manner, ten per cent of even Raphael's later, purely classical
presentments" (*MS*, p. 48). (I take "accept . . . ten per cent" to mean
"accept *as little as* ten per cent.") And now for the first time medieval
Catholicism—and not merely its aesthetic aspects but its "whole creed"
—is seen as an essential component of the Renaissance imagination;
whereas earlier, the Renaissance was a reinstatement of "pagan" ideals
tout court, or the Middle Ages were seen, in the Morris review of 1868
and elsewhere, as at most providing an overwrought "mystical" climate in which a rather sinister and antinomian "liberty" of the heart
and senses could fluorish. In his greatest, "partly symbolic," paintings,

Raphael asserts, interprets the power and charm of the Catholic ideal as
realised in history. A scholar, a student of the visible world, of the natural
man, yet even more ardently of the books, the art, the life of the old pagan
world, the age of the Renaissance, through all its varied activity, had, in
spite of the weakened hold of Catholicism on the critical intellect, been still
under its influence, the glow of it, as a religious ideal, and in the presence

of Raphael you cannot think it a mere after-glow. Independently, that is, of less or more evidence for it, the whole creed of the Middle Age, as a scheme of the world as it should be, as we should be glad to find it, was still welcome to the heart, the imagination. (*MS*, p. 58)

Orthodox Christianity itself is now conceived as compatible with "humanistic developments." In 1894 Pater remarks that the Gothic churches of the thirteenth century "concurred . . . with certain novel humanistic movements of religion itself at that period," especially in Marian devotion; or, put differently, Gothic architecture "had a large share in that inventive and motivating genius, that expansion of the natural human soul, of which the art, the literature, the religious movements of the thirteenth century in France, as in Italy, where it ends with Dante, bear witness" (*MS*, pp. 110, 128). In what is probably Pater's most favorable comment on the Catholic Church of history, comparable to the opening of Arnold's "Pagan and Mediaeval Religious Sentiment," he states that, "in contrast with the classic manner, and the Romanesque survivals from it, the vast complexity of the Gothic style seemed, as if consciously, to correspond to the richness, the expressiveness, the thousandfold influence of the Catholic religion, in the thirteenth century still in natural movement in every direction" (*MS*, p. 114). The clear implication of all these references, however, is that orthodox "Catholic" Christianity is by no means in these latter days "in natural movement," that its hold on the critical intellect has indeed even further declined. The reader is left somewhat baffled, as indeed Pater himself may have been, as to the place of this historic Christianity in the even more emphatically skeptical culture of the nineteenth-century aesthete. The "hold" of orthodoxy upon the intellect has been reduced to a "bare concession of possibility"; if Pater's generation wishes to embrace the medieval as openly as the pagan in a "seductively mixed" cultural conflation, will not Christianity be the merest "after-glow" and its power and claim purely picturesque? The terms of the contract for the marriage of religion and culture, holiness and beauty, remain moot.

Part of the difficulty here is that the role of the "pagan" element in life remains almost equally enigmatic. For example, Heine's theme

of the gods in exile, of Apollo redivivus in the Middle Ages—referred
to in the Raphael essay, but first mentioned in the Renaissance studies
—becomes the central motif in a number of Pater's fictional works of
the final decade. Many years ago, John Smith Harrison helpfully explored Pater's use of the idea of the gods in exile, but beyond a vagrant suggestion that Pater's intentions involved the reconciliation of
Christianity and paganism,[1] he did not link the theme with his life-
long exploration of cultural antagonism and synthesis. More recently
R. T. Lenaghan has identified as the central pattern of Pater's fiction,
the opposition of the two gods, Dionysus and Apollo. In Apollo, he
finds "the concentration of mortal achievement, an ideal of human
development"; in Dionysus, "the power of a massive vitality external
to man" and "the promise of the continuity of life in nature."[2] The
difference is not that between intellect and passion, since Apollonian
religion embodies both intellect and passion, but is a matter of scope:
"the Greeks under Apollonian guidance had concentrated value on
man and had achieved a marvelous ethical depth and purity, but their
achievement was circumscribed within relatively narrow human limits
and it neglected the wider spiritual sense of the more than human vitality which Dionysus proclaims."[3]

For Lenaghan Pater's various "Portraits" then become so many examples of the different balance of these two elements—ranging from
conflict, through the varying predominance of one or the other, to different kinds of reconciliation. But Lenaghan's exemplary study is dis-
appointing in suggesting that "Pater's purpose seems to have been to
reset the old myths in a Christian era, not just to show how the world
has changed, but to show also, in the continued vitality of the old myths,
how it has not changed."[4] For vitality and continuity, while unquestionably conferring validity, are not sufficient to suggest the precise

[1] John Smith Harrison, "Pater, Heine, and the Old Gods of Greece," *PMLA,*
XXXIX (September 1924), pp. 657–658, 679. Harrison seems unaware of the
major shifts of emphasis in Pater's career.

[2] R. T. Lenaghan, "Pattern in Walter Pater's Fiction," *Studies in Philology,* LVIII
(January 1961), p. 70.

[3] *Ibid.,* p. 73.

[4] *Ibid.,* p. 75.

weight these pagan themes are to have in Pater's cultural synthesis. Moreover, the *content* of these pagan views, lightly touched on by Lenaghan, has undergone a decisive change. First of all, the Apollonian-Dionysan distinction is substantially the same as the contrast, made in the *Greek Studies* of the late seventies, between the Ionian and the Doric aspects of Greek religion and Greek culture. But in those earlier essays Pater's intention was clearly to praise the richness and adequacy of the Greek religious ideal at the expense of Christian pretensions to spiritual uniqueness; whereas in the portraits of the years after *Marius,* only one—"Apollo in Picardy," and that arguably—can be said to represent Christianity unfavorably. For now the desired combination of these two religious ideals, discernible in Greek religion, is simply seen as observable in medieval Christianity too. There is no question of setting off Christian against pagan in the spirit of Pater's earlier cultural polemics. The prevailing religious norm of Pater's writings after *Marius* is that of historic Christianity. Pater's Ionian-Doric, or Apollonian-Dionysan, distinction now designates perennial aspects of human consciousness, and if only a special version of Christianity will fully meet his test, it will be a version of Christianity nevertheless. The older, cruder antagonism between Christianity and paganism—suggestive of the vehemence of Pater's rejection of traditional Christianity in his early adult life—is no longer adequate to the complexity of his new view of the religious problem. Lenaghan illuminatingly refers to the Christianity of Cornelius and Cecilia as "a humane Apollonian ideal." Marius' own "natural Christianity" is evidently even richer, giving "full recognition both to Apollo and to Dionysus," by offering to the intellect "an ideal of humanity perfected in love" and by suggesting that this love is "the bond between the individual and the powers beyond mortality" which man senses in the vitality of nature.[5]

But the content of Pater's "pagan" religious synthesis, somehow compatible with historic Christianity, is not yet fully clarified by these distinctions and continuities. Certainly it is only in the two longest portraits, *Marius* and *Gaston de Latour* (1886), that there is a suf-

---

[5] *Ibid.*, pp. 85–86.

ficiently developed adjustment of these disparate forces to suggest exactly the view of man which Pater projected in his last years. *Gaston* is significant for its further exploration of a "third condition" of humanity and, in its unfinished state, for its inconclusiveness. The first five chapters, published from June to October 1889 in *Macmillan's*, have a certain coherency in themselves, and recapitulate much of the dialectical progression of *Marius*, though with some altered emphases. Gaston, as an observer of the religious wars in France in the late sixteenth century, is like Marius in living in a society in fundamental transition. In his youth he possessed an "imaginative heat, that might one day enter into dangerous rivalry with simple old-fashioned faith"; but for now the two are "hardly distinguishable elements of an amiable character, . . . two neighbourly apprehensions of a single ideal" (*GL*, pp. 22–23), an ideal not otherwise explained. This susceptibility to beauty is predictably challenged by a growing recognition of sorrow in the world. As Gaston develops into manhood his naturally religious nature is questioned, "as by a rival new religion claiming to supersede the religion he knew, to identify himself conclusively with this so tangible world"—in other words, the Epicureanism of *Marius* or the aesthetic Hellenism of the heroes of the *Renaissance*. The dilemma is familiar: "Two worlds, two antagonistic ideals, were in evidence before him. Could a third condition supervene, to mend their discord, or only to vex him perhaps, from time to time, with efforts towards an impossible adjustment?" (*GL*, pp. 38–39)

In the poetry of the Pléiade, Gaston finds the mode for his "new imaginative culture" (*GL*, p. 60). The contemporary relevance of his ideal—variously described as "a discovery, a new faculty, a privileged apprehension," "a manner, a habit of thought"—is evident in Pater's reference to "the power of 'modernity,' as renewed in every successive age for genial youth, protesting, defiant of all sanctions in these matters" (*GL*, p. 57). The moral ambiguities of the new religion are dwelt on at length. The devotee will wait "devoutly, rapturously, . . . for the manifestation . . . of flawless humanity, in some undreamed-of depth and perfection of the loveliness of bodily form" (*GL*, p. 71). This may well be the most openly erotic statement of the "worship of

physical beauty" in Pater's writings. At any rate, Gaston is fully aware
of the incompatibility of these "two rival claimants": "Might that new
religion be a religion not altogether of goodness, a profane religion
. . . ?" (*GL*, p. 71) The tone of the eighties, which had suffused
Marius, reappears as Gaston hopes either to be rid of the traces of his
youthful religious idealism or to have it "speak with irresistible decision and effect." Gaston seeks for "some penetrative mind" or a
theory "which might harmonise for him his earlier and later preference, . . . or, failing that, establish, to his pacification, the exclusive
supremacy of the latter" (*GL*, p. 72). Pater is explicit that Gaston's
position exactly parallels the dilemma of radical spirits in an earlier
generation of the Renaissance: mankind haunted by an older moral and
religious ideal in actual possession of the world, at the very moment it
was "called, through a full knowledge of the past, to enjoy the present
with an unrestricted expansion of its own capacities" (*GL*, pp. 82–83).
If one were to "enjoy," to "eat of all the trees," there was needed
"some new reading of human nature itself," as a sanction for the always rather suspicious Paterian "liberty of heart" (*GL*, p. 83).

That justification is attributed, *ex post facto*, to Montaigne. For he
is made the propagator of "that emancipating ethic" through his demonstration that "the essential dialogue was that of the mind with
itself"—the famous phrase from the Preface to the *Poems* of 1853
which Arnold had in disapproval applied to the "modern" consciousness. Montaigne's essays are about the "variableness, the complexity,
the miraculous surprises of man, concurrent with the variety, the complexity, the surprises of nature, making all true knowledge of either
wholly relative and provisional," and "a likely insecurity in one's self"
(*GL*, p. 89). Since these diversities are ultimate, truth is not to be
sought "in large theoretic apprehension of the general, but in minute
vision of the particular" (*GL*, p. 93). Thus his own experience was the
"ultimate ground of judgment," providing "what undulancy, complexity, surprises!" (*GL*, pp. 106, 107) This ultimate epistemological
defense of subjectivity, which Pater here and in *Plato and Platonism*
attributes to Socrates and Plato, may have a more immediate source in
Arnold despite Arnold's disapproval of the dialogue of the mind with

itself. In effect the ideal that Arnold demanded of the adequate critic in the Homer lectures of 1861, Pater characteristically applies, as he had done in the Coleridge essay of 1866, to a new mode of life:

The 'thing itself' [Arnold said] with which one is here dealing,—the critical perception of poetic truth,—is of all things the most volatile, elusive, and evanescent; by even pressing too impetuously after it, one runs the risk of losing it. The critic of poetry should have the finest tact, the nicest moderation, the most free, flexible, and elastic spirit imaginable; he should be indeed the 'ondoyant et divers,' the *undulating and diverse* being of Montaigne. (*CPW*, I, 174)

Indeed, Arnold's appeal for "the nicest moderation" may be behind Gaston's reflection that in a world of insane heroism like that of sixteenth-century France, "as regards all that belongs to the spirit, the one thing needful was moderation" (*GL*, p. 109). But whatever Arnold's possible role in these passages, Pater at the end draws back from his rather innocent if tendentious reading of Montaigne and finds in this "two-sided thinker" a religious recognition "of a certain great possibility, which might be among the conditions of so complex a world." For the "secret and subtle" center of Montaigne's thought was "the opinion that things as we find them would bear a certain old-fashioned construction"—even if it was not "this side of that double philosophy which recommended itself just now to Gaston" (*GL*, p. 113).

This is, dialectically, the ambiguous state in which Pater leaves his hero. His account simply reproduces the doubleness of the aesthetic "openness" of Marius' deathbed consciousness, which is somehow susceptible also to religious hope or possibility—though the balance is now shifted somewhat toward the skeptical and aesthetic side. But Pater was to use Gaston once again as the vehicle for the exploration of a far more radical "third condition" of man, in the "pantheism" of Giordano Bruno. Entirely out of the sequence with the other essays of the series, this piece appeared a year later in another periodical (*Fortnightly*, August 1889). Pater's ambiguity is revealed in the title, "The Lower Pantheism." In his later years in Paris, Gaston, apparently content in his Montaignean double consciousness, remains alert to theories of "divine assistance" and "inspiration." In a pantheism that tends to cancel differences between matter and spirit, spirit and flesh, good and evil, Gaston saw at once the possibility of "a freer way of taking, a possible modification of, certain moral precepts" (*GL*, pp. 141–142). And yet, though this was no doubt a "primitive morality," Pater hastens to point out that there is no evidence that Bruno was prepared "to sacrifice to the antinomianism, which is certainly part of its rigid logic, the austerities, the purity of his own youth" (*GL*, p. 145). Bruno's counsel was certainly, "Touch! see! listen! eat freely of all the trees of the garden of Paradise, with the voice of the Lord God literally everywhere!—here was the final counsel of perfection. . . . How petty in comparison seemed those sins, the purging of which was man's chief motive in coming to places like this convent. . . ." (*GL*, pp. 152–153) This doctrine of "indifference" is nevertheless a genuine *religion* and Bruno "but the instrument of some subtly materialised spiritual force" (*GL*, pp. 153–154). Pater's final stance, however, is one of tolerant rejection. At first his disapproval seems moral: Bruno's "large, antique, pagan ideas" seem to deny the deepest antagonism, that between "Christ and the world, say!—Christ and the flesh!" or even that between good and evil (*GL*, p. 159). For Pater recognizes that if Bruno was cautious about the practical application of his theory,

there was that in his very manner of speech, in that rank, un-weeded eloquence of his, which seemed naturally to discourage any effort at selection, any sense of fine difference, of *nuances* or proportion, in things. The loose sympathies of his genius were allied to nature, nursing, with equable maternity of soul, good, bad, and indifferent alike, rather than to art, distinguishing, rejecting, refining. Commission and omission! sins of the former surely had the natural preference. . . . How would . . . susceptible persons . . . read it ["this lesson"] especially if the opposition between practical good and evil traversed diametrically another distinction, the "opposed points" of which, to Gaston for instance, could never by any possibility become "indifferent," the distinction, namely, between the precious and the base, aesthetically; between what was right and wrong in the matter of art? (*GL*, p. 161)

In short, Pater's rejection of this ultimate Renaissance statement of Greek "liberty of heart" is based, finally, on fastidious aesthetic grounds. The grosser amoralities are unartistic, because indiscriminate, and hence unacceptable.

CHAPTER TWENTY-ONE Plato and Pater's
Double Vision

P*lato and Platonism* (1894) is as indecisive as *Gaston* and in no way derogates from the claim of *Marius* to be the ultimate statement, however ambiguous, of Pater's religious position. I accept the assertion of U. C. Knoepflmacher, in the finest reading of *Plato and Platonism* to date, that this last work of Pater's is his "final, most elaborate, but still characteristically hesitant and irresolute, iteration" of the question first imperfectly raised in the *Renaissance*, that of "the reconciliation of the religion of antiquity with the religion of Christ."[1] However, I question the climactic importance he attaches to the work ("an ambitious synthesis of all the assumptions that underlie his scattered essays and works of fiction," "the culmination of Pater's search for an aesthetic religion of form")[2] and his reading of the connection between Pater's Greek "religion of sanity" and his view of Christianity. In the first place, *Plato and Platonism* is a decidedly imperfect unity—part undergraduate lecture series, part the restatement of his reconciling ideas of the period of the *Greek Studies* (1875–1880).[3] More centrally, the balance of forces has been

[1] U. C. Knoepflmacher, "Pater's Religion of Sanity: 'Plato and Platonism' as a Document of Victorian Unbelief." *Victorian Studies*, VI (December 1962), 152–153.

[2] *Ibid.*, pp. 151, 155–156.

[3] For example, a central passage on the Ionian and Dorian "tendencies" in Greek life, including politics (*PP*, pp. 103–105), is borrowed almost verbatim from a passage on Greek art in "The Marbles of Aegina," an essay of 1880 (*GS*, pp. 252–253).

permanently and significantly tipped: always in the background, unlike the essays of the late seventies, looms the Christian standard.

Knoepflmacher feels that, for Pater, "the Greek love of form merely survives in the humanism of Christianity," that "Pagan gnôsis merely becomes Christian 'vision'," that Christianity is simply the "outgrowth" of Pater's "independent" Platonism, that Christianity represents "offshoots" of "Pater's 'true' pre-Christian Hellenism," and that the medieval cathedrals are "after all the evolutionary end-product of 'the Platonic aesthetics'."[4] Admittedly Knoepflmacher has no difficulty in showing that the "soothing mental atmosphere" of the Lacedaemonian religion of sanity can be found in Christianity (see *PP*, pp. 33, 278–279), but certain contradictions in this view remain imperfectly resolved. For example, at one point he admits that the Spartan religion of sanity in *Plato and Platonism* is *unlike* the Greco-Christian "religion of cheerfulness" of *Marius* in being "a curiously shrivelled cult of moral form, a pseudo-Christianity," and yet shortly thereafter speaks of "Pater's Hellenistic Christianity" as if this described the ideal of *Plato and Platonism* as well as the "Christianity" of *Marius*.[5] Similarly, it is hard to see how Knoepflmacher's definition of Pater's Christianity as a mere survival of Greek form is compatible with his view (with which I concur) that in *Plato and Platonism* Pater's "frame of reference is unmistakably Christian."[6]

My own view is that *Marius* and the essays of the eighties and nineties represent a fundamental and permanent realignment of the dialectically struggling forces in the Paterian synthesis and that *Plato and Platonism* does not mark a retreat from that final adjustment. Admittedly, the opening chapter strikes the tone of *Culture and Anarchy* in its insistence that "Perfection . . . is attainable only through a certain combination of opposites" (*PP*, p. 24). But the entire polemical thrust of *Plato and Platonism* exalts the Hebraic Lacedaemonian morality as

---

[4] Knoepflmacher, "Pater's Religion of Sanity," pp. 157, 158, 166.

[5] *Ibid.*, pp. 156, 157.

[6] *Ibid.*, p. 158. The closest Knoepflmacher comes to a final resolution is the formula that as Pater moves from "Winckelmann" to *Plato and Platonism*, his "humanistic" standards remain unchanged; Pater simply alters the "atmosphere" in which he places them and, in particular, has "become more and more sympathetic to Christianity and to its 'humanized' symbols" (p. 161 n).

"the saving Dorian soul," a source of discipline and order in the total "true Hellenism" Pater projects, and questions Athenian or Ionian intellectualism as somehow shallow, unstable, and excessively individualistic (*PP*, pp. 23–24).[7] This latter beginning of the scholastic mentality is condemned as having put the European mind "on a quest (vain quest it may prove to be) after a kind of knowledge perhaps not properly attainable" (*PP*, p. 40). Of course Pater's suspicion of the Parmenidean "One" springs from his own nineteenth-century relativism and skepticism, his temperamental commitment to the "philosophy of motion." Nevertheless, the important fact for present purposes is that the absolutist, Greek line of European thought—akin to Indian self-annihilation, embodied in Christian mystics like Johannes Eckhart and Johannes Tauler and in "the hard and ambitious intellectualism" of Spinoza—is consistently disparaged for falling below the "deeper *Gnôsis*" of the Old Testament (*PP*, p. 49). The Parmenidean One "was like the revelation to Israel in the midst of picturesque idolatries, 'The Lord thy God is one Lord'; only that here it made no claim to touch the affections, or even to warm the imagination" (*PP*, p. 38). That Christianity is the norm in this last work of Pater's is evident in the crucial Chapter VI on "The Genius of Plato." However historically suspect may be Pater's attempt to combine in the figure of Plato "the utmost degree of Ionian sensibility" and a "desire towards the Dorian order and *ascêsis*" (*PP*, p. 110)—in order later to unravel this

---

[7] Interestingly, Pater's regret that the loss of the "objective, unconscious, pleasantly sensuous mind of the Greek" has permanently impaired the health, sanity, and naturalness of the mind parallels Arnold's famous statement in the Preface of 1853 about the loss of "the calm, the cheerfulness, the disinterested objectivity" of the early Greeks (*PP*, pp. 31; *CPW*, I, 1). But where Arnold disapproves of the succeeding "modern" dialogue of the mind with itself, a state of doubt and discouragement, Pater welcomes the "wholesome scepticism" of the modern world, "beset now with insane speculative figments," as "an appeal from the preconceptions of the understanding to the authority of the senses" (*PP*, p. 31).

The Arnoldian echoes are so numerous and so casual as to suggest that *Plato and Platonism*, far from being the careful ultimate statement of Pater's position, is in fact in some ways careless and that it did not receive the attention other volumes of his did. In addition to a number of Arnold's key religious phrases and Biblical citations, there are such familiar Arnoldianisms as the criticism of life, the dialogue of the mind with itself, intellectual solvent, the modern spirit, disinterestedness, the imaginative reason, the "mechanic" aspects of life, and having one's eye on the object.

garment into two very different Platonic traditions—it is significant that Pater defends his Platonic "fusion" by reference to a higher, Christian standard:

Not to be "pure" from the body, but to identify it, in its utmost fairness, with the fair soul, by a gymnastic "fused in music," became, from first to last, the aim of education as he conceived it. That the body is but "a hindrance to the attainment of philosophy, if one takes it along with one as a companion in one's search" (a notion which Christianity, at least in its later though wholly legitimate developments, will correct) can hardly have been the last thought of Plato himself on quitting it. . . . and, Plato thus qualifying the Manichean or Puritan element in Socrates by his own capacity for the world of sense, Platonism has contributed largely, has been an immense encouragement towards, the redemption of matter, of the world of sense, by art, by all right education, by the creeds and worship of the Christian Church—towards the vindication of the dignity of the body. (*PP*, pp. 145–146)

This is to judge by historic Christian standards and not merely by those of Pater's "Hellenic" Christianity.

The "opposed tendencies" that Pater presents as somehow embodied in the historical Plato undoubtedly reflect divergent pulls in his own personality, as they also recapitulate the carefully poised irresolution of the conclusion of *Marius*. Indeed, the verbal parallels with Marius suggest that Chapter VII, which distinguishes the two tendencies reconciled in Plato, is dialectically the climax of *Plato and Platonism*. The paradox is the union of "the largest possible demand for infallible certainty in knowledge" with "the utmost possible inexactness, or contingency, in the method by which actually he proposes to attain it" (*PP*, p. 188). The first of these "two opposite Platonic traditions" is "the ideal, the world of 'ideas,' 'the great perhaps,' " which "we may assume to be objective and real"; plainly this corresponds to the religiously conceived "revelation" and "undeniable possibilities," an "ampler vision" or "the great hope," to which Marius finally and tentatively opens himself (*PP*, p. 196; *ME*, II, 218–221). Similarly, "the dialectical spirit, which to the last will have its diffidence and reserve, its scruples and second thoughts," is a "condition of suspended judgment" and is simply "the expectation, the receptivity, of the faithful scholar, deter-

mined not to foreclose what is still a question" (*PP*, p. 196). This
receptivity parallels Marius' "elaborate and lifelong education of his
receptive powers," his "unclouded receptivity of soul," cherished to
the end, which not so much contradicts those possibilities as prepares
him for the acceptance of revelation (*ME*, II, 219–220).

The two following chapters not only make Christianity the standard
of reference but unmistakably set it above Greek religion. In Chapter
VIII historical Platonism is declared to be the continuation of one of
the two components of the Hellenic genius; its origin is in the severe
Lacedaemonian religious spirit, "the specially Hellenic element in Hellenism" (*PP*, pp. 200–201). This was not "a religion of gloom," for
the Lacedaemonians, "like those monastic persons of whom they so
often remind one, . . . were a very cheerful people" (*PP*, p. 227).
This "religion of sanity," which works for "the establishment of a
kind of cheerful daylight in men's tempers," has a "tincture of asceticism" which "may remind us again of the monasticism of the Middle
Ages. But then, monastic severity was for the purging of a troubled
conscience, or for the hope of an immense prize . . ." (*PP*, pp. 227,
223). Even more emphatically, Pater concludes his discussion of the
Republic in Chapter IX by a cautious judgment on "the greatness of
the claim Plato makes for philosophy—a promise, you may perhaps
think, larger than anything he has actually presented to his readers in
the way of a philosophic revelation justifies. He seems, in fact, to
promise all, or almost all, that in a later age natures great and high
have certainly found in the Christian religion" (*PP*, p. 264). Moreover, when Pater comes to seek the historical realization of Plato's
philosopher-king, he inverts Matthew Arnold's evaluations of 1863,
contrasting Marcus Aurelius unfavorably with Saint Louis: "Look inward, and what is strange and inexplicable in [Marcus Aurelius'] realisation of the Platonic scheme—strange, if we consider how cold and
feeble after all were the rays of light on which he waited so devoutly
—becomes clear in the person of Saint Louis," whose "whole being
was full of heavenly vision" (*PP*, pp. 265–266). Pater finishes with
a flourish concerning "this vision of the City of the Perfect, *The Republic*, Καλλίπολις *Uranopolis, Utopia, Civitas Dei, The Kingdom of
God*" (*PP*, p. 266). Again, Christianity is the culmination both his-

torically and intrinsically—for, in effect, Pater is endorsing the essence of Arnold's earlier judgment that Christianity, by supplying "an inspiration, a joyful emotion, to make moral action perfect," "has *lighted up* morality" and that Marcus Aurelius, the noblest pagan moralist, remains unsatisfied, reaching out for the "tears" and "happy self-sacrifice" of Christianity (*CPW*, III, 134, 156–157).[8]

Indeed, the incomplete evidence suggests that the calculated skeptical poise and double-consciousness of Pater's later religious period were in fact tipped even further toward orthodoxy during the final decade of his life. Edmund Chandler's study of the textual changes in *Marius* between 1885 and 1892 indicates this general movement. Pater's defense of the antinomian morality of Cyrenaicism and its compatibility with the "old morality" is excised, as are "passages plainly critical of Christianity as a religion, passages which imply a 'historical' approach, and even passages which might be taken as derogatory at first sight."[9] This omission of criticism of Christianity, and "a hardening of his attitude towards pagan thought and belief,"[10] are exactly what the reviews of Amiel's *Journal Intime* and *Robert Elsmere* and the essay on "Style" would lead one to expect. The deliberately maintained mood of those last years seems to have been one of religious *hope*, "the sort of hope which is a great factor in life" that he wrote about to Mrs. Humphry Ward in 1885. The beliefs and functions of the Church remain, he explained, one of the "obscure but all-important possibilities," "a workable hypothesis." Where Arnold, in "The Study of Poetry" and "Literature and Science," spoke of "the supposed fact" or the "supposed knowledge" underlying Christian theology with the clear sense that it was exploded, Pater's tone here is markedly different as he says, "The supposed facts on which Christianity rests, utterly incapable as they have become of any ordinary test, seem to me matters of very much the same sort of assent we give to any assumptions, in the strict and

---

[8] Chapter X, "Plato's Aesthetics," does not further the dialectic of Christian and pagan, except perhaps in so far as Pater, self-consciously and by verbal sleight of hand, identifies Plato's insistence on the connection between aesthetic experience and moral development, with the modern view that art has no end but its own perfection.

[9] Edmund Chandler, *Pater on Style*, pp. 65–67.

[10] *Ibid.*, p. 68.

ultimate sense, moral."[11] In fact, the almost Virgilian image of the dying aesthete Marius still open to the ampler vision, or of Plato and Marcus Aurelius in *Plato and Platonism* reaching out unsatisfied for the fulfillment of their hope, remained Pater's favorite religious image of this period, one which very likely reflects his sense of his own religious position. The two motifs of Pater's later career meet in a difficult passage in "The Age of Athletic Prizemen" (1894), one of the last publications of his life. The "Greek," Pater says, whose cultural achievement is summed up in the "pure humanity" of the Discobolus, "has been faithful" in the "administration" of the visible world: "he merited Revelation, something which should solace his heart in the inevitable fading of that"—that is, the world of sense (*GS*, p. 298). As the climax to this essay Pater quotes from "the Hebrew Scriptures," words given to "the Wisdom, the *Logos*, by whom God made the world"— "I was by him, as one brought up with him, rejoicing in the habitable parts of the earth. My delights were with the sons of men" (*GS*, pp. 298–299).

[11] Mrs. Humphry Ward, *A Writer's Recollections*, p. 210. The predominantly Christian tone of the period is evident in Grant Duff's diary entry for December 11, 1892: "Pater, who came down to dine, told me that his *Plato* would soon be out, and that he had planned a theological work in three divisions, the first to be called *Hebrew and Hellene*, the second *The Genius of Christ*, and the third *The Poetry of Anglicanism*" (see Mountstuart E. Grant Duff, *Notes from a Diary, 1892–95*, I, 134).

Pater and Newman:
The Road to the Nineties

CHAPTER TWENTY-TWO Newman and the Rhetoric
of Aestheticism

The purpose of T. S. Eliot's "Arnold and Pater" (1930) was "to indicate a direction from Arnold, through Pater, to the 'nineties, with, of course, the solitary figure of Newman in the background."[1] That "direction" had to do with a progressive confusion as to the place of religion in life in the later nineteenth century; but the "of course" regarding the solitary Newman in the background remained a suggestive but undeveloped notion. Ferris Greenslet long ago indicated a basis for this line of continuity in the tradition of Oxford and in Pater's style found "something of the spirit of her moods as Matthew Arnold found another trace of it in Newman's."[2] In seeking to define, as part of his secular humanism of the sixties, the qualities of mind which he grouped under the labels of "criticism" and "culture," Arnold, as seen in Chapters 2–4, repeatedly associated those qualities with Oxford and, above all, with the person and writings of Newman. Pater, in his attempt to trace out the lineaments of highly refined religious-aesthetic aware-

[1] T. S. Eliot, *Selected Essays*, p. 431. As early as January 1925, Eliot had remarked provocatively ("The Return of Matthew Arnold," *The Criterion*, III, 162) that "[Arnold's] thought lacks the logical rigour of his master Newman."

[2] Ferris Greenslet, *Walter Pater*, p. 17. Oscar Wilde, speaking in 1890 of modern prose styles, said, "in Mr. Pater, as in Cardinal Newman, we find the union of personality and perfection" (*Reviews by Oscar Wilde*, p. 545). George Sampson, in his Introduction (dated 1902) to Newman's *University Sketches*, p. xxxiii, discusses Newman as "an influence on prose writing": "Arnold's admirable clearness and gentle acidity are echoes of these qualities in Newman; while the fastidious phrases of Pater, his delicate use of words, even his little mannerisms, have all been fostered by his admiration for the elder writer, though of course there is a wide difference between the symphonic completeness of Newman's style and Pater's perpetual Adagio."

ness, especially in the eighties and nineties, found Newman and Newman's example an equally essential point of departure. The three men
are linked primarily by the description and advocacy of a peculiar,
highly Oxonian, version of perfected human consciousness. To study
the totality of the relationships among the three men is to witness the
transformation—and in some ways the dilution and debasement—of
the older, theologically oriented Oxford humanism. This older tradition of "letters and philosophy," no longer intact after mid-century
in an increasingly skeptical, secularized, and science-oriented Oxford,
was, significantly, most fully and adequately described by Newman in
works like the *Idea of a University* and the *Grammar of Assent* only
after he had felt compelled to leave Oxford for good.

   While Arnold and Pater always found in Newman a "miracle" of
aesthetic and religious perception, they decisively diverged in their
reaction to his theology. Where the strenuously "moral" Arnold in his
religious writings of the seventies regularly manipulated Newman's
position on such matters as faith, development, and prophecy in order
consistently to subvert the totality of orthodox theology, the "aesthetic" Pater of the eighties and nineties used, if rather tentatively, a simplified and attenuated version of Newman's most characteristic arguments in favor of "assent" and ecclesiastical tradition. Men like T. H.
Huxley agreed with Newman that the Oxford literary humanism was
historically, and by implication intrinsically, dependent on theological
values.[3] With differing emphases, Arnold and Pater also insisted that,
even in the absence of faith, a religiously tinged richness of perception
is the crown of the perfected life; for both, the role of religion thus
becomes the crux of a modern literary humanism. The most fertile
source of confusion in tracing the connection among the three men is

   [3] I read this as the clear implication of Huxley's dual attack on Christianity and
classical studies in "Science and Culture" (1880), where Newman's claims in "Christianity and Letters" seem the most direct object of attack. Manning, in a letter to
Talbot of 1866, shows an awareness of the Oxford character of Newman's theological
humanism: "I see much danger [he says] of an English Catholicism, of which Newman is the highest type. It is the old Anglican patristic, literary, Oxford tone trans-
planted into the Church" (see Edmund Sheridan Purcell, *Life of Cardinal Manning,
Archbishop of Westminster*, II, 332–323).

the fact that Arnold and Pater became the most influential advocates of an historic humanist consciousness, while rejecting the theological and metaphysical underpinnings of that heritage.

Before his religious crisis of the late fifties, Pater was an enthusiastic High-Church ritualist who already knew a considerable amount about the Tractarian Movement. He had visited John Keble at the age of fifteen and had even written an "Essay on Justification," which is now lost.[4] But a now skeptical and scoffing Pater learned, in the sixties, to see Newman through the distorting spectacles provided by Arnold's early essays. Before the appearance of Pater's first published essay, in 1866, Arnold had established the reading of Newman the man, the thinker, and the artist which was to color Pater's view for the rest of his life. In January 1863, amid the glare of the Colenso controversy, Arnold had associated Newman with the theory of a spiritual and intellectual elite who are alone the privileged bearers of truth. Speaking in the name of "literary criticism" and as the spokesman of "culture," Arnold attributes the view that "Knowledge and truth . . . are not attainable by the great mass of the human race at all" to "Dr. Newman": " 'The few (those who can have a saving knowledge) can never mean the many,' says, in one of his noblest sermons, Dr. Newman" (*CPW*, III, 43–44). In the following year, Arnold sought to define the qualities of mind which made Newman the embodiment and exponent par excellence of the Oxford "sentiment." He speaks of the *Apologia* as marked throughout with an "*urbanity*" that is the product of "a miracle of intellectual delicacy," and as "the work of a man never to be named by any son of Oxford without sympathy, a man who alone in Oxford of his generation, alone of many generations, conveyed to us in his genius that same charm, that same ineffable sentiment which this exquisite place itself conveys" (*CPW*, III, 250, 244).

These ideas are reflected in the first two essays published by Pater. In his study of Coleridge's prose writings (January 1866), Pater had

[4] Thomas Wright, *The Life of Walter Pater*, I, 77, xix.

this double-edged remark to make concerning conservative thinkers of "the highest order."

Communicating in this way to the passing stage of culture the charm of what is chastened, high-strung, athletic, they yet detach the highest minds from the past by pressing home its difficulties and finally proving it impossible. Such is the charm of Julian, of St. Louis, perhaps of Luther; in the narrower compass of modern times, of Dr. Newman and Lacordaire; it is also the peculiar charm of Coleridge.[5]

Before he ends, Pater exclaims: "How often in the higher class of theological writings—writings which really spring from an original religious genius, such as those of Dr. Newman—does the modern aspirant to perfect culture seem to find the expression of the inmost delicacies of his own life, the same yet different!"[6] *Culture, genius, charm, delicacy*: the words and the ideas are Arnold's; and both he and Pater associate them centrally with Newman. Similarly, in the crucial essay on "Winckelmann," of January 1867, Pater develops the view of ancient Greek religion as "the religion of art and beauty," even if only to question it by quite unexpectedly citing Newman's *Development of Christian Doctrine*: "Thus Dr. Newman speaks of 'the classical polytheism which was gay and graceful, as was natural in a civilized age'" (*Ren-1*, p. 171; see *EDD*, p. 209). Further on in the same paragraph he asserts: "Religious progress, like all purely spiritual progress, is confined to a few" (*Ren-1*, p. 172).

In the "Winckelmann" essay, too, there appeared an echo of a theme Newman had developed masterfully in one of his Dublin lectures, "Christianity and Letters." Pater sees Winckelmann as a late Renaissance exponent of what he variously calls "the classical spirit," "intellectual culture," "Hellenic humanism." This classical tradition, "the supreme tradition of beauty," provides the unity of European culture. Pater describes a fresco of Raphael's which depicts Apollo and the classical and Renaissance poets as embodying this "orthodoxy of taste." The "general history of culture" testifies to "the authority of

[5] [Walter Pater], "Coleridge's Writings," *Westminster Review*, N.S. XXIX (January 1866), 106–107.
[6] *Ibid.*, p. 127.

the Hellenic tradition, its fitness to satisfy some vital requirement of the intellect." Spiritual forces of the past must now live an underground life: "The Hellenic element alone has not been so absorbed or content with this underground life; from time to time it has started to the surface; culture has been drawn back to its sources to be clarified and corrected. Hellenism is not merely an element in our intellectual life; it is a constant tradition in it" (*Ren-1*, pp. 168–169). This "element of permanence, a standard of taste," in European art, "is maintained in a purely intellectual tradition . . . [and] takes its rise in Greece at a definite historical period. A tradition for all succeeding generations, it originates in a spontaneous growth out of the influences of Greek society" (*Ren-1*, p. 170).

Though the idea is by no means unique to Newman, Pater seems to be following rather closely Newman's description of "a great association of nations . . . not political, but mental, based on the same intellectual ideas, and advancing by common intellectual methods," which, for all the changes of history, "continues down to this day," continuously "one and the same" (*Idea*, p. 220). Newman, too, finds Greece "the fountain head of intellectual gifts" (*Idea*, p. 224). Of course Newman is concerned with "the formation of the course of liberal education," whereas Pater characteristically in his "supreme tradition of beauty" is thinking primarily of the fine arts; but the emphasis on "a conscious tradition," "a purely intellectual tradition," of culture is held in common. Newman, in defining his "tradition of intellectual training," insists that classical literature "has been the instrument of education, and the food of civilization, from the first times of the world down to this day" (*Idea*, p. 228). Paradoxically, perhaps nowhere do Pater and Newman stand closer, even in this early period, than on the essential *unity* of the Western tradition, at once Hellenic and Christian. Despite Pater's hostility to Christianity in the essay, he insists on the view "which preserves the identity of European culture. The two [pagan and Christian art] are really continuous: and there is a sense in which it may be said that the Renaissance was an uninterrupted effort of the Middle Ages, that it was ever taking place" (*Ren-1*, p. 199). Taking an even more comprehensive, and perhaps tenden-

tious, view, Newman asserts the historical unity of the classical intellectual heritage and Christian religious experience: "Jerusalem is the
fountainhead of religious knowledge, as Athens is of secular. . . . The
grace stored in Jerusalem, the gifts which radiate from Athens, are
made over and concentrated in Rome. . . . Rome has inherited both
sacred and profane learning" (*Idea*, pp. 230–231).

As one might suspect, however, it was not Newman the Christian
apologist who was of most interest to Pater during the years before
Marius was begun in the late seventies—the years of the essays in the
first two editions of the *Renaissance* and of the majority of the *Greek
Studies*. Except for his role in the "Winckelmann" essay, Newman
makes no explicit appearance in either of these two collections of Pater's work of the sixties and seventies.[7] During this early period, however, there first appear certain lines of revisionist rhetoric which at
least partially justify Eliot's view of "the solitary figure of Newman"
at the beginning of the route from Arnold through Pater to the nineties. There is, first, the frequent iteration of the Calvinistically tinged
doctrine of the few and the many in characteristically "aesthetic" con-

---

[7] Though Arnold's presence is not far to seek (see Chap. 14, n. 13, above), Newman's example in Discourse V of the *Idea of a University* ("Knowledge Its Own
End") also seems very apparent in the conclusion of "Wordsworth" (1874), one
of the most important statements of Pater's view of the mind in its highest reaches.
"Contemplation—impassioned contemplation" is, says Pater, "the end-in-itself, the
perfect end." The principle of the new "higher morality" is that "the end of life is
not action but contemplation—*being* as distinct from *doing*—a certain disposition of
mind." "To treat life in the spirit of art, is to make life a thing in which means and
ends are identified" (*Appr.*, pp. 59–64). This is an "aesthetic" version of Newman's
extended argument that "Knowledge is, not merely a means to something beyond it,
. . . but an end sufficient to rest in and pursue for its own sake," "not only an instrument, but an end," "worth possessing for what it is, and not merely for what it does."
Thus Pater in making the end of the whole of life a state of contemplation, "a certain disposition of mind," seems to be drawing on Newman's defense of "the cultivation of the intellect" as "a state or condition of mind," "an acquired illumination,
. . . a habit, a personal possession, and an inward endowment." Even Pater's elaborate
rejection of the "machinery" of life (borrowed also from Arnold) is paralleled by
Newman's repeatedly playing off of the "philosophical" against the "mechanical."
Though Arnold is an important intermediary in the larger shift of values, Pater was
quite capable of appropriating, and transforming, even Newman's secular values for
the purposes of the new aestheticism and morality.

texts. Certainly the idea of a "clerisy" or an intellectual elite was a commonplace in nineteenth-century England, from Coleridge to Mill and beyond, but Pater's continuous use of the "few" as opposed to the "many," in the very restricted sense of a special class of aesthetically susceptible souls, seems strongly to suggest a further extension of Arnold's quotation from Newman. A glaring example occurs in "Aucassin and Nicolette," first published in 1873. "The central love-poetry of Provence," Pater announces, "the poetry of the *Tenson* and the *Aubade*, of Bernard de Ventadour and Pierre Vidal, is poetry for the few, for the elect and peculiar people of the kingdom of sentiment" (*Ren-1*, p. 6). That kingdom of sentiment, a parody of the Kingdom of God, is of course a realm of calculated spiritual snobbishness. The transformation of values, however, seems even more intentionally offensive when the doctrine is applied in specifically religious contexts, with the implication that certain refined religious experiences are the highest states of aesthetic consciousness, open only to certain elite souls. In the *Greek Studies* generally, Pater was reassessing the whole of the ancient religious tradition, anticipating his partial accommodation with Christianity in *Marius*. In "Demeter and Persephone," for example, he claims with a kind of complacent contemptuousness that "coarser minds" might misunderstand the deeper significance of Greek religious ritual, whereas "more elevated spirits," "the nobler kind of souls," could adapt religious myth at will in the name of "culture" and as the embodiment of their own "susceptibilities and intuitions" (*GS*, pp. 136–137). In "A Study of Dionysus," he maintains that Dionysus, like Persephone, "has also a peculiar message for a certain number of refined minds, seeking, in the later days of Greek religion, such modifications of the old legend as may minister to ethical culture, to the perfecting of the moral nature" (*GS*, p. 49). This is "the finer, mystical sentiment of the few, detached from the coarser and more material religion of the many" (*GS*, p. 50). Arnold had quite consciously wrenched Newman's Biblical paraphrase—" 'The few (those who can have a saving knowledge) can never mean the many' "—into a defense of the freedom of a small intellectual elite whom, "in the field of free religious speculation" as in other areas of "the higher culture

of Europe," "literary criticism regards as exempt from all concern
with edification" (*CPW*, III, 49, 79). Pater, whose "culture" had
even less claim than Arnold's to inhabit "the sphere of speculative
life, of intellect, of pure thought" (*CPW*, III, 67), decisively extends
the process of redefinition by making the language of religious doctrine a vindication of the life of pure aesthetic apprehension. Throughout his career Pater has a good deal to say about those "elect souls"
and "the purely aesthetic beauty of the old morality."

The process of transformation is equally clear in the remarkably
similar images used by Newman and Pater in presenting the human
condition. In some of the best known words of the Conclusion to the
Renaissance, Pater discusses "the inward world of thought and feeling," associated with images of whirlpool and flame, as a "drift of momentary acts of sight and passion and thought" (*Ren-1*, p. 208). If we
dwell on "impressions unstable, flickering, inconsistent, which burn
and are extinguished with our consciousness of them," the world is
contracted still further:

the whole scope of observation is dwarfed to the narrow chamber of the
individual mind. Experience, already reduced to a swarm of impressions, is
ringed round for each one of us by that thick wall of personality through
which no real voice has ever pierced on its way to us, or from us to that
which we can only conjecture to be without. Every one of those impressions
is the impression of the individual in his isolation, each mind keeping as a
solitary prisoner its own dream of a world. (*Ren-1*, p. 209)

In a sermon of 1836, "The Individuality of the Soul," Newman had
in a memorable panorama presented his version of the reality underlying the appearances of life:

Or again, survey some populous town: crowds are pouring through the
streets; some on foot, some in carriages; while the shops are full, and the
houses too, could we see into them. Every part of it is full of life. . . . But
what is the truth? why, that every being in that great concourse is his own
centre, and all things about him are but shades, but a "vain shadow," in
which he "walketh and disquieteth himself in vain." He has his own hopes
and fears, desires, judgments, and aims; he is everything to himself, and no
one else is really any thing. No one outside of him can really touch him, can

touch his soul, his immortality; he must live with himself for ever. He has a depth within him unfathomable, an infinite abyss of existence; and the scene in which he bears part for the moment is but like a gleam of sunshine upon its surface.[8] (*PPS*, IV, 82–83)

The differences of intention in the two passages are of course very marked. Newman's thesis is "the doctrine of the distinct individuality of the human soul," destined for immortality, whereas Pater makes his vision of the "continual vanishing away, that strange perpetual weaving and unweaving of ourselves," the ground of an appeal to live a life of "sharp and eager observation," for the moment's sake, before the final darkness descends (*Ren-1*, p. 210). But what is shared, in tone and implication, is of great significance. Newman's view that every man "is as whole and independent a being in himself, as if there were no one else in the whole world but he" (*PPS*, IV, 81)—that for every man "no one else is really any thing. No one outside of him can really touch him, can touch his soul"—is easily transmuted, once the transcendental escape route has been sealed off, into the near solipsism of Pater's solitary prisoner for whom "no real voice has ever pierced" the wall of personality. The two men also share a strong sense of the impermanence and even unreality of "material phenomena" (*Apologia*, p. 4). Newman's image of the activities of life as a momentary "gleam of sunshine" on the surface of the "infinite abyss of existence" is carried over into Pater's more desperate view of life as "this short day of frost and sun" (*Ren-1*, p. 211). Pater may well have come on Newman's sermon opportunely: the *Parochial and Plain Sermons* were reissued in the spring of 1868, and Pater, already a reader of New-

[8] The unsettling undertone of Newman's passage is made the explicit substance of the powerful view of the "condition of the whole race" developed in Chapter V of the *Apologia* (pp. 218 ff.) as the basis of Newman's apologetic. Human life is there presented as largely aimless, random, blind, unreasoning, passionate, willful energy, and experience as a matter of pain, anguish, sin, corruption, and disappointment— truly "a vision to dizzy and appal." The fundamental unintelligibility of life, as well as a spiritually fastidious removal from the *grossièreté* of experience, are similarly suggested in the lecture "English Catholic Literature," where literature is said to reflect "the untutored movements of the reason, imagination, passions, and affections of the natural man, the leapings and the friskings, the plungings and the snortings, the sportings and the buffoonings, the clumsy play and the aimless toil, of the noble, lawless savage of God's intellectual creation" (*Idea*, p. 275).

man's sermons in the sixties, published his famous passage first in October 1868 as the conclusion of the Morris review. Nevertheless, the issue here is not precisely that of a direct source, but of a more general transformation of a special religious tone and imagery for new "aesthetic" purposes. The "inwardness" and spiritual individualism of Newman's Tractarian ethos, in its most characteristic formulation, could be directly exploited in the new submetaphysical and sensationalist world of refined spiritual and aesthetic apprehension.

CHAPTER TWENTY-THREE Newman and the
                      Theology of *Marius*

Pater's most sustained engagement with Newman's thought occurs in *Marius the Epicurean* (1885), which Pater claimed to have written "to show the necessity of religion."[1] The large number of direct and indirect references to Newman's characteristic ideas—especially as found in *Loss and Gain,* the *Idea of a University,* and the *Grammar of Assent*—suggests that a rereading of Newman played an important role in Pater's own partial reconciliation with Christianity during the five or six years of the composition of *Marius.* Indeed, it is now known that, probably sometime in the eighties, Pater read deeply enough in Newman's major works to make extensive notes toward an uncompleted essay to be called "The Writings of Cardinal Newman."[2]

[1] Thomas Wright, *The Life of Walter Pater,* II, 87.

[2] Professor Lawrence Evans of Northwestern University is now editing the manuscript of this fragmentary essay, a copy of which he has graciously allowed me to read. He has also provided me with a list of Newman's works borrowed by Pater from the Brasenose College Library: *Sermons on Subjects of the Day* in 1865, *University Education* in 1867, and, between 1879 and 1889, two volumes of *Tracts for the*

The idea of an historical novel set in early Christian times and designed to illuminate the nineteenth-century religious dilemma may
well have been derived from Newman, whose *Callista*, subtitled *A
Tale of the Third Century*, had appeared in 1855. Though both Wiseman's *Fabiola* and Kingsley's *Hypatia* had provided examples of the
type, Newman's altogether more subtle exploration of the stages of
conversion is far closer to Pater's analytical method. Moreover, both
works culminate in "conversion" and martyrdom; and the plague leading to an outbreak of violence against the Christians in *Marius* is paralleled by the plague of locusts and the resulting persecution in *Callista*.[3]
There are positive signs that Newman's earlier novel of religious controversy, *Loss and Gain* (1848), was in Pater's thoughts while composing *Marius* and may have provided at least a remote pattern for its
dialectical structure. *Loss and Gain* seeks to capture, in faintly novelistic
form, the climate of religious debate at Oxford during the Tractarian
period and to systematize and recapitulate in relatively popular terms
the arguments of the various contending parties. Like Marius, Charles
Reding struggles through alternative positions; he ends, as Newman
himself had, in the camp of Roman Catholic orthodoxy.

Pater used the phrase "loss and gain" pointedly on four occasions
in *Marius* (*ME*, II, 14–15, 28, 189, 219). Though one cannot argue
any strong case from Pater's various, but obviously calculated, use of
Newman's phrase, it is nevertheless hard to shake off the impression
that Newman's fictionalized and partly autobiographical presentation
of the various religious possibilities open to a sensitive young man of
the eighteen-forties was somehow part of the matrix of Pater's similarly
dialectical and autobiographical marking out of philosophical and religious avenues open to an aesthetic youth of forty years later.[4] Marius,

---

Times; two volumes of the Oxford sermons, the essays on Miracles, and the *Arians of
the Fourth Century.* One suspects Pater owned copies of the *Apologia,* the *Grammar,*
and perhaps the *Development of Christian Doctrine.*

[3] This is not to overlook or exclude a further, more immediate source in Lemaitre's
Sérénus. See Louise M. Rosenblatt, "The Genesis of Pater's *Marius the Epicurean,*"
XIV (Summer 1962), 242–260. And see Chapter 19, above.

[4] Just before one of the passages on loss and gain, Pater makes the contemporary
relevance perfectly explicit: "That age and ours have much in common—many difficulties and hopes. Let the reader pardon me if here and there I seem to be passing

the sadly reflective, morally upright, and emotionally withdrawn pagan, though not entirely unlike certain other heroes of Victorian conversion and anticonversion novels, seems to have a special affinity with Newman's Oxford hero, who "was naturally timid and retiring, oversensitive, and, though lively and cheerful, yet not without a tinge of melancholy in his character" (*LG*, pp. 2–3). Moreover, a tutor at Eton "gave his mind a religious impression, which secured him against the allurement of bad company, whether at the school itself, or afterwards at Oxford" (*LG*, p. 3). The Marius who to the end of his life was accompanied by "the sense . . . of a living person at his side" (*ME*, II, 218) was not unlike Charles, whose "characteristic, perhaps above everything else, was an habitual sense of the Divine Presence" (*LG*, 230–231).

Pater's novel is deeply and primarily indebted to Newman, however, because the central argument of Marius' "conversion" is taken almost bodily from the *Grammar of Assent* (1870) and other writings of Newman. The issue is that of the grounds of religious "assent," which both men place in a convergence of "probabilities." And both are concerned in strikingly similar ways with the role of the "will" and "personality" in the act of faith. At each stage of Marius' dialectical advance, the conflicts are expressed in Newman's terms. Early in his career, when in process of giving up the religion of his childhood, the "visionary idealism of the villa," in favor of his new Cyrenaicism, Marius reflects that the new comprehensive ideal "demanded entire liberty of heart and brain," whereas

that old, staid, conservative religion of his childhood certainly had its being in a world of somewhat narrow restrictions. But then, the one was absolutely real, with nothing less than the reality of seeing and hearing—the other, how vague, shadowy, problematical! Could its so limited probabilities be worth taking into account in any practical question as to the rejecting or receiving of what was indeed so real, and, on the face of it, so desirable? (*ME,* I, 48–49)

The passage is doubly indebted to Newman. First, as we shall see in

---

from Marius to his modern representatives—from Rome, to Paris or London" (*ME,* II, 14).

detail, there is the problem that religious belief seems grounded on "so limited probabilities." But Newman had also developed at length the conflict in modes of vision between "the old Theology" and "the great Sciences which are the characteristics of this era." Putting words into the mouths of his opponents, Newman argued, in "A Form of Infidelity of the Day," that the aggressive new branches of positive knowledge are the

indirect but effectual means of overturning Religion! They do but need to be seen in order to be pursued; you will put an end, in the Schools of learning, to the long reign of the unseen shadowy world, by the mere exhibition of the visible. This was impossible heretofore, for the visible world was so little known itself; but now, thanks to the New Philosophy, sight is able to contest the field with faith. (*Idea*, p. 301)

Later, on the brink of accepting Cyrenaicism, Pater's hero muses on the "sentimental or ethical equivalent" of metaphysical principles, and on how "a rich and genial nature" can transform even "the most depressing of theories":

in the reception of metaphysical *formulae*, all depends, as regards their actual and ulterior result, on the pre-existent qualities of that soil of human nature into which they fall—the company they find already present there, on their admission into the house of thought; there being at least so much truth as this involves in the theological maxim, that the reception of this or that speculative conclusion is really a matter of the will. (*ME*, I, 135-136)

But it is not until Volume II that Marius, under the influence now of the Stoic Cornelius Fronto, considers (in a passage already strongly reminiscent of Newman for other reasons) the possibility of and the need for "moral assents" and "a place for duty and righteousness in his house of thought" (*ME*, II, 7). The Newmanesque flavor is strengthened by Pater's twice emphatically setting off "assent" in quotation marks. Speculating on an inherited, almost unconscious, code embodied in the "observances, customs, usages" of the "old morality," Cornelius hinted at "a remnant of right conduct, what he does, still more what he abstains from doing, not so much through his own free election, as from a deference, an 'assent,' entire, habitual, unconscious, to custom—to the actual habit or fashion of others" (*ME*, II, 9). So critical had Marius become of the failure of the "old Cyrenaics" to take account of "that whole complex system of manners or morals" embodied in hereditary Greek religion, that he can now complain: "A little more of such 'walking by faith,' a little more of such not unreasonable 'assent,' and they might have profited by a hundred services to their culture, from Greek religion and Greek morality, as they actually were" (*ME*, II, 24).

The argument shifts slightly in Chapter XIX, "The Will as Vision," perhaps theologically the center of the whole work, by emphasizing the role of appetency—choice, volition, hope, will—in achieving "certitude of intellect" in matters of belief. Concerning the writings of Marcus Aurelius, Marius inquires:

And were the cheerful, sociable, restorative beliefs, of which he had there read so much, that bold adhesion, for instance, to the hypothesis of an eternal friend to man, just hidden behind the veil of a mechanical and material order, but only just behind it, ready perhaps even now to break through:— were they, after all, really a matter of choice, dependent on some deliberate act of volition on his part? Were they doctrines one might take for granted, generously take for granted, and led on by them, at first as but well-defined objects of hope, come at last into the region of a corresponding certitude of the intellect? (*ME,* II, 63–64)

About Cornelius' remarks "concerning the practicability of a methodical and self-forced assent to certain principles or presuppositions 'one could not do without,' " Marius asks, "Were there, as the expression *'one could not do without'* seemed to hint, beliefs, without which life itself must be almost impossible, principles which had their sufficient ground of evidence in that very fact?" (*ME*, II, 64.) Similarly, if by an act of will one could attend to this or that color or sound,

Might it be not otherwise with those various and competing hypotheses, the permissible hypotheses, which, in that open field for hypothesis—one's own actual ignorance of the origin and tendency of our being—present themselves so importunately, some of them with so emphatic a reiteration, through all the mental changes of successive ages? Might the will itself be an organ of knowledge, of vision? (*ME*, II, 64–65)

In Chapter XX Marius, now deeply immersed in the early Christian culture, receives further impetus in his quest through a discourse of the "Platonist" Apuleius expounding a "boldly mystical . . . view of man and his position in the world" (*ME*, II, 90). Even in frivolous surroundings Apuleius' conviction was evident. "Yes!" Marius concurs, "the reception of theory, of hypothesis, of beliefs, did depend a great deal on temperament."

The notion that assent or belief is arrived at by "the whole man"—mind, feelings, imagination, etc.—is evident throughout Newman's career. For example, in *Loss and Gain* Pater would have found the Roman Catholic priest whom Reding conveniently meets on the train discussing the role of the will in the act of faith: " 'Certainty, in its highest sense, is the reward of those who, by an act of the will, and at the dictate of reason and prudence, embrace the truth, when nature, like a coward, shrinks' " (*LG*, p. 385). And again: "They will not be blessed, they will effect nothing in religious matters, till they begin by an act of unreserved faith in the word of God, whatever it be; till they go out of themselves; till they cease to make something within them their standard; till they oblige their will to perfect what reason leaves sufficient, indeed, but incomplete' " (*LG*, p. 386). However, it was in the *Grammar of Assent*, now little more than a decade old, that Newman had developed at length the "personal" and "subjective" quality of the apprehension of truth. Only a few of the many relevant passages need be indicated. Newman's fascinating exploration of the complexities of Shakespearean textual study suggests "how little syllogisms have to do with the formation of opinion; . . . and how much upon those pre-existing beliefs and views, in which men either already agree with each other or hopelessly differ, before they begin in dispute, and which are hidden deep in our nature, or, it may be, in our personal peculiarities" (*GA*, p. 210). Moreover, "thought is too keen and manifold, its sources are too remote and hidden, its path too personal, delicate, and circuitous, its subject matter too various and intricate, to admit of the trammels of any language, of whatever subtlety and of whatever compass" (*GA*, p. 216). Similarly, the "cumulation of probabilities" in the process of concrete inference varies "according to the particular intellect which is employed upon it" (*GA*, p. 223).

This is the "personal element" in proof, the "living *organon*" or the "supra-logical judgment" of the prudent man (*GA*, pp. 240–241). This prudential "personal endowment" ensures that the discovery of truth is a moral as well as an intellectual activity: "truth there is, and attainable it is, but . . . its rays stream in upon us through the medium of our moral as well as our intellectual being; and . . . in consequence that perception of its first principles which is natural to us is enfeebled, obstructed, perverted, by allurements of sense and the supremacy of self, and, on the other hand, quickened by aspirations after the supernatural" (*GA*, p. 237). Put differently, a characteristic of the argumentative process is "the moral state of the parties inquiring or disputing"; that is, "the personality (so to speak) of the parties reasoning is an important element in proving propositions in concrete matter" (*GA*, p. 243).

The echoes of thought and phrasing from the *Grammar* are too full to be accidental or casual, and they extend well beyond the role of will and personality in the act of faith. For example, Pater's insistence on a deference to an authoritative "tradition" in religious matters, "a system or order . . . in possession," reflects a central preoccupation of Newman's, as in this passage in the *Grammar*: "tradition, though unauthenticated, being (what is called) in possession, has a prescription in its favour, and may, *prima facie*, or provisionally, be received" (*GA*, p. 286).[5] But, as Newman's Victorian critics saw, there was a joker in his argument. For all his agreement as to the psychological conditions of belief, Pater was evidently unprepared to accept in its entirety Newman's conclusion that the differences discernible in men's religious and moral perceptions, far from casting doubt on objective truth, suggest that "there is something deeper in our differences than the accident of external circumstances; and that we need the interposition of a Power, greater than human teaching and human argument,

---

[5] On the role of "hope" as indicative of religious "possibilities," see *ME*, II, 90–91, and *GA*, p. 262; on the relativity of sense perception, *ME*, I, 146, and *GA*, p. 283. Pater's reference to principles " 'one could not do without' " (*ME*, II, 64) may reflect Newman's discussion in the *Apologia* (p. 261) of "first principles," especially in religion, as a prime example of the Liberals' "false liberty of thought, or the exercise of thought upon matters, in which, from the constitution of the human mind, thought cannot be brought to any successful issue."

to make our beliefs true and our minds one" (*GA*, p. 285). Marius, and his creator, seem more willing to exist in a kind of negative capability, content with religious "possibilities."[6]

Newman's voice reechoes, in important contexts, in many other places in *Marius*. Not surprisingly, Marius, Pater's supreme elite soul, is intrigued by Heraclitus' emphasis on "the difference between the many and the few"; throughout much is heard of the mingled aesthetic and moral superiorities of "the select few," "the rare minority of *elite* intelligences," "certain elect souls" (*ME*, I, 128, 133, 242; II, 7, 57). Though Pater may have discovered the Calvinistically tinged doctrine of the few and the many in Newman's sermons, and as mediated and transformed by Matthew Arnold, he could have found it more immediately in the *Grammar* itself. Newman cites as an example of informal inference a certain writer's driving at a conclusion about the

[6] Pater's characteristic hesitancy is evident in a letter of March 1885 to William Sharp (*Papers Critical and Reminiscent*, pp. 213–214): "As to the ethical drift of *Marius* . . . I *did* mean it to be more anti-Epicurean than it has struck you as being. In one way, however, I am glad that you have mistaken me a little on this point, as I had some fears that I might seem to be pleading for a formal thesis of 'parti pris'."

Bernard Duffey ("The Religion of Pater's *Marius*," *Texas Studies in Literature and Language*, II [Spring 1960], 103–114) has argued the strongest case yet made for the genuinely supernatural character of the religion of *Marius*. I cannot accept his conclusions concerning Pater's orthodoxy, but what I especially wish to question here is his assigning (pp. 107 ff.) to Pater's views on the limits of reason and the role of the will in religious belief a source in the *Kingdom of Christ* (1838) by F. D. Maurice. Professor Duffey cites the very passages in *Marius* which I have shown to echo Newman's *Grammar* very closely. Though Thomas Wright shows (*Walter Pater*, I, xix, 136, 167) that Maurice played a role in Pater's early *loss* of faith, he seems to have played a very small role in the mature Pater's thought (see Germain d'Hangest, *Walter Pater, L'Homme et L'Oeuvre* I, 58), and any verbal resemblances between the arguments of the *Kingdom of Christ* and *Marius* are unapparent to me. Of course Maurice's work may remain as a more remote background for *Marius*.

Martha Salmon Vogeler ("The Religious Meaning of *Marius the Epicurean*," *Nineteenth-Century Fiction*, XIX [December 1964], 287–299) also argues for the seriousness of Pater's religious intentions and lightly touches on the parallel with Newman. *Marius*, she observes, "is Pater's *Grammar of Assent*" (p. 291). David Anthony Downes, *Victorian Portraits: Hopkins and Pater*, emphasizes, largely by implication, the authenticity of Pater's religious views. He briefly cites (pp. 122–123) three passages from "The Will as Vision" as parallel to the *Grammar*, though the relationship is not made clear beyond defining Pater's "natural theology" as the view that "religious faith is based on real knowledge and comes by way of an intuitive understanding which can never come from notional knowledge alone."

authorship of a book, not "by mere argumentation" but by "delicate" and "intricate" processes, "invisible, except to those who from circumstances have an intellectual perception of what does not appear to the many" (*GA*, p. 250). Even more explicitly, Newman had devoted a long paragraph to the text, "Many are called, few are chosen" (*GA*, pp. 346–347). The process of Marius' conversion also draws upon Newman's *Idea of a University*—for example, Marius' growing apprehension that the fragments of human speculation form a great "whole," a "supreme system of knowledge and doctrine" (*ME*, II 19, *Idea*, pp. 24, 44, 45, 46, 64; ME, II, 134, *Idea*, pp. 40, 41).

Pater drew even more substantively from the *Idea* in the first two chapters of Volume II of *Marius*, the crucial period when Marius contemplates the basis for a broader and deeper morality than his Cyrenaicism had provided. In Chapter XV, "Stoicism at Court," in which Newman's emphasis on an elite and on "an 'assent' . . . to custom" has already been noted, Marius, under the sway of the aged Stoic moralist, Fronto, sees the glimmering possibility of "an adjustment between his own elaborately thought-out intellectual scheme and the 'old morality' " (*ME*, II, 6). To a young Epicurean seeking "moral assents," Fronto offered "the key to this problem in the purely aesthetic beauty of the old morality, as an element in things, fascinating to the imagination, to good taste in its most highly developed form, through association—a system or order, as a matter of fact, in possession, not only of the larger world, but of the rare minority of *elite* intelligences" (*ME*, II, 7). This lowest level of motivation, highly "aesthetic" as it might seem, at least presupposed a sincere

search after some principle of conduct . . . which might give unity of motive to an actual rectitude, a cleanness and probity of life, determined partly by natural affection, partly by enlightened self-interest or the feeling of honour, due in part even to the mere fear of penalties; no element of which, however, was distinctively moral in the agent himself as such, and providing him, therefore, no common ground with a really moral being like Cornelius, or even like the philosophic emperor. Performing the same offices; actually satisfying, even as they, the external claims of others; rendering to all their dues —one thus circumstanced would be wanting, nevertheless, in the secret of inward adjustment to the moral agents around him. How tenderly—more ten-

derly than many stricter souls—he might yield himself to kindly instinct!
what fineness of charity in passing judgment on others! what an exquisite
conscience of other men's susceptibilities! He knows for how much the manner, because the heart itself, counts, in doing a kindness. He goes beyond
most people in his care for all weakly creatures; judging, instinctively, that to
be but sentient is to possess rights. He conceives a hundred duties, though he
may not call them by that name, of the existence of which purely duteous
souls may have no suspicion. He has a kind of pride in doing more than
they, in a way of his own. Sometimes, he may think that those men of line
and rule do not really understand their own business. How narrow, inflexible, unintelligent! what poor guardians (he may reason) of the inward
spirit of righteousness, are some supposed careful walkers according to its
letter and form. And yet all the while he admits, as such, no moral world
at all: no theoretic equivalent to so large a proportion of the facts of life.
(*ME*, II, 7–9)

This excerpt seems clearly to show the influence of Newman's famous double-edged description of the "gentleman" in the *Idea*—double-
edged, because while the gentleman is the characteristic product of a
liberal education, his qualities make him the dangerous simulacrum of
a true Christian. Those qualities—"a cultivated intellect, a delicate
taste, a candid, equitable, dispassionate mind, a noble and courteous
bearing in the conduct of life"—"may attach to the man of the world,
to the profligate, to the heartless. . . . Taken by themselves, they do but
seem to be what they are not; they look like virtue at a distance, but they
are detected by close observers, and on the long run" (*Idea*, p. 107).
The ethics of the mere gentleman are those endorsed by what Newman
in Discourse VIII scathingly describes as the Religion of Philosophy.
This standard, "the ethical temperament of a civilized age," makes virtue a mere point of good taste, and vice vulgar and ungentlemanlike.
. . . To *seem* becomes to *be*; what looks fair will be good, what causes
offense will be evil; virtue will be what pleases, vice what pains" (*Idea*,
p. 178). He goes on:

And from this shallowness of philosophical Religion it comes to pass that
its disciples seem able to fulfil certain precepts of Christianity more readily
and exactly than Christians themselves. St. Paul . . . gives us a pattern of
evangelical perfection; he draws the Christian character in its most graceful

form, and its most beautiful hues. He discourses of that charity which is patient and meek, humble and single-minded, disinterested, contented, and persevering. He tells us to prefer each the other before himself, to give way to each other, to abstain from rude words and evil speech, to avoid self-conceit, to be calm and grave, to be cheerful and happy, to observe peace with all men, truth and justice, courtesy and gentleness, all that is modest, amiable, virtuous, and of good repute. . . . The school of the world seems to send out living copies of this typical excellence with greater success than the Church. (*Idea*, p. 180)

Pater has, it is evident, not only reproduced the substance of Newman's argument, but has retained much of the openly disparaging tone.[7] It is clear that Marius, whatever the ambiguities of his final state, is *not* to stop short in a pseudo ethic based on "the purely aesthetic beauty of the old morality."

From Fronto, too, Marius learns that, beyond this motive of "natural affection or self-love or fear," there is a further spring of morality in that " 'assent,' entire, habitual, unconscious, to custom" (*ME*, II, 9). This conformity to precedent is associated with the Stoic principle of "Humanity—of a universal commonwealth of mind," embodied in an elite whose observances and customs have now become a "weighty tradition" and are indeed the sum of the "old morality." Marius' thoughts go beyond the speaker's intention, not toward a theory of the ideal commonwealth, "but rather as if in search of its visible locality and abiding-place" (*ME*, II, 11)—presumably the Christian Church he will increasingly turn toward. In the following chapter, Marius now worries that in broadening and deepening the admittedly narrow perfection of his present philosophy by turning to inherited moral standards, he would be forced to forego his claim to "an entire personal liberty, liberty of heart and mind" (*ME*, II, 26). But he sees that in attaching oneself to this "venerable system of sentiment and idea,

[7] That these passages of Newman's are what Pater had in mind, at least remotely, while composing Chapter XV of *Marius* is confirmed by a remark in his "Art Notes in North Italy" (1890). In the art of Romanino, Pater claims, almost as if recalling the central aspiration of *Marius*, "Catholicism and the Renaissance, religion and culture, holiness and beauty" seem "reconciled" (*MS*, p. 107). The elegance of Romanino's martyr "reminds one how the great Apostle Paul has made courtesy part of the content of the Divine charity itself" (*MS*, p. 108).

widely extended in time and place" (which he compares with membership in the "catholic church" or the old Roman citizenship), one makes
one's own a great tide of human experience. This "wonderful order,
actually in possession of human life," has penetrated law, language,
and habit; the authority of the elect spirits is "like that of classic taste"
(*ME*, II, 26–27). Marius adopts this ideal of Humanity (in a sense
"beyond the actual intention of the speaker") and is now prepared for
his final engagement with Christianity.

There can be little doubt that Pater's "universal commonwealth of
mind," that "venerable system of sentiment and idea, widely extended
in time and place," a "wonderful order, actually in possession of human
life," is a version of the "great association of nations" or "social commonwealth," "from time immemorial" and with "visible continuity"
the seat of a unique "association of intellect and mind," described by
Newman in "Christianity and Letters." This is undoubtedly a more
authentic version than the one detected in Pater's "Winckelmann"
nearly twenty years earlier. The later version is, for one thing, notice-
ably less fixed on "the supreme tradition of beauty" which so absorbed
the younger Pater and at least makes an obeisance toward a "universal
commonwealth of *mind*," which was Newman's central concern. Most
significant, perhaps, is the strongly ethical complexion of Pater's revised version of the great tradition in the West. For an important
extension of Newman's argument was the implication that, among the
numerous analogies between "Civilization" and Christianity, classical
studies had providentially been maintained as the instrument of education in Christian countries. In a kind of polemical pun, Newman had
declared, "Rome has inherited both sacred and profane learning"
(*Idea*, p. 231). By 1885 that notion would probably have seemed more
acceptable to Pater than it had in 1867. Although his hero does not follow out their full implications, a number of the central arguments of
Pater's theology in *Marius*—on the nature of religious "assent" and
the role of will and personality in belief; on the inadequacy of a religion of mere "taste"; on the authority of a great religious-humanistic
tradition "in possession" of the Western mind—are those he had found
in Newman's writings. The conclusion to be drawn is that Pater by the
eighties had moved well beyond the vision of life embodied in the

Renaissance and that Newman had played a crucial part in the focusing of the new vision, for all of Marius' concern to the end with an aesthetic "receptivity."

The extent of that shift of spiritual focus and the degree to which Newman can be seen as its agent are strikingly evident in Pater's review, a year after the publication of *Marius*, of Amiel's *Journal Intime*. Pater shows impatience with a kind of spiritual pusillanimity he detects in Amiel with regard to the historic Catholic Church:

And as that abstract condition of *Maia,* to the kind and quantity of concrete literary production we hold to have been originally possible for him; so was the religion he actually attained, to what might have been the development of his profoundly religious spirit, had he been able to see that the old-fashioned Christianity is itself but the proper historic development of the true "essence" of the New Testament. There, again, is the constitutional shrinking, through a kind of metaphysical prejudice, from the concrete— that fear of the actual—in this case, of the Church of history. . . . Assenting, on probable evidence, to so many of the judgments of the religious sense, he failed to see the equally probable evidence there is for the beliefs, the peculiar directions of men's hopes, which complete those judgments harmoniously, and bring them into connection with the facts, the venerable institutions of the past—with the lives of the saints. By failure, as we think, of that historic sense, of which he could speak so well, he got no further in this direction than the glacial condition of rationalistic Geneva. . . . "I miss something," he himself confesses, "common worship, a positive religion, shared with other people. Ah! when will the Church to which I belong in heart rise into being?" To many at least of those who can detect the ideal through the disturbing circumstances which belong to all actual institutions in the world, it was already there. Pascal, from considerations to which Amiel was no stranger, came to the larger hopes of the Catholic Church: Amiel stopped short at a faith almost hopeless; and by stopping short just there he really failed, as we think, of intellectual consistency, and missed that appeasing influence which his nature demanded as the condition of its full activity, as a force, an intellectual force, in the world—in the special business of his life. (*EG,* pp. 33–34) [8]

[8] See also Pater's important review (1888) of Mrs. Humphry Ward's *Robert Elsmere,* where he expresses vexation at the hero's leaving the Anglican communion. With probable autobiographical overtones, he argues against precipitate measures on

The historic Catholic Church as "the proper historic development" of the New Testament, and "assenting" to Catholic doctrine on "probable evidence": these phrases neatly summarize the drift of Newman's most original defenses of orthodoxy in works like the *Development of Christian Doctrine* and the *Grammar of Assent*. The tone of the conscious polemicist, the impatience with religious hesitancy, the appeal to "intellectual consistency," and the yearning for a higher "appeasing influence" —these mark stages beyond the careful irresolutions of *Marius* and are, I think, unmistakably autobiographical.

Newman's was thus a decisive role, perhaps intellectually the most decisive, in that rather enigmatic High Churchmanship Pater practiced in the final years of his life. Pater's theological arguments, in *Marius* and elsewhere, are unquestionably less subtle and less precise than Newman's, primarily because he was unwilling to follow out Newman's logic in its entirety. Pater, for whom Newman's concatenated proofs remained more suggestive than cogent, characteristically emphasizes the elements of Newman's arguments which opened the latter to persistent charges of "scepticism." Pater found the *Grammar* especially suited to his purposes: he chose to stress the "personal" and relative quality in religious apprehension (rather than the commitment to which Newman's arguments inherently led) and assimilated Newman's subtle exploration of the modes of assent to his own preoccupation with rarified states of religious-aesthetic perception (to the neglect of the fact that Newman claimed to be describing processes employed by all men). Similarly, though Newman is very penetrating on the role of will and personality in religious assent, Pater's major emphasis is on the religious "possibility" this line of argument opens up, instead of on Newman's emphasis on will acting "at the dictate of reason and prudence." For Pater, as much as for Arnold, post-Kantian religion was to

---

the part of the now large class of those who "cannot be sure that the sacred story is true," and makes "a great possibility" sufficient grounds for remaining within the existing Church (*EG,* pp. 67, 68). Pater's final balance of attitudes is conveyed, almost amusingly, in his praise of Anglicanism, in conversation with Lionel Johnson in 1889, for its "reverent doubt and sober mysticism" (see Arthur W. Patrick, *Lionel Johnson: Poète et Critique,* pp. 20–21; cited in Lawrence G. Evans, "Some Letters of Walter Pater," [Ph.D. dissertation, Harvard University], p. x).

be incapable of receiving a coherent *intellectual* formulation: his version of Christianity, almost as much as Arnold's, was to lie beyond the assault of logic or reason because, as he wrote in 1886, "The supposed facts on which Christianity rests, utterly incapable as they have become of any ordinary test, seem to me matters of very much the same sort of assent we give to any assumptions, in the strict and ultimate sense, moral."[9] Nevertheless, Pater's use of Newman's chief arguments in favor of orthodox belief is notably straightforward in the Amiel review, and even in *Marius* there is an essentially serious concern with Newman's views on the psychology of belief and on the credentials of the historic Church. This is quite the reverse of Matthew Arnold's annoyed rejection, in his writings of the seventies, of Newman's characteristic reasoning as either self-defeating or prima facie "impossible." While Pater drew heavily on Arnold's theological writings for his own "natural" Christianity, under Newman's tutelage he had, by the mid-eighties, entered a country beyond the boundaries of Arnold's ethical idealism—though Pater probably did not take up full citizenship there. In a special sense of his own, Pater could say in his later years that the Roman Catholic Church "is what we are all tending to."[10]

[9] A letter quoted in Mrs. Humphry Ward, *A Writer's Recollections* p. 210. He speaks there of the claims of the historic church as an "obscure but all-important" possibility, "a workable hypothesis." This attitude of sympathetic but suspended judgment before the claims of historic Christianity lies behind the phrase Pater used in a letter to Violet Paget in July 1883, discussing his intentions in writing *Marius*: "I think there is a fourth sort of religious phase possible for the modern mind" (Evans, "Some Letters of Walter Pater," p. 64). In her dialogue, "The Responsibilities of Unbelief: A Conversation between Three Rationalists" (*Contemporary Review*, XLIII [May 1883], 685–710), she had divided the possibilities among an "optimistic Voltairean" and intellectual epicure, an "aesthetic pessimist," and (much like herself) a positivist who is a "militant humanitarian atheist." See also Peter Gunn, *Vernon Lee: Violet Paget, 1856–1935*, pp. 112–114.

[10] Father Dessain informs me that F. V. Reade, a relative of Pater's and a Catholic convert who later became Superior of the Oratory, wrote the following at the end of his copy of *Marius*: "Sir William Richmond, whom I met at Assisi in August 1905, told me that Pater had once said to him (it was towards the end of Pater's life) —'That [sc. the Roman Catholic church] is what we are all tending to'." Richmond (1852–1921) was Slade Professor of Art at Oxford, 1879–1883, and thus was in a position to become aware of Pater's changing religious views during the writing of *Marius*.

CHAPTER TWENTY-FOUR The "Style" of Humanism

Newman's ideas were to be of decisive importance in what is perhaps Pater's best-known essay, that on "Style," first published in 1888. Pater also looked to Newman for a "personalist" doctrine of style which would be the adequate vehicle of his favored religious-aesthetic consciousness. As early as 1886, in a review of several books including George Saintsbury's *Specimens of English Prose*, Pater had anticipated much of the central argument of "Style" and firmly linked Newman's essay on "Literature" with his own crucial views on the relations between "style" and "matter":

If there be a weakness in Mr. Saintsbury's view, it is perhaps in a tendency to regard style a little too independently of matter. And there are still some who think that, after all, the style is the man; justified, in very great varieties, by the simple consideration of what he himself has to say, quite independently of any real or supposed connection with this or that literary age or school. Let us close with the words of a most versatile master of English—happily not yet included in Mr. Saintsbury's book—a writer who has dealt with all the perturbing influences of our century in a manner as classical, as idiomatic, as easy and elegant, as Steele's:

"I wish you to observe," says Cardinal Newman, "that the mere dealer in words cares little or nothing for the subject which he is embellishing, but can paint and gild anything whatever to order; whereas the artist, whom I am acknowledging, has his great or rich visions before him, and his only aim is to bring out what he thinks or what he feels in a way adequate to the thing spoken of, and appropriate to the speaker." (*EG*, pp. 15–16; see *Idea*, pp. 248–249)

"Literature," like "Christianity and Letters," is from the set of occasional lectures comprising the second half of Newman's *Idea of a University* and must have been familiar to Pater from a very early date.

There is evidence that it began to influence Pater's views even before 1886.

It may be best to begin by showing that, even apart from the testimony of the 1886 review, Newman and the *Idea* are quite explicitly at the center of Pater's "Style." Pater notes early that among the many varieties of possible style, the prose of Cicero and Newman is "musical" (*Appr.*, p. 6). This is later expanded, in Pater's defense of imaginative prose as the "special art of the modern world," into the observation that nineteenth-century prose will be

as varied in its excellence as humanity itself reflecting on the facts of its latest experience—an instrument of many stops, meditative, observant, descriptive, eloquent, analytic, plaintive, fervid. Its beauties will not be exclusively "pedestrian": it will exert, in due measure, all the varied charms of poetry, down to the rhythm which, as in Cicero, or Michelet, or Newman, at their best, gives its musical value to every syllable. (*Appr.*, pp. 11–12)

It has been observed by more than one reader that this latter description properly fits, of the three writers named, only Newman. Further on, the *Idea* is associated with the now familiar "select few" and with a quasi-religious view of the function of the arts:

scholars, I suppose, and not only scholars, but all disinterested lovers of books, will always look to it [literature], as to all other fine art, for a refuge, a sort of cloistral refuge, from a certain vulgarity in the actual world. A perfect poem like *Lycidas*, a perfect fiction like *Esmond*, the perfect handling of a theory like Newman's *Idea of a University*, has for them something of the uses of a religious "retreat." Here, then, with a view to the central need of a select few, those "men of a finer thread" who have formed and maintain the literary ideal, everything, every component element, will have undergone exact trial, and above all, there will be no uncharacteristic or tarnished or vulgar decoration, permissible ornament being for the most part structural, or necessary. (*Appr.*, pp. 17–18)[1]

Finally, when defining "soul in style," which communicates "through vagrant sympathy and a kind of immediate contact," Pater finds it primarily embodied in such religious works as the Vulgate, the English

---

[1] Pater's judgment that the *Idea* is "the perfect handling of a theory" is challenged by Fergal McGrath (*Newman's University: Idea and Reality*, pp. 291–292).

Bible, the Prayer-Book, and the *Tracts for the Times* (*Appr.*, pp. 25–26)—which would of course bring Newman to the reader's mind again.

In all these instances, Newman is viewed as himself a supreme practitioner of the sort of "style" Pater most admired. The major concern here, however, is with the doctrine of Newman's lecture, which Martin J. Svaglic has recently placed in its nineteenth-century setting in this way:

> The best known of the lectures is probably that on "Literature," which anticipates Pater's essay "On Style" [sic] in its insistence on the inseparability of thought and word and in its definition of literature as "the personal use or exercise of language"; and which looks back to Romantics like Coleridge and DeQuincey in its sharp disjunction (perhaps too sharp) between literature and science, the former expressing "not objective truth, as it is called, but subjective; not things, but thoughts."[2]

Pater's prolonged emphasis on the fusion of form and matter in art, which might be called the aesthetic analogue of his humanistic attempt to cancel any opposition between morality and the world of intellectual and aesthetic perception, is one of the unifying themes of his whole career. From 1873 onward, his views on the unity of both art and literature were expressed most frequently in terms of matter and form, the ambiguous correlatives of Aristotelian hylomorphism, themselves originally metaphors. While the theoretical aim is generally one of the union or fusion or interpenetration of the two, the constant bias is toward a state in which *"form . . . is everything, and the mere matter is nothing"* (*PP*, p. 8; see also *Ren-1*, pp. 9, 143–144). The most extended statement of this view, of considerable influence on late nineteenth- and early twentieth-century aesthetics, appears in "The School of Giorgione" (1877).[3] *"All art constantly aspires towards the condition of music"*—in the sense that music above all other arts "obliterates" the distinction between matter and form (*Ren-3*, p. 135).

The Giorgione essay is probably the most persuasive and responsible statement in nineteenth-century England of the cult of form. But it also

---

[2] John Henry Newman, *The Idea of a University*, ed. Martin J. Svaglic, p. xxiv.

[3] On that influence, see Solomon Fishman, *The Interpretation of Art*, pp. 67 ff.

marks Pater's distance from the position of Coleridge, to whom he is sometimes linked, since Coleridge—in his concern for the unity, the totality, or the wholeness of art works—keeps a better balance between part and whole.[4] Moreover, Pater was much more interested in the fine arts than was Coleridge and constantly tended to assimilate literature to the condition of the fine arts—and the disparagement of "mere matter" can be applied to painting or music or architecture far more successfully than to verbal structures. Further, Coleridge's interest in unity and wholeness is fundamentally a concern for the organic relation of the parts to the whole, that is, of the parts to a seminal vision in the "imagination" of the creative artist. Pater, by contrast, seems by "matter" to mean (in art) the subject matter depicted and (in literature) both the narrative subject and the logical, denotative "meaning" of words, phrases, and larger units—and by "form" to mean (in art) technique, "manner," and (in literature) "expression," the suggestive and evocative power of language beyond the denotative. Only once does Pater approach the Coleridgean position, when he declares style to be giving "the phrase, the sentence, the structural member, the entire composition, song, or essay, a . . . unity with its subject and with itself. . . . All depends on the original unity, the vital wholeness and identity, of the initiatory apprehension or view" (*Appr.*, p. 22). He even stresses the need for an "architectural design, . . . a single, almost visual, image, vigorously informing an entire, perhaps very intricate, composition," and disparages an original vision "not organically complete" (*Appr.*, p. 23).[5] Nevertheless, the drift of Pater's reiterated reflections on form and matter, thought and word, is atomic, fractionary, a matter of this or that expressive unit, far more than the development or growth of an entire work from a unitary Coleridgean germ. Even in the quoted section on unity of conception, Pater charac-

---

[4] René Wellek, *A History of Modern Criticism: 1750–1950*, Vol. II: *The Romantic Age*, p. 171.

[5] On the basis of this quotation and two references in *Greek Studies* (*GS*, pp. 215, 239), I do not see why Professor Wellek (*A History of Modern Criticism*, Vol. IV: *The Later Nineteenth-Century*, p. 390) implies that Pater simply rejects the organic analogy, unless it be because of the prevailing atomism of Pater's views as I have developed them here. (I am of course aware of Pater's hesitations concerning organicism, *Appr.*, pp. 80–81.)

teristically stresses variety, expressiveness, the inevitability of "many irregularities, surprises, and afterthoughts" in composition. In fact Pater's emphasis on the exact relation of inner thought and outward expression is far more probably derived immediately from Newman's "Literature" than from Coleridge.

Newman's central doctrine—"Thought and speech are inseparable from each other. Matter and expression are parts of one: style is a thinking out into language" (*Idea*, p. 241)—is at least echoed as early as Pater's 1874 essay on "Wordsworth": "in him [Wordsworth], when the really poetic motive worked at all, it united, with absolute justice, the word and the idea; each, in the imaginative flame, becoming inseparably one with the other, by that fusion of matter and form, which is the characteristic of the highest poetical expression. His words are themselves thought and feeling" (*Appr.*, p. 58). Even the strongest "formalist" passage in the Giorgione essay contains a key metaphor anticipated by Newman—in ideal poetry and painting "form and matter, in their common identity, present one single effect to the 'imaginative reason,' that complex faculty for which every thought and feeling is twin-born with its sensible analogue or symbol" (*Ren-3*, p. 138); Newman had said: "according to the well-known line, 'facit indignatio *versus*;' not the words alone, but even the rhythm, the metre, the verse, will be the contemporaneous offspring of the emotion or imagination which possesses him" (*Idea*, p. 243). In *Marius*, too, Flavian, the companion of the hero's youth, sought to save Latin literature from "routine and languor" by re-establishing "the natural and direct relationship between thought and expression" (*ME*, I, 96). The other chief doctrine of Newman's "Literature" to be embodied in "Style" was the related view that "literature is personal," "the faithful expression of [the writer's] intense personality, attending on his inward world of thought as its very shadow" (*Idea*, pp. 240–241). This idea, too, was earlier broached in *Marius*, where Marius learns from Flavian the "demand for a matter, in all art, derived immediately from lively personal intuition"; for Marius, the word or phrase became "valuable in exact proportion to the transparency with which it conveyed to others the apprehension, the emotion, the mood, so vividly real within himself" (*ME*, I, 103, 155).

That Pater had Newman's lecture at his elbow while composing the essay on "Style" is scarcely to be questioned. Nevertheless, it is well to beware of breaking down into a myriad of "sources" any complex exercise of thought and sensibility like Pater's essay. Moreover, behind Newman's and (explicitly) Pater's distinction between science and literature lay De Quincey—and behind him, Hazlitt, Coleridge, and Wordsworth.[6] De Quincey had also spoken of style as "the incarnation of thoughts,"[7] but Pater's phrasing and development of argument suggest that Newman is the major direct influence in these as in certain other matters. Some of the more revealing coincidences of thought and expression will suffice to show the indebtedness.

When Pater says the historian "must needs select, and in selecting assert something of his own humor, something that comes not of the world without but of a vision within" (*Appr.*, p. 9), he echoes Newman's remarks that literature is the shadow of the writer's "own inward world of thought," "the poetry of his inner soul," the very "image" of his mind (*Idea*, pp. 241, 243, 244).[8] Or when Pater calls literary art "the representation . . . of a specific personality, in its preferences, its volition and power" (*Appr.*, p. 10), he recalls Newman's view

---

[6] M. H. Abrams, *The Mirror and the Lamp: Romantic Theory and the Critical Tradition*, p. 143.

[7] *Ibid.*, p. 291. De Quincey's contrast in "Style" (1840–1841; *Collected Writings of Thomas De Quincy*, ed. David Masson, X, 137 ff.) is between the matter and style (or manner); the vocabulary for their marriage includes metaphors like inextricably interwoven, embedded, entangled, interfused, interpenetration, intertexture, embodiment, confluence. He attributes to Wordsworth (p. 230) the remark that language is "the *incarnation* of thoughts." His final analogy (p. 230) is the union of the human body and soul. De Quincey anticipates (pp. 229 ff.) not only Newman's distinction between a "subjective" and an "objective" exercise of the mind, but even Pater's emphasis on the need to strip away *"surplusage"* (p. 162). De Quincey approaches the more extreme formalism of the "Giorgione" essay in "Language" (*ibid.*, p. 260), when he insists: "style has an *absolute* value, like the product of any other exquisite art, quite distinct from the value of the subject about which it is employed, and irrelatively to the subject."

[8] Pater's remarks on the writing of history are also very close to Newman's observations in the *Grammar of Assent* on "how little [historical] judgment will be helped on by logic, and how intimately it will be dependent upon the intellectual complexion of the writer" (*GA*, p. 364; and *GA*, p. 367, on point of view).

of language as the expression of a man's "inward mental action" and
of "his intense personality" (*Idea*, p. 241). Pater's similar remark that
language must be adapted to express "every lineament of the vision
within" and that style is the man "in absolutely sincere apprehension
of what is most real to him" (*Appr.*, p. 36) harkens back to the passage from Newman cited in Pater's 1886 review: "the artist . . . has
his great or rich visions before him, and his only aim is to bring out
what he thinks or what he feels in a way adequate to the thing spoken
of, and appropriate to the speaker" (*Idea*, p. 249). Both men are
highly conscious of the artist's power of shaping and transforming
language for his own special purposes. Newman observes that "while
the many use language as they find it, the man of genius uses it indeed, but subjects it withal to his own purposes, and moulds it to his
own peculiarities" (*Idea*, p. 240). Similarly, in defining "soul" in
style, Pater speaks of the way certain writers have "of absorbing language, of attracting it into the peculiar spirit they are of, with a subtlety
which makes the actual result seem like some inexplicable inspiration"
(*Appr.*, p. 25).

The instances could be multiplied: for example, the discussion of
Cicero (*Idea*, p. 245; *Appr.*, p. 36); the correlation of idea and expression (*Idea*, pp. 241 ff.; *Appr.*, pp. 34, 37–38); or the emphasis
on personal "colour and intensity" (*Appr.*, p. 37; *Idea*, p. 240). More
significant, I think, is the dependence of Pater's much-decried finale
on Newman's conclusion. Pater distinguishes there between good and
great art, no longer according to form but according to matter—that
is, by adding to the criteria of good art (the fusion of substance and
matter, "the absolute correspondence of the term to its import") certain moral efficacies. This is, says René Wellek, not only the entire
revocation of Pater's aestheticism: "It is a recantation at the expense of
any unified, coherent view of art."[9] Pater's statement may not satisfy
the theorists, but surely Wellek's dismissal of Pater's ending leaves a
persistent critical problem equally unsolved since formalist doctrine
has been notoriously unequal to the task of moral judgment and of

[9] Wellek, *Modern Criticism*, IV, 395. As Wellek sees, Pater's view anticipates
T. S. Eliot's distinction between art and great art (see *Selected Essays*, p. 388).

accounting for both the "value" and the "wisdom" of certain works of literature which do *not* pass muster according to formalist criteria. At any rate, Wellek is convincing when he attributes this new view of "art as an agency of sympathy and even of humanitarianism" to Pater's new involvement with Christianity.[10] In fact, it seems likely that Newman's example inspired the famous conclusion. Pater wrote:

Given the conditions I have tried to explain as constituting good art;—then, if it be devoted further to the increase of men's happiness, to the redemption of the oppressed, or the enlargement of our sympathies with each other, or to such presentment of new or old truth about ourselves and our relation to the world as may ennoble and fortify us in our sojourn here, or immediately, as with Dante, to the glory of God, it will be also great art; if, over and above those qualities I summed up as mind and soul—that colour and mystic perfume, and that reasonable structure, it has something of the soul of humanity in it, and finds its logical, its architectural place, in the great structure of human life. (*Appr.*, p. 38)

This flourish, even in its rhythm and syntax, was anticipated in Newman's own conclusion:

If by means of words the secrets of the heart are brought to light, pain of soul is relieved, hidden grief is carried off, sympathy conveyed, counsel imparted, experience recorded, and wisdom perpetuated,—if by great authors the many are drawn up into unity, national character is fixed, a people speaks, the past and the future, the East and the West are brought into communication with each other,—if such men are, in a word, the spokesmen and prophets of the human family,—it will not answer to make light of Literature or to neglect its study. (*Idea*, pp. 255–256)

It is hardly surprising that Newman's "spokesmen and prophets of the human family" should, in Pater, create a literature with "the soul of humanity in it" which shall find its place "in the great structure of human life." For it was Newman who had had a chief share in formulating Pater's explicit religious position—Newman who had given Pater a vision of "the great structure of human life."

---

[10] Wellek, *Modern Criticism*, IV, 395. Wellek's statement, however, that Pater had "returned to the Church" is incautious, as are Wright's unqualified words: "Pater had again become a Christian" (Thomas Wright, *The Life of Walter Pater*, II, 208).

This is not of course to argue that Newman had somehow "converted" Pater. The ending of *Marius* is both too passive and too deliberately inconclusive to permit such a hypothesis. Moreover, *Plato and Platonism* (1893), Pater's other major attempt to provide a religious basis for life, is—in its endorsement of dialectic, the product of a detached, rather disembodied skepticism and relativism—even more remote from historic Christianity in any authentic or recognizable form. Yet even here, as shown in Chapter 21, Pater's attempt is to effect a synthesis, a harmony, of his own "independent" Platonism and a special (if rather shadowy) version of Christian religious experience, embodied chiefly in art and ritual. Here again, significantly, Newman's ideas figure prominently.

There are the inevitable references to an elite band of souls of special receptivity. The notion, "Many are called, but few chosen," is implicated in "the very essence of Platonism" (*PP*, p. 98; see also p. 22). More central is Pater's continued concern with the psychology of apprehension, both in philosophy and art, especially as Newman had developed it under the theological notion of the "economy" or "reserve." Though a considerable body of Victorian anti-intellectualism underlay Pater's skepticism, the tone and phrasing of Pater's argument reflect a rereading of Newman's *Apologia*. Behind Pater's remark concerning the Socratic irony, "for we judge truth not by the intellect exclusively, and on reasons that can be adequately embodied in propositions; but with the whole complex man" (*PP*, p. 88), lies Newman's famous statement concerning his own theological progress: "I had a great dislike of paper logic. For myself, it was not logic that carried me on. . . . It is the concrete being that reasons; pass a number of years, and I find my mind in a new place; how? the whole man moves; paper logic is but the record of it" (*Apologia*, p. 153). Thus, when Pater speaks of Plato's myths and fables as "medicinable lies or fictions, with a provisional or economised truth in them, set forth under such terms as simple souls could best receive" (*PP*, p. 247) or when he declares that the "manly" artist "will be apt . . . to express more than he seems actually to say. He economises" (*PP*, p. 281), he reminds the reader that Kingsley's chief charge against the Catholic priesthood, the charge that provoked the *Apologia*, had centered on the use of the "economy."[11] Newman's economy and the argument of the *Grammar* are enlisted in behalf of a Paterian relativism; the result is that Plato is made to sound like an aestheticized Newman. Despite Plato's demand "for certainty and exactness and what is absolute," he is represented as thinking "that truth, precisely because it resembles some high kind of relationship of persons to persons, depends a good deal on the receiver; and must be, in that degree, elusive, provisional, contingent, a matter of various approximation, and of an 'economy,' as is said; that it is partly a subjective attitude of mind:—that philosophic truth consists in the philosophical temper" (*PP*, p. 187).

There was to be one final use of the *Apologia* in an anti-intellectual context. Pater's last, uncompleted essay, on "Pascal," published posthumously in December 1894, sympathetically reviews the case against "mere argument" in matters of religious persuasion. Rather obliquely, Pater compares Pascal's manner to Newman's: "The spirit in which Pascal deals with his opponents, his irony, may remind us of the 'Apology' of Socrates; the style which secured them immediate access to people who, as a rule, find the subjects there treated hopelessly dry, reminds us of the 'Apology' of Newman" (*MS*, pp. 66–67). Just what in the *Apologia* makes it accessible is not explained.[12] The larger context of these late references to Newman is a correspondence between the two men in the late eighties, evidently irrecoverable.[13]

---

[11] See *Apologia*, pp. 245 ff., 310 ff. Newman defines the principle of the economy there: "that out of various courses, in religious conduct or statement, all and each *allowable antecedently and in themselves*, that ought to be taken which is most expedient and most suitable at the time for the object in hand" (*Apologia*, p. 311). See also *GA*, p. 37.

[12] The reference to the *Apologia* is succeeded by a flurry of elitist references that wrench predestinarian theology into the familiar pattern of spiritual snobbishness (*MS*, pp. 69, 71).

[13] Thomas Wright, *Pater* II, 106. Wright mistakenly declares (p. 174) that Pater contributed verses, "'In Memoriam Cardinal Newman," to the *Oxford University Herald* after Newman's death in August 1890. Interestingly, a poem of that title *was* published there on August 23, 1890 (p. 8), by Richard C. Jackson, the alleged original of Marius. It seems very likely that there was also an important link between these two men who probably never met, in the person of a younger and then more obscure Oxonian, Gerard Manley Hopkins. Hopkins, who received his degree in

CHAPTER TWENTY-FIVE   Newman, Arnold, Pater,
and the Future

Newman's claims upon Pater's attention were multiple and persistent—and, especially toward the end of Pater's career, they struck close to the center of a new focus in the Paterian view of life. Newman was always a master of "style," both its definer and its practitioner. In the first of these roles, Newman had played a part in the lineage of modern formalist theory larger than is usually guessed at.[1] As practitioner, Newman from the first was the "original religious genius" who advocated a cause "impossible" to the passing stage of culture but who had somehow revealed, to "the modern aspirant to perfect culture," "the inmost delicacies of his own life, the same yet different." Similarly, near the last Newman's special

---

the spring of 1867, had read essays to Pater while an undergraduate and seems to have been an especial favorite of the older man. Newman took an important part in Hopkins' conversion in 1866, and Hopkins taught at Newman's Oratory School from September to December 1867. Hopkins' correspondence with Newman continued until the former's death in 1889. The friendship between Pater and Hopkins lapsed for twenty years, until Hopkins was assigned to parish duties at St. Aloysius', St. Giles's, Oxford, for ten months (December 1878–October 1879). There, Hopkins said, "Pater was one of the men I saw most of" (*Further Letters of Gerard Manley Hopkins,* ed. Claude Colleer Abbott, p. 246). Inevitably, the two men would have discussed Newman at length, at a time when Pater was beginning the composition of *Marius.* It would be of interest to know whether Pater saw or met Newman early in 1878, when Newman visited Trinity College as its first Honorary Fellow, or in May 1880, when Newman was guest of honor there for a weekend.

Ingram Bywater, an undergraduate with Pater at Queen's, recalled in later life: "I always thought there was a possibility of his [Pater's] ending his days as a Catholic. If he had come across a really great Catholic like Cardinal Newman he would have satisfied his emotional and aesthetic nature" (William Walrond Jackson, *Ingram Bywater, The Memoir of an Oxford Scholar, 1840–1914,* p. 79).

[1] Newman's overlooked but important place in the critical tradition has been stressed recently by Norman Friedman: see Introduction, n. 8, above.

distinction was that he "has dealt with all the perturbing influences of our century in a manner as classical, as idiomatic, as easy and elegant, as Steele's." Perhaps here is the clue to the strange remoteness that one ultimately feels between these two eminent Oxonians, united by definable qualities of personality and of humanist aspiration, yet divided by two generations of cultural erosion and a world of late-nineteenth-century cultural assumptions. Pater's constant references to Newman, explicit and implicit, have a ghostly, parodic quality; Newman the man and the thinker is invoked—"the same yet different"—to buttress a structure he would have judged dangerously insubstantial.

Newman was, secondly, associated with an elitism essential to the Paterian estimate of things. Again, Newman's almost Calvinistic emphasis on the painful text of the few and the many is easily transformed, in the convolutions of Pater's prose, into a defense of a select community of "elite souls" who, blessed with a specially receptive sensibility, draw on the cultural capital of the West yet remain consciously disengaged from the enormous energy and faith which produced it. What I have referred to as Pater's snobbishness is not, to be sure, mere artiness or posing. It is in fact an integral and coherent version of humanism, mindful of tradition, the intellectual urgencies of the present, and the needs of "special" souls. It was never proffered as an energizing creed for the many, for society at large, or as a substitute for traditional beliefs. Less a countertradition than a complement, Pater's humanism was the imaginatively reconstructed residue of the Christian-classical synthesis after the science and skepticism of the century had taken their toll. It was in no sense a positive alternative, based on that science and skepticism, after the fashion of the new scientific humanisms. The "great structure" of life, a vision of which Pater caught in Newman's Oxford humanism, was not disassembled, reduced, and reconstructed according to new blueprints, as in T. H. Huxley. Instead, there is a tastefully simplified renovation of the old edifice, its emotional and imaginative facade and superstructure still intact, although the metaphysical substructure had in fact been systematically if unobtrusively removed. For Pater's delicately framed "temperament" was able to take into its architectural pattern large amounts of what was central in Newman, sometimes almost verbatim, and systematically change its import, its focus, its spiritual exigency. The Paterian "House Beautiful," or Marius' "house of thought," was lodged in the sands of special temperament, itself the unique product of a passing stage of culture. It now lies in ruins.

Perhaps Newman and Pater coincided most centrally in suggesting the continuity and complex unity of European culture. Newman defended, with a lucidity and assurance and largeness of view not available to a later generation, a comprehensive tradition in the West—an educational structure at once theological, literary, and social—of which Pater also felt himself the continuator and defender. The two men apprehended this central theological-literary tradition (which was precisely the object of attack for the new secularist advocates of a scientific education) from different perspectives. From "Winckelmann" to *Marius*, the theological component was steadily deepened and strengthened, even if the tradition remained for Pater primarily secular, a religiously colored "Commonwealth" of elite spirits, the saints and heroes and martyrs of taste and culture.

The paradoxes inherent in this perplexing relationship are abundant enough. Despite a temperamental affinity and a gradual narrowing of the explicit distance between them, Newman and Pater remain divided by divergences of basic commitment. Even the temperaments are easily distinguishable. For all the awesome subtlety of intellect and of psychological insight in Newman, and the personal depths that remained forever out of sight, there was a fundamental simplicity and openness of aspect in his writings. In Pater, by contrast, there is a certain evasiveness and finicalness, both of style and thought, forbidding commitment, which unquestionably reflect the man. Certainly Newman, had he turned his attention to Pater's works, would not have approved. He might not even have understood. What would he have made, for example, of Marius' interest in the idea that morals are simply "one mode of comeliness in things," or of Pater's near-identification of the saint and "the Cyrenaic lover of beauty" (*ME*, II, 4, 20)? In Discourse VIII of the *Idea of a University*, which Pater knew well, Newman had brilliantly portrayed the "religion . . . of imagination and sentiment," which, since for it "virtue is only one kind of beauty," substitutes "a moral sense or taste for conscience in the true meaning of the word"

(*Idea*, pp. 170 ff.). Many would say this description applied obviously enough to Pater (especially the best-known Pater of the *Renaissance*) and declare the passage prophetic—as, for example, "A Form of Infidelity of the Day" neatly states the agnostic position and strategy before they were formally named or enunciated. But Newman's examples in Discourse VIII, characteristically, are from Gibbon and Shaftesbury, and he is attacking a form of eighteenth-century benevolence and rationalism. Pater's case—especially in the writings most influenced by Newman, *Marius*, "Style," *Plato and Platonism*, and the *Guardian* essays—seems significantly different. Pater did not conceive himself as standing *ab extra* to Christianity, as did the inheritors of eighteenth-century Deism, the new secularists and rationalists: Leslie Stephen, John Morley, T. H. Huxley. Instead, in Pater the older Oxford theological humanism—classically summed up by Newman just after its decisive disappearance—emerges in the late state of deliquescence. Pater's bloodless aestheticism is a pale reflection of the central European and English tradition that had united intellectual refinement with devoutness of spirit. (One thinks of the ghostly, immobile classical figures in the paintings and murals of Pater's contemporary, Puvis de Chavannes.)

In this limited but decisive sense Newman is, in Eliot's words, "the solitary figure . . . in the background" for both Arnold and Pater. Speaking of Arnold, Eliot elsewhere says: "All his writing in the kind of *Literature and Dogma* seems to me a valiant attempt to dodge the issue, to mediate between Newman and Huxley."[2] In his review of Pater's *Renaissance*, John Morley had, with considerable prescience and from his own rationalist point of view, suggested a similar dialectical line of inheritance, though he could not define the kind of transvaluation involved. He welcomed Pater's aestheticism as being divorced from theology and yet meaningfully related to the Oxford Movement:

this more recent pagan movement is one more wave of the great current of reactionary force which the Oxford movement first released. It is infinitely less powerful, among other reasons because it only appeals to persons with

---

[2] T. S. Eliot, *The Use of Poetry and the Use of Criticism*, pp. 105–106.

some culture, but it is equally a protest against the mechanical and graceless formalism of the modern era, equally an attempt to find a substitute for a narrow popular creed in a return upon the older manifestations of the human spirit, and equally a craving for the infusion of something harmonious and beautiful about the bare lines of daily living. Since the first powerful attempt to revive a gracious spirituality in the country by a renovation of sacramentalism, science has come. . . . here is Mr. Pater courageously saying that the love of art for art's sake has most of the true wisdom that makes life full. The fact that such a saying is possible in the mouth of an able and shrewd-witted man of wide culture and knowledge, and that a serious writer should thus raise aesthetic interest to the throne lately filled by religion, only shows how void the old theologies have become.[3]

Both Arnold and Pater had derived the rationale and the tonality for their ideal of full consciousness (including a religious "sense") from the older Oxford, and above all from such works of Newman's as the *Idea of a University* and the *Apologia*, but in response to the challenge of T. H. Huxley and company they were forced to assert it in increasingly subphilosophical forms, contentless, as "states of mind" detached from any metaphysical substance. The European past—mind, imagination, devotion—was to be somehow preserved for the future, apart from belief, through refinement of taste and the pursuit of a self-regarding "culture." This "style" of life and consciousness seemed able, in carefully controlled circumstances, to persist for a time in the absence of the ballast which, historically and intellectually, had given balance and stability to that kind of apprehension. The line from Newman to some of the untidy private lives of the nineties of which Eliot speaks is an intelligible and swift descent. That Newman's thought has proved renewable in other ways—in European existentialism and personalism and in modern theological studies—is another story.

Newman's thought and personality provided a continuous touchstone for Arnold's developing view of what would remain most essential for man as science and democracy swept away the securities and institutions of the past. Similarly, Newman emerges as a strikingly central figure in the later development of Pater's thought, in effect a

[3] John Morley, Review of *Studies in the History of the Renaissance* by Walter Pater, *Fortnightly Review*, N. S. XIII (April 1873), 476.

guide pointing beyond the more destructive and skeptical influences that had earlier set the limits of Pater's range of vision. Both Arnold and Pater were essentially mediators, honest brokers between past and future. The past was a set of human values with which they identified their efforts but whose metaphysical basis they could not finally accept; the future was a numbing visita of poetryless mechanism and (as Arnold might have said) the "Americanization" of the human personality. Caught as they were between two colliding worlds of value, they remain remarkably representative modern men, since the pulls and counterpulls of their careers remain the unresolved, perhaps unresolvable, tensions in the humanist consciousness even a century later.[4] Arnold and Pater are valuable to us because, among other reasons, they were among the first to analyze the conditions of an adequate modern humanism, and to pay in their own lives the full price of such an attempt. If their "great critical effort" was finally inconclusive, it is not surprising that the precise degree and kind of transformation of value which their reliance on Newman involved still baffle our attempts at understanding. Perhaps the deepest paradox here is the finality with which these two men, both conscious continuators of the older Oxford humanism, in effect assisted in eliminating from the educational and cultural enterprise the inner spirit of the tradition that Newman classically represented. The breakdown of the spiritual center of the European tradition is in retrospect a rapid, and, to men of many points of view, an appalling sight. What this signifies as to the viability of a "Christian humanism" in the West in our time cannot even today be fully grasped.

[4] This seems to me the significance of the Leavis-Snow debate, which repeated so much of the Arnold-Huxley clash of the early eighteen-eighties, and as inconclusively. I have discussed the theological implications of modern literary humanism more polemically in "Newman as Prophet," *The Dublin Review*, No. 513 (Autumn 1967), pp. 222–235.

APPENDIX I

In a letter to John Duke Coleridge of January 8, 1843,[1] following a paragraph on the memorial and scholarship fund to be collected in honor of Dr. Thomas Arnold, Matthew Arnold continues: "I am extremely glad that you like the sermons. I always wished that you should read them. They seem to me the most delightful and most satisfactory to read, of all his writings. The last sermon but two in the last volume preached on Whitsunday, is, I think, the most beautiful of all of them. I neither expect nor desire that they should change your admiration for Newman. I should be very unwilling to think they did so in my own case, but owing to my utter want of prejudice . . . I find it perfectly possible to admire them both. You cannot expect that very detailed and complete controversial sermons, going at once to the root of all the subjects in dispute, should be preached to a congregation of boys. It would be very unfit that they should. The peculiar nature of Newman's congregation gives him, I think, a great advantage, in enabling him to state his views and to dwell on them, in all their completeness." Louis Bonnerot garbles the significance of this passage by suggesting that "the sermons" and "his writings" are Newman's.[2] No sermon of Newman's, published by this date, however, fulfills Arnold's conditions; the only supposition on which the passage is intelligible is that the sermons alluded to are those of Dr. Arnold. "The last sermon but two in the last volume preached on Whitsunday" is Sermon XXXII ("Waiting for God in Christ," preached on Whitsunday, 1842), which appeared in the second volume of sermons titled *Christian Life*, and subtitled *Its Hopes, Its Fears, and Its Close*. The volume was edited by Dr. Arnold's widow, and its preface is dated October 20, 1842; it appeared later in the same year. The elegiac note ("I always wished that you should read them") is accounted for by the fact of Dr. Arnold's death on June 12, of the preceding year, within a week of Whitsunday. Arnold's reference to a particular volume of sermons ("the last volume") seems to indicate that he had given Coleridge two or more

[1] Ernest Hartley Coleridge, ed., *Life and Correspondence of John Duke Lord Coleridge*, I, 122–123.

[2] Louis Bonnerot, *Matthew Arnold, Poète*, pp. 26–27.

of his father's volumes. Clearly, moreover, *Newman's* sermons would not
alter Coleridge's "admiration" for Newman; the reference is, instead, to
Christian Life: Its Course, Its Hindrances, and Its Helps, Thomas Arnold's
fourth volume of sermons, published in 1841, the sixty-eight–page introduction to which Thomas Arnold makes his most detailed attack on "the new
counter-reformation" of "Mr. Newman and his friends."[3] Dr. Arnold pleads
at the end (p. lxvii) that "in naming Mr. Newman as the chief author of
the system which I have been considering, I have in no degree wished to
make the question personal." Nevertheless, despite the attempt at measured
judgment, Dr. Arnold insists that the doctrines of Newman and his companions "are not of God" (p. xxvii), and he bears down heavily on the
serious "moral and intellectual faults" found in "the writings of the supporters of Mr. Newman's system" (p. xxxiv n). Moreover, all the sermons
of these two volumes of Dr. Arnold's were "preached to a congregation of
boys" at Rugby. Finally, despite Arnold's evident interest in "the peculiar
nature of Newman's congregation," the letter cited above gives us no special
warrant to assume that Arnold was at this time (early in 1843) *reading* the
published volumes of Newman's sermons. (E. K. Brown sees that the volume of sermons is not Newman's but speaks of it only as being "by some
cleric who differed from J. H. Newman."[4])

[3] Page references to quotations from this edition are given in the text.
[4] E. K. Brown, *Matthew Arnold, A Study in Conflict,* pp. 192–193 n.

APPENDIX II

The sources of Arnold's and Pater's views of the Renaissance need further study. Certainly Pater knew at first hand Hegel's view of the Renaissance, in Wallace Ferguson's words, "as both the antithesis of the Middle Ages and the forerunner of the Reformation," and his view of medieval feudalism and the Church as combining "to destroy freedom and to barbarize and debase the spirit."[1] Of course Hegel was summing up a long-held German view, alluded to earlier in this study, which tended to identify the Renaissance "with the ideas of reaction against medieval transcendentalism and of the reassertion of man's self-consciousness, his moral and intellectual autonomy, and his spiritual reconciliation with this present world."[2] The Hegelian version of this familiar view, in the broadest sense "Protestant," Arnold would have absorbed in his wide reading in Continental periodicals in the fifties and sixties. Certainly both Arnold's and Pater's careers antedate all Burckhardtian revisionist attempts to reread the relations between medieval and Renaissance. Of course neither man anticipated the rehabilitation of medieval thought which a later generation effected; scholastic philosophy is a matter of contemptuous indifference to Pater, and to Arnold, especially in the religious writings, one of deep ignorance and hyper-Protestant prejudice. They anticipate later views only with regard to the Reformation: Pater scarcely mentions it (see, *Ren-1*, p. 128), while Arnold, throughout the sixties, almost invariably refers to it with either carefully qualified praise or with outright criticism. Arnold and Pater diverge most in their evaluation of the medieval religious achievement. Pater nowhere shows the warm appreciation of the "wide-embracing" spirit of the medieval Church, "the Church of the multitude," which Arnold displayed in the opening pages of "Pagan and Mediaeval Religious Sentiment." And even amid the defense of Hellenism in *Culture and Anarchy*, Arnold could say of Christian self-sacrifice: "Of this endeavour, the animating labours and afflictions of early Christianity, the touching asceticism of mediaeval Chris-

[1] Wallace K. Ferguson, *The Renaissance in Historical Thought: Five Centuries of Interpretation*, p. 171.
[2] *Ibid.*, p. 172.

tianity are the great historical manifestations. Literary monuments of it, each in its own way incomparable, remain in the Epistles of St. Paul, in St. Augustine's Confessions, and in the two original and simplest books of the Imitation" (*CPW*, V, 170).

Jules Michelet seems to have played an important role in forming the views of both men. *The Renaissance*, volume seven of his great *History of France* (1833–1862), appeared in 1855. He shared Hegel's view of the antithesis between the medieval and Renaissance spirits. Though Michelet underplays the importance of the Italian Renaissance proper from Leonardo da Vinci, he does see art as vital: the Renaissance is the reconciliation of art and reason, the beautiful and the true.[3] While he includes the Reformation within the Renaissance, as Hegel did not, Michelet's view of the Renaissance as a rebirth of the human spirit has the essential Hegelian ingredients: "art and the rebirth of antiquity, reconciliation with nature, the rediscovery of man's inner nature and his external world."[4]

That Pater knew Michelet's *History* is proved by a citation concerning Abelard, in 1873 (*Ren-1*, p. 5). Sir Kenneth Clark, in his Introduction to the *Renaissance* (pp. 15–16) notes the importance of Michelet in Pater's early thought, and comments (p. 16): "It was Michelet who first saw the spirit of the Renaissance foreshadowed in Abelard and Joachim of Flora [sic] and Michelet who saw this spirit reaching its perfection in Leonardo da Vinci." Arnold's notebooks contain numerous citations from Michelet, and the reading lists from 1856 on refer again and again to the *History*. In February 1863 Arnold read an article in French on Michelet and the Middle Ages (*NB*, pp. 569, 628). "Preface to Michelet's Renaissance" (*NB*, p. 570) is listed for March 1863 and is on the list of books for 1864: "re-read Heine's articles on Germany, and Michelet on the Renaissance" (*NB*, p. 577). "Pagan and Mediaeval Religious Sentiment" appeared in April 1864.

---

[3] *Ibid.*, pp. 176–177.
[4] *Ibid,*. p. 177.

BIBLIOGRAPHY

I. BOOKS AND DISSERTATIONS

Abrams, M. H. *The Mirror and the Lamp: Romantic Theory and the Critical Tradition.* 2nd ed. New York: W. W. Norton and Company, 1958.

Altholz, Josef L. *The Liberal Catholic Movement in England: The "Rambler" and Its Contributors, 1848–1864.* London: Burns and Oates, 1962.

Anderson, Warren D. *Matthew Arnold and the Classical Tradition.* Ann Arbor: University of Michigan Press, 1965.

Appleman, Philip, William A. Madden, and Michael Wolff, eds. *1859: Entering An Age of Crisis.* Bloomington: Indiana University Press, 1959.

Arnold, Matthew. *A Bible-Reading for Schools: The Great Prophecy of Israel's Restoration (Isaiah, Chapters 40–66).* London: Macmillan and Co., 1872.

—————. *The Complete Prose Works of Matthew Arnold,* ed. R. H. Super. Vol. I: *On the Classical Tradition* (1960); Vol. III: *Lectures and Essays in Criticism* (1962); Vol. V: *Culture and Anarchy* (1965). Ann Arbor: University of Michigan Press, 1960—————.

—————. *Culture and Anarchy,* ed. J. Dover Wilson. Cambridge: Cambridge University Press, 1932.

—————. *Discourses in America.* New York: The Macmillan Company, 1896.

—————. *Essays in Criticism, Second Series.* London: Macmillan and Company, 1895.

—————. *Essays, Letters, and Reviews by Matthew Arnold,* ed. Fraser Neiman. Cambridge, Massachusetts: Harvard University Press, 1960.

—————. *Five Uncollected Essays of Matthew Arnold,* ed. Kenneth Allott. Liverpool, England: Liverpool University Press, 1953.

—————. *God and the Bible.* New York: Macmillan and Company, 1883.

—————. *Higher Schools and Universities in Germany.* London: Macmillan and Co., 1874.

—————. *Isaiah XL–LXVI: With the Shorter Prophecies Allied to It.* London: Macmillan and Co., 1875.

————. *Letters of Matthew Arnold, 1848–1888*, ed. G. W. E. Russell. 2 vols. in one. New York: The Macmillan Company, 1900.

————. *The Letters of Matthew Arnold to Arthur Hugh Clough*, ed. Howard Foster Lowry. London and New York: Oxford University Press, 1932.

————. *Literature and Dogma.* New York: The Macmillan Company, 1883.

————. *Mixed Essays* and *Irish Essays and Others.* 2 vols. in one. New York: The Macmillan Company, 1883.

————. *The Note-books of Matthew Arnold*, eds. Howard Foster Lowry, Karl Young, and Waldo Hilary Dunn. London: Oxford University Press, 1952.

————. *The Poems of Matthew Arnold*, ed. Kenneth Allott. London: Longmans, 1965.

————. *The Poetical Works of Matthew Arnold*, eds. C. B. Tinker and H. F. Lowry. London: Oxford University Press, 1950.

————. *Poetry and Criticism of Matthew Arnold*, ed. A. Dwight Culler. Boston: Houghton Mifflin Company, 1961.

————. *St. Paul and Protestantism.* Popular Edition (1887). London: Smith, Elder, and Company, 1912.

————. *St. Paul and Protestantism* and *Last Essays on Church and Religion.* 2 vols. in one. New York: Macmillan and Co., 1883.

————. *Unpublished Letters of Matthew Arnold*, ed. Arnold Whitridge, New Haven: Yale University Press, 1923.

Arnold, Thomas. *Christian Life: Its Course, Its Hindrances, and Its Helps.* 2nd ed. London: B. Fellowes, 1842.

————. *Christian Life: Its Hopes, Its Fears, and Its Close.* 2nd ed. London: B. Fellowes, 1843.

Arnold, Thomas [Jr.]. *Passages in a Wandering Life.* London: E. Arnold, 1900.

Bamford, T. W. *Thomas Arnold.* London: Cresset Press, 1960.

Benson, A. C. *Walter Pater.* English Men of Letters. London: Macmillan and Company, 1906.

Bonnerot, Louis. *Matthew Arnold, Poète: Essai de Biographie Psychologique.* Paris: Librairie Marcel Didier, 1947.

Brown, E. K. *Matthew Arnold: A Study in Conflict.* Chicago: University of Chicago Press, 1948.

Bruford, W. H. *Culture and Society in Classical Weimar, 1775–1806.* Cambridge: Cambridge University Press, 1962.

Buckley, Vincent. *Poetry and Morality: Studies in the Criticism of Matthew Arnold, T. S. Eliot and F. R. Leavis.* London: Chatto and Windus, 1959.

Carlyle, Thomas. *The Works of Thomas Carlyle,* ed. H. D. Traill. 30 vols. Centenary Edition. Boston: Charles Scribner's Sons, 1897–1901.

Chadwick, Owen, ed. *The Mind of the Oxford Movement.* Stanford, California: Stanford University Press, 1960.

Chandler, Edmund. *Pater on Style. Anglistica,* Vol. XI. Copenhagen: Rosenkilde and Bagger, 1958.

Charlesworth, Barbara. *Dark Passages: The Decadent Consciousness in Victorian Literature.* Madison and Milwaukee: University of Wisconsin Press, 1965.

Child, Ruth C. *The Aesthetic of Walter Pater.* New York: The Macmillan Company, 1940.

Clough, Arthur Hugh. *The Correspondence of Arthur Hugh Clough,* ed. Frederick L. Mulhauser. 2 vols. Oxford: Clarendon Press, 1957.

Coleridge, Ernest Hartley. *Life and Correspondence of John Duke Lord Coleridge.* 2 vols. New York: D. Appleton and Company, 1904.

Coleridge, John Taylor. *A Memoir of the Rev. John Keble.* 2nd ed.; 2 vols. Oxford and London: J. Parker and Company, 1869.

Coleridge, Stephen. *Famous Victorians I Have Known.* London: Simpkin, Marshall, 1928.

———. *Memories.* London: John Lane; New York: John Lane Company, 1913.

Culler, A. Dwight. *Imaginative Reason: The Poetry of Matthew Arnold.* New Haven and London: Yale University Press, 1966.

———. *The Imperial Intellect: A Study of Cardinal Newman's Educational Ideal.* New Haven: Yale University Press, 1955.

Davies, Hugh Sykes, and George Watson, eds. *The English Mind: Studies in the English Moralists Presented to Basil Willey.* Cambridge: Cambridge University Press, 1964.

De Quincey, Thomas. *Collected Writings of Thomas De Quincey,* ed. David Masson. 14 vols. London: A. C. Black, 1896–1897.

Downes, David Anthony. *Victorian Portraits: Hopkins and Pater.* New York: Bookman Associates, 1965.

Eaker, J. Gordon. *Walter Pater: A Study in Methods and Effects.* University of Iowa Studies: Humanistic Studies, Vol. V, No. 4. Iowa City: University of Iowa, 1933.

Eliot, T. S. *Selected Essays.* 3rd ed. London: Faber and Faber, 1951.

————. *The Use of Poetry and the Use of Criticism.* London: Faber and Faber, 1933.

Ellmann, Richard, ed. *Edwardians and Late Victorians.* English Institute Essays 1959. New York: Columbia University Press, 1960.

Evans, Lawrence G. "Some Letters of Walter Pater." Unpublished Ph.D. dissertation, Harvard University, 1961.

Eversley, Lord [George John Shaw Lefevre]. *Gladstone and Ireland: The Irish Policy of Parliament from 1850–1894.* London: Methuen and Company, 1912.

Ferguson, Wallace K. *The Renaissance in Historical Thought: Five Centuries of Interpretation.* Boston: Houghton Mifflin Company, 1948.

Fishman, Soloman. *The Interpretation of Art.* Berkeley: University of California Press, 1963.

Fletcher, Iain. *Walter Pater.* Writers and Their Work. London: Longmans, Green, 1959.

Foster, Richard. *The New Romantics: A Reappraisal of the New Criticism.* Bloomington: Indiana University Press, 1962.

Grant Duff, Mountstuart E. *Notes From a Diary, 1892–1895.* 2 vols. London: John Murray, 1904.

Greenslet, Ferris. *Walter Pater.* Boston and New York: Houghton Mifflin Company, 1911.

Gunn, Peter. *Vernon Lee: Violet Paget, 1856–1935.* London and New York: Oxford University Press, 1964.

d'Hangest, Germain. *Walter Pater: l'Homme et l'Oeuvre.* 2 vols. Paris: Librairie Marcel Didier, 1961.

Harrold, Charles Frederick. *John Henry Newman: An Expository and Critical Study of His Mind, Thought and Art.* New York: Longmans, Green and Co., 1945.

Hatfield, Henry. *Aesthetic Paganism in German Literature: From Winckelmann to the Death of Goethe.* Cambridge, Massachusetts: Harvard University Press, 1964.

Holloway, John. *The Victorian Sage: Studies in Argument.* London: Macmillan & Co., 1953.

Hopkins, Gerard Manley. *Further Letters of Gerard Manley Hopkins,* ed. Claude Colleer Abbott. 2nd ed. London: Oxford University Press, 1956.

Hough, Graham. *The Last Romantics.* 2nd ed. London: Methuen; New York, Barnes and Noble, 1961.

Houghton, Walter E. *The Victorian Frame of Mind, 1830–1870.* New Haven: Yale University Press, 1957.

Hutton, Richard Holt. *Essays on Some of the Modern Guides to English Thought in Matters of Faith*. London and New York: Macmillan and Company, 1888.

Huxley, Thomas Henry. *Collected Essays of Thomas Henry Huxley,* ed. Leonard Huxley. 9 vols. London: Macmillan and Company, 1893–1894.

Iser, Wolfgang. *Walter Pater: Die Autonomie des Aesthetischen*. Tübingen: M. Niemeyer, 1960.

Jackson, William Walrond. *Ingram Bywater, The Memoir of an Oxford Scholar, 1840-1914*. Oxford: Clarendon Press, 1917.

Jump, J. D. *Matthew Arnold*. Men and Books. New York: Longmans, Green, 1955.

Knickerbocker, William S. *Creative Oxford: Its Influence in Victorian Literature*. Syracuse, New York: University Press, 1925.

Knoepflmacher, U. C. *Religious Humanism and the Victorian Novel: George Eliot, Walter Pater, and Samuel Butler*. Princeton, New Jersey: Princeton University Press, 1965.

Liptzin, Sol. *The English Legend of Heinrich Heine*. New York: Bloch Publishing Company, 1954.

Madden, William A. *Matthew Arnold: A Study of the Aesthetic Temperament in Victorian England*. Bloomington and London: Indiana University Press, 1967.

Maritain, Jacques. *Art and Scholasticism, and The Frontiers of Poetry*. New York: Charles Scribner's Sons, 1962.

McGrath, Fergal. *Newman's University: Idea and Reality*. London: Longmans, Green, 1951.

Milman, Henry Hart. *Savonarola, Erasmus, and Other Essays*. London: John Murray, 1870.

Moore, George. *Confessions of a Young Man*. New York: Capricorn Books, 1959.

More, Paul Elmer. *The Drift of Romanticism: Shelburne Essays, Eighth Series*. Boston and New York: Houghton Mifflin Company, 1913.

Mozley, Thomas. *Reminiscences, Chiefly of Oriel College and the Oxford Movement*. 2 vols. Boston and New York: Houghton, Mifflin and Company, 1882.

Newman, John Henry. *Apologia Pro Vita Sua,* ed. A. Dwight Culler. Boston: Houghton Mifflin Company, 1956.

———. *Apologia Pro Vita Sua,* ed. Charles Frederick Harrold. New York: Longmans, Green, and Co., 1947.

———. *Autobiographical Writings,* ed. Henry Tristram. London: Sheed and Ward, 1956.

———. *Certain Difficulties Felt by Anglicans in Catholic Teaching.* 2 vols. London: Longmans, Green, and Co., 1897.

———. *Correspondence of John Henry Newman with John Keble and Others, 1839–1845.* London: Longmans, Green, and Co., 1917.

———. *Discussions and Arguments on Various Subjects.* London: Longmans, Green, and Co., 1897.

———. *An Essay in Aid of a Grammar of Assent,* ed. Charles Frederick Harrold. New York: Longmans, Green, and Co., 1947.

———. *An Essay on the Development of Christian Doctrine.* London: J. Toovey, 1945.

———. *Essays Critical and Historical.* 2 vols. London: Longmans, Green, and Co., 1897.

———. *Fifteen Sermons Preached before the University of Oxford.* London: Longmans, Green, and Co., 1898.

———. *The Idea of a University,* ed. Charles Frederick Harrold. New York: Longmans, Green, and Co., 1947.

———. *The Idea of A University,* ed. Martin J. Svaglic. New York: Rinehart and Company, 1960.

———. *Lectures on the Present Position of Catholics in England.* London: Longmans, Green & Co., 1899.

———. *Letters and Correspondence of John Henry Newman,* ed. Anne Mozley. 2 vols. London: Longmans, Green, and Co., 1898.

———. *Loss and Gain: The Story of a Convert.* 9th ed. London: Longmans, Green, and Co., 1891.

———. *Parochial and Plain Sermons.* 8 vols. London: Longmans, Green, and Co., 1899.

———. *Sermons Bearing on Subjects of the Day.* London: Longmans, Green, and Co., 1898.

———. *University Sketches,* ed. George Sampson. London and Newcastle-on-Tyne: Walter Scott Publishing Company, [1903].

———. *Verses on Various Occasions.* London: Longmans, Green, and Co., 1896.

Ojala, Aatos. *Aestheticism and Oscar Wilde.* Part I: *Life and Letters.* Helsinki: Academia Scientiarum Fennica, 1954.

Olivero, Federico. *Il Pensiero Religioso ed Estetico di Walter Pater.* Turin: Società Editrice Internazionale, 1939.

Pater, Walter. *Appreciations*. Library Edition. London: Macmillan & Co., 1910.

————. *Essays from 'The Guardian.'* Library Edition. London: Macmillan & Co., 1910.

————. *Gaston de Latour: An Unfinished Romance*. Library Edition. London: Macmillan & Co., 1910.

————. *Greek Studies*. Library Edition. London: Macmillan & Co., 1910.

————. *Marius the Epicurean: His Sensations and Ideas*. 2 vols. Library Edition. London: Macmillan & Co., 1910.

————. *Miscellaneous Studies*. Library Edition. London: Macmillan & Co., 1910.

————. *Plato and Platonism*. Library Edition. London: Macmillan & Co., 1910.

————. *The Renaissance,* ed. Kenneth Clark. London: Collins, The Fontana Library, 1961.

————. *The Renaissance: Studies in Art and Poetry*. 3rd ed. Library Edition. London: Macmillan & Co., 1910.

————. *Sketches and Reviews,* ed. Albert Mordell. New York: Boni and Liveright, 1919.

————. *Studies in the History of the Renaissance*. London: Macmillan and Company, 1873.

Peters, Robert L., ed. *Victorians on Literature and Art*. New York: Appleton-Century-Crofts, 1961.

Purcell, Edmund Sheridan. *Life of Cardinal Manning, Archbishop of Westminster*. 2 vols. London: Macmillan and Company, 1895.

Robbins, William. *The Ethical Idealism of Matthew Arnold*. London: William Heinemann, 1959.

Rosenblatt, Louise. *L'Idée de l'Art pour l'Art dans la Littérature Anglaise pendant la Période Victorienne*. Paris: H. Champion, 1931.

Russell, G. W. E. *Matthew Arnold*. New York: Charles Scribner's Sons, 1904.

Selkirk, J. B. *Ethics and Aesthetics of Modern Poetry*. London: Smith, Elder, and Company, 1878.

Sharp, William. *Selected Writings of William Sharp*. Vol. III: *Papers Critical and Reminiscent*. New York: Duffield and Company, 1912.

Stanley, Arthur Penrhyn. *The Life and Correspondence of Thomas Arnold*. 2 vols. in one. New York: Charles Scribner's Sons, 1910.

Starkie, Enid. *From Gautier to Eliot: The Influence of France on English Literature, 1851–1939*. London: Hutchinson, 1960.

Stephen, Leslie. *Studies of a Biographer.* 2 vols. New York: G. P. Putnam's Son; London: Duckworth and Company, 1898.

Temple, Ruth Zabriskie. *Critic's Alchemy: A Study of the Introduction of French Symbolism into England.* New York: Twayne Publishers, 1953.

Thomas, Edward. *Walter Pater: A Critical Study.* London: M. Secker, 1913.

Tillotson, Geoffrey. *Criticism and the Nineteenth Century.* London: University of London, The Athlone Press, 1951.

Tinker, C. B., and H. F. Lowry. *The Poetry of Matthew Arnold: A Commentary.* London: Oxford University Press, 1940.

Trevelyan, Humphry. *Goethe and the Greeks.* Cambridge: Cambridge University Press, 1941.

Trilling, Lionel. *Matthew Arnold.* 3rd ed. New York: Meridian Books, 1955.

Ward, Mrs. Humphry [Mary Augusta Arnold Ward]. *A Writer's Recollections.* London: W. Collins Sons, 1918.

Ward, Wilfrid. *The Life of John Henry Cardinal Newman.* 2 vols. in one. London: Longmans, Green, and Company, 1927.

Wellek, René. *A History of Modern Criticism.* Vol. II: *The Romantic Age* (1955); Vol. IV: *The Later Nineteenth Century* (1965). New Haven: Yale University Press, 1955———.

Whitridge, Arnold. *Dr. Arnold of Rugby.* London: Constable and Company, 1928.

Wilde, Oscar. *The Letters of Oscar Wilde,* ed. Rupert Hart-Davis. London: R. Hart-Davis, 1962.

———. *Reviews by Oscar Wilde.* 2 vols. Toronto: The Musson Book Company; Boston: John W. Luce and Company, n.d.

Will, Frederic, ed. *Hereditas: Seven Essays on the Modern Experience of the Classical.* Austin: University of Texas Press, 1964.

Williams, Raymond. *Culture and Society, 1780–1950.* 2nd ed. New York: Anchor Books, 1959.

Wright, Charles D. "Matthew Arnold's Response to German Culture." Unpublished Ph.D. dissertation, University of Iowa, 1963.

Wright, Thomas. *The Life of Walter Pater.* 2 vols. New York: G. P. Putnam's Sons, 1907.

II. Articles

Allott, Kenneth. "Matthew Arnold's Reading-Lists in Three Early Diaries," *Victorian Studies,* II (March 1959), 254–266.

———. "Pater and Arnold," *Essays in Criticism*, II (April 1952), 219–221.

Arnold, Matthew. "Literature and Science," *The Nineteenth Century*, XII (August 1882), 216–230.

Blackburn, William. "Matthew Arnold and the Oriel Noetics," *Philological Quarterly*, XXV (January 1946), 70–78.

Bowra, C. M. "Walter Pater," *Sewanee Review*, LVII (Summer 1949), 378–400.

Brown, E. K. "Pater's Appreciations: A Bibliographical Note," *Modern Language Notes*, LXV (April 1950), 247–249.

Bruford, W. H. "Goethe and Some Victorian Humanists," *Publications of the English Goethe Society*, N.S. XVIII (1949), 34–67.

Burgum, Edwin Berry. "Walter Pater and the Good Life," *Sewanee Review*, XL (July 1932), 276–293.

Butts, Denis. "Newman's Influence on Matthew Arnold's Theory of Poetry," *Notes and Queries*, N.S. V (June 1958), 255–256.

Coulling, Sidney M.B. "The Background of 'The Function of Criticism at the Present Time'," *Philological Quarterly*, XLII (January 1963), 36–54.

Culler, A. Dwight. "Method in the Study of Victorian Prose," *The Victorian Newsletter*, No. 9 (Spring 1956), pp. 1–4.

DeLaura, David J. "Newman as Prophet," *The Dublin Review*, No. 513 (Autumn 1967), pp. 222–235.

———. "*Romola* and the Origin of the Paterian View of Life," *Nineteenth-Century Fiction*, XXI (December 1966), 225–233.

———. "The 'Wordsworth' of Pater and Arnold: 'The Supreme, Artistic View of Life'," *Studies in English Literature*, VI (Autumn 1966), 651–667.

Duffey, Bernard. "The Religion of Pater's *Marius*," *Texas Studies in Literature and Language*, II (Spring 1960), 103–114.

[Eliot, T. S.] "The Return of Matthew Arnold," *The Criterion*, III (January 1925), 162.

Friedman, Norman. "Newman, Aristotle, and the New Criticism: On the Modern Element in Newman's Poetics," *PMLA*, LXXXI (June 1966), 261–271.

Fulweiler, Howard W. "Tractarians and Philistines: *The Tracts for the Times* Versus Victorian Middle-Class Values," *Historical Magazine of the Protestant Episcopal Church*, XXXI (March 1962), 36–53.

Gillispie, Charles Coulston. Review of *The Autobiography of Charles*

Darwin, ed. N. Barlow, and of *Evolutionary Theory and Christian Belief,* by David Lack, *Victorian Studies,* II (December 1958), 166–169.

Griffin, John R. "In Defense of Newman's 'Gentleman'," *Dublin Review,* No. 505 (Autumn 1965), pp. 245–254.

Harris, Alan. "Matthew Arnold: The 'Unknown Years'," *The Nineteenth Century,* CXIII (April 1933), 498–509.

Harris, Wendell V. "Pater as Prophet," *Criticism,* VI (Fall 1964), 349–360.

Harrison, John Smith. "Pater, Heine, and the Old Gods of Greece," *PMLA,* XXXIX (September 1924), 655–686.

Hutton, Richard Holt. "Dr. Newman's Anglican Essays," *The Spectator,* XLIV (November 11, 1871), 1369–1371.

Inman, Billie Andrew. "The Organic Structure of *Marius the Epicurean,*" *Philological Quarterly,* XLI (April 1962), 475–491.

Kerpneck, Harvey. " 'Kings of Modern Thought'," *Modern Language Quarterly,* XXIV (December 1963), 392–395.

Kissane, James. "Victorian Mythology," *Victorian Studies,* VI (September 1962), 5–28.

Knoepflmacher, U. C. "Pater's Religion of Sanity: 'Plato and Platonism' as a Document of Victorian Unbelief," *Victorian Studies,* VI (December 1962), 151–168.

Lee, Vernon [Violet Paget]. "The Responsibilities of Unbelief: A Conversation Between Three Rationalists," *Contemporary Review,* XLIII (May 1883), 685–710.

Lenaghan, R. T. "Pattern in Walter Pater's Fiction," *Studies in Philology,* LVIII (January 1961), 69–91.

"W. M." [Wilfrid Maynell?] "Afterthoughts on Cardinal Newman as a Man of Letters," *The Athenaeum,* No. 3278 (August 23, 1890), pp. 257–258.

Madden, William A. "The Divided Tradition of English Criticism," *PMLA,* LXXIII (March 1958), 69–80.

[Morley, John.] Review of *Studies in the History of the Renaissance,* by Walter Pater. *Fortnightly Review,* N.S. XIII (April 1873), 469–577.

Murphy, Howard R. "The Ethical Revolt Against Christian Orthodoxy in Early Victorian England," *American Historical Review,* LX (July 1955), 800–817.

Orrick, James Bentley. "Matthew Arnold and Goethe," *Publications of the English Goethe Society,* N.S. IV (1928), 5–54.

Osbourn, R. V. "*Marius the Epicurean,*" *Essays in Criticism,* I (October 1951), 387–403.

[Pater, Walter.] "Coleridge's Writings," *Westminster Review,* N.S. XXIX (January 1866), 106–132.

———. "The Myth of Demeter and Persephone," Part II, *Fortnightly Review,* N.S. XIX (February 1876), 260–276.

[———.] "Poems by William Morris," *Westminster Review,* N.S. XXXIV (October 1868), 300–312.

[———]. "Winckelmann," *Westminster Review,* N.S. XXXI (January 1867), 80–110.

Pick, John. "Divergent Disciples of Walter Pater," *Thought: Fordham University Quarterly,* XXIII (March 1948), 114–128.

Roellinger, Francis X. "Intimations of Winckelmann in Pater's Diaphanéitè," *English Language Notes,* II (June 1965), 277–282.

Rosenblatt, Louise M. "The Genesis of Pater's *Marius the Epicurean,*" *Comparative Literature,* XIV (Summer 1962), 242–260.

Ryals, Clyde de L. "The Nineteenth-Century Cult of Inaction," *Tennessee Studies in Literature,* IV (1959), 51–60.

Shafer, Robert. "Walter Pater Redivivus," *The Open Court,* XXXIV (April 1920), 217–231.

Shumaker, Wayne. "Matthew Arnold's Humanism: Literature as a Criticism of Life," *Studies in English Literature,* II (Autumn 1962), 385–402.

Sidgwick, Henry. "The Prophet of Culture," *Macmillan's Magazine,* XVI (August 1867), 271–280.

Stephenson, Anthony. "The Development and Immutability of Christian Doctrine," *Theological Studies,* XIX (December 1958), 481–532.

Super, R. H. "Documents in the Matthew Arnold–Sainte-Beuve Relationship," *Modern Philology,* LX (February 1963), 206–210.

Tillotson, Kathleen. "Matthew Arnold and Carlyle" (Warton Lecture on English Poetry), *Proceedings of the British Academy,* XLII (1956), 133–153.

Townsend, Francis G. "The Third Instalment of Arnold's *Literature and Dogma,*" *Modern Philology,* L (February 1953), 195–200.

Tristram, Henry. "Newman and Matthew Arnold," *The Cornhill,* N.S. LX (March 1926), 309–319.

Vogeler, Martha Salmon. "The Religious Meaning of *Marius the Epicurean,*" *Nineteenth-Century Fiction,* XIX (December 1964), 287–299.

INDEX

Abelard, Peter: Arnold on, 184; Pater on, 223, 241 and n. 5, 243, 259, 348

Aberdeen, George Hamilton-Gordon, 4th Earl of: 46

Acton, John Emerich Edward Dalberg, 1st Baron: 44

Aeschylus: 205, 250

aestheticism: ix–x, xi, xix, 342–343

Allott, Kenneth: 21 n. 34

Anderson, Warren D.: 171 n. 1

Anselm (Saint): 85 n.4

Apollinaris: 124

Appleman, Philip: 174–175 and n. 10

Aristotle: 64

Arius: 124

Arnold, Frances Lucy Wightman (Matthew Arnold's wife): 5, 23

Arnold, Matthew: and God, xii, 102–113 passim, 118, 158, 276–278, 284; first meeting of, with Newman, 5–6, 140; on the language of the Bible, 8; and the dual Oriel tradition, 8–10, 37–39, 48–49, 50–51, 57–59, 153–154; and the Oxford Movement, 7–12 passim; reasons for loss of faith of, 13–14; influence of Newman on, at Oxford, 14–19; influence of Carlyle on, 14, 18, 62, 73, 113, 148, 153, 182; interest of, in Newman in the eighteen-fifties, 22–24; on culture, 25–26, 70–79, 109–110, 176, 180; and Newman, on criticism, 25–26; acknowledges Newman's influence, 21, 94–95, 100–101; and Roman Catholic Church, 27–28; and Newman, on a spiritual elite, 28–32; and Newman, on morality vs. intellect, 30–33; Arnold on, 31, 43–48, 62– 70, 109–110, 180; and Newman, on reason and faith, 33–39; and Newman, on economy of faith, 35–36; on imaginative reason, 37, 64–65, 205– 206; and Newman, on Bentham, 56– 57, 105; on place of religion in modern life, 60–61, 203–206; on disinterestedness, 66–67; and Newman, on history, 72–75; on development of doctrine, 82–91, 103–104, 133, 155; on the Bible, 102–120 passim; attacks Unitarians, 103; on Catholic University of Ireland, 123–128, 131–132; on Newman and Liberalism, 137–138; on poetry and religion, 139–140; second meeting of, with Newman, 141; on Newman's power and personality, 148– 151; style and tone of, contrasted with those of Newman, 153 and n. 1; attitude of, toward Newman, 158–161; Hellenism of, 165–181 passim; and science, 173–177; development of ethical doctrine of, 180–181, 267–271; dualism of, 181, 286; sources of Hellenism of, 181–191; and Goethe, 182–190 passim; and Abelard, 184; and Lessing, 184–185; and Herder, 184– 186; and Humboldt, 186–187; and Heine, 191; influence of, on "Winckelmann," 202–222 passim; on tragedy, 214–215 n. 7; and Pater's ideal "type," 220 n. 13; influence of, on Conclusion to Renaissance, 221–230; and aestheticism, 229–230; influence of, on Renaissance, 231–232; influence of, on "Pico della Mirandola," 233– 234, 236; influence of, on Pater's views of Renaissance and Christianity, 242–244; on the life of the senses, 243–244; influence of, on Preface to *Renaissance*, 244 n. 8; influence of, on Pater's "Wordsworth," 245; influence of, on *Greek Studies*, 245–255 *passim*; influence of, on "Romanticism," 257 n. 1; influence of, on "The Child in the House," 262, n. 3; influence of, on *Marius the Epicurean*, 263–285 *passim*; on culture and religion, 267–271; influence of, on *Gaston de Latour*, 293–294; influence of, on *Plato and Platonism*, 298 n. 7, 300; prose style of, 305 n. 2; influence of, on Pater's view of Newman, 307–308; relation of, to Newman, 342–344; early reading of Newman's sermons of, 345–346; sources for views of the Renaissance of, 347–348

—, works of: *A Bible-Reading for Schools*, 98–101, 122, 125, 126; "The Bishop and the Philosopher," 30–32, 34; "A Comment on Christmas," 87 n. 5, 282 n. 10; "Cromwell," 20, 129 n. 7; *Culture and Anarchy*, 27, 30, 32, 37, 39, 42, 49–51, 58, 59 and n. 20, 64, 70–73, 78, 79, 81, 109, 138, 154, 156, 165–166, 171, 173–174, 180, 181 n. 27, 183, 185, 186, 187, 197, 199, 231–232, 233, 236, 242–243, 245, 255, 264, 268, 270–271, 273, 285, 297; "Dante and Beatrice," 224 n. 2; *Discourses in America*, 142–151; "Dr. Stanley's Lectures," 31, 34–35, 66; "Dover Beach," 22; "Ecce, Convertimur, ad Gentes," 134–137; "Emerson," 15, 148–151, 160; "Empedocles on Etna," 25, 264 n. 1; *Essays in Criticism*, 42, 48, 58, 92, 109, 154, 171, 180, 193, 202, 257 n. 1, 285; *Friendship's Garland*, 51, 190; "The Function of Criticism at the Present Time," 32 and n. 8, 43–48, 66–68, 70, 143, 187, 198, 228–229, 267; *God and the Bible*, 38, 88, 121, 135, 159; "Heinrich Heine," 28, 231, 233; *Higher*

Schools and Universities in Germany, 122–128, 131; "In Utrumque Paratus," 264 n. 1; "De Maistre's Lettres et opuscules inédits," 137–138, 152; "Irish Catholicism and British Liberalism," 131–134, 283; *Isaiah XL–LXVI*, 122; "Joubert," 32 and n. 8, 236–237 n. 3; *Last Essays on Church and Religion*, 129–130, 129 n. 7, 155, 166; "The Literary Influence of Academies," 40–43, 47, 198; *Literature and Dogma*, 18, 27, 38, 58 n. 19, 59 n. 20, 78, 88, 95, 96, 101–120, 121, 127, 129, 134, 135, 140, 155, 159, 160, 174, 176, 185, 189, 200, 262 n. 3, 267, 268–270, 273, 277–278, 279, 283, 342; "Literature and Science," 35, 134, 142–147, 175 n. 12, 238 n. 4, 301; "A Liverpool Address," 60, 141; "The Lord's Messengers," 30; "Marcus Aurelius," 34, 262 n. 3, 263–264, 267, 300–301; "Maurice de Guérin," 202, 216, 227; *Mixed Essays*, 129 n. 7; "The Nadir of Liberalism," 151–152; "Numbers; or, The Majority and the Remnant," 147–148; "On the Modern Element in Literature," 62, 188 n. 17, 231, 232, n. 1, 263–264; *On the Study of Celtic Literature*, 49, 160, 171, 172–173 n. 3, 183, 184 n. 10, 187; *On Translating Homer*, 171, 189, 198, 294; "Pagan and Mediaeval Religious Sentiment," 23 n. 38, 37, 64, 183, 191, 201, 203–221 *passim*, 231, 234, 236, 243, 245–255 *passim*, 278–279, 289, 347–348; "A Persian Passion Play," 92–93; Preface to *Merope*, 171, 184, 214–215 n. 7; Preface to *Poems* of 1853, 24–26, 171, 214–215 n. 7, 293, 298 n. 7; "A Psychological Parallel," 129–130; "Rugby Chapel," 30; *St. Paul and Protestantism*, 73, 81–92, 112, 114, 116, 119, 134, 155, 173, 200, 271, 277, 279, 282–283; "The Scholar-Gipsy," 24, 94 and n. 10, 192, 193, 196; *Schools and Universities on the Continent*, 122; "A Speech* at Eton," 181 n. 27; "Spinoza and the Bible," 32, 34; "Stanzas from the Grande Chartreuse," 20–22; "Stanzas in Memory of the Author of 'Obermann'," 30; "The Study of Poetry," 139–140, 199, 238 n. 4, 301; "Thyrsis," 19; "The Voice," 22 n. 37

Arnold, Thomas (Matthew Arnold's father): and Oxford, 7–10 passim, 40, 53, 54, 82, 152; and Newman, 10–12; influence of, on Matthew Arnold, 16–17, 38, 91, 158; as subject of Cromwell, 21; last sermon of, discussed, 345–346; mentioned 85 n. 4, 148 n. 8

Arnold, Thomas [Jr.] (Matthew Arnold's brother): 6, 12, 14, 15, 17, 18, 19, 23–24, 44 n. 4, 49, 125, 127

Augustine (Saint): 194, 248, 348

Austin, John: 195

Bacon, Francis: 64

Beer, John: xiii

Bentham, Jeremy: utilitarianism of, criticized by Newman and Arnold, 56–57, 105; Pater on, 195

Benthamism: 56

Bhagavad-Gita: 182

Boethius: 85 n. 4

Bonnerot, Louis: 345

Bowra, C. M.: 179 n. 21

Bradlaugh, Charles: 58 n. 19

Bright, John: 55

Brougham, Henry Peter, Baron: 136, 138

Brown, E. K.: 28, 75, 223 n. 1, 346

Browning, Robert: 192 n. 1

Bruford, W. H.: 189 n. 18

Buchanan, Robert: 191

Buckley, Vincent: xix n. 9

Bunsen, Christian Charles Josias: 172, 172–173 n. 3

Burckhardt, Jakob: 347

Burgoyne, Sir John: 46

Burgum, Edwin: 178, 181 n. 28

Burke, Edmund: influence of, on Arnold, 62, 70, 137, 156

Butler, Joseph: 81, 95, 96, 103–104, 106, 107

Butts, Denis: 139–140

Byron, George Gordon Noel, 6th Baron: 9, 54, 201

Bywater, Ingram: 338–339 n. 13

Calvinism: 28

Carlyle, Thomas: influence of, on Arnold, 14, 18, 62, 73, 113, 148, 153, 182

Catholic University of Ireland: Arnold supports, 123–128 passim, 131–132; mentioned, 24, 49

Chadwick, Owen: 18, 37–38

Chambers, Robert: 113

Chandler, Edmund: 301

Chateaubriand, Francois René: 201

Cherbuliez, Victor: 184

Clark, Sir Kenneth: 348

Clough, Arthur Hugh: 14, 17–18, 19

Cobbe, Frances: 59 and n. 21

Colenso, Bishop John William: 28, 30, 34, 307

Coleridge, John Duke: 16, 141, 345

Coleridge, John Taylor: 9, 58 and n. 19

Coleridge, Samuel Taylor: 24, 62, 64, 82, 193–201 passim, 308, 331–333, 334

Coleridge, Stephen: 141

Copleston, Edward: 9, 152

Comte, Auguste: 210–211 n. 4

Comteanism: 56

Cousin, Victor: 182

criticism: Newman and Arnold on, 25–26; Arnold on, 31, 109–110, 180; influence of Newman on Arnold's view of, 43–48, 62–80 passim; influence of Arnold's view of, on Pater, 193–199 passim, 202–203, 228–229, 245, 255; evolution of concept of, in Newman, Arnold, and Pater, 305–306, 307, 312. SEE ALSO culture

Cullen, Archbishop Paul: 128

Culler, A. Dwight: xvi n. 7, 21 n. 34, 47, 75, 76, 77, 157

culture: general discussion of, xi–xii, xix, 118, 343; and religion, xv, xviii, 267–271; Newman and Arnold on, 25–26; Arnold on, 70–79, 109–110, 180; Arnold and Pater on, 176; Pater on, 193–199 *passim,* 245–246, 253, 255, 263–296 *passim,* 305–312 *passim*; Pater's "House Beautiful" as element of, 260–262. SEE ALSO criticism, religion

Dante: 32 n. 8, 85 n. 4, 205, 224 n. 2, 233, 237, 257, 258, 263, 281, 336
Darwin, Charles: 174, 174–175 n. 10, 175 n .12
Decadence: ix
De Quincey, Thomas: 334 and n. 7
Dessain, C. Stephen: 328 n. 10
development of doctrine: view of Newman on, xv; view of Arnold on, 82–91, 103–104, 133, 155
disinterestedness: Arnold on, 66–67
Döllinger, Ignatius: 45
Dowden, Edward: 9, 152
Dublin Review: 27, 44, 45

Eckhart, Johannes: 298
economy of faith: Arnold and Newman on, 35–36
Edinburgh Review: 26, 68
elitism: defined, xi; influence of Newman's view of, on Arnold, 16, 28–33, 148 and n. 8, 307; Pater's view of, 246–250, 308; influence of Newman's view of, on Pater, 310–312, 321–322, 338 n. 12
Eliot, George: 13, 168
Eliot, T. S.: x, xviii n. 8, 172, 173, 305, 310, 335 n. 9
Emerson, Ralph Waldo: influence of, on Arnold, 14, 15, 18, 113, 148, 153
Evangelical movement: 18
Evans, Lawrence G.: 314 n. 2
Eversley, Charles Shaw-Lefevre, Viscount: 127

faith: influence of Newman's view of, on Arnold, 33–39, 112, 114; Arnold defines view of, 115–116; Pater on, 199–201. SEE ALSO reason vs. morality, Hebraism and Hellenism

Falkland, Lucius Cary, 2nd Viscount: 59 n. 20
Ferguson, Wallace: 347–348
Florentine Platonists: 233
Fontanès, Ernest: 59
Foster, Richard: xviii n. 9
Fra Angelico: 211, 215, 218
Francis of Assisi (Saint): 204, 206, 267, 281
Francis de Sales (Saint): 248
Friedman, Norman: xviii n. 8
Froude, James Anthony: 13–14, 20, 113, 141, 168
Froude, Richard Hurrell: 11, 56, 96
Fulweiler, Howard W.: 55 n. 12

German Hellenism: 165–170 *passim*
Gibbon, Edward: 342
Giotto: 281
Gladstone, William E.: 46, 127–128, 151
Goethe, J. W.: influence of, on Pater, xvi, 167, 207–222 *passim,* 229, 251, 257; influence of, on Arnold, 18, 25, 26, 94 n. 10, 170, 172, 173, 182–183, 186, 189–190, 189 n. 18; influence of, on Arnold acknowledged, 100, 149, 153; influence of, at Oxford cited by Arnold, 148; influence of, on Arnold evaluated, 161; Hellenic ideals of, 165, 166; Pater's ideal of culture modeled on, 177; influence of, on European thought cited by Arnold, 184; mentioned, 168
Godwin, William: 9, 152
Gondon, Jules: 27
Grant Duff, M. E.: 302 n. 11
Greenslet, Ferris: 178 and n. 15, 179 n. 21, 305
Gregory the Great, Pope: 95

Hampden, R. D.: 8–9, 11, 54
d'Hangest, Germain: 210–211 n. 4, 262 n. 2, 264 n. 1
Harris, Wendell V.: x n. 2
Harrold, Charles F.: 24–25
Hatfield, Henry: 168, n. 3, 173
Hawkins, Edward: 9, 152

Hazlitt, William: 334

Hebraism and Hellenism: conflict of, discussed, xvii, 165–170; Arnold on, 33; as central to *Culture and Anarchy*, 37, 72–73; Pater and, 202–221 *passim*, 233–237, 263, 266–267, 268, 273; influence of Arnold's views of, on Pater, 278, 281–283

Hegel, G. W. F.: inufluence of, on Pater's view of art history, xvi, 170, 202, 209–220 *passim*, 286; as one of Arnold's intellectual elite, 31; Arnold praises, 190–191 n. 19; influence of views of Renaissance of, on Arnold and Pater, 347–348

Heine, Heinrich: influence of, on Pater's view of aesthetics, xvi, 288; and aesthetic movement, 170; as source of Arnold's Hellenism, 181, 201, 204–205; influence of, on Pater's view of Middle Ages, 223, 234, 241 n. 5, 243, 289–290

Hellenism: of Arnold and Pater, 171–181. SEE ALSO Hebraism and Hellenism

Herbert, Sidney: 46

Herder, J. G.: 171, 182, 184–186

history: Newman and, xv; Arnold's view of, 84–90, 107–112, 156; Pater's view of, 220, 234–235, 279–282; mentioned, xvii. SEE ALSO *Zeitgeist*

Hobbes, Thomas: 56

Holloway, John: 153

Home and Foreign Review: 44, 45

Homer: 32 n. 8, 147

Hooker, Thomas: 106, 107

Hopkins, Gerard Manley: 154, 338–339 n. 13

Hough, Graham: ix, 179, 180, 272 n. 9

Houghton, Walter E.: 192 n. 1

House Beautiful: 260–262. SEE ALSO culture

Hugh of St. Victor: 64

Hugo, Victor: 223, 229

Humboldt, Alexander von: 172, 182, 186–187

Hume, David: 56

Hunt, Leigh: 9

Hutton, R. H.: 94, 112–113, 153 n. 1, 157–158, 172

Huxley, T. H.: 58 n. 19, 142–147, 168, 173, 174 and n. 7, 175 n. 13, 176, 306 n. 3, 340, 342, 343, 344 n. 4

imaginative reason: Arnold's concept of, 37, 64–65, 205–206; influence of Arnold's concept of, on Pater, 236; Pater and, 261–262, 262 n. 2, SEE ALSO reason vs. morality, modern spirit

Imitation of Christ, The: 194

Inman, Billie Andrew: 265–266

inwardness: concept of, transformed, xi; Pater and, 240

Iser, Wolfgang: 257 n. 1

Jackson, Richard C.: 338 n. 13

Joachim of Floris: 242, 348

Johnson, Lionel: x and n. 2

Julian the Apostate: 308

Kant, Immanuel: 182, 262 n. 2, 327

Keats, John: 230

Keble, John: 9, 12, 24, 58 n. 19, 152, 307

Keble, Thomas: 9, 152

Kerpneck, Harvey: 22 n. 35

Kingsley, Charles: 35 n. 10, 41–42, 173, 315

Kissane, James: 246–247

Knickerbocker, William S.: xv n. 6

Knoepflmacher, U. C.: 264 n. 4, 296–297, 297 n. 6

Lacordaire, Père J. B. H.: 27, 308

Lamennais, l'Abbé F. de: 95–97

Leavis, F. R.: xx, 344 n. 4

Lemaître, Jules: 264 n. 1

Leonardo da Vinci: 230–232, 260, 348

Lessing, G. E.: Arnold and, 184–185, 184 n 10; Pater and, 180, 234

Liberalism: Newman and Arnold and, 6, 50–57; Thomas Arnold and, 9; Newman opposed to, 36 n. 11; Arnold opposed to, 95, 102, 105, 144, 157; Arnold on Newman's views of, 122,

137–138; influence of Newman's views of, acknowledged by Arnold, 130, 134–135, 154–156; Arnold defines, 151
Locke, John: 68, 199
Lowry, H. F.: 20, 21
Luther, Martin: 206, 267, 308

McGrath, Fergal: 76, 330 n. 1
Madden, William A.: xviii n. 9
Maistre, Joseph de: 137–138, 156
Mallock, W. H.: 266
Manning, Henry Edward, Cardinal: 23, 27, 44, 121, 122, 128, 306 n. 3
Maritain, Jacques: 252 and n. 6
Marcus Aurelius Antoninus: 180, 266–267, 300–301, 302, 318
Mayo, Richard Southwell Bourke, 6th Earl of: 124, 125
Mechanics' Institutes: 136–137, 137 n. 10
medievalism: xiii–xiv. SEE ALSO Middle Ages
Michelangelo Buonarroti: 238, 239–240
Michelet, Jules: 348
Middle Ages: Oxford and, 23, 48; attitude of Arnold toward, 23 n. 38, 116–118, 347–348; Pater and, 177, 199–201, 222–224, 240–244, 256–261, 347–348; and "Pagan and Mediaeval Religious Sentiment," 203–206; and "Winckelmann," 207–218 *passim*; and *The Renaissance,* 239–240. SEE ALSO medievalism
Mill, John Stuart: 73, 151, 154
Milman, Henry Hart: xiii, 85 n. 4, 92–93
Modernism, in theology: xiv n. 5, xvii, 87
modern spirit: and imaginative reason, 37, 236; opposition of, to morality and aestheticism, 133–134; role of, in Arnold, 172, 206; role of, in Pater, 193–194, 200, 203, 206, 231, 242–244. SEE ALSO reason vs. morality (and faith), imaginative reason
Mohammedanism: 92
Mommsen, Theodor: 151

Montaigne, Michel de: 293
Moore, George: x n. 2
More, Paul Elmer: xv
Morley, John: 342–343
Morris, William: ix, xv, 222–224
Mozley, Thomas: 141

Newcastle, Henry Pelham Fiennes Pelham, 5th Duke of: 46
Newman, Francis William: 20, 168
Newman, John Henry: place of, in critical tradition, xii-xiii, 329–336, 339; and Oxford tradition, xv n. 6, 122, 149–150; personalist theory of literature of, xvi; first meeting of, with Matthew Arnold, 5–6; central to Arnold's development, 6–7; and Thomas Arnold, 7–12 *passim;* influence of, on Arnold's early poetry, 19–22; influence of, on Preface to *Poems* of 1853, 24–26; and Arnold's ideal of culture, 25–26, 70–75; on a spiritual elite, 28–32; on morality vs. intellect, 30–32; and Arnold, on reason and faith, 33–39; and Arnold, on economy of faith: 35–36; role of, in "Literary Influence of Academies," 40–43; role of, in "Function of Criticism," 43–48; role of, in *Culture and Anarchy,* 49–51; and Arnold, on Bentham, 56–57, 105; and Arnold's ideal of criticism, 62–80 *passim;* failure of, to synthesize man's impulses, 75–77; on the "gentleman," 76–77, 322–324; role of, in *Literature and Dogma,* 101–120; as supreme representative of Oxford tradition, 110–111; as model for Arnold's theological inquiry, 111–112; on Catholic University of Ireland, 123–124; and Arnold's view of religion and poetry, 139–140; and Arnold's defense of letters, 142–147; on classical polytheism, 248; influence of, on "Winckelmann," 308–310; influence of, on "Wordsworth," 310 n. 7; influence of, on *Marius,* 314–326; influence of, on "Style," 329–336;

role of, in *Plato and Platonism,* 337–
338; relations of, with Gerard Manley
Hopkins, 338–339 n. 13
—, works of: *Apologia,* 7, 11, 35, 36, 40–
41, 50, 52–54, 73–74, 91, 111–112,
313 and n. 8, 337–338, 338 n. 12, 343;
Gallista, 315; "The Course of Truth,"
29; "Christianity and Letters," 47,
308–310, 324–325; *Certain Difficulties
Felt by Anglicans in Catholic Teaching,* 56; *Discussions and Arguments,*
97, 129; "English Catholic Literature,"
313 n. 8; *Essay in Aid of a Grammar
of Assent,* xii, 112, 314, 316, 319–322,
327, 338; *Essay on the Development of
Christian Doctrine,* xvi, 15, 82–91 *passim,* 102–120 *passim,* 327; *Essays Critical and Historical,* 92–93, 99, 102–
120 *passim,* 139–140; "Faith and Reason, contrasted as Habits of Mind," 22;
"A Form of Infidelity of the Day," 317,
342; *The Idea of a University,* xii, xiii,
24, 36–37, 39, 43, 56, 57, 63–64, 66,
68–70, 75–77, 137, 143–144, 146, 147,
310 n. 7, 314, 322–324, 343; "Implicit
and Explicit Reason," 29, 65; "Letter
to the Duke of Norfolk," 122, 127;
"Literature," 329–336 *passim; Loss and
Gain,* 314–316, 319; *Parochial and
Plain Sermons,* 15, 147–150; "Poetry,
with Reference to Aristotle's Poetics,"
24; *The Present Position of Catholics,*
57, 84, 129; *Sermons Bearing on Subjects of the Day,* 16; "The Tamworth
Reading Room," 32–33, 36, 55–56,
56–57, 68, 134–138, 144; "The Theory of Developments in Religious Doctrine," 15, 35, 38; Tract 85, 33–34,
120; Tract 90, 7; *Verses on Various
Occasions,* 79; "Who's to Blame?"
45–46, 57; "Wisdom, as Contrasted
with Faith and with Bigotry," 63, 65
Norfolk, Duke of: 5

O'Curry, Eugene: 49
Oriel College tradition: 8–10
Oriel Noetics: 53

Osbourn, R. V.: 264
Oxford Movement: xiii, xiv, 7–12 *passim,* 50–51, 52, 57–59, 140–141, 307,
314, 315, 342–343. SEE ALSO Oxford
tradition
Oxford tradition: central importance of,
discussed, xiv–xv, xix, 23–24; Newman and, xv n. 6, 122, 149–150; Pater
and, xv n. 6, 257 n. 1, 305–307, 342–
343, 344; Arnold and, 8–10, 37–39,
40, 48–49, 50–51, 57–59, 142, 147,
153–154, 230, 344; Newman's concept of "gentleman" and, 76–77, 322–
324; Newman as supreme representative of, 110–111. SEE ALSO Oxford
Movement

Paget, Violet (Vernon Lee): 328 n. 9
Paley, William: 38
Parmenides: 31, 190 n. 19, 298
Pater, Walter Horatio: and importance of
religion, xii; and Oxford tradition, xv
n. 6, 257 n. 1; 305–307, 342–343, 344;
dual character of religious position of,
xvi; Hellenism of, 165–181 *passim;*
and evolutionary theory, 174–175; and
science, 174–177, 180; influence of
Huxley on, 175 and n. 13; and Arnold,
on culture, 176; on the Middle Ages,
177, 199–201, 222–224, 256–260, 347–
348; dualism in, 178–180, 286; personality of, 178–179; ethical crisis of, 179–
180; attitudes of, toward Arnold, 192
and n. 1; on culture and religion, 193–
199, 263–296 *passim;* transforms Arnold's view of culture, 194–199; on
Bentham, 195; on reason vs. faith, 199–
201; on art in Greek and medieval religion, 206–218; view of life of, 220–
222; on history, 220, 234–235, 279–
282; on religion and art, 222–224, 230–
244 *passim;* on Abelard, 223, 241 and
n. 5, 243, 259, 348; on relation of truth
to beauty, 224–227; contrasted with
Arnold, 228–230; on the Renaissance,
230–244; on Christianity and Greek
religion, 233–237, 245–255, 296–302;

on Christianity vs. Platonism, 237–238; on a religion above creeds, 238; on religious and artistic inwardness, 239–240; on the Middle Ages vs. the Renaissance, 240–244, 258–261; on the life of the senses, 243–244; on myth, 245–255; on classical vs. medieval, 245–255; on a spiritual elite, 246–250, 310–312, 321–322, 338 n. 12; on classical vs. romantic, 256–258; on Christianity and Hellenism, 256–263 *passim*; on the House Beautiful, 260–262; on God, 276–278, 284; final religious position of, 301–302, 325–328; early attitudes of, toward Newman, 307–308; on pagan and Christian art, 309–310, 329; on role of personality in religious faith, 316–320; authenticity of later religion of, 321 n. 6; on the "gentleman," 322–324; doctrine of style of, 329–336; compared to Coleridge on organic unity, 331–333; relations of, with Gerard Manley Hopkins, 338–339 n. 13; relation of, to Newman, 339–344; sources of views of the Renaissance of, 347–348
—, works of: "The Age of Athletic Prizemen," 302; "Apollo in Picardy," 180; "Art Notes in North Italy," 287–298, 324 n. 7; "Aucassin and Nicolette," 240–244; "The Child in the House," 262–263; "Coleridge's Writings," 193–201, 228, 238 n. 4, 241, 245, 248, 307–308; Conclusion to the *Renaissance,* 224–227, 241; "Dante Gabriel Rossetti," 262; "Diaphanéitè," 193, 227, 228; *Essays from the "Guardian,"* 342; Gaston de Latour, 291–296; *Greek Studies,* 245–255, 291, 296 and n. 3, 310, 311; "Leonardo da Vinci," 230–232; "Luca della Robbia," 239–244; *Marius the Epicurean,* 179–180, 185–186, 207, 238, 256, 261, 262, 263–285, 286, 291, 292, 297, 299–300, 310, 311, 314–326, 328 and nn. 9 and 10, 333, 337, 342; "The Myth of Demeter and Persephone," 246–249;

"Pascal," 338; "Pico della Mirandola," 233–237; *Plato and Platonism,* 178, 286, 293, 296–302, 337, 342; "Poems by William Morris," 222–227, 288, 314; "The Poetry of Michelangelo," 237–238; Preface to the *Renaissance,* 243; *The Renaissance,* 175, 176, 178, 179, 197–198, 230–244, 263, 266, 275, 278, 282, 286, 292, 296, 310, 311, 312–313, 326, 342–343, 348; review of Amiel's *Journal Intime,* 301, 326–327; review of *Robert Elsmere,* 180, 287, 301, 326–327 n. 8; "Romanticism," 256–258, 260; "Sandro Botticelli," 232–233; "The School of Giorgione," 261–262; "Style," 301, 342; "Two Early French Stories," 258–261; "Winckelmann," 166, 175, 175–176 n. 13, 183, 190–191 n. 19, 202–221, 228–229, 245, 247, 248, 297 n. 6, 308; "Wordsworth," 245, 310 n. 7, 333; "The Writings of Cardinal Newman," 314 and n. 2

Patmore, Coventry: 154
Paul (the Apostle): 348
Peel, Sir Robert: 55 n. 17
Perugino: 217
Peters, Robert L.: xiii n. 3
Philistines: opposition of Arnold to, 42, 48–49, 57, 81, 129, 130, 155; as subject of "Who's to Blame," 46 n. 9; supersession of, 50–51. SEE ALSO Liberalism
Pick, John: x n. 2
Pico della Mirandola: 233–237, 238
Pindar: 205–206
Plato: 143, 172–173 n. 3, 190 n. 19, 238, 293, 299, 300, 338
Pre-Raphaelites: 230
Pusey, E. B.: 11, 17, 20
Puvis de Chavannes, Pierre: 342

Raglan, Fitzroy James Henry Somerset, 1st Baron: 46
Rambler, The: 44
Reade, F. V.: 328 n. 10

reason vs. morality (and faith): Arnold and, 30–39, 70–79, 133, 146, 156, 165–181, 233; Pater and, 165–181, 199–201, 233–234. SEE ALSO Hebraism and Hellenism, imaginative reason
Reform Bill of 1832: 50
Reform Bill of 1867: 50
religion: role of, in the modern world, xii, 60–61, 170, 203–206; and culture, xv, xviii, 267–271; central to Arnold and Pater's vision, xvii. SEE ALSO faith, culture
Renan, Ernest: 41, 244, 264 n. 1
Revue des Deux Mondes: 43
Rhymers' Club: ix
Richmond, Sir William: 328 n. 10
Ritualism: 59–61
Robbins, William: 29, 65, 81, 147 n. 7
Roellinger, F. X.: 213
Roman Catholic Church: xiv and n. 5, 73–74, 83–84, 88, 95–97, 104, 121–128 *passim*, 130, 131–134, 138, 200, 237–238, 238 n. 4, 240, 283–284, 286–289, 328 and n. 10
Rossetti, Dante Gabriel: ix, xv, 192 n. 1, 262
Romanino: 287–288
Rosenblatt, Louise: 264 n. 1
Ruskin, John: ix, 190, 192 n. 1, 230, 246
Ryals, Clyde deL.: 227–228 n. 7

Sainte-Beuve, Charles Augustin: as "centre of correct taste," 41; influence of, on Matthew Arnold, 100 and n. 17, 149, 153
St. Louis: 300, 308
Saintsbury, George: 329
Salvation Army: 60
Sampson, George: 305 n. 2
Sand, George: 14, 18, 100 n. 17
Savonarola, Girolamo: 238
Schelling, F. W. J. von: 182
Scherer, Edmond: 188
Schiller, Friedrich: 165, 182, 190, 272
Schleiermacher, Friedrich: 172, 172–173 n. 3
Science: Arnold and, 143–146, 172, 173,

176–177; specter of, in Arnold and Pater, 168, 229; Pater and, 174–177, 210, 220, 235, 286, 287, 340, 343; and Oxford tradition, 306; Newman and, 317; influence of Newman's view of, on Pater, 334
Scott, Sir Walter: 222
secularity: xvii
Sénancour, Étienne Pivert de: 30
Shadwell, C. L.: 250
Shafer, Robert: 176
Shaftesbury, Anthony Ashley Cooper, 3rd Earl of: 342
Shakespeare, William: 32 n. 8, 41, 138
Sharp, William: 192 n. 1
Shelley, Percy Bysshe: 9, 152, 172
Sidgwick, Henry: 51–52
Simonides: 205
Snow, Charles Percy: xx, 344 n. 4
Socrates: 172–173 n. 3, 293, 299, 338
Sophocles: 62, 172, 188, 205–206
Spencer, Herbert: 105
Spinoza, Baruch: 18, 26, 31, 190 n. 19, 195, 298
Stanley, Arthur Penrhyn: 5, 10, 12, 17
Stephen, Leslie: 342
Svaglic, Martin J.: 331
Swinburne, Algernon Charles: xvi, 174 and n. 7, 191, 192 n. 1, 230
Symonds, John Addington: 246

Talbot, Edward: 122, 306 n. 3
Tauler, Johannes: 298
Taylor, Jeremy: 199
Temple, Ruth Z.: x n. 2, 100 n. 17
Tennyson, Alfred, 1st Baron: 23 n. 38, 94 and n. 10, 192 n. 1
Theocritus: 203–204
Thomas, Edward: 178 n. 17
Thomson, James: 191
Tieck, Ludwig: 257
Tinker, C. B.: 20, 21
Tillotson, Geoffrey: 225 n. 3, 226, 229
Tillotson, Kathleen: 20
Titian: 218
Tristram, Henry: 6, 57, 62
Trilling, Lionel: 37, 69

urbanity: Arnold on, 40–41
utilitarianism: 26, 56, 68. SEE ALSO Jeremy Bentham

Ventadour, Bernard de: 311
Veuillot, Louis: 122
Vidal, Pierre: 311
Vinci, Leonardo da: SEE Leonardo da Vinci
Virgil: 284
Voltaire: 151, 184

Ward, Mrs. Humphry (Mary Augusta Arnold Ward): 14, 287, 301, 326–327 n. 8, 328 n. 9
Ward, Wilfrid: 45
Ward, William George Ward: 44, 122
Wellek, René: 174 and n. 10, 332 n. 5, 335–336, 336 n. 10

Whately, Richard: 8, 38, 54, 126
Wilde, Oscar: x and n. 2, 159, 305 n. 2
Williams, Raymond: 62, 70, 75
Wilson, J. Dover: 39, 62
Winckelmann, J. J.: 170, 171, 181, 183, 206–218 *passim*
Wiseman, Nicholas, Cardinal: 27, 44, 315
Wolf, Friedrich: 188
Wordsworth, William: Newman and, 24; key influence of, on Arnold, 100, 149, 153; importance of, on Arnold evaluated, 161; Arnold quotes, 221 n. 14; and Pater, 334

Yeats, William Butler: ix

Zeitgeist: xv, 86–88, 107–112, 118, 160, 170. SEE ALSO history

Date Due